Handbook for Coding Interviews

Master the *Method* to Solve Coding Interview Questions

One Book to *Rule it All*

With complete Solutions to the
122 *Most Frequently Asked Questions*

Preface

The *Handbook for Coding Interviews* book is written with one goal in mind: *to equip you with the essential problem-solving skills needed to excel in coding interviews.* As someone who has both faced and conducted hundreds of interviews, I understand the importance of not just solving problems, but doing so efficiently and articulately.

This book covers a wide range of coding interview topics—*from basic to advanced*—all presented in a structured format to simulate real interview scenarios. Each problem is accompanied by detailed explanations, brute force and optimal solutions, Java code, and complexity analysis to help you grasp both the "*how*" and "*why*" of each approach.

Whether you're preparing for interviews at top tech companies or refining your problem-solving skills, I hope this book will serve as a valuable resource on your journey to success.

Good luck, and happy coding!

Format of the Book

This book is designed to guide you through coding interview preparation with a consistent and structured format for each problem.

Here's the format of the every chapter in this book:

1. **Introduction and Core Concepts**
   Each chapter provides key details about the current topic and just what you need to know about it from a coding interview point of view. Then it covers the most frequently asked questions on that particular topic/pattern.

2. **Problem Statement**
   Each problem comes with a problem statement presented in a similar fashion as you might be faced with in a real life interview setting.

3. **Clarifying Questions**
   Solution to each problem starts with clarifying questions simulating a real interview with back-and-forth dialogue between a candidate and an interviewer. This section emphasizes the importance of asking clarifying questions to fully understand the problem.

4. **Example**
   Provides one or more sample inputs and the expected output to help you visualize the problem.

5. **Brute Force Approach**
   Outlines a straightforward, less efficient solution. This gives you more clarity about the problem, stimulating your thought process to optimize it subsequently by analyzing tradeoffs about time and space complexity.

6. **Optimal Approach**
   Describes the most efficient solution using appropriate problem-solving patterns.

7. **Code Solution**
   Provides a well-commented Java solution that demonstrates how to implement the optimal approach.

8. **Time and Space Complexity Analysis**
   Each problem includes an explanation of the time and space complexity.

This consistent format helps you approach each problem methodically and prepares you to think and communicate effectively during real interviews.

Table of Contents

Chapter 1: Problem Solving *Method*

To succeed in coding interviews, it's essential to follow a structured approach. I recommend following ***method*** for solving coding questions:

1. Understand the Problem

- **Reword the Problem:** Simplify the problem statement in your own words to ensure you understand it fully.
- **Ask Clarifying Questions:** Identify any unclear points early. Ask questions about edge cases, constraints, and expected input/output.

2. Examples and Edge Cases

- **Walk Through an Example:** Create sample input and manually work through it to identify patterns or edge cases.
- **Consider Edge Cases:** Think of boundary conditions, such as empty input, large numbers, zeros or negative values, depending on the problem.

3. Choose a Strategy

- **Brute Force First:** Always start by considering a simple, brute force approach. This helps solidify your understanding.
- **Optimal Approach:** Identify patterns (*e.g., two pointers, sliding window, dynamic programming, bfs, dfs etc*) that lead to an efficient solution. Consider trade offs with time and space complexity at this stage.

4. Write the Code

- **Iterative Approach:** Begin coding with the brute force solution if needed, then optimize.
- **Break It Down:** Divide the problem into smaller, manageable steps. Use helper functions where appropriate.

5. Test and Validate

- **Run Multiple Test Cases:** Test your solution with typical cases and edge cases to validate correctness.

6. Explain Your Solution

- **Communication Is Key:** In an interview, explain your thought process clearly while you work through the solution.
- **Iterate:** If the interviewer suggests improvements, adjust your approach and show how you'd refactor your solution.

This *problem-solving method* ensures clarity, efficiency, and a structured approach in coding interviews.

Chapter 2: Arrays

In this chapter, we will look at what you *need to know about Arrays* from a coding interview point of view. We will also go over a few most commonly asked array based coding interview problems, and how to approach them with complete solutions in Java.

Introduction to Arrays

An array is a ***collection of elements***, each identified by an index. Arrays store elements of *a fixed size and type*, and the elements are stored in *contiguous memory locations.*

Arrays provide *efficient random access* to elements. Accessing an element by its index is a constant-time operation, `O(1)`.

Arrays can be used to implement other data structures like *stacks*, *queues*, *heaps* and *hash tables.*

Basic Array Operations: Java examples

1. Creating an Array

```
int[] numbers = new int[5]; // Declaration and initialization
numbers[0] = 10;
numbers[1] = 20;
numbers[2] = 30;
numbers[3] = 40;
numbers[4] = 50;
```

2. Accessing Elements

```
int firstNumber = numbers[0]; // Accessing the first element
System.out.println("First number: " + firstNumber); // Output: 10
```

3. Updating Elements

```
numbers[2] = 35; // Updating the third element
System.out.println("Updated third number: " + numbers[2]); // Output: 
35
```

4. Traversing the Array

```
for (int i = 0; i < numbers.length; i++) {
   System.out.println("Element at index " + i + ": " + numbers[i]);
}
```

5. Insertion

Inserting an element requires shifting elements to the right to make space.

```
int[] newNumbers = new int[6];
```

```
System.arraycopy(numbers, 0, newNumbers, 0, 3); // Copy first 3
elements
newNumbers[3] = 25; // Insert new element
System.arraycopy(numbers, 3, newNumbers, 4, 2); // Copy remaining
elements


// Resulting array: [10, 20, 35, 25, 40, 50]
```

6. Deletion
Deleting an element requires shifting elements to the left to fill the gap.

```
int deleteIndex = 2; // Index of element to delete
for (int i = deleteIndex; i < numbers.length - 1; i++) {
   numbers[i] = numbers[i + 1];
}
// Resulting array after deletion: [10, 20, 40, 50, 0]
```

Popular Coding Interview Questions on Arrays

In this section, we will cover the most popular coding interview questions on arrays along with their complete solution in Java. We will apply the structured approach to systematically solve these coding questions.

Problem 1: Two Sum Problem

Problem Statement

You are given an array of integers called `nums` and an integer called `target`. Your task is to find and return the indices of the two numbers in the array that add up to the `target`. Each input will have exactly one solution, and you cannot use the same element more than once.

Solution

Let's dive into this problem as if we're in a real life interview setting.

> **Note**: We will follow the ***same structured approach*** throughout this book, so that it becomes your *natural habit* while approaching a coding interview question in a real life interview setting.

Clarifying Questions

Candidate: Before I proceed, I'd like to clarify a few things to ensure I understand the problem correctly. Is that alright?
Interviewer: Of course, go ahead.

Candidate: First, regarding the array *nums*, can I assume that the array may contain both positive and negative integers?
Interviewer: Yes, the array can contain both positive and negative integers.

Candidate: Great! Also, since each input has exactly one solution, should I assume that the array has at least two elements?
Interviewer: Yes, that's correct. The array will always have at least two elements.

Candidate: Lastly, should I return the indices in any specific order, or does it not matter?
Interviewer: The order of the indices does not matter, as long as the correct indices are returned.

Candidate: Understood. I think I have a clear understanding of the problem now.

Example

Let's consider an example:

- `Input: nums = [2, 7, 11, 15], target = 9`
- `Expected Output: [0, 1]`

Here, `nums[0] + nums[1]` equals `9`, which matches the target, so the output is `[0, 1]`.

Brute Force Approach

Let me first discuss a brute force approach to solve this problem.

The simplest way to solve this would be to *use a nested loop*. I would iterate over each element in the array and for each element, check every other element to see if their sum equals the target. If a pair is found, I would return their indices.

This approach would have a time complexity of $O(n^2)$, where n is the number of elements in the array. This is because we would be checking each pair of elements, which leads to a quadratic number of operations.

Optimal Approach

I believe we can improve the efficiency using a HashMap.

Here is the idea:

1. I will use a *HashMap* to store each element's value as the key and its index as the value while iterating through the array.
2. For each element in the array, I would calculate the *complement* that, when added to the current element, *equals the target*.
3. If this complement exists in the HashMap, it means we've already encountered the corresponding number, and I can return the current index and the stored index of the complement.

Code Solution

Here is how I would implement this in Java:

```
import java.util.HashMap;
```

```
public class TwoSum {
   public int[] twoSum(int[] nums, int target) {
        // HashMap to store the value and its index
        HashMap<Integer, Integer> map = new HashMap<>();

        // Iterate over the array
        for (int i = 0; i < nums.length; i++) {
            int complement = target - nums[i];

            // Check if the complement exists in the map
            if (map.containsKey(complement)) {
                // Return the indices of the two numbers that add up
to the target
                return new int[]{map.get(complement), i};
            }

            // Add the current number and its index to the map
            map.put(nums[i], i);
        }

        // In case no solution is found, which shouldn't happen as
per the problem statement
        throw new IllegalArgumentException("No two sum solution");
   }

   public static void main(String[] args) {
        TwoSum solver = new TwoSum();

        // Test cases
        int[] nums1 = {2, 7, 11, 15};
        int target1 = 9;
        int[] result1 = solver.twoSum(nums1, target1);
        System.out.println("Indices: [" + result1[0] + ", " +
result1[1] + "]");

        int[] nums2 = {3, 2, 4};
        int target2 = 6;
        int[] result2 = solver.twoSum(nums2, target2);
        System.out.println("Indices: [" + result2[0] + ", " +
result2[1] + "]");

        int[] nums3 = {3, 3};
        int target3 = 6;
        int[] result3 = solver.twoSum(nums3, target3);
        System.out.println("Indices: [" + result3[0] + ", " +
result3[1] + "]");
   }
}
```

Time and Space Complexity

- The time complexity of this solution is `O(n)`, where `n` is the number of elements in the array. This is because we're only iterating through the array once.
- The space complexity is also `O(n)` because we are storing elements and their indices in a HashMap.

Problem 2: Best Time to Buy and Sell Stock for Profit

Problem Statement

You are given an array called `prices` where `prices[i]` represents the price of a stock on the `i-th` day. Your task is to find the maximum profit you can achieve by making exactly one transaction (buying one share of the stock and selling it later). You can only buy and sell the stock once.

Solution

Let's follow our structured approach to solve this problem.

Clarifying Questions

Candidate: I'd like to ask a few clarifying questions to make sure I fully understand the problem.
Interviewer: Absolutely, go ahead.

Candidate: First, is it correct that the *prices* array contains the stock prices for consecutive days, and I need to find the maximum profit by buying on one day and selling on a later day?
Interviewer: Yes, that's correct. You must buy before you sell, meaning the purchase has to happen on an earlier day than the sale.

Candidate: Understood. Also, is it possible for the prices array to be empty or have only one element? If so, what should the output be?
Interviewer: Good question. If the array is empty or has only one element, no transaction can be made, so the profit should be `0`.

Candidate: Got it. Lastly, is there a restriction on the price values? For example, can the prices be negative?
Interviewer: No, all prices will be non-negative integers.

Candidate: Perfect, I have all the information I need to proceed.

Example

Let's consider an example:

- `Input: prices = [7, 1, 5, 3, 6, 4]`
- `Expected Output: 5`

Here, we can achieve the maximum profit by buying on *day* 2 (`prices[1] = 1`) and selling on *day* 5 (`prices[4] = 6`). The profit would be `6 - 1 = 5`.

Brute Force Approach

The brute force approach would be to check the profit for every possible pair of days.

For each day, I would iterate through the remaining days to calculate the potential profit by selling on those days, and I would keep track of the maximum profit encountered.
This approach has a time complexity of $O(n^2)$ because for each day, I would need to check all subsequent days to compute the profit. This isn't the most efficient solution, but it would work.

Optimal Approach

The more optimal solution would be using a single pass through the array.

Here is how it would work:

1. As we iterate through the array, we keep track of the *minimum price* encountered so far.
2. For each price, we *calculate the profit* if we were to *sell* at that price.
3. If this profit is greater than the *maximum profit* we've seen so far, we update the maximum profit.

Code Solution

Here is how I would implement this in Java:

```
public class BestTimeToBuyAndSellStock {
   public int maxProfit(int[] prices) {
        // Initialize variables to keep track of minimum price and
maximum profit
        int minPrice = Integer.MAX_VALUE;
        int maxProfit = 0;

        // Iterate through the array of prices
        for (int i = 0; i < prices.length; i++) {
            // If we find a new minimum price, update minPrice
            if (prices[i] < minPrice) {
                minPrice = prices[i];
            }
            // Otherwise, calculate the profit if we sold at the
current price
            else {
                int profit = prices[i] - minPrice;
                // Update maxProfit if the current profit is greater
                if (profit > maxProfit) {
                    maxProfit = profit;
                }
            }
        }
```

```
        // Return the maximum profit found
        return maxProfit;
    }

    public static void main(String[] args) {
        BestTimeToBuyAndSellStock solver = new
BestTimeToBuyAndSellStock();

        // Test cases
        int[] prices1 = {7, 1, 5, 3, 6, 4};
        System.out.println("Max Profit: " +
solver.maxProfit(prices1));  // Expected: 5

        int[] prices2 = {7, 6, 4, 3, 1};
        System.out.println("Max Profit: " +
solver.maxProfit(prices2));  // Expected: 0

        int[] prices3 = {1, 2, 3, 4, 5};
        System.out.println("Max Profit: " +
solver.maxProfit(prices3));  // Expected: 4
    }
}
```

Time and Space Complexity

- The time complexity of this solution is `O(n)`, where `n` is the number of elements in the array. This is because we only iterate through the array once.
- The space complexity is `O(1)` since we are using only a constant amount of additional memory for the variables minPrice and maxProfit.

Problem 3: Product of Array Except Self

Problem Statement

You are given an array `nums` containing `n` integers, where `n > 1`. Your task is to return a new array `output` such that each element `output[i]` is equal to the product of all the elements in `nums` except for `nums[i]`.

You should solve this without using division.

Solution

Let's follow our structured approach to solve this problem.

Clarifying Questions

Candidate: I'd like to clarify a few points about the problem before proceeding.
Interviewer: Sure, go ahead.

Candidate: First, you mentioned that `n > 1`, so should I assume that the array will always contain at least two elements?
Interviewer: Yes, that's correct. The array will always have more than one element.

Candidate: Understood. Also, should the solution handle both positive and negative integers, as well as zeros, in the array?
Interviewer: Yes, the array can contain positive numbers, negative numbers, and zeros.

Candidate: Thanks for the clarification.

Example

Let's consider an example:

- `Input: nums = [1, 2, 3, 4]`
- `Expected Output: [24, 12, 8, 6]`

Here, the *output* array would be `[24, 12, 8, 6]` because:

- `output[0] = 2 * 3 * 4 = 24`
- `output[1] = 1 * 3 * 4 = 12`
- `output[2] = 1 * 2 * 4 = 8`
- `output[3] = 1 * 2 * 3 = 6`

Brute Force Approach

The brute force approach would involve calculating the product of all elements except `nums[i]` for each `i` by iterating through the array *multiple times*.

For each element `nums[i]`, I would loop through the entire array, skipping `nums[i]`, to calculate the product.

This approach would result in a time complexity of $O(n^2)$, which is inefficient for large arrays.

Optimal Approach

We can optimize the solution by using a *two-pass approach* with the help of auxiliary arrays.

The idea is to create *two additional arrays*, left and right. The `left[i]` array will store the product of all elements to the left of `nums[i]`, and the `right[i]` array will store the product of all elements to the right of `nums[i]`.

Once we have these two arrays, we can calculate `output[i]` as `left[i] * right[i]`.

However, ***we can further optimize this to use just the output array***, avoiding the need for additional arrays by *calculating the `left` and `right` products on the fly.*

Code Solution

Here is how I would implement the optimized version in Java:

```
public class ProductOfArrayExceptSelf {
   public int[] productExceptSelf(int[] nums) {
       int n = nums.length;
       int[] output = new int[n];

       // Initialize the first element of output array as 1 (no
elements to the left of index 0)
       output[0] = 1;

       // Fill the output array with the left products
       for (int i = 1; i < n; i++) {
           output[i] = output[i - 1] * nums[i - 1];
       }

       // Variable to store the product of elements to the right of
the current element
       int rightProduct = 1;

       // Multiply the current output with the right products
       for (int i = n - 1; i >= 0; i--) {
           output[i] *= rightProduct;
           rightProduct *= nums[i];  // Update rightProduct
       }

       return output;
   }

   public static void main(String[] args) {
       ProductOfArrayExceptSelf solver = new
ProductOfArrayExceptSelf();

       // Test cases
       int[] nums1 = {1, 2, 3, 4};
       int[] result1 = solver.productExceptSelf(nums1);
       System.out.println("Output: " +
java.util.Arrays.toString(result1));  // Expected: [24, 12, 8, 6]

       int[] nums2 = {-1, 1, 0, -3, 3};
       int[] result2 = solver.productExceptSelf(nums2);
       System.out.println("Output: " +
java.util.Arrays.toString(result2));  // Expected: [0, 0, 9, 0, 0]

       int[] nums3 = {2, 3, 4, 5};
       int[] result3 = solver.productExceptSelf(nums3);
       System.out.println("Output: " +
java.util.Arrays.toString(result3));  // Expected: [60, 40, 30, 24]
   }
}
```

Time and Space Complexity

- The time complexity of this solution is `O(n)`, where `n` is the number of elements in the array. We iterate through the array twice: once for calculating the left products and once for the right products.
- The space complexity is `O(1)` if we exclude the space used for the output array. We only use a few extra variables (*rightProduct*), making it constant space.

Problem 4: Maximum Subarray Sum

Problem Statement

You are given an integer array `nums`. Your task is to find the contiguous subarray within `nums` that has the largest sum and return that sum.

Solution

Let's follow our structured approach to tackle this problem.

Clarifying Questions

Candidate: I'd like to clarify a few points before starting. Is that alright?
Interviewer: Absolutely, go ahead.

Candidate:Should I assume that the array *nums* will always contain at least one element?
Interviewer: Yes, you can assume that nums will always have at least one element.

Candidate: Got it. Also, can the array contain both positive and negative numbers, and is there any constraint on the size of the array?
Interviewer: Yes, the array can contain both positive and negative numbers. There is no specific constraint on the size of the array, but it could be large, so an efficient solution is preferred.

Candidate: Understood. Lastly, in case the array contains all negative numbers, I should return the smallest negative number as the maximum sum, right?
Interviewer: Yes, that's correct.

Candidate: I believe I have all the information I need to proceed.

Example

Let's consider an example:

- `Input: nums = [-2, 1, -3, 4, -1, 2, 1, -5, 4]`
- `Expected Output: 6`

Here, the contiguous subarray `[4, -1, 2, 1]` has the largest sum of `6`.

Brute Force Approach

The brute force approach would be to check the sum of every possible subarray and keep track of the maximum sum encountered.

We would iterate over all possible starting points and for each starting point, iterate over all possible ending points to calculate the sum of the subarray.

This approach has a time complexity of $O(n^2)$, where n is the length of the array, because we would be calculating the sum for every possible subarray. This is not efficient for large arrays.

Optimal Approach

We can use a well-known algorithm called ***Kadane's Algorithm*** to solve this problem in linear time.

The idea behind Kadane's Algorithm is to iterate through the array while maintaining a *running sum* of the subarray (*currentSum*).

We also keep track of the *maximum sum encountered* so far (*maxSum*) during this iteration.

Code Solution

Here is the implementation of the solution using Kadane's algorithm:

```
public class MaxSubArraySum {
    public int maxSubArray(int[] nums) {
         // Initialize variables to keep track of the maximum sum and
current sum
         int maxSum = nums[0];
         int currentSum = nums[0];

         // Iterate through the array starting from the second
element
         for (int i = 1; i < nums.length; i++) {
             // Update currentSum: either extend the current subarray
or start a new subarray
             currentSum = Math.max(nums[i], currentSum + nums[i]);

             // Update maxSum if currentSum is greater
             maxSum = Math.max(maxSum, currentSum);
         }

         return maxSum;
    }

    public static void main(String[] args) {
         MaxSubArraySum solver = new MaxSubArraySum();

         // Test cases
         int[] nums1 = {-2, 1, -3, 4, -1, 2, 1, -5, 4};
```

```
        System.out.println("Max Subarray Sum: " +
solver.maxSubArray(nums1));   // Expected: 6

        int[] nums2 = {1};
        System.out.println("Max Subarray Sum: " +
solver.maxSubArray(nums2));   // Expected: 1

        int[] nums3 = {5, 4, -1, 7, 8};
        System.out.println("Max Subarray Sum: " +
solver.maxSubArray(nums3));   // Expected: 23

        int[] nums4 = {-1, -2, -3, -4};
        System.out.println("Max Subarray Sum: " +
solver.maxSubArray(nums4));   // Expected: -1
    }
}
```

Time and Space Complexity

- The time complexity of this solution is O(n), where n is the number of elements in the array. We only iterate through the array once.
- The space complexity is O(1) because we are only using a few variables (*maxSum and currentSum*).

Problem 5: Rotate Array to the Right

Problem Statement

You are given an array of integers. Your task is to rotate the array to the right by k steps, where k is a non-negative integer.

Solution

Let's follow our structured approach to solve this problem.

Clarifying Questions

Candidate: I'd like to ask a few clarifying questions to make sure I understand the problem correctly.
Interviewer: Sure, go ahead.

Candidate: First, when you say "rotate the array", I assume that if an element is *shifted past the last position in the array*, it should wrap around to the beginning. Is that correct?
Interviewer: Yes, that's correct. The elements that go past the last position should wrap around to the front of the array.

Candidate: Got it. Also, should I consider the case where k is greater than the length of the array? If so, should I take k % n as the effective number of rotations, where n is the length of the array?

Interviewer: Yes, that's correct!

Candidate: Understood. Finally, does the problem have any constraints regarding the input size or the allowed space complexity?
Interviewer: The array can be large, so an efficient solution is preferred. Try to solve the problem with `O(1)` additional space if possible, meaning in-place rotation.

Candidate: Perfect, I think I have a clear understanding of the requirements.

Example

Let's consider an example to clarify:

- `Input: nums = [1, 2, 3, 4, 5, 6, 7], k = 3`
- `Expected Output: [5, 6, 7, 1, 2, 3, 4]`

Here, the array is rotated to the right by `3` steps. After rotating, the last `3` elements `[5, 6, 7]` move to the front, and the rest of the elements `[1, 2, 3, 4]` follow.

Brute Force Approach

The brute force approach would be to shift each element one step to the right, and repeat this process k times. After each full pass through the array, the last element would be placed at the beginning, and every other element would shift one position to the right.

This approach would have a time complexity of `O(nk)`, where `n` is the length of the array. Each rotation involves shifting all `n` elements, and this is repeated `k` times. This is not efficient, especially when `k` is large.

Optimal Approach

We can solve this problem efficiently using a *three-step reversal algorithm.*

The idea is to break down the problem into three steps:

1. Reverse the *entire array.*
2. Reverse the first `k` elements.
3. Reverse the remaining `n - k` elements.

This approach works because reversing the array shifts all elements, and then reversing specific portions of the array places the elements in the correct rotated order.

Code Solution

Here's how I would implement this in Java:

```
public class RotateArray {
   public void rotate(int[] nums, int k) {
        int n = nums.length;

        // If k is greater than n, take k modulo n
        k = k % n;
```

```
        // Step 1: Reverse the entire array
        reverse(nums, 0, n - 1);

        // Step 2: Reverse the first k elements
        reverse(nums, 0, k - 1);

        // Step 3: Reverse the remaining n-k elements
        reverse(nums, k, n - 1);
    }

    // Helper method to reverse a portion of the array
    private void reverse(int[] nums, int start, int end) {
        while (start < end) {
            int temp = nums[start];
            nums[start] = nums[end];
            nums[end] = temp;
            start++;
            end--;
        }
    }

    public static void main(String[] args) {
        RotateArray solver = new RotateArray();

        // Test cases
        int[] nums1 = {1, 2, 3, 4, 5, 6, 7};
        solver.rotate(nums1, 3);
        System.out.println("Rotated Array: " +
java.util.Arrays.toString(nums1));  // Expected: [5, 6, 7, 1, 2, 3,
4]

        int[] nums2 = {-1, -100, 3, 99};
        solver.rotate(nums2, 2);
        System.out.println("Rotated Array: " +
java.util.Arrays.toString(nums2));  // Expected: [3, 99, -1, -100]

        int[] nums3 = {1, 2};
        solver.rotate(nums3, 3);
        System.out.println("Rotated Array: " +
java.util.Arrays.toString(nums3));  // Expected: [2, 1]
    }
}
```

Time and Space Complexity

- The time complexity of this solution is O(n), where n is the length of the array. We reverse the array three times, each taking O(n) time.
- The space complexity is O(1) since we are performing the rotations in place and using only a constant amount of extra space.

Chapter 3: Strings

Introduction

Strings represent *sequences of characters.*

Strings are essential for processing text and managing data. Mastering string manipulation is crucial for solving many coding problems efficiently.

This chapter will cover the key concepts about String, common operations, and solutions to the most commonly asked String based coding interview questions solved using our structured approach learned in chapter 1.

Key Concepts and Operations

1. **String Initialization and Immutability**:
   - In Java, strings are immutable, meaning once created, their values cannot be changed.
   - String objects are created using *literals* or the `new` keyword.
2. **Common String Operations**:
   - **Concatenation**: Combining two or more strings using the + operator or `concat()` method.
   - **Substring**: Extracting a portion of a string using the `substring()` method.
   - **Length**: Determining the number of characters in a string using the `length()` method.
   - **Character Access**: Accessing individual characters using the `charAt()` method.
   - **Comparison**: Comparing strings using `equals()`, `compareTo()`, or `==` (for reference comparison).
   - **Searching**: Finding characters or substrings using `indexOf()`, `lastIndexOf()`, or regular expressions.
3. **StringBuilder**:
   - `StringBuilder` is a mutable sequence of characters, ideal for situations requiring frequent modifications.
   - Common operations include `append()`, `insert()`, `delete()`, and `reverse()`.
4. **String Manipulation Techniques**:
   - **Splitting**: Dividing a string into an array of substrings using the `split()` method.
   - **Joining**: Combining an array of strings into a single string using `String.join()`.
   - **Trimming**: Removing whitespace from the beginning and end of a string using `trim()`.
   - **Replacing**: Substituting characters or substrings using `replace()` and `replaceAll()`.

Most Popular String Questions

Now, let's look at five most popular coding interview questions on Strings with complete solutions.

Problem 1: Longest Substring Without Repeating Characters

Problem Statement

You are given a string `s`. Your task is to find the length of the longest substring in `s` that does not contain any repeating characters.

Solution

Let's follow the structured approach to solve this problem.

Clarifying Questions

Candidate: I'd like to ask a few clarifying questions before starting.
Interviewer: Of course, go ahead.

Candidate: First, should I consider only English alphabet characters, or does the string contain other characters, such as digits or symbols?
Interviewer: The string can contain any character, including digits and symbols.

Candidate: Got it. Also, should I assume that the string can be very large?
Interviewer: Yes, the string can be large, so an efficient solution would be preferred.

Candidate: Lastly, does the entire input string fits in memory, or should I consider streaming input?
Interviewer: You can assume that the input fits in memory, so you don't need to worry about streaming.

Candidate: Perfect. I have all the information I need to proceed.

Example

Let's consider an example to clarify:

- `Input: s = "abcabcbb"`
- `Expected Output: 3`

The longest substring without repeating characters is `abc`, which has a length of `3`.

Brute Force Approach

A brute force approach would involve checking all possible substrings of the string and verifying whether each substring contains unique characters. We would keep track of the longest substring that meets the condition.

To generate all substrings, we can use two nested loops. The outer loop selects the starting character, and the inner loop selects the ending character.
For each substring, we would need to check if it contains any duplicate characters, which could be done using a data structure like a set.

This approach would have a time complexity of $O(n^3)$, where n is the length of the string. This is because we would need to generate all substrings ($O(n^2)$) and check each substring for duplicates ($O(n)$). Hence, this solution is not efficient.

Optimal Approach

We can optimize this problem using a ***sliding window technique along with a HashMap***.

> **Note**: We will cover the *Sliding Window Pattern* in detail in a separate chapter.

*The idea is to use two pointers, **left** and **right**, to represent a **sliding window** over the string.*

The window will contain a substring without repeating characters. We will move the *right pointer to expand* the window and the *left pointer to shrink* it when we encounter a duplicate character.

We can use a *HashMap to keep track of the characters in the current window* and their indices. This allows us to efficiently skip over repeated characters by adjusting the left pointer.

Code Solution

Here is how I would implement this in Java:

```
import java.util.HashMap;

public class LongestSubstringWithoutRepeatingCharacters {
   public int lengthOfLongestSubstring(String s) {
        // HashMap to store the last index of each character
        HashMap<Character, Integer> map = new HashMap<>();
        int maxLength = 0;
        int left = 0;

        // Iterate through the string with the right pointer
        for (int right = 0; right < s.length(); right++) {
            char currentChar = s.charAt(right);

            // If the character is already in the window, move the
left pointer
            if (map.containsKey(currentChar)) {
                left = Math.max(left, map.get(currentChar) + 1);
            }
```

```
            // Update the character's index in the map
            map.put(currentChar, right);

            // Update the maximum length of the substring
            maxLength = Math.max(maxLength, right - left + 1);
        }

        return maxLength;
    }

    public static void main(String[] args) {
        LongestSubstringWithoutRepeatingCharacters solver = new
LongestSubstringWithoutRepeatingCharacters();

        // Test cases
        String s1 = "abcabcbb";
        System.out.println("Longest Substring Length: " +
solver.lengthOfLongestSubstring(s1));  // Expected: 3

        String s2 = "bbbbb";
        System.out.println("Longest Substring Length: " +
solver.lengthOfLongestSubstring(s2));  // Expected: 1

        String s3 = "pwwkew";
        System.out.println("Longest Substring Length: " +
solver.lengthOfLongestSubstring(s3));  // Expected: 3

        String s4 = "";
        System.out.println("Longest Substring Length: " +
solver.lengthOfLongestSubstring(s4));  // Expected: 0
    }
}
```

Time and Space Complexity

- The time complexity of this solution is `O(n)`, where `n` is the length of the string. Each character is processed at most twice—once when expanding the window with the right pointer and potentially again when contracting it with the left pointer.
- The space complexity is `O(min(n,m))`, where `n` is the length of the string and `m` is the size of the character set (for example, 128 for ASCII). This is because we use a HashMap to store the indices of characters

---

Problem 2: Longest Palindromic Substring

Problem Statement

You are given a string `s`. Your task is to find and return the longest substring within `s` that is a palindrome.

A palindrome is a string that reads the same forward and backward.

Solution

Let's follow the structured approach to solve this problem.

Clarifying Questions

Candidate: Should I consider all characters, including digits and special characters, when identifying palindromes?
Interviewer: Yes, the input string can include any characters, not just alphabetic characters.

Candidate: Thanks, I'm ready to proceed.

Example

Let's consider an example:

- `Input: s = "babad"`
- `Expected Output: "bab" or "aba"`

Both "*bab*" and "*aba*" are valid longest palindromic substrings, as both have the same maximum length of 3.

Brute Force Approach

The brute force approach would involve generating all possible substrings of s and checking each one to see if it is a palindrome. We would then return the longest palindrome found.

This approach has a time complexity of $O(n^3)$, where n is the length of the string. This is because we generate all substrings ($O(n^2)$) and check each substring for being a palindrome ($O(n)$). Hence, this approach is not optimal.

Optimal Approach

We can use the ***Expand Around Center*** approach to solve this problem efficiently.

The idea is to consider each character (and the gap between each pair of characters) as the center of a potential palindrome and *expand outward* while the characters on both sides are the same.

This allows us to identify palindromic substrings centered around each character.

Code Solution

Here's how I would implement it in Java:

```
public class LongestPalindromicSubstring {
   public String longestPalindrome(String s) {
       if (s == null || s.isEmpty()) {
```

```
            return "";
        }

        int start = 0, end = 0;

        for (int i = 0; i < s.length(); i++) {
            // Check for the longest odd-length palindrome
            int len1 = expandAroundCenter(s, i, i);
            // Check for the longest even-length palindrome
            int len2 = expandAroundCenter(s, i, i + 1);
            // Find the maximum length between the two
            int len = Math.max(len1, len2);
            // Update start and end indices if we found a longer
palindrome
            if (len > end - start) {
                start = i - (len - 1) / 2;
                end = i + len / 2;
            }
        }

        return s.substring(start, end + 1);
    }

    // Helper method to expand around the center
    private int expandAroundCenter(String s, int left, int right) {
        while (left >= 0 && right < s.length() && s.charAt(left) ==
s.charAt(right)) {
            left--;
            right++;
        }
        return right - left - 1;
    }

    public static void main(String[] args) {
        LongestPalindromicSubstring solver = new
LongestPalindromicSubstring();

        // Test cases
        String s1 = "babad";
        System.out.println("Longest Palindromic Substring: " +
solver.longestPalindrome(s1));  // Expected: "bab" or "aba"

        String s2 = "cbbd";
        System.out.println("Longest Palindromic Substring: " +
solver.longestPalindrome(s2));  // Expected: "bb"

        String s3 = "a";
        System.out.println("Longest Palindromic Substring: " +
solver.longestPalindrome(s3));  // Expected: "a"

        String s4 = "ac";
        System.out.println("Longest Palindromic Substring: " +
solver.longestPalindrome(s4));  // Expected: "a" or "c"
```

```
    }
}
```

Time and Space Complexity

- The time complexity of this solution is `O(n²)`, where `n` is the length of the string. This is because we expand around each center for palindromes, and this expansion takes `O(n)` time for each of the `n` centers.
- The space complexity is `O(1)` since we are only using a few variables for indices and lengths, and no additional data structures are used.

Problem 3: String to Integer

Problem Statement

You are tasked with implementing the function `myAtoi(string s)`, which converts the input string s into a 32-bit signed integer.

The function should handle various edge cases and return the corresponding integer value.

Solution

Let's follow the structured approach to solve this problem.

Clarifying Questions

Candidate: I have a few clarifying questions before starting. Is that okay?
Interviewer: Absolutely, go ahead.

Candidate: Can the string contain non-numeric characters, and if so, what should I do when I encounter them?
Interviewer: The string can contain non-numeric characters. You should stop the conversion as soon as a non-numeric character is encountered after parsing any initial spaces and the optional sign.

Candidate: Got it. Should I handle the case where the converted number exceeds the range of a 32-bit signed integer?
Interviewer: Yes, if the number exceeds $2^{31} - 1$, return *INT_MAX*. If it's less than -2^{31}, return *INT_MIN*.

Candidate: Perfect, I believe I have all the information to proceed.

Example

Let's consider an example:

- `Input: s = " -42"`
- `Expected Output: -42`

The function ignores the leading spaces, reads the - sign, and then converts 42 to an integer.

Approach

To solve this problem, I'll break the implementation into the following steps:

1. *Ignore Leading Whitespaces*: I'll skip any leading whitespace characters.
2. *Check for Optional Sign*: I'll check if the next character is either a + or - to determine the sign of the number.
3. *Convert Digits to Integer*: I'll iterate over the digits in the string and build the integer value.
4. *Handle Overflow*: If the resulting number exceeds the 32-bit signed integer range, I'll return either INT_MAX or INT_MIN.
5. *Stop on Non-Numeric Characters*: As soon as a non-numeric character is encountered, the conversion stops.

Code Solution

Here's how I would implement it in Java:

```
public class MyAtoi {
    public int myAtoi(String s) {
        int index = 0, n = s.length();
        int result = 0;
        int sign = 1;

        // Step 1: Ignore leading whitespace
        while (index < n && s.charAt(index) == ' ') {
            index++;
        }

        // Step 2: Check for optional sign
        if (index < n && (s.charAt(index) == '+' || s.charAt(index)
== '-')) {
            sign = s.charAt(index) == '-' ? -1 : 1;
            index++;
        }

        // Step 3: Convert digits to integer
        while (index < n && Character.isDigit(s.charAt(index))) {
            int digit = s.charAt(index) - '0';

            // Step 4: Check for overflow and handle it
            if (result > (Integer.MAX_VALUE - digit) / 10) {
                return sign == 1 ? Integer.MAX_VALUE :
Integer.MIN_VALUE;
            }

            result = result * 10 + digit;
            index++;
        }
```

```
        // Step 5: Return the final result with the sign applied
        return result * sign;
    }

    public static void main(String[] args) {
        MyAtoi solver = new MyAtoi();

        // Test cases
        System.out.println(solver.myAtoi("42"));              //
Expected: 42
        System.out.println(solver.myAtoi("   -42"));          //
Expected: -42
        System.out.println(solver.myAtoi("4193 with words")); //
Expected: 4193
        System.out.println(solver.myAtoi("words and 987"));   //
Expected: 0
        System.out.println(solver.myAtoi("-91283472332")); //
Expected: -2147483648 (INT_MIN)
    }
}
```

Time and Space Complexity

- The time complexity of this solution is O(n), where n is the length of the input string. We scan through the string once.
- The space complexity is O(1) since we only use a few variables for processing and do not use any additional data structures.

Problem 4: Group Anagrams

Problem Statement

You are given an array of strings. Your task is to group the anagrams together.

An anagram is a word formed by rearranging the letters of another word, using all the original letters exactly once.

Return a list of groups where each group contains words that are anagrams of each other.

Solution

Let's follow the structured approach to solve this problem.

Clarifying Questions

Candidate: I'd like to ask a few clarifying questions to make sure I understand the problem correctly.
Interviewer: Sure, go ahead.

Candidate: First, should I assume that all strings in the input array consist only of lowercase English letters?
Interviewer: Yes, you can assume that all strings consist of lowercase English letters.

Candidate: Understood. Also, should I return the groups in any specific order, or does the order not matter?
Interviewer: The order of the groups or the words within the groups does not matter.

Candidate: Got it. Lastly, can the input contain duplicate strings, and if so, should duplicates be treated normally in the group?
Interviewer: Yes, duplicates are possible, and they should be grouped normally with other anagrams.

Candidate: Great! I think I have all the necessary information to proceed.

Example

Let's consider an example:

- `Input: strs = ["eat", "tea", "tan", "ate", "nat", "bat"]`
- `Expected Output: [["eat", "tea", "ate"], ["tan", "nat"], ["bat"]]`

Here, "eat", "tea", and "ate" are anagrams and grouped together, "tan" and "nat" are another group, and "bat" is in a group by itself.

Brute Force Approach

A brute force approach would involve comparing each string to every other string to check if they are anagrams. This would involve sorting each string and comparing the sorted versions. We would then group strings that have the same sorted version.

Sorting each string takes `O(m log m)`, where `m` is the length of the string, and comparing all pairs would lead to a time complexity of `O(n × m log m)`, where `n` is the number of strings. This is not the most efficient approach, as there would be a lot of repetition in terms of sorting the same string and comparing with every other string.

Optimal Approach (Using HashMap)

We can optimize this problem by using a ***HashMap*** to group the anagrams. Instead of comparing each string with every other string, we can sort the characters of each string and use the sorted string as the key in the HashMap.

All strings that are anagrams of each other will have the same sorted string and will be grouped together.

The plan is as follows.

For each string in the input array:

1. We sort the string to generate a key.
2. If the sorted string is already in the HashMap, we append the original string to the corresponding list.
3. If the sorted string is not in the HashMap, we create a new entry with the sorted string as the key and the original string as the value in the list.
4. At the end, we return the values of the HashMap as the groups of anagrams.

Code Solution

Here's how I would implement this in Java:

```
import java.util.*;

public class GroupAnagrams {
    public List<List<String>> groupAnagrams(String[] strs) {
        // HashMap to store the grouped anagrams
        HashMap<String, List<String>> map = new HashMap<>();

        // Iterate over each string in the input array
        for (String str : strs) {
            // Convert the string to a character array, sort it, and
convert it back to a string
            char[] charArray = str.toCharArray();
            Arrays.sort(charArray);
            String sortedStr = new String(charArray);

            // Add the original string to the group in the HashMap
            if (!map.containsKey(sortedStr)) {
                map.put(sortedStr, new ArrayList<>());
            }
            map.get(sortedStr).add(str);
        }

        // Return all the values (grouped anagrams) from the HashMap
        return new ArrayList<>(map.values());
    }

    public static void main(String[] args) {
        GroupAnagrams solver = new GroupAnagrams();

        // Test cases
        String[] strs1 = {"eat", "tea", "tan", "ate", "nat", "bat"};
        System.out.println(solver.groupAnagrams(strs1));
        // Expected: [["eat", "tea", "ate"], ["tan", "nat"],
["bat"]]

        String[] strs2 = {""};
        System.out.println(solver.groupAnagrams(strs2));
        // Expected: [[""]]
```

```
        String[] strs3 = {"a"};
        System.out.println(solver.groupAnagrams(strs3));
        // Expected: [["a"]]
    }
}
```

Time and Space Complexity

- The time complexity is `O(n × m log m)`, where `n` is the number of strings in the input array and `m` is the maximum length of a string. Sorting each string takes `O(m log m)`, and we do this for each of the `n` strings.
- The space complexity is `O(n × m)`, where `n` is the number of strings and mm is the length of the strings. This space is used by the HashMap and the list of strings.

Problem 5: Valid Parentheses

Problem Statement

You are given a string that contains just the characters `(`, `)`, `{`, `}`, `[`, and `]`. Your task is to determine if the input string is **valid**. A string is considered valid if:

1. Open brackets are closed by the same type of brackets.
2. Open brackets are closed in the correct order.

Solution

Let's follow the structured approach to solve this problem.

Clarifying Questions

Candidate: I'd like to clarify a few points about the problem before starting.
Interviewer: Sure, go ahead.

Candidate: First, should I assume that the input string only contains the characters `()[]{}`?
Interviewer: Yes, the string will contain only those six characters.

Candidate: Got it. Also, should I return true if the string is empty since there are no unmatched brackets?
Interviewer: Yes, an empty string should be considered valid.

Candidate: Understood. Lastly, does the string have a length limit?
Interviewer: There's no specific length limit, so an efficient solution is preferred.

Candidate: Great, I have a clear understanding now.

Example

Let's consider few examples:

1) `Input: s = "()", Expected Output: true`
   The string contains a valid pair of parentheses.

2) `Input: s = "(]", Expected Output: false`
   The string has mismatched brackets.

Brute Force Approach

A brute force approach would involve checking for balanced parentheses by iterating over the string and ensuring that each closing bracket has a matching opening bracket.
However, this approach can be tricky to implement without an appropriate data structure.

Optimal Approach

We can efficiently solve this problem using a stack data structure.

The idea is to use a stack to keep track of opening brackets. Whenever we encounter a closing bracket, we check if it matches the most recent opening bracket by popping from the stack.

If there is no matching opening bracket or if they are mismatched, the string is invalid. At the end, if the stack is empty, the string is valid.

Code Solution

Here's how I would implement this in Java:

```
import java.util.Stack;

public class ValidParentheses {
   public boolean isValid(String s) {
        // Stack to keep track of opening brackets
        Stack<Character> stack = new Stack<>();

        // Iterate over the characters in the string
        for (char c : s.toCharArray()) {
            // If it's an opening bracket, push it onto the stack
            if (c == '(' || c == '{' || c == '[') {
                stack.push(c);
            }
            // If it's a closing bracket, check for matching opening
bracket
            else {
                if (stack.isEmpty()) {
                    return false;  // No matching opening bracket
                }
                char top = stack.pop();
                if ((c == ')' && top != '(') ||
```

```
                        (c == '}' && top != '{') ||
                        (c == ']' && top != '[')) {
                    return false;  // Mismatched brackets
                }
            }
        }

        // In the end, the stack should be empty if the string is
valid
        return stack.isEmpty();
    }

    public static void main(String[] args) {
        ValidParentheses solver = new ValidParentheses();

        // Test cases
        System.out.println(solver.isValid("()"));       // Expected:
true
        System.out.println(solver.isValid("()[]{}")); // Expected:
true
        System.out.println(solver.isValid("(]"));       // Expected:
false
        System.out.println(solver.isValid("([)]"));     // Expected:
false
        System.out.println(solver.isValid("{[]}"));     // Expected:
true
    }
}
```

Time and Space Complexity

- The time complexity is O(n), where n is the length of the input string. We iterate through the string once, pushing and popping elements from the stack.
- The space complexity is O(n), where n is the length of the string, because in the worst case, all opening brackets may be pushed onto the stack.

Chapter 4: Two Pointers Pattern

The two pointers pattern is a popular and efficient technique often used to solve *array and string problems* in coding interviews.

This approach involves using *two pointers to iterate through the data structure*, which helps reduce the time complexity by avoiding nested loops.

This chapter will cover the fundamentals of the two pointers pattern and demonstrate how to apply it to solve some of the most frequently asked questions in this category.

Fundamentals of Two Pointers Pattern

In the two pointers pattern, two pointers are used to traverse an array or a string from different directions or at different speeds.

Depending on the problem, the pointers can move towards each other, away from each other, or in the same direction with one moving faster than the other.

This pattern is particularly useful for problems involving *searching*, *sorting*, and *partitioning*.

Common Scenarios for Two Pointers

1. **Opposite Direction**: One pointer starts from the beginning, and the other starts from the end, moving towards each other until they meet.
2. **Same Direction**: Both pointers start from the same position but move at different speeds.
3. **Fixed Distance**: One pointer remains fixed while the other moves.

Most Popular Questions

Let's apply the two pointers pattern to solve the popular questions in this category.

Problem 1: Two Sum in Sorted Array

Problem Statement

You are given a sorted array of integers in non-decreasing order. Your task is to find two numbers in the array such that their sum equals a given target number.

Return the 1-indexed positions of the two numbers. There will be exactly one solution, and you should not use the same element twice.

Solution

Let's follow the structured approach to solve this problem.

Clarifying Questions

Candidate: I'd like to clarify a few points before starting.
Interviewer: Sure, go ahead.

Candidate: First, should I assume that the input array will always have at least two elements?
Interviewer: Yes, you can assume that the array will always contain at least two elements.

Candidate: Lastly, should I return the indices as *1-indexed*, meaning the first element in the array has an index of 1?
Interviewer: Correct, the output should be 1-indexed.

Candidate: Understood. I have everything I need to proceed.

Example

Let's consider an example:

- `Input: numbers = [2, 7, 11, 15], target = 9`
- `Expected Output: [1, 2]`

Here, `numbers[1] + numbers[2] = 2 + 7 = 9`, which equals the `target`, so the answer is `[1, 2]`.

Brute Force Approach

A brute force approach would involve using *two nested loops*. For each element in the array, I would iterate over the remaining elements to check if their sum equals the target. If a match is found, I would return the indices of those two elements.

This approach would have a time complexity of $O(n^2)$, where n is the length of the array. Since we are checking each pair of elements, this is not the most efficient solution.

Optimal Approach

Since the array is sorted, we can use the ***two pointers approach*** to solve this in `O(n)` time.

The idea is to maintain two pointers: one starting at the beginning (*left*) and the other at the end (*right*) of the array. We then check the sum of the elements at these two pointers:

- If the sum *equals* the target, we return their indices.
- If the sum is *less* than the target, we move the left pointer to the right to increase the sum.

- If the sum is *greater* than the target, we move the right pointer to the left to decrease the sum.

This ensures that we find the solution in one pass through the array.

Code Solution

Here's how I would implement it in Java:

```
public class TwoSumSortedArray {
   public int[] twoSum(int[] numbers, int target) {
       // Initialize two pointers
       int left = 0;
       int right = numbers.length - 1;

       // Iterate while the two pointers do not overlap
       while (left < right) {
           int sum = numbers[left] + numbers[right];

           // If the sum matches the target, return 1-indexed
positions
           if (sum == target) {
               return new int[]{left + 1, right + 1};
           }
           // If the sum is too small, move the left pointer to the
right
           else if (sum < target) {
               left++;
           }
           // If the sum is too large, move the right pointer to
the left
           else {
               right--;
           }
       }

       // In case no solution is found, which shouldn't happen per
the problem statement
       throw new IllegalArgumentException("No two sum solution");
   }

   public static void main(String[] args) {
       TwoSumSortedArray solver = new TwoSumSortedArray();

       // Test cases
       int[] numbers1 = {2, 7, 11, 15};
       int target1 = 9;
       int[] result1 = solver.twoSum(numbers1, target1);
       System.out.println("Indices: " + result1[0] + ", " +
result1[1]);  // Expected: 1, 2

       int[] numbers2 = {2, 3, 4};
       int target2 = 6;
```

```
        int[] result2 = solver.twoSum(numbers2, target2);
        System.out.println("Indices: " + result2[0] + ", " +
result2[1]);  // Expected: 1, 3

        int[] numbers3 = {-1, 0};
        int target3 = -1;
        int[] result3 = solver.twoSum(numbers3, target3);
        System.out.println("Indices: " + result3[0] + ", " +
result3[1]);  // Expected: 1, 2
    }
}
```

Time and Space Complexity

- The time complexity of this solution is `O(n)`, where `n` is the length of the array. We only pass through the array once using the two pointers.
- The space complexity is `O(1)` because we only use a constant amount of extra space for the two pointers.

Problem 2: Remove Duplicates from Sorted Array

Problem Statement

You are given a sorted array `nums`. Your task is to remove the duplicates **in-place** such that each unique element appears only once and return the new length of the array.

The array should be modified in-place, and you cannot use any extra space for another array.

You are required to return the new length of the array after removing duplicates, but do not worry about elements beyond the returned length.

Solution

Let's follow the structured approach to solve this problem.

Clarifying Questions

Candidate: I'd like to ask a few clarifying questions to ensure I understand the problem correctly.
Interviewer: Sure, go ahead.

Candidate: Got it. Also, since the operation is to be done in-place, can I modify the input array directly and return the new length?
Interviewer: Yes, you should modify the input array in-place and return the new length. Elements beyond the new length can remain unchanged.

Candidate: Understood. Lastly, is there any specific constraint on the size of the array?
Interviewer: The array can be large, but you can assume it fits in memory. An efficient solution is preferred.

Candidate: Perfect. I think I have all the information to proceed.

Example

Let's consider an example:

- Input: `nums = [0, 0, 1, 1, 1, 2, 2, 3, 3, 4]`
- Expected Output: `5`, with `nums` modified to `[0, 1, 2, 3, 4]` and the remaining elements irrelevant.

Brute Force Approach

A brute force approach would involve iterating through the array and creating a new array containing only the unique elements. However, this would require additional space, which violates the problem's constraints.

Optimal Approach

Since the array is sorted, we can solve the problem efficiently using the two pointers technique.

We can use one pointer (`i`) to track the current position where the next unique element should be placed, and another pointer (`j`) to iterate through the array.

The idea is to compare each element at position `j` with the element at position `i - 1`. If the elements are different, it means we have found a new unique element, and we can place it at `i` and increment `i`.

Code Solution

Here is the implementation in Java:

```
public class RemoveDuplicatesSortedArray {
    public int removeDuplicates(int[] nums) {
        // Edge case: If the array is empty, return 0
        if (nums.length == 0) {
            return 0;
        }

        // Initialize the first pointer
        int i = 1;

        // Iterate through the array starting from the second
element
        for (int j = 1; j < nums.length; j++) {
            // If the current element is different from the previous
element
```

```
            if (nums[j] != nums[i - 1]) {
                // Place the current element at the i-th position
                nums[i] = nums[j];
                i++;
            }
        }

        // Return the new length of the array (number of unique
elements)
        return i;
    }

    public static void main(String[] args) {
        RemoveDuplicatesSortedArray solver = new
RemoveDuplicatesSortedArray();

        // Test cases
        int[] nums1 = {1, 1, 2};
        int newLength1 = solver.removeDuplicates(nums1);
        System.out.println("New Length: " + newLength1);   //
Expected: 2
        System.out.println("Modified Array: " +
java.util.Arrays.toString(java.util.Arrays.copyOfRange(nums1, 0,
newLength1)));  // Expected: [1, 2]

        int[] nums2 = {0, 0, 1, 1, 1, 2, 2, 3, 3, 4};
        int newLength2 = solver.removeDuplicates(nums2);
        System.out.println("New Length: " + newLength2);   //
Expected: 5
        System.out.println("Modified Array: " +
java.util.Arrays.toString(java.util.Arrays.copyOfRange(nums2, 0,
newLength2)));  // Expected: [0, 1, 2, 3, 4]
    }
}
```

Time and Space Complexity

- The time complexity is `O(n)`, where `n` is the length of the array. We pass through the array once using the two pointers.
- The space complexity is `O(1)` because we are not using any extra space other than a few variables for pointers.

Problem 3: Container With the Most Water

Problem Statement

You are given `n` non-negative integers, where each integer represents the height of a vertical line at the `i-th` position.

Your task is to find two lines that, together with the x-axis, form a container that holds the most water.

Return the maximum amount of water the container can contain.

Solution

Let's follow the structured approach to solve this problem.

Clarifying Questions

Candidate: I'd like to clarify a few points before starting.
Interviewer: Sure, go ahead.

Candidate: First, should I assume that the height of each line is represented by a non-negative integer and that the x-axis is formed between these lines?
Interviewer: Yes, that's correct. Each line's height is represented by a non-negative integer, and the x-axis is between the lines.

Candidate: Got it. Also, should the width of the container be the distance between the two lines, which is the difference in their indices?
Interviewer: Yes, the width of the container is the difference between the indices of the two lines.

Candidate: Understood. I believe I have all the information to proceed.

Example

Let's consider an example:

- Input: `height = [1,8,6,2,5,4,8,3,7]`
- Expected Output: `49`

Here, the two lines at indices 1 and 8 (with heights 8 and 7) form the container that can hold the most water, with an area of 49.

Brute Force Approach

A brute force approach would involve calculating the area for every possible pair of lines.

The area between two lines is the minimum of their heights multiplied by the distance between them (the difference in their indices).

We would iterate through all pairs of lines and keep track of the maximum area encountered.

This approach would have a time complexity of $O(n^2)$, where n is the number of lines. This is because we would check every possible pair of lines. It's inefficient for large arrays.

Optimal Approach

We can use the two pointers approach to solve this problem efficiently.

The idea is to start with two pointers: one at the beginning (*left*) and one at the end (*right*) of the array. We calculate the area formed by these two lines and then move the pointer pointing to the *shorter line* inward.

This is because moving the taller line won't help increase the area (since the height is limited by the shorter line), *so we move the shorter line to try and find a taller line that might increase the area.*

Code Solution

Here is the implementation in Java:

```
public class ContainerWithMostWater {
    public int maxArea(int[] height) {
        // Initialize two pointers
        int left = 0;
        int right = height.length - 1;
        int maxArea = 0;

        // Loop until the two pointers meet
        while (left < right) {
            // Calculate the area formed by the two lines
            int currentArea = Math.min(height[left], height[right]) *
(right - left);
            // Update maxArea if the current area is greater
            maxArea = Math.max(maxArea, currentArea);

            // Move the pointer pointing to the shorter line
            if (height[left] < height[right]) {
                left++;
            } else {
                right--;
            }
        }

        // Return the maximum area found
        return maxArea;
    }

    public static void main(String[] args) {
        ContainerWithMostWater solver = new ContainerWithMostWater();

        // Test cases
        int[] height1 = {1, 8, 6, 2, 5, 4, 8, 3, 7};
        System.out.println("Max Area: " + solver.maxArea(height1));
// Expected: 49

        int[] height2 = {1, 1};
        System.out.println("Max Area: " + solver.maxArea(height2));
// Expected: 1

        int[] height3 = {4, 3, 2, 1, 4};
        System.out.println("Max Area: " + solver.maxArea(height3));
// Expected: 16
```

```
        int[] height4 = {1, 2, 1};
        System.out.println("Max Area: " + solver.maxArea(height4));
// Expected: 2
    }
}
```

Time and Space Complexity

- The time complexity of this solution is `O(n)`, where `n` is the length of the array. We iterate through the array once using the two pointers.
- The space complexity is `O(1)`, since we are only using a few variables to keep track of the pointers and the maximum area.

Problem 4: Maximum Operations to Pair Sum to given Target

Problem Statement

You are given an integer array `nums` and an integer `k`.

In one operation, you can select two numbers from the array whose sum equals `k` and remove both numbers from the array.

Your task is to return the maximum number of operations you can perform on the array.

Solution

Let's follow the structured approach to solve this problem.

Clarifying Questions

Candidate: I'd like to clarify a few points before jumping into a solution.
Interviewer: Sure, go ahead.

Candidate: First, should I assume that the elements of the array can be both positive and negative?
Interviewer: Yes, the array can contain both positive and negative integers.

Candidate: Is there any constraint on the size of the array or the value of `k` that I should consider for efficiency?
Interviewer: There are no specific constraints beyond ensuring the solution is efficient, especially for large arrays.

Candidate: Understood. I think I have everything I need to proceed.

Example

Let's consider an example to clarify:

- Input: `nums = [3, 1, 3, 4, 3], k =` 6

- Expected Output: 1

Here, you can only remove one pair of numbers whose sum is equal to 6 (for example, 3 + 3).

Brute Force Approach

A brute force approach would involve checking every pair of numbers to see if their sum equals k.

For each valid pair, we would remove both numbers from the array and increment the count of operations.

This approach would have a time complexity of $O(n^2)$ because for each number, we would need to check every other number to find a pair. This is inefficient for large arrays.

Optimal Approach

We can optimize the solution using a HashMap to store the frequency of each number in the array.

The idea is to iterate over the array and for each number *num*, check if there is a complement k - num that we've encountered before (stored in the HashMap). If such a complement exists, it means we can form a pair that sums to k. We then decrement the frequency of the complement and continue. If no complement exists, we add the current number to the HashMap.

Code Solution

Here is the implementation in Java:

```
import java.util.HashMap;

public class MaxOperationsPairSumK {
    public int maxOperations(int[] nums, int k) {
        // HashMap to store the frequency of elements
        HashMap<Integer, Integer> map = new HashMap<>();
        int operations = 0;

        // Iterate through the array
        for (int num : nums) {
            // Check if there is a complement (k - num) in the map
            int complement = k - num;

            if (map.getOrDefault(complement, 0) > 0) {
                // If a complement exists, perform the operation
                operations++;
                // Decrease the count of the complement in the map
                map.put(complement, map.get(complement) - 1);
            } else {
                // Otherwise, increase the count of the current
number
```

```
                map.put(num, map.getOrDefault(num, 0) + 1);
            }
        }

        return operations;
    }

    public static void main(String[] args) {
        MaxOperationsPairSumK solver = new MaxOperationsPairSumK();

        // Test cases
        int[] nums1 = {3, 1, 3, 4, 3};
        int k1 = 6;
        System.out.println("Max Operations: " +
solver.maxOperations(nums1, k1));  // Expected: 1

        int[] nums2 = {1, 2, 3, 4};
        int k2 = 5;
        System.out.println("Max Operations: " +
solver.maxOperations(nums2, k2));  // Expected: 2

        int[] nums3 = {1, 1, 1, 1};
        int k3 = 2;
        System.out.println("Max Operations: " +
solver.maxOperations(nums3, k3));  // Expected: 2
    }
}
```

Time and Space Complexity

- The time complexity of this solution is `O(n)`, where `n` is the length of the array. We iterate through the array once, and each HashMap operation (insertion, lookup) takes `O(1)` on average.
- The space complexity is `O(n)` due to the HashMap storing the frequency of elements in the array.

Problem 5: Move Zeroes to End

Problem Statement

You are given an array `nums`. Your task is to write a function that moves all the `0`s in the array to the end while maintaining the relative order of the non-zero elements.

Solution

Let's follow the structured approach to solve this problem.

Clarifying Questions

Candidate: I'd like to clarify a few points before jumping into a solution.
Interviewer: Sure, go ahead.

Candidate: Understood. Also, should I maintain the relative order of the non-zero elements, meaning their positions in the array should not change?
Interviewer: Yes, you should maintain the relative order of all non-zero elements.

Candidate: Got it. Lastly, should the solution be done in-place?
Interviewer: Correct. The solution should be done in-place, without extra space.

Candidate: Perfect. I believe I have all the information to proceed.

Example

Let's consider an example to clarify:

- Input: `nums = [0, 1, 0, 3, 12]`
- Expected Output: `[1, 3, 12, 0, 0]`

Here, all `0`s are moved to the end of the array while maintaining the order of the non-zero elements.

Brute Force Approach

A brute force approach might involve creating a new array and copying all non-zero elements to it, then appending zeros at the end. However, this would require extra space, which violates the problem constraints.

Optimal Approach

We can solve this efficiently using a two pointers approach.

The idea is to use one pointer (*nonZeroIndex*) to keep track of the position where the next non-zero element should be placed.
We then iterate through the array using another pointer (`i`). Every time we encounter a non-zero element at `i`, we move it to `nonZeroIndex` and increment `nonZeroIndex`.

After all non-zero elements have been processed, we fill the remaining positions in the array with `0`s.

Code Solution

Here's how I would implement this in Java:

```
public class MoveZeros {
   public void moveZeroes(int[] nums) {
        int nonZeroIndex = 0;

        // First pass: Move all non-zero elements to the front
        for (int i = 0; i < nums.length; i++) {
            if (nums[i] != 0) {
                nums[nonZeroIndex] = nums[i];
                nonZeroIndex++;
            }
        }
```

```
        // Second pass: Fill the rest of the array with zeros
        for (int i = nonZeroIndex; i < nums.length; i++) {
            nums[i] = 0;
        }
    }

    public static void main(String[] args) {
        MoveZeros solver = new MoveZeros();

        // Test cases
        int[] nums1 = {0, 1, 0, 3, 12};
        solver.moveZeroes(nums1);
        System.out.println("Modified Array: " +
java.util.Arrays.toString(nums1));  // Expected: [1, 3, 12, 0, 0]

        int[] nums2 = {0, 0, 1};
        solver.moveZeroes(nums2);
        System.out.println("Modified Array: " +
java.util.Arrays.toString(nums2));  // Expected: [1, 0, 0]

        int[] nums3 = {2, 1};
        solver.moveZeroes(nums3);
        System.out.println("Modified Array: " +
java.util.Arrays.toString(nums3));  // Expected: [2, 1]

        int[] nums4 = {0};
        solver.moveZeroes(nums4);
        System.out.println("Modified Array: " +
java.util.Arrays.toString(nums4));  // Expected: [0]
    }
}
```

Time and Space Complexity

- The time complexity of this solution is `O(n)`, where `n` is the length of the array. We iterate through the array twice: once to move non-zero elements and once to fill zeros.
- The space complexity is `O(1)` since the operation is done in-place and we only use a few variables for tracking indices.

Chapter 5: Sliding Window Pattern

The Sliding Window pattern is a commonly used technique in solving array and string problems, especially those that involve ***finding a subarray or substring** that meets a specific condition.*

Introduction

The Sliding Window pattern is based on the idea of *maintaining a window that satisfies a certain condition* as it slides over the input data. The window can be either fixed-size or dynamic, depending on the problem at hand.

- **Fixed-size Window:** The window has a constant size, and we move it one element at a time.
- **Dynamic-size Window:** The window's size adjusts based on the conditions defined by the problem.

When to Use Sliding Window Pattern

You should consider using the Sliding Window pattern when:

- You need to examine or process all possible *contiguous subarrays/substrings* of a given size.
- You are asked to find the *maximum, minimum, or average of a subarray or substring* of a fixed size.
- You need to find the *smallest or largest subarray/substring* that meets a specific condition.

How to Implement Sliding Window Pattern

The Sliding Window pattern can be implemented as follows:

1. **Initialize:** Start by defining the window's boundaries (usually the *start* and *end* indices).
2. **Expand:** Move the end boundary to include new elements until the window meets the condition.
3. **Shrink:** If the window exceeds the required condition, move the start boundary to shrink the window.
4. **Track:** Keep track of the best or required result as the window slides over the data.

Most Popular Sliding Window Problems

Problem 1: Maximum Sum Subarray of Size K

Problem Statement

You are given an *array* of positive integers and an integer `k`.

Your task is to find the maximum sum of any contiguous subarray of size `k` from the array.

Solution

Let's follow the structured approach to solve this problem.

Clarifying Questions

Candidate: I'd like to clarify a few points before jumping into a solution.
Interviewer: Sure, go ahead.

Candidate: First, should I assume that the array always contains at least `k` elements?
Interviewer: Yes, the array will always have at least k elements.

Candidate: Got it. Also, can I assume that the input array only contains positive integers?
Interviewer: Yes, the array consists of positive integers.

Candidate: Perfect, I think I have everything I need to proceed.

Example

Let's consider an example to clarify:

- Input: `nums = [2, 1, 5, 1, 3, 2], k = 3`
- Expected Output: `9`

The subarray `[5, 1, 3]` has the maximum sum of `9`.

Brute Force Approach

A brute force approach would involve checking the sum of every possible contiguous subarray of size `k`.

We would iterate over all starting points of the subarray, compute the sum of each subarray, and keep track of the maximum sum encountered.

This brute force approach would have a time complexity of `O(nk)`, where `n` is the length of the array. For each starting index, we would sum up the next `k` elements, making it inefficient for large arrays.

Optimal Approach

We can solve this problem efficiently using the sliding window technique.

In the sliding window approach, we will first calculate the sum of the first k elements (this will be our initial window). Then, for each subsequent element, we slide the window one position to the right by subtracting the element that's leaving the window and adding the element that's entering the window.

This way, we can compute the sum of the subarray in constant time as we move the window across the array.

Code Solution

Here's how I would implement this in Java:

```
public class MaxSumSubarraySizeK {
    public int maxSumSubarray(int[] nums, int k) {
        // Edge case: if the array is empty or k is invalid, return
0
        if (nums.length == 0 || k <= 0 || k > nums.length) {
            return 0;
        }

        // Initialize the sum of the first window
        int maxSum = 0;
        int windowSum = 0;

        // Calculate the sum of the first window of size k
        for (int i = 0; i < k; i++) {
            windowSum += nums[i];
        }

        // Set the initial maxSum to the first windowSum
        maxSum = windowSum;

        // Slide the window across the array
        for (int i = k; i < nums.length; i++) {
            // Slide the window: subtract the element going out and
add the element coming in
            windowSum = windowSum - nums[i - k] + nums[i];
            // Update maxSum if the current windowSum is greater
            maxSum = Math.max(maxSum, windowSum);
        }

        return maxSum;
    }

    public static void main(String[] args) {
        MaxSumSubarraySizeK solver = new MaxSumSubarraySizeK();

        // Test cases
        int[] nums1 = {2, 1, 5, 1, 3, 2};
        int k1 = 3;
        System.out.println("Max Sum: " + solver.maxSumSubarray(nums1,
k1));  // Expected: 9
```

```
        int[] nums2 = {2, 3, 4, 1, 5};
        int k2 = 2;
        System.out.println("Max Sum: " + solver.maxSumSubarray(nums2,
k2));  // Expected: 7

        int[] nums3 = {1, 2, 3, 4, 5, 6};
        int k3 = 3;
        System.out.println("Max Sum: " + solver.maxSumSubarray(nums3,
k3));  // Expected: 15

        int[] nums4 = {10, 10, 10, 10};
        int k4 = 4;
        System.out.println("Max Sum: " + solver.maxSumSubarray(nums4,
k4));  // Expected: 40
    }
}
```

Time and Space Complexity

- The time complexity of this solution is `O(n)`, where `n` is the length of the array. We traverse the array once while sliding the window.
- The space complexity is `O(1)` since we are only using a few variables to store the current window sum and the maximum sum.

Problem 2: Minimum Size Subarray with a Given Sum

Problem Statement

You are given an array of positive integers called `nums` and a positive integer called `target`. Your task is to return the minimal length of a contiguous subarray whose sum is greater than or equal to `target`. If there is no such subarray, return `0`.

Solution

Let's follow the structured approach to solve this problem.

Clarifying Questions

Candidate: From the problem statement, it looks like I have to write a code to find the minimum size of a contiguous subarray whose sum is greater than or equal to given target?.
Interviewer: Yes, that's right.

Candidate: Also the array only contains *positive* numbers, right?
Interviewer: Yes.

Candidate: Thank you. I believe I have all the information I need to proceed.

Example

Let's consider an example:

- Input: `nums = [2, 3, 1, 2, 4, 3], target = 7`
- Expected Output: `2`

Here, the subarray `[4, 3]` has the minimal length of 2 with a sum of 7, which is greater than or equal to the target.

Brute Force Approach

A brute force approach would involve checking the sum of every possible subarray and keeping track of the shortest subarray whose sum is greater than or equal to the target.

We would start at each index, compute the sum for every possible subarray starting from that index, and track the minimal length.

This brute force approach would have a time complexity of $O(n^2)$, where n is the length of the array. For each starting index, we would need to iterate over the remaining elements to calculate the sum of the subarrays, making it inefficient for large arrays.

Optimal Approach

We can solve this problem more efficiently using the sliding window technique.

The sliding window approach involves maintaining a window that expands to include elements until the sum of the elements in the window is greater than or equal to the target.

Once the sum is greater than or equal to the target, we try to *shrink the window* from the left to find the smallest subarray that meets the condition. We repeat this process while updating the minimal length.

Code Solution

Here's the implementation in Java:

```
public class MinSubarraySum {
   public int minSubArrayLen(int target, int[] nums) {
        int minLength = Integer.MAX_VALUE;  // Initialize minLength
to a large value
        int windowSum = 0;
        int left = 0;

        // Iterate over the array with the right pointer
        for (int right = 0; right < nums.length; right++) {
            windowSum += nums[right];  // Add the current element to
the window sum

            // Shrink the window from the left while the window sum
is greater than or equal to the target
            while (windowSum >= target) {
                minLength = Math.min(minLength, right - left + 1);
```

```
// Update the minimal length
                windowSum -= nums[left];  // Shrink the window from
the left
                left++;  // Move the left pointer to the right
            }
        }

        // If no valid subarray is found, return 0
        return minLength == Integer.MAX_VALUE ? 0 : minLength;
    }

    public static void main(String[] args) {
        MinSubarraySum solver = new MinSubarraySum();

        // Test cases
        int[] nums1 = {2, 3, 1, 2, 4, 3};
        int target1 = 7;
        System.out.println("Minimal Length: " +
solver.minSubArrayLen(target1, nums1));  // Expected: 2

        int[] nums2 = {1, 4, 4};
        int target2 = 4;
        System.out.println("Minimal Length: " +
solver.minSubArrayLen(target2, nums2));  // Expected: 1

        int[] nums3 = {1, 1, 1, 1, 1, 1, 1, 1};
        int target3 = 11;
        System.out.println("Minimal Length: " +
solver.minSubArrayLen(target3, nums3));  // Expected: 0
    }
}
```

Time and Space Complexity

- The time complexity of this solution is `O(n)`, where `n` is the length of the array. We traverse the array only once.
- The space complexity is `O(1)`, as we are only using a few extra variables to keep track of the window sum, pointers, and the minimal length.

Problem 3: Longest Substring with At Most K Distinct Characters

Problem Statement

You are given a string `s` and an integer `k`. Your task is to return the length of the longest contiguous substring of `s` that contains at most `k` distinct characters.

Solution

Let's follow the structured approach to solve the problem:

Clarifying Questions

Candidate: I'd like to clarify a few points before starting.
Interviewer: Sure, go ahead.

Candidate: First, should I consider that `k` can be `0`, meaning no characters are allowed in the substring?
Interviewer: Yes, if `k = 0`, the result should be `0`, as no valid substring can exist.

Candidate: Got it. Can the input string s contain both uppercase and lowercase letters, digits, and special characters?
Interviewer: Yes, the string s can contain any character, including digits and special characters.

Candidate: Understood. I have all the information I need to proceed.

Example

Let's consider an example:

- Input: `s = "eceba", k = 2`
- Expected Output: `3`

The longest substring with at most 2 distinct characters is `"ece"`, which has a length of `3`.

Brute Force Approach

A brute force approach would involve checking every possible substring of the string `s` and counting the number of distinct characters in each substring. We would then return the length of the longest substring that contains at most `k` distinct characters.

This brute force approach would have a time complexity of $O(n^3)$, where `n` is the length of the string. This is because we would generate all possible substrings ($O(n^2)$) and for each substring, we would count the distinct characters ($O(n)$). This is inefficient for large strings.

Optimal Approach

We can solve this problem efficiently using the sliding window technique with a *HashMap* to track the distinct characters in the current window.

The idea is to use two pointers (left and right) to represent the boundaries of the sliding window.

As we move the right pointer across the string, we add characters to the window. We maintain a HashMap that tracks the frequency of each character in the window.

If the number of distinct characters exceeds `k`, we shrink the window by moving the left pointer until we have at most `k` distinct characters.

Code Solution

Here's how I would implement it in Java:

```
import java.util.HashMap;

public class LongestSubstringKDistinct {
   public int lengthOfLongestSubstringKDistinct(String s, int k) {
        if (k == 0 || s.length() == 0) {
            return 0;  // If k is 0, return 0 as no valid substring
can exist
        }

        // HashMap to track the frequency of characters in the
current window
        HashMap<Character, Integer> map = new HashMap<>();
        int left = 0, maxLength = 0;

        // Iterate through the string with the right pointer
        for (int right = 0; right < s.length(); right++) {
            char currentChar = s.charAt(right);
            map.put(currentChar, map.getOrDefault(currentChar, 0) +
1);

            // Shrink the window until there are at most k distinct
characters
            while (map.size() > k) {
                char leftChar = s.charAt(left);
                map.put(leftChar, map.get(leftChar) - 1);
                if (map.get(leftChar) == 0) {
                    map.remove(leftChar);  // Remove the character
when its count becomes 0
                }
                left++;  // Move the left pointer to the right
            }

            // Update the maximum length of the valid window
            maxLength = Math.max(maxLength, right - left + 1);
        }

        return maxLength;
    }

   public static void main(String[] args) {
        LongestSubstringKDistinct solver = new
LongestSubstringKDistinct();

        // Test cases
        String s1 = "eceba";
        int k1 = 2;
        System.out.println("Longest Length: " +
solver.lengthOfLongestSubstringKDistinct(s1, k1));  // Expected: 3

        String s2 = "aa";
        int k2 = 1;
```

```
        System.out.println("Longest Length: " +
solver.lengthOfLongestSubstringKDistinct(s2, k2));   // Expected: 2

        String s3 = "a";
        int k3 = 1;
        System.out.println("Longest Length: " +
solver.lengthOfLongestSubstringKDistinct(s3, k3));   // Expected: 1

        String s4 = "abcabcabc";
        int k4 = 2;
        System.out.println("Longest Length: " +
solver.lengthOfLongestSubstringKDistinct(s4, k4));   // Expected: 2
    }
}
```

Time and Space Complexity

- The time complexity is `O(n)`, where `n` is the length of the string. Both pointers (left and right) traverse the string once, and HashMap operations are `O(1)` on average.
- The space complexity is `O(k)`, where `k` is the number of distinct characters in the window, since the HashMap stores at most k characters.

Problem 4: Fruits into Baskets

Problem Statement

You are visiting a farm where there is a row of fruit trees, represented by an array called `fruits`, where each element `fruits[i]`represents the type of fruit produced by the `i-th` tree.

You have two baskets, and each basket can only hold one type of fruit. You want to collect as much fruit as possible starting from any tree and moving to the right, but you must follow these rules:

- Each basket can hold only one type of fruit.
- You must pick exactly one fruit from every tree as you move to the right.
- Once you encounter a tree with fruit that doesn't fit in either basket, you must stop.

Return the maximum number of fruits you can collect while adhering to these rules.

Solution

Let's follow the structured approach to solve this problem.

Clarifying Questions

Candidate: I'd like to clarify a few points before starting.

Interviewer: Sure, go ahead.

Candidate: As per the problem statement, the array called *fruits* can contain multiple types of fruits, and the goal is to collect fruits from a contiguous subarray containing at most two distinct types of fruits, is that correct?
Interviewer: Yes, that's correct.

Candidate: Got it. Should I return the total number of fruits collected, which is simply the length of the subarray?
Interviewer: Exactly!

Candidate: Understood. I believe I have all the information to proceed.

Example

Let's consider an example:

- Input: `fruits = [1, 2, 1]`
- Expected Output: `3`

Here, you can collect all 3 fruits since they contain only two distinct types: 1 and 2.

Brute Force Approach

A brute force approach would involve checking every possible starting point in the array and counting how many fruits can be collected before encountering a third distinct fruit.

For each starting point, we would scan the array to the right until we encounter more than two distinct types of fruits.

This brute force approach would have a time complexity of $O(n^2)$, where n is the length of the array. For each starting point, we would need to scan through the remaining elements, which is inefficient for large arrays.

Optimal Approach

We can solve this problem efficiently using the sliding window technique with a HashMap to track the types of fruits in the current window.

The idea is to use two pointers (left and right) to represent the boundaries of a sliding window. As we move the right pointer across the array, we add fruits to the window.

We use a HashMap to track the frequency of each fruit type in the window. If the window contains *more than two distinct types of fruits*, we shrink the window by moving the left pointer until there are only two distinct types of fruits left.

Code Solution

Here's how I would implement this in Java:

```
import java.util.HashMap;
```

```
public class MaxFruitCollection {
   public int totalFruit(int[] fruits) {
        // HashMap to store the count of each fruit type in the
current window
        HashMap<Integer, Integer> map = new HashMap<>();
        int left = 0, maxFruits = 0;

        // Iterate through the array with the right pointer
        for (int right = 0; right < fruits.length; right++) {
            int currentFruit = fruits[right];
            map.put(currentFruit, map.getOrDefault(currentFruit, 0) +
1);

            // Shrink the window until we have at most 2 distinct
fruit types
            while (map.size() > 2) {
                int leftFruit = fruits[left];
                map.put(leftFruit, map.get(leftFruit) - 1);
                if (map.get(leftFruit) == 0) {
                    map.remove(leftFruit);  // Remove the fruit from
the map when its count becomes 0
                }
                left++;  // Move the left pointer to the right
            }

            // Update the maximum number of fruits we can collect
            maxFruits = Math.max(maxFruits, right - left + 1);
        }

        return maxFruits;
    }

    public static void main(String[] args) {
        MaxFruitCollection solver = new MaxFruitCollection();

        // Test cases
        int[] fruits1 = {1, 2, 1};
        System.out.println("Max Fruits: " +
solver.totalFruit(fruits1));  // Expected: 3

        int[] fruits2 = {0, 1, 2, 2};
        System.out.println("Max Fruits: " +
solver.totalFruit(fruits2));  // Expected: 3

        int[] fruits3 = {1, 2, 3, 2, 2};
        System.out.println("Max Fruits: " +
solver.totalFruit(fruits3));  // Expected: 4

        int[] fruits4 = {3, 3, 3, 1, 2, 1, 1, 2, 3, 3, 4};
        System.out.println("Max Fruits: " +
solver.totalFruit(fruits4));  // Expected: 5
    }
}
```

Time and Space Complexity

- The time complexity is `O(n)`, where `n` is the length of the array. Both pointers (left and right) traverse the array once, and HashMap operations take `O(1)` on average.
- The space complexity is `O(1)` in terms of the number of distinct fruit types, as we only store up to *two* distinct fruit types in the HashMap.

Problem 5: Permutation in a String

Problem Statement

You are given two strings, `s1` and `s2`. Your task is to return `true` if `s2` contains any permutation of `s1` as a substring, and `false` otherwise.

A permutation of `s1` is any rearrangement of its characters.

Solution

Let's follow the structured approach to solve this problem.

Clarifying Questions

Candidate: I'd like to clarify a few points before starting.
Interviewer: Sure, go ahead.

Candidate: Should I assume that both strings s1 and s2 contain only lowercase English letters?
Interviewer: Yes, you can assume both strings consist of only lowercase English letters.

Candidate: If `s1` is longer than `s2`, then no permutation of `s1` can fit inside `s2`, in that case I can just return `false`, right?
Interviewer: Yes, if `s1` is longer than `s2`, return false.

Candidate: Perfect, I think I have everything I need to proceed.

Example

Let's consider an example:

- Input: `s1 = "ab", s2 = "eidbaooo"`
- Expected Output: `true`

Here, one permutation of `"ab"` is `"ba"`, and it exists as a substring in `s2`.

Brute Force Approach

A brute force approach would involve generating all permutations of `s1` and checking if any of them exist as a substring in `s2`.

However, generating all permutations would have a time complexity of O(n!), where n is the length of s1, which is very inefficient.

Optimal Approach

We can solve this efficiently using the sliding window technique with a frequency count array.

The idea is to create a frequency array for the characters in s1 and use a sliding window of the same length as s1 to traverse s2.
At each step, we compare the frequency of characters in the current window of s2 with the frequency of characters in s1. If the frequencies match, we know we have found a permutation of s1 in s2.

Code Solution

Here's the implementation in Java:

```
import java.util.Arrays;

public class PermutationInString {
   public boolean checkInclusion(String s1, String s2) {
        // Edge case: if s1 is longer than s2, no permutation is
possible
        if (s1.length() > s2.length()) {
            return false;
        }

        // Frequency arrays for s1 and the sliding window in s2
        int[] s1Freq = new int[26];
        int[] windowFreq = new int[26];

        // Populate the frequency array for s1
        for (int i = 0; i < s1.length(); i++) {
            s1Freq[s1.charAt(i) - 'a']++;
            windowFreq[s2.charAt(i) - 'a']++;
        }

        // Slide the window over s2
        for (int i = s1.length(); i < s2.length(); i++) {
            // If the frequency arrays match, we found a permutation
            if (Arrays.equals(s1Freq, windowFreq)) {
                return true;
            }

            // Slide the window: add the next character and remove
the leftmost character
            windowFreq[s2.charAt(i) - 'a']++;
            windowFreq[s2.charAt(i - s1.length()) - 'a']--;
        }

        // Check the last window
        return Arrays.equals(s1Freq, windowFreq);
```

```
    }

    public static void main(String[] args) {
        PermutationInString solver = new PermutationInString();

        // Test cases
        String s1 = "ab";
        String s2 = "eidbaooo";
        System.out.println("Contains Permutation: " +
solver.checkInclusion(s1, s2));  // Expected: true

        s1 = "ab";
        s2 = "eidboaoo";
        System.out.println("Contains Permutation: " +
solver.checkInclusion(s1, s2));  // Expected: false
    }
}
```

Time and Space Complexity

- The time complexity of this solution is `O(n)`, where `n` is the length of s2. We iterate over s2 once, and comparing the frequency arrays takes `O(1)` since they always have a fixed size of 26 (for lowercase English letters).
- The space complexity is `O(1)`, since the frequency arrays have a fixed size of 26.

Chapter 6: Prefix Sum Pattern

The Prefix Sum pattern is a technique used to solve problems *involving arrays* where you need to calculate the ***sum of elements in a subarray*** or determine certain properties of subarrays.

In this chapter, we will explore the basics of the Prefix Sum pattern, walk through common problem types, and discuss how to apply this pattern effectively.

We will also solve the top 5 most frequently asked prefix sum-based coding interview questions with detailed explanations, code in Java, and analysis of time and space complexity.

What is the Prefix Sum Pattern?

The Prefix Sum pattern involves creating a *prefix sum array*, where each element at index `i` in the prefix sum array represents the sum of all elements in the original array from the *start up to index* `i`.

This allows us to quickly *calculate the sum of any subarray* in ***constant time*** by using the difference between two elements in the prefix sum array.

Example

Given an array `arr = [3, 1, 4, 1, 5]`, the prefix sum array would be:

```
prefixSum = [3, 4, 8, 9, 14]
```

To calculate the sum of the subarray from index 1 to 3, you can use the prefix sum array as follows:

```
Subarray sum (index 1:3) = prefixSum[3] - prefixSum[0] = 9 - 3 = 6
```

Why is the Prefix Sum Pattern Important?

The Prefix Sum pattern is useful because it significantly reduces the time complexity for solving *problems that require* ***multiple*** *sum calculations.*

Without using this pattern, calculating the sum of subarrays might take `O(n)` time for each query, but with the Prefix Sum pattern, it can be done in `O(1)` time, making it much more efficient, especially for large inputs.

Popular Prefix Sum Pattern Questions

Now, Let's dive into solving some of the most frequently asked Prefix Sum pattern-based coding interview questions.

Problem 1: Count Subarrays with Target Sum

Problem Statement

We are given an array of integers called `nums` and a target integer `k`. The task is to find how many contiguous subarrays from the array sum up to exactly `k`.

Solution

Let's solve this problem using a structured approach.

Clarifying Questions

Candidate: Just to clarify, when you say "continuous subarrays," you mean that the subarrays must be made up of consecutive elements from the array, correct?
Interviewer: Yes, that's correct.

Candidate: Great. Is there any specific constraint on the size of the array or the values of nums and k that I should be aware of?
Interviewer: The size of the array can be up to 10,000 elements, and the values of the integers in nums can range from -10,000 to 10,000.

Candidate: Got it. One last question: are there any special cases like if `k` is `0`, or if the array contains all negative numbers?
Interviewer: Good question. `k` can be any integer, including `0`, and the array may have a mix of positive, negative, and zero values. You should handle all cases.

Candidate: Perfect. I think I have everything I need to get started.

Example

Let's consider an example:

- Input: `nums = [1, 2, 3], k = 3`
- Output: `2`

Explanation: The subarrays `[1, 2]` and `[3]` both sum to `3`.

Brute Force Approach

To start off, a brute force solution would involve checking every possible subarray, calculating its sum, and then checking if it equals `k`.

The approach would be:

1. Iterate over each starting point of the subarray.

2. For each starting point, iterate through the subsequent elements to calculate the sum of the subarray.
3. If the sum equals k, increment a counter.

However, this approach has a time complexity of $O(n^2)$ because we're calculating the sum of subarrays repeatedly, which can be inefficient for large arrays.

Optimal Approach

The optimal approach is to leverage a prefix sum pattern combined with a hashmap to store the cumulative sums we've seen so far.

Here's the idea:

- As we iterate through the array, we calculate the cumulative sum (or prefix sum) at each index.
- If at some point, the difference between the current cumulative sum and k has been seen before, it means that there exists a subarray that sums up to k.
- We can efficiently track the number of such subarrays using a hashmap.

This allows us to find subarrays in linear time.

Code Solution

Here's is how I would implement it in Java:

```
import java.util.HashMap;

public class SubarraySumEqualsK {

    // Function to count the number of subarrays with sum equal to k
    public static int subarraySum(int[] nums, int k) {
        // HashMap to store the cumulative sum and its frequency
        HashMap<Integer, Integer> cumulativeSumMap = new HashMap<>();

        // Initialize the map with 0 cumulative sum at the beginning
        cumulativeSumMap.put(0, 1);

        int cumulativeSum = 0; // To track the running cumulative sum
        int count = 0; // To track the number of subarrays

        // Iterate through the array
        for (int num : nums) {
            // Add the current number to the cumulative sum
            cumulativeSum += num;

            // Check if there exists a subarray ending at the
current index
            // whose sum is equal to k
            if (cumulativeSumMap.containsKey(cumulativeSum - k)) {
                count += cumulativeSumMap.get(cumulativeSum - k);
            }

            // Update the cumulative sum in the map
```

```
            cumulativeSumMap.put(cumulativeSum,
cumulativeSumMap.getOrDefault(cumulativeSum, 0) + 1);
        }

        return count; // Return the total count of subarrays
    }

    // Main method to test the function
    public static void main(String[] args) {
        int[] nums1 = {1, 1, 1};
        int k1 = 2;
        System.out.println("Number of subarrays: " +
subarraySum(nums1, k1)); // Output: 2

        int[] nums2 = {1, 2, 3};
        int k2 = 3;
        System.out.println("Number of subarrays: " +
subarraySum(nums2, k2)); // Output: 2

        int[] nums3 = {-1, -1, 1};
        int k3 = 0;
        System.out.println("Number of subarrays: " +
subarraySum(nums3, k3)); // Output: 1
    }
}
```

Time and Space Complexity

- The time complexity is `O(n)` where `n` is the number of elements in the array. We are iterating through the array once and performing constant-time operations for each element.
- The space complexity is `O(n)` as we are using a hashmap to store cumulative sums, which in the worst case could store all the sums.

Problem 2: Maximum Length Subarray with Target Sum

Problem Statement

We are given an array of integers called `nums` and a target integer `k`. The goal is to find the maximum length of a continuous subarray from the array whose sum equals `k`. If no such subarray exists, return `0`.

Solution

Let's follow the structured approach to solve this problem.

Clarifying Questions

Candidate: Just to clarify, the subarray must consist of consecutive elements, correct?
Interviewer: Yes, the subarray must be continuous.

Candidate: Understood. And the subarray should have a sum exactly equal to `k`?
Interviewer: Correct.

Candidate: Got it. Are there any constraints on the size of the array or the values in the array?
Interviewer: Yes, the array can have up to 10,000 elements, and the values in nums can range between -10,000 and 10,000.
Candidate: Perfect. Also, should I assume that there could be negative numbers in the array, or will it consist only of positive numbers?
Interviewer: Yes, the array can contain negative, positive, and zero values.

Candidate: Thanks for the clarification. I think I'm ready to proceed.

Example

Let's walk through an example:

- Input: `nums = [1, -1, 5, -2, 3], k = 3`
- Output: `4`

Explanation: The subarray `[1, -1, 5, -2]` sums to `3`, and its length is `4`, which is the maximum possible.

Brute Force Approach

To start off, a brute force solution would involve checking every possible subarray, calculating its sum, and comparing it with `k`.

If the sum equals `k`, we keep track of the length of the subarray and update the maximum length if needed.

However, this approach has a time complexity of $O(n^2)$, as it involves checking the sum of all possible subarrays. This would be inefficient for large arrays.

Optimal Approach

To improve the efficiency, we can leverage the prefix sum technique combined with a hashmap.

Here's the approach:

- As we iterate through the array, we maintain a cumulative sum (or prefix sum).
- We use a hashmap to store the earliest occurrence of each cumulative sum. This helps in identifying subarrays that sum to `k` in constant time.
- For each element, we check if `cumulative_sum - k` exists in the hashmap. If it does, the subarray between the earliest occurrence of `cumulative_sum - k` and the current index sums to `k`, and we can calculate its length.

This approach allows us to find the maximum length of the subarray in linear time.

Code Solution

Here's the Java implementation for the optimal solution:

```
import java.util.HashMap;

public class MaximumLengthSubarraySumK {

   // Function to find the maximum length of a subarray that sums
to k
   public static int maxSubArrayLen(int[] nums, int k) {
        // HashMap to store the cumulative sum and the earliest
index where it occurs
        HashMap<Integer, Integer> cumulativeSumMap = new HashMap<>();

        int cumulativeSum = 0; // To track the running cumulative sum
        int maxLength = 0; // To store the maximum length of the
subarray

        // Initialize the map with 0 cumulative sum at index -1 (to
handle cases where the subarray starts at index 0)
        cumulativeSumMap.put(0, -1);

        // Iterate through the array
        for (int i = 0; i < nums.length; i++) {
            // Add the current number to the cumulative sum
            cumulativeSum += nums[i];

            // Check if there's a cumulative sum that, when
subtracted from the current sum, equals k
            if (cumulativeSumMap.containsKey(cumulativeSum - k)) {
                // Calculate the length of the subarray
                int length = i - cumulativeSumMap.get(cumulativeSum -
k);
                // Update the maximum length if this subarray is
longer
                maxLength = Math.max(maxLength, length);
            }

            // Only add the current cumulative sum to the map if
it's not already present
            // This ensures we keep the earliest index of each
cumulative sum
            if (!cumulativeSumMap.containsKey(cumulativeSum)) {
                cumulativeSumMap.put(cumulativeSum, i);
            }
        }

        return maxLength; // Return the maximum length of the
subarray
   }

   // Main method to test the function
   public static void main(String[] args) {
        int[] nums1 = {1, -1, 5, -2, 3};
        int k1 = 3;
```

```
        System.out.println("Max Length of subarray: " +
maxSubArrayLen(nums1, k1)); // Output: 4

        int[] nums2 = {-2, -1, 2, 1};
        int k2 = 1;
        System.out.println("Max Length of subarray: " +
maxSubArrayLen(nums2, k2)); // Output: 2

        int[] nums3 = {1, 2, 3};
        int k3 = 6;
        System.out.println("Max Length of subarray: " +
maxSubArrayLen(nums3, k3)); // Output: 3

        int[] nums4 = {1, -1, 1, -1};
        int k4 = 0;
        System.out.println("Max Length of subarray: " +
maxSubArrayLen(nums4, k4)); // Output: 4
    }
}
```

Time and Space Complexity

- The time complexity is `O(n)` because we iterate through the array once, and all operations involving the hashmap are done in constant time.
- The space complexity is `O(n)` as we are storing the cumulative sums in a hashmap, which in the worst case could store all the sums.

Problem 3: Find the Pivot Index

Problem Statement

You are given an array of integers called `nums`.

The pivot index is an index where the sum of all numbers to the left of the index is equal to the sum of all numbers to the right of it. Your task is to return the pivot index. If no such index exists, return `-1`.

Solution

Let's solve this problem using the structured approach.

Clarifying Questions

Candidate: To clarify, the pivot index divides the array into two parts where the sum of elements on the left is equal to the sum of elements on the right, excluding the element at the pivot index itself, correct?
Interviewer: Yes, that's correct. The element at the pivot index is not included in either the left or right sums.

Candidate: Understood. If there are multiple valid pivot indices, should we return the first one?
Interviewer: Yes, return the smallest index where the condition is met.

Candidate: Perfect. One last question: if the array is empty, should I return `-1` as there would be no pivot index?
Interviewer: Yes, return `-1` in that case.

Candidate: Great, thanks for the clarification.

Example

Let's go through an example:

- Input: `nums = [1, 7, 3, 6, 5, 6]`
- Output: `3`

Explanation: The sum of numbers to the left of index 3 (i.e., `1 + 7 + 3 = 11`) is equal to the sum of numbers to the right of index 3 (i.e., `5 + 6 = 11`).

Brute Force Approach

A brute force approach would be to check every index in the array. For each index `i`, I would:

1. Compute the sum of all elements to the left of `i`.
2. Compute the sum of all elements to the right of `i`.
3. If these sums are equal, return `i`.

This approach would involve iterating through the array for each index to calculate the left and right sums, making the time complexity $O(n^2)$.

However, this brute force approach is inefficient for large arrays.

Optimal Approach

To optimize this, we can use a prefix sum strategy to compute the total sum of the array and then dynamically calculate the left and right sums as we iterate through the array.

The idea is:

1. Calculate the *total sum* of the array.
2. As we iterate through the array, keep track of the *cumulative sum* (or left sum) up to the current index.
3. The right sum at any index `i` is simply the total sum minus the left sum and the current element at index `i`.
4. If at any index `i`, the *left sum equals the right sum*, then that index is the pivot.

This approach reduces the time complexity to `O(n)`.

Code Solution

Here's the Java implementation using the optimal approach:

```
public class PivotIndex {

    // Function to find the pivot index
    public static int pivotIndex(int[] nums) {
        int totalSum = 0;  // Calculate the total sum of the array
        for (int num : nums) {
            totalSum += num;
        }

        int leftSum = 0;  // Initialize left sum to 0

        // Iterate through the array to find the pivot index
        for (int i = 0; i < nums.length; i++) {
            // The right sum at index i is totalSum - leftSum -
nums[i]
            int rightSum = totalSum - leftSum - nums[i];

            // Check if left sum is equal to right sum
            if (leftSum == rightSum) {
                return i;  // Pivot index found
            }

            // Update the left sum by adding the current element
            leftSum += nums[i];
        }

        return -1;  // No pivot index found
    }

    // Main method to test the function
    public static void main(String[] args) {
        int[] nums1 = {1, 7, 3, 6, 5, 6};
        System.out.println("Pivot Index: " + pivotIndex(nums1)); //
Output: 3

        int[] nums2 = {1, 2, 3};
        System.out.println("Pivot Index: " + pivotIndex(nums2)); //
Output: -1

        int[] nums3 = {2, 1, -1};
        System.out.println("Pivot Index: " + pivotIndex(nums3)); //
Output: 0
    }
}
```

Time and Space Complexity

- The time complexity is `O(n)` where `n` is the number of elements in the array. We iterate through the array twice: once to compute the total sum and once to find the pivot index.
- The space complexity is `O(1)` since we are only using a few extra variables to store the total sum and the left sum.

Problem 4: Range Sum Query for an Array

Problem Statement

You are given an integer array `nums`. You need to handle multiple queries, where each query asks for the sum of the elements between two indices `i` and `j`.

You are required to implement a `NumArray` class with the following methods:

1. `NumArray(int[] nums)`: Initializes the object with the integer array `nums`.
2. `int sumRange(int left, int right)`: Returns the sum of the elements between the indices `left` and `right` (inclusive).

Solution

Let's solve this problem using the structured approach.

Clarifying Questions

Candidate: Just to clarify, when you say the sum of elements between indices `i` and `j`, that includes both the `i-th` and `j-th` elements, right?
Interviewer: Yes, the sum should include the elements at both indices `i` and `j`.

Candidate: Got it. Should we expect negative numbers in the array, or will it only contain positive integers?
Interviewer: The array can contain both positive and negative integers.

Candidate: Perfect. One last question: should I optimize for multiple queries, or is it acceptable to simply sum up the elements for each query as it comes in?
Interviewer: You should optimize for multiple queries. Each query should be handled efficiently.

Candidate: Great! I think I have everything I need to get started.

Example

Let's go through an example to ensure the problem is clear.

- Input:
    1. `nums = [-2, 0, 3, -5, 2, -1]`
    2. Queries:
        1. `sumRange(0, 2)`
        2. `sumRange(2, 5)`
        3. `sumRange(0, 5)`
- Output:
    1. 1 (sum of `[-2, 0, 3]`)
    2. -1 (sum of `[3, -5, 2, -1]`)
    3. -3 (sum of `[-2, 0, 3, -5, 2, -1]`)

Brute Force Approach

The brute force approach would involve calculating the sum for each query directly. For every call to `sumRange(left, right)`, we would iterate from index left to right, summing up the elements in that range.

While this works, the time complexity for each query is `O(n)`, which can be inefficient when there are many queries, especially for large arrays.

Optimal Approach

To optimize for *multiple queries*, we can use a prefix sum approach. The idea is to *preprocess the array* such that we can quickly calculate the sum for any range in constant time.

Here's the approach:

1. Create a *prefixSum* array, where `prefixSum[i]` stores the sum of elements from the start of the array up to index `i`.
2. For each query, the sum of elements between left and right is simply `prefixSum[right] - prefixSum[left - 1]` (if left is greater than 0).

This allows us to answer each query in constant time `O(1)` after an initial preprocessing step that takes `O(n)` time.

Code Solution

Let me implement this using the optimal approach:

```
public class NumArray {

    private final int[] prefixSum; // Array to store the cumulative
sums

    // Constructor to initialize the prefixSum array
    public NumArray(int[] nums) {
        prefixSum = new int[nums.length + 1]; // Initialize the
prefix sum array with an extra element for convenience

        // Calculate the prefix sums
        for (int i = 0; i < nums.length; i++) {
            prefixSum[i + 1] = prefixSum[i] + nums[i]; // prefixSum[i
+ 1] stores the sum from index 0 to i
        }
    }

    // Method to return the sum of elements between indices left and
right
    public int sumRange(int left, int right) {
        // The sum of elements between left and right is the
difference between prefixSum[right + 1] and prefixSum[left]
```

```
        return prefixSum[right + 1] - prefixSum[left];
    }

    // Main method to test the implementation
    public static void main(String[] args) {
        int[] nums = {-2, 0, 3, -5, 2, -1};
        NumArray obj = new NumArray(nums);

        System.out.println("Sum of range (0, 2): " + obj.sumRange(0,
2)); // Output: 1
        System.out.println("Sum of range (2, 5): " + obj.sumRange(2,
5)); // Output: -1
        System.out.println("Sum of range (0, 5): " + obj.sumRange(0,
5)); // Output: -3
    }
}
```

Time and Space Complexity

- The time complexity for preprocessing the prefixSum array is `O(n)`, where `n` is the length of the input array nums. After preprocessing, each query is answered in `O(1)` time, since it only involves subtracting two values from the prefixSum array.
- The space complexity is `O(n)` because we store an additional *prefixSum* array of the same size as the input array.

Problem 5: Subarrays with Zero Sum

Problem Statement

You are given an array of integers called `nums`. The task is to find all the subarrays whose sum equals zero and return the list of those subarrays. Each subarray should consist of consecutive elements.

Solution

Let's solve this problem using a structured approach.

Clarifying Questions

Candidate: Just to clarify, when you say "find all subarrays", do you mean I should return the subarrays themselves or their starting and ending indices?
Interviewer: Good question. You should return the starting and ending indices of each subarray that has a sum equal to zero.

Candidate: Got it. Should I assume the array can contain both positive and negative numbers?

Interviewer: Yes, the array can have positive, negative, and zero values.

Candidate: Understood. Is there any constraint on the size of the array?
Interviewer: The array can have up to 10,000 elements.

Candidate: Perfect. One last thing: If there are no subarrays whose sum equals zero, should I return an empty list?
Interviewer: Yes, if there are no such subarrays, return an empty list.

Candidate: Great! I think I'm ready to proceed.

Example

Let's go through an example to make sure the problem is well-understood.

- Input: `nums = [1, -1, 2, -2, 3, 0]`
- Output: `[(0, 1), (2, 3), (5, 5)]`

Explanation:

- Subarray `[1, -1]` (from index 0 to 1) sums to 0.
- Subarray `[2, -2]` (from index 2 to 3) sums to 0.
- Subarray `[0]` (at index 5) sums to 0.

Brute Force Approach

The brute force approach would involve checking the sum of every possible subarray in the array.
For each starting index `i`, I would:

1. Iterate through each ending index `j` (where `j >= i`).
2. Calculate the sum of the subarray from `i` to `j`.
3. If the sum equals zero, I would record the indices `(i, j)`.

However, this approach has a time complexity of $O(n^2)$, where n is the length of the array, because we're recalculating the sum for every possible subarray. This would be inefficient for large arrays.

Optimal Approach

To optimize this, we can use a prefix sum approach along with a hashmap to store previously seen cumulative sums. This will allow us to identify subarrays that sum to zero in linear time.

Here's the idea:

- We calculate a running cumulative sum as we iterate through the array.
- If at any point the cumulative sum becomes zero, or if we encounter the same cumulative sum twice, it means that the elements between the two occurrences of the sum form a subarray with a sum of zero.
- We store the cumulative sum and the index where it occurred in a hashmap, which allows us to efficiently find all subarrays.

Code Solution

Here's the Java implementation using the optimal approach:

```
import java.util.ArrayList;
import java.util.HashMap;
import java.util.List;

public class SubarraySumZero {

    // Function to find all subarrays with sum equal to zero
    public static List<int[]> findSubarraysWithZeroSum(int[] nums) {
        // List to store the result: each element is an array
containing the start and end indices of a subarray
        List<int[]> result = new ArrayList<>();

        // HashMap to store the cumulative sum and the list of
indices where the sum occurred
        HashMap<Integer, List<Integer>> sumMap = new HashMap<>();

        int cumulativeSum = 0; // To track the running cumulative sum

        // Initialize the map with a cumulative sum of 0 at index -1
(this helps to handle subarrays that start at index 0)
        sumMap.put(0, new ArrayList<>());
        sumMap.get(0).add(-1);

        // Iterate through the array
        for (int i = 0; i < nums.length; i++) {
            // Update the cumulative sum
            cumulativeSum += nums[i];

            // Check if the cumulative sum has been seen before
            if (sumMap.containsKey(cumulativeSum)) {
                // For each occurrence of this sum, a subarray with
zero sum exists between that index + 1 and the current index
                for (int start : sumMap.get(cumulativeSum)) {
                    result.add(new int[]{start + 1, i});
                }
            }

            // Add the current index to the list of indices where
this cumulative sum has occurred
            sumMap.putIfAbsent(cumulativeSum, new ArrayList<>());
            sumMap.get(cumulativeSum).add(i);
        }

        return result; // Return the list of subarrays
    }

    // Main method to test the function
    public static void main(String[] args) {
        int[] nums1 = {1, -1, 2, -2, 3, 0};
        List<int[]> result1 = findSubarraysWithZeroSum(nums1);
        System.out.println("Subarrays with zero sum:");
        for (int[] subarray : result1) {
            System.out.println("(" + subarray[0] + ", " + subarray[1]
+ ")");
```

```
        }

        int[] nums2 = {3, 4, -7, 1, 2, -6, 3, 1};
        List<int[]> result2 = findSubarraysWithZeroSum(nums2);
        System.out.println("Subarrays with zero sum:");
        for (int[] subarray : result2) {
            System.out.println("(" + subarray[0] + ", " + subarray[1]
+ ")");
        }
    }
}
```

Time and Space Complexity

- The time complexity is `O(n)` where `n` is the length of the array, because we iterate through the array once, and all operations on the hashmap are done in constant time.
- The space complexity is `O(n)` since we are storing the cumulative sums and their corresponding indices in the hashmap.

Chapter 7: Binary Search

Binary Search is an efficient algorithm for *searching in a sorted array (or list).*

It's a *divide-and-conquer type of algorithm* that ***reduces the problem size by half with each step***, making it highly efficient with a time complexity of `O(log n)`.

Understanding Binary Search is crucial for coding interviews, as it forms the basis for solving many complex problems in an optimal way.

Understanding Binary Search

Binary Search works on the principle of ***dividing*** a sorted array into two halves and ***determining*** which half contains the target element.

The algorithm *repeatedly halves the search space* until it either finds the target element or concludes that the element is not present in the array.

Key Concepts

- **Sorted Array:** Binary Search only works on a sorted array or list. If the array is not sorted, Binary Search is not applicable.
- **Midpoint Calculation:** At each step, the algorithm calculates the middle index of the current search space.
- **Comparison:** The middle element is compared with the target. If it matches, the search is complete. If not, the algorithm decides whether to search the left half or the right half.

Time and Space Complexity

- Time Complexity: `O(log n)`, where `n` is the number of elements in the array.
- Space Complexity: `O(1)` for iterative implementation and `O(log n)` for recursive implementation due to stack space.

Binary Search Implementation in Java

Let's look at an implementation of Binary Search in Java:

```
public class BinarySearch {
    public static int binarySearch(int[] array, int target) {
        int left = 0;
        int right = array.length - 1;
```

```
        while (left <= right) {
            int mid = left + (right - left) / 2;

            // Check if the target is present at mid
            if (array[mid] == target) {
                return mid; // Target found
            }

            // If target is greater, ignore left half
            if (array[mid] < target) {
                left = mid + 1;
            } else {
                // If target is smaller, ignore right half
                right = mid - 1;
            }
        }

        // Target is not present in the array
        return -1;
    }

    public static void main(String[] args) {
        int[] array = {2, 3, 4, 10, 40};
        int target = 10;
        int result = binarySearch(array, target);
        if (result == -1) {
            System.out.println("Element not found in the array.");
        } else {
            System.out.println("Element found at index " + result);
        }
    }
}
```

Explanation

- **Initialization:** left and right pointers are initialized to the first and last indices of the array.
- **Midpoint Calculation**: mid is calculated using `left + (right - left) / 2` to avoid overflow.
- **Comparison:** The value at array[mid] is compared to the target. Based on the comparison, either the left or right half is selected for the next iteration.
- **Termination:** The loop continues until left exceeds right, at which point the search space is empty, indicating the target is not in the array.

Why Not Just Use (left + right) / 2?

In a straightforward Binary Search, one might be tempted to calculate the midpoint using:

```
int mid = (left + right) / 2;
```

While this is mathematically correct, it can lead to an integer overflow when `left` and `right` are *large* integers.

In languages like Java, integers have a fixed size (32-bit), and *adding two large numbers can cause the sum to exceed the maximum value an integer can hold*, resulting in an overflow.

The Overflow Problem

Consider the scenario where `left` and `right` are both large numbers close to the maximum integer value (`Integer.MAX_VALUE`):

- If `left = Integer.MAX_VALUE - 1` and `right = Integer.MAX_VALUE`, then:
  - `left + right = (Integer.MAX_VALUE - 1) + Integer.MAX_VALUE = 2 * Integer.MAX_VALUE - 1`

This sum exceeds the maximum value an integer can hold, leading to an incorrect calculation of the midpoint, *which might cause the algorithm to behave unpredictably or crash.*

Avoiding Overflow Problem

To avoid this issue, the midpoint is calculated using:

```
int mid = left + (right - left) / 2;
```

Here's why this works:

- **Subtraction First:** The expression `right - left` is calculated first. Since `right` is always greater than or equal to `left`, `right - left` is always a non-negative number that won't cause an overflow.
- **Adding to `left`:** The result is then added to `left`, ensuring that the sum stays within the range of valid integers.

This method guarantees that you avoid overflow while still correctly calculating the midpoint of the current search space.

The expression `left + (right - left) / 2` is a safer and more reliable way to calculate the midpoint in Binary Search, especially in cases where `left` and `right` can be large integers.

It ensures the algorithm remains ***robust and free from overflow-related errors***, which is crucial for maintaining the correctness of Binary Search.

Recursive Implementation

The earlier implementation is *iterative*, which is generally preferred for its simplicity and avoidance of stack overflow.

However, Binary Search can also be implemented recursively as follows:

```
public class BinarySearchRecursive {
   public static int binarySearch(int[] array, int target, int left,
int right) {
        if (left <= right) {
            int mid = left + (right - left) / 2;

            if (array[mid] == target) {
                return mid;
            }

            if (array[mid] < target) {
                return binarySearch(array, target, mid + 1, right);
            } else {
                return binarySearch(array, target, left, mid - 1);
            }
        }

        return -1; // Target is not present in the array
    }

    public static void main(String[] args) {
        int[] array = {2, 3, 4, 10, 40};
        int target = 10;
        int result = binarySearch(array, target, 0, array.length -
1);
        if (result == -1) {
            System.out.println("Element not found in the array.");
        } else {
            System.out.println("Element found at index " + result);
        }
    }
}
```

Efficiency of Binary Search

Let's dive into why the Binary Search algorithm is so efficient.

1. **Initial Search Space:** The search starts with the entire array, which has n elements.
2. **Halving the Search Space:**
    a. At each step, *the search space is divided in half.* This means after one comparison, the size of the array to search through is reduced from n to n/2.
    b. After two comparisons, the search space is n/4, then n/8, and so on.
3. **Number of Steps:**
    a. The *process of halving the array* continues until the size of the search space is 1, which is when the algorithm terminates.
    b. The number of times you can halve n before you reach 1 is given by $\log_2 n$.
4. **Total Comparisons:** In the worst case, the binary search will make $\log_2 n$ comparisons, where n is the number of elements in the array.

Hence, the time complexity of Binary Search is **`O(log n)`**, where **`n`** is the number of elements in the array. The logarithmic time complexity makes Binary Search very efficient, especially for large datasets, ***as the number of operations grows very slowly with the size of the input.***

Interview Questions Based on Binary Search

Binary Search is a versatile algorithm that can be adapted to solve various other problems.

In this section, we will look at a few most commonly asked coding interview questions which can be solved by using a variant of binary search algorithm.

Problem 1: First & Last Position of a Target in a Sorted Array

Problem Statement

You are given a sorted array of integers in non-decreasing order, and your task is to find the first and last positions of a given target value.

If the target is not present in the array, return `[-1, -1]`.

Solution

Let's break down the question and follow the structured approach to solve it.

Clarifying Questions

Candidate: To confirm, the array is sorted, and I need to find the first and last position of a target value. If the value is not present, I should return [-1, -1]. Is that correct?
Interviewer: Yes, that's correct.

Candidate: Can I assume the array contains only integers? Also, are there any constraints on the size of the array or the values of the elements?
Interviewer: Yes, you can assume the array contains integers. The size of the array can be large. The values in the array could be negative, positive, or zero. Expected time complexity is `O(log n)`.

Candidate: Understood. I think I can proceed with this information.

Example

- Input: `nums = [5, 7, 7, 8, 8, 10], target = 8`
- Output: `[3, 4]` (since the target 8 appears at index 3 and 4)

Brute Force Approach

One straightforward method would be to iterate through the entire array, find the first index where the target matches, and then continue until I find the last index. This would require scanning the whole array, so it would take `O(n)` time.

However, this approach doesn't meet the `O(log n)` time complexity requirement, so it's not optimal.

Optimal Approach

Since the array is sorted, I can take advantage of binary search to find the target in `O(log n)` time.
Here's my plan:

1. Use binary search twice — once to find the first occurrence of the target and once to find the last occurrence of the target.
2. If the target is not found, return `[-1, -1]`.

For the first binary search, I'll look for the leftmost index where the target appears. For the second binary search, I'll look for the rightmost index where the target appears.

Code Solution

Here's how I would implement this in Java:

```
import java.util.Arrays;

public class FirstAndLastOccurrence {
   // Method to find the first and last position of the target
   public static int[] searchRange(int[] nums, int target) {
       int[] result = new int[]{-1, -1};

       // Find the first occurrence of the target
       result[0] = findPosition(nums, target, true);

       // If the first occurrence was found, find the last
occurrence
       if (result[0] != -1) {
           result[1] = findPosition(nums, target, false);
       }

       return result;
   }

   // Helper method to perform binary search and find either first
or last occurrence
   private static int findPosition(int[] nums, int target, boolean
findFirst) {
       int left = 0, right = nums.length - 1;
       int position = -1;

       while (left <= right) {
```

```
            int mid = left + (right - left) / 2;

            if (nums[mid] == target) {
                position = mid; // Store the potential position

                if (findFirst) {
                    right = mid - 1; // Continue searching in the
left half
                } else {
                    left = mid + 1; // Continue searching in the
right half
                }
            } else if (nums[mid] < target) {
                left = mid + 1; // Move to the right half
            } else {
                right = mid - 1; // Move to the left half
            }
        }

        return position;
    }

    // Main method to test the solution
    public static void main(String[] args) {
        int[] nums1 = {5, 7, 7, 8, 8, 10};
        int[] nums2 = {5, 7, 7, 8, 8, 10};
        int[] nums3 = {};

        // Test case 1: Target found
        System.out.println(Arrays.toString(searchRange(nums1, 8)));
// Expected output: [3, 4]

        // Test case 2: Target not found
        System.out.println(Arrays.toString(searchRange(nums2, 6)));
// Expected output: [-1, -1]

        // Test case 3: Empty array
        System.out.println(Arrays.toString(searchRange(nums3, 8)));
// Expected output: [-1, -1]
    }
}
```

Time and Space Complexity

- Time Complexity: `O(log n)` for each binary search, so the overall time complexity is `O(log n)`.
- Space Complexity: `O(1)` since we're only using a fixed amount of additional space for variables.

Problem 2: Searching in a Rotated Sorted Array

Problem Statement

You are given a sorted array that has been possibly rotated at an unknown pivot.

Your task is to find the index of a given target value in the array. If the target is not present, return `-1`. You need to find the target in `O(log n)` time.

Solution

Let's break down the question and follow the structured approach to solve this problem.

Clarifying Questions

Candidate: Got it. A couple of clarifications to ensure I understand the problem correctly:

1. Can I assume the array contains distinct values?
2. Can I assume the array size will be at least 1?
3. Does the array wrap around at the pivot, meaning the values after the pivot are smaller than the ones before?

Interviewer: Yes, the array contains distinct values, and it will always have at least one element. Also, the array wraps around at the pivot point, as you described.

Candidate: Great! To summarize, I need to find the target in a rotated sorted array, and I must achieve this in `O(log n)` time complexity.

Example

- Input: `nums = [4,5,6,7,0,1,2],target = 0`
- Output: 4 (target `0` is found at index 4)

Brute Force Approach

The brute force approach would be to linearly search through the array, looking for the target. However, this would take `O(n)` time. Since the problem requires `O(log n)` time complexity, this is not an optimal approach, so I'll avoid it.

Optimal Approach

Since the array is rotated but still consists of two sorted subarrays, I can take advantage of binary search to solve this in `O(log n)` time.

Here's my approach:

1. I will perform binary search on the array. While doing so, I'll check which side of the array is sorted (left or right).
2. Depending on where the target could be, I'll either search the left or right half.

There are two main cases to consider during the binary search:

- The left side is sorted: If the target lies within the left side, I search there. Otherwise, I search the right side.

- The right side is sorted: Similarly, if the target lies within the right side, I search there. Otherwise, I search the left side.

Code Solution

Here's how I would implement this in Java:

```
public class SearchRotatedArray {
    public static int search(int[] nums, int target) {
        int left = 0, right = nums.length - 1;

        while (left <= right) {
            int mid = left + (right - left) / 2;

            // Check if mid is the target
            if (nums[mid] == target) {
                return mid;
            }

            // Determine which half is sorted
            if (nums[left] <= nums[mid]) {
                // Left half is sorted
                if (nums[left] <= target && target < nums[mid]) {
                    right = mid - 1; // Target is in the left half
                } else {
                    left = mid + 1; // Target is in the right half
                }
            } else {
                // Right half is sorted
                if (nums[mid] < target && target <= nums[right]) {
                    left = mid + 1; // Target is in the right half
                } else {
                    right = mid - 1; // Target is in the left half
                }
            }
        }

        // If we exit the loop, target was not found
        return -1;
    }

    // Main method to test the solution
    public static void main(String[] args) {
        int[] nums1 = {4, 5, 6, 7, 0, 1, 2};
        int[] nums2 = {4, 5, 6, 7, 0, 1, 2};
        int[] nums3 = {1};

        // Test case 1: Target found
        System.out.println(search(nums1, 0)); // Expected output: 4

        // Test case 2: Target not found
        System.out.println(search(nums2, 3)); // Expected output: -1

        // Test case 3: Single element array
```

```
        System.out.println(search(nums3, 1)); // Expected output: 0
    }
}
```

Time and Space Complexity

- Time Complexity: `O(log n)` because we are using binary search to reduce the search space by half at each step.
- Space Complexity: `O(1)` as no additional space is required other than a few variables.

Problem 3: Find Peak Element in an Array

Problem Statement

You are given an array of integers. You need to find and return the index of any peak element in `O(log n)` time.

A peak element is defined as an element that is strictly greater than its neighbors. If there are multiple peak elements, you can return the index of any one of them.

Solution

Let's break down the problem and follow the structured approach to solve it.

Clarifying Questions

Candidate: A couple of clarifications to ensure I understand the problem correctly:

1. Can I assume the array has at least one element?
2. Are the values in the array distinct or could they repeat?

Interviewer: Yes, the array will have at least one element, and the values do not have to be distinct. They could repeat.

Candidate: Understood. One last clarification: The array is 0-indexed, and I can assume that the elements beyond the boundaries (i.e., `nums[-1]` and `nums[n]`) are effectively -∞, correct?

Interviewer: Yes, you can imagine `nums[-1]` and `nums[n]` as -∞ for the purpose of comparison.
Candidate: Great, thanks for the clarifications!

Example

- Input: `nums = [1, 2, 3, 1]`
- Output: 2 (as nums[2] = 3 is a peak element)
- Input: `nums = [1, 2, 1, 3, 5, 6, 4]`
- Output: 5 (as nums[5] = 6 is a peak element, though nums[1] = 2 is also a peak)

Brute Force Approach

A brute force approach would be to scan through the entire array and check if each element is greater than both its neighbors. If we find such an element, we return its index. However, this would require `O(n)` time since we would need to check every element.

Since the problem requires `O(log n)` time, this brute force approach is not optimal, so I'll avoid it.

Optimal Approach

Since the problem requires `O(log n)` time, the optimal approach would be to use binary search.

Here's the plan:

1. I'll perform a binary search to find a peak element.
2. At each step, I'll compare the middle element with its neighbors. If `nums[mid]` is greater than both `nums[mid-1]` and `nums[mid+1]`, then `nums[mid]` is a peak element.
3. If `nums[mid]` is not a peak, I can determine whether to move left or right by comparing `nums[mid]` with its neighbors. Specifically:
    - If `nums[mid] < nums[mid+1]`, the peak must lie to the right.
    - Otherwise, the peak must lie to the left.

Code Solution

Hers is the implementation in Java:

```
public class PeakElement {
   public static int findPeakElement(int[] nums) {
       int left = 0, right = nums.length - 1;

       while (left < right) {
           int mid = left + (right - left) / 2;

           // Compare middle element with its next element
           if (nums[mid] < nums[mid + 1]) {
               // Peak is to the right
               left = mid + 1;
           } else {
               // Peak is to the left, or mid itself is a peak
               right = mid;
           }
       }

       // left and right will converge to the peak
       return left;
   }

   // Main method to test the solution
   public static void main(String[] args) {
```

```
        int[] nums1 = {1, 2, 3, 1};
        int[] nums2 = {1, 2, 1, 3, 5, 6, 4};
        int[] nums3 = {1};

        // Test case 1: Single peak
        System.out.println(findPeakElement(nums1)); // Expected
output: 2

        // Test case 2: Multiple peaks, return any
        System.out.println(findPeakElement(nums2)); // Expected
output: 5 (or any peak index like 1)

        // Test case 3: Single element array
        System.out.println(findPeakElement(nums3)); // Expected
output: 0
    }
}
```

Time and Space Complexity

- Time Complexity: `O(log n)` because we're using binary search to divide the search space by half in each iteration.
- Space Complexity: `O(1)` since we're using only a fixed amount of extra space for variables.

Problem 4: Find the Minimum Element in a Rotated Sorted Array

Problem Statement

You are given a sorted array of unique integers that has been rotated between 1 and n times.

Your task is to find and return the minimum element in this rotated array.

Solution

Let's break down the problem and follow the structured approach to solve it.

Clarifying Questions

Candidate: A couple of clarifying questions:

1. Can I assume that the array is not empty and contains at least one element?
2. Should I assume the array is rotated at least once, or could it still be in its original sorted form?

Interviewer: Yes, the array will have at least one element, and the array might not be rotated at all. It could still be sorted in its original order.

Candidate: Understood. If the array is not rotated, the first element will be the minimum. Otherwise, I will need to find the pivot point where the rotation happened, which is where the minimum element will be.

Example

- Input: `nums = [4,5,6,7,0,1,2]`
- Output: `0` (since 0 is the minimum element)
- Input: `nums = [0,1,2,4,5,6,7]`
- Output: `0` (since the array is not rotated, the first element is the minimum)

Brute Force Approach

The brute force approach would be to iterate through the array and find the minimum element by comparing each element with the current minimum.

However, this would take `O(n)` time and is not efficient for large arrays.

Optimal Approach

Since the array is sorted, I can apply binary search to solve this in `O(log n)` time. The key observation is that, in a rotated sorted array, the minimum element is the only element that breaks the sorted order.

More specifically:

1. If the middle element is greater than the rightmost element, it means the minimum element is in the right half.
2. If the middle element is smaller than or equal to the rightmost element, the minimum element is in the left half.

Here's the plan:

- Use binary search to find the minimum element.
- Compare the middle element with the rightmost element to determine which half of the array contains the minimum.

Code Solution

Here is the implementation in Java:

```
public class FindMinimumInRotatedSortedArray {
   public static int findMin(int[] nums) {
        int left = 0;
        int right = nums.length - 1;

        while (left < right) {
            int mid = left + (right - left) / 2;

            // Compare middle element with the rightmost element
            if (nums[mid] > nums[right]) {
                // The minimum is in the right half
                left = mid + 1;
            } else {
                // The minimum is in the left half (or mid is the
minimum)
                right = mid;
            }
```

```
        }

        // When left == right, we have found the minimum element
        return nums[left];
    }

    // Main method to test the solution
    public static void main(String[] args) {
        int[] nums1 = {4, 5, 6, 7, 0, 1, 2};
        int[] nums2 = {0, 1, 2, 4, 5, 6, 7};
        int[] nums3 = {3, 4, 5, 1, 2};
        int[] nums4 = {11, 13, 15, 17};

        // Test case 1: Rotated array
        System.out.println(findMin(nums1)); // Expected output: 0

        // Test case 2: No rotation
        System.out.println(findMin(nums2)); // Expected output: 0

        // Test case 3: Rotated array
        System.out.println(findMin(nums3)); // Expected output: 1

        // Test case 4: No rotation
        System.out.println(findMin(nums4)); // Expected output: 11
    }
}
```

Time and Space Complexity

- Time Complexity: `O(log n)` because we use binary search to reduce the search space by half at each step.
- Space Complexity: `O(1)` because we only use a few extra variables (no additional data structures).

Problem 5: Find the Square Root of a Non-Negative Integer

Problem Statement

You are given a non-negative integer `x`, and your task is to return the ***square root*** of `x`, rounded down to the nearest integer.

You cannot use any built-in exponentiation function or operator.

Solution

Let's break down the question and follow the structured approach to solve it.

Clarifying Questions

Candidate: One clarifying question: Can I assume that the input `x` is always a non-negative integer, and the result should also be non-negative?

Interviewer: Yes, x is always a non-negative integer, and the result should also be non-negative.

Candidate: Thanks. I will take an example and then proceed with the approach to solve the problem.

Example

- Input: `x = 8`
- Output: 2 (since the square root of 8 is approximately 2.828, and the integer part is 2)
- Input: `x = 16`
- Output: 4 (since the square root of 16 is exactly 4)

Brute Force Approach

A brute force approach would be to try all integers from 0 to x, and for each integer i, check if `i * i <= x`. Once `i * i` exceeds x, I will return `i - 1` because that's the largest integer whose square is still less than or equal to x.

However, this approach would take `O(√x)` time in the worst case, which can be inefficient for large values of x.

Optimal Approach

We can solve this problem more efficiently by using binary search.

Since the square root of x must lie between `0` and x, and we are looking for an integer value, I can apply binary search to find the largest integer `mid` such that `mid * mid <= x`.

Here's the plan:

1. I'll initialize two pointers, *left* = 0 and *right* = x.
2. I'll use binary search to narrow down the range. In each iteration:
    - I calculate `mid = (left + right) / 2`.
    - If `mid * mid == x`, then `mid` is the square root, so I return `mid`.
    - If `mid * mid < x`, then the square root must be greater than `mid`, so I move the left pointer to `mid + 1`.
    - If `mid * mid > x`, then the square root must be less than `mid`, so I move the right pointer to `mid - 1`.
3. After the binary search ends, *right will hold the integer part of the square root of x.*

Code Solution

Here's how I would implement it in Java:

```
public class SquareRoot {
    public static int mySqrt(int x) {
        // Base case for 0 and 1
```

```
        if (x == 0 || x == 1) {
            return x;
        }

        int left = 0, right = x;
        int result = 0;

        while (left <= right) {
            int mid = left + (right - left) / 2;

            // Check if mid*mid is equal to x
            if (mid == x / mid) {
                return mid;
            }

            // If mid*mid is less than x, discard left half
            if (mid < x / mid) {
                left = mid + 1;
                result = mid;  // Keep track of the closest possible
answer
            } else {
                // If mid*mid is greater than x, discard right half
                right = mid - 1;
            }
        }

        // Return the floor of the square root
        return result;
    }

    // Main method to test the solution
    public static void main(String[] args) {
        // Test case 1: Non-perfect square
        System.out.println(mySqrt(8)); // Expected output: 2

        // Test case 2: Perfect square
        System.out.println(mySqrt(16)); // Expected output: 4

        // Test case 3: Very small input
        System.out.println(mySqrt(1)); // Expected output: 1

        // Test case 4: Large input
        System.out.println(mySqrt(2147395599)); // Expected output:
46339
    }
}
```

Time and Space Complexity

- **Time Complexity:** `O(log x)` because we're performing binary search over the range of possible square roots.
- **Space Complexity:** `O(1)` because we're only using a few variables for the binary search.

Chapter 8: Linked Lists

In this chapter, we'll cover everything you need to know about the linked list data structure to confidently tackle any coding question on this topic.

Understanding Linked Lists

A **linked list** is a linear data structure where elements are stored in nodes. Each node contains two parts:

- **Data**: The actual data or value.
- **Pointer**: A pointer to the next node in the sequence.

> Unlike arrays, linked lists *do not store elements in contiguous memory locations*. This characteristic allows linked lists to *grow and shrink dynamically*, making them highly flexible for scenarios where *memory allocation is unpredictable*.

Types of Linked Lists:

1. **Singly Linked List**: Each node has a single pointer to the next node.
2. **Doubly Linked List**: Each node has two pointers—one to the next node and one to the previous node.
3. **Circular Linked List**: The last node points back to the first node, forming a circle.

Common Operations on Linked Lists

Before diving into interview questions, let's understand the basic operations on linked lists:

1. **Insertion**: Adding a node to the linked list.
    - **At the beginning**: O(1)
    - **At the end**: O(n) for singly linked lists; O(1) for doubly linked lists with a tail pointer.
    - **At a given position**: O(n)
2. **Deletion**: Removing a node from the linked list.
    - **From the beginning**: O(1)
    - **From the end**: O(n) for singly linked lists; O(1) for doubly linked lists.
    - **From a given position**: O(n)
3. **Traversal**: Accessing or printing each node in the linked list. This operation is O(n).
4. **Searching**: Finding a node with a specific value. This operation is O(n).
5. **Reversal**: Reversing the order of nodes in a linked list. This is a common interview problem and can be solved in O(n).

Dummy Node Technique

Linked list problems often involve operations at the head of the list, such as inserting or deleting a node. These operations can be tricky because the head node itself may need to be changed, leading to special cases in your code.

By introducing a *dummy node at the beginning of the list*, you create a *non-changing* "anchor" that simplifies these operations.

The dummy node provides a stable reference point, so you *don't have to handle the head node differently from other nodes.*

Using a dummy node is a good idea while solving linked list-based questions for several reasons:

1. Simplifies Edge Case Handling
2. Eliminates the Need for Special Conditions
3. Makes Iteration and Manipulation Easier
4. Facilitates Multiple Operations in a Single Pass
5. Consistency Across Different Linked List Problems

We will demonstrate the use and benefits of using dummy node technique in the Linked Lists based problem section (specifically with the problem "*Remove Nth Node from End of Linked List*").

Popular Linked List Questions

Now, let's look at the most popular interview questions based on Linked Lists.

Problem 1: Remove Nth Node from End of Linked List

Problem Statement

You are given the head of a linked list. Your task is to remove the nth node from the end of the list and return the modified linked list.

Solution

Let's follow the structured approach to solve this problem.

Clarifying Questions

Candidate: I'd like to clarify a few points before starting.
Interviewer: Sure, go ahead.

Candidate: Should I assume that n is always valid, meaning there is at least one node in the list and n will not be greater than the length of the list?
Interviewer: Yes, you can assume that n is always valid and the list has at least one node.

Candidate: Got it. Also, do we need to handle edge cases, such as when the head itself needs to be removed?
Interviewer: Yes, you should handle that case as well.

Candidate: Perfect. I think I have all the information I need to proceed.

Example

Let's consider an example:

- Input: `head = [1, 2, 3, 4, 5], n = 2`
- Expected Output: `[1, 2, 3, 5]`

Here, the 2nd node from the end (node with value 4) is removed, and the modified list is `[1, 2, 3, 5]`.

Brute Force Approach

A brute force approach would involve calculating the total length of the linked list first, and then finding the position of the node to remove by iterating through the list a second time.

The time complexity would be `O(n)`, where `n` is the length of the linked list, but since we traverse the list twice, it is not the most efficient solution.

Optimal Approach

We can solve this problem in one pass using the two pointers technique. We can use two pointers: fast and slow.

The idea is to move the fast pointer `n` steps ahead of the slow pointer. Then, we move both pointers together until fast reaches the end of the list. *At this point, the slow pointer will be at the node just before the one to be removed.* We can then adjust the pointers to remove the target node.

Code Solution

Here's how I would implement this in Java:

```
public class RemoveNthNodeFromEnd {
    public static class ListNode {
        int val;
        ListNode next;

        ListNode(int x) {
            val = x;
        }
    }
```

```
    public ListNode removeNthFromEnd(ListNode head, int n) {
        // Create a dummy node to handle edge cases like removing
the head
        ListNode dummy = new ListNode(0);
        dummy.next = head;

        // Initialize two pointers, both starting from the dummy
node
        ListNode fast = dummy;
        ListNode slow = dummy;

        // Move the fast pointer n steps ahead
        for (int i = 0; i < n; i++) {
            fast = fast.next;
        }

        // Move both fast and slow pointers until fast reaches the
end
        while (fast.next != null) {
            fast = fast.next;
            slow = slow.next;
        }

        // Remove the nth node from the end by adjusting pointers
        slow.next = slow.next.next;

        // Return the new head of the list
        return dummy.next;
    }

    public static void main(String[] args) {
        // Test case: Create a linked list [1, 2, 3, 4, 5]
        ListNode head = new ListNode(1);
        head.next = new ListNode(2);
        head.next.next = new ListNode(3);
        head.next.next.next = new ListNode(4);
        head.next.next.next.next = new ListNode(5);

        // Remove the 2nd node from the end
        RemoveNthNodeFromEnd solver = new RemoveNthNodeFromEnd();
        ListNode newHead = solver.removeNthFromEnd(head, 2);

        // Print the modified list: Expected [1, 2, 3, 5]
        while (newHead != null) {
            System.out.print(newHead.val + " ");
            newHead = newHead.next;
        }
    }
}
```

Note: *We create a dummy node that points to the head of the list. This helps handle edge cases like removing the head node.*

Time and Space Complexity

- The time complexity of this solution is `O(n)`, where `n` is the length of the linked list. We only make one pass through the list.
- The space complexity is `O(1)`, as we only use a few extra pointers.

Problem 2: Detect a Cycle in a Linked List

Problem Statement

You are given the head of a linked list. Your task is to determine whether the linked list contains a cycle.

A cycle occurs when a node's `next` pointer points to a previous node in the list, forming a loop.

Solution

Let's solve this problem using a structured approach.

Clarifying Questions

Candidate: I'd like to clarify a few points before starting.
Candidate: Sure, go ahead.

Candidate: Should I assume that the linked list contains at least one node?
Candidate: Yes, you can assume that the list contains at least one node.

Candidate: Got it. Should the cycle always point to one of the previous nodes, or could it also point back to the head node?
Candidate: The cycle can point to any of the previous nodes, including the head.

Candidate: Understood. I think I have all the information I need to proceed.

Example

Let's consider an example to clarify:

- Input: `head = [3, 2, 0, -4]`, where `tail.next` points to the node with value 2 (forming a cycle).
- Expected Output: `true`

In this case, the list has a cycle, as the last node points back to an earlier node.

Brute Force Approach

A brute force approach could involve using a data structure like a HashSet to store each node as we traverse the linked list. If we encounter a node that already exists in the set, we know there is a cycle.

The time complexity would be `O(n)`, where `n` is the length of the linked list, since we traverse the list once. The space complexity would also be `O(n)`, as we need to store each node in the HashSet.

Optimal Approach

We can solve this problem more efficiently using Floyd's Cycle Detection Algorithm, also known as the Tortoise and Hare algorithm.

The idea is to use two pointers:

- The slow pointer (tortoise) moves one step at a time.
- The fast pointer (hare) moves two steps at a time.

If there is a cycle in the list, the fast pointer will eventually meet the slow pointer inside the cycle. If the fast pointer reaches the end of the list (null), we know there is no cycle.

Code Solution

Here is the implementation in Java:

```
public class LinkedListCycle {
   public static class ListNode {
        int val;
        ListNode next;

        ListNode(int x) {
            val = x;
            next = null;
        }
   }

   public boolean hasCycle(ListNode head) {
        // Edge case: if the list is empty or has only one node, no
cycle is possible
        if (head == null || head.next == null) {
            return false;
        }

        // Initialize two pointers: slow (tortoise) and fast (hare)
        ListNode slow = head;
        ListNode fast = head;

        // Traverse the list with the two pointers
        while (fast != null && fast.next != null) {
            slow = slow.next;          // Move slow pointer by one
step
```

```
            fast = fast.next.next;     // Move fast pointer by two
steps

            // If slow and fast pointers meet, there is a cycle
            if (slow == fast) {
                return true;
            }
        }

        // If the fast pointer reaches the end of the list, there is
no cycle
        return false;
    }

    public static void main(String[] args) {
        // Test case 1: Create a linked list with a cycle
        ListNode head1 = new ListNode(3);
        ListNode node2 = new ListNode(2);
        ListNode node3 = new ListNode(0);
        ListNode node4 = new ListNode(-4);
        head1.next = node2;
        node2.next = node3;
        node3.next = node4;
        node4.next = node2;  // Create a cycle

        LinkedListCycle solver = new LinkedListCycle();
        System.out.println("Has Cycle: " + solver.hasCycle(head1));
// Expected: true

        // Test case 2: Create a linked list without a cycle
        ListNode head2 = new ListNode(1);
        ListNode node5 = new ListNode(2);
        head2.next = node5;

        System.out.println("Has Cycle: " + solver.hasCycle(head2));
// Expected: false
    }
}
```

Time and Space Complexity

- The time complexity of this solution is O(n), where n is the number of nodes in the linked list. The slow pointer and fast pointer both traverse the list at most once.
- The space complexity is O(1), as we only use two extra pointers.

Problem 3: Reverse a Singly Linked List

Problem Statement

You are given the head of a singly linked list. Your task is to reverse the linked list in place and return the head of the reversed list.

Solution

Let's follow the structured approach to solve this problem.

Clarifying Questions

Candidate: I'd like to clarify a few points before starting.
Interviewer: Sure, go ahead.

Candidate: Should I assume the list contains at least one node?
Interviewer: Yes, you can assume the list contains at least one node.

Candidate: Got it. Should I reverse the list in place without using extra space?
Interviewer: Yes, please reverse the list in place using constant space.

Candidate: Perfect, I think I have all the information I need to proceed.

Example

Let's consider an example:

- `Input: head = [1, 2, 3, 4, 5]`
- `Expected Output: [5, 4, 3, 2, 1]`

The list is reversed, and the head of the reversed list is returned.

Brute Force Approach

A brute force approach would involve using a stack to store all the nodes as we traverse the list. After storing the nodes, we pop them from the stack and reconstruct the list in reverse order.

The time complexity would be `O(n)`, where `n` is the length of the linked list, but the space complexity would also be `O(n)` due to the use of the stack.

Optimal Approach

We can reverse the list in place using an iterative approach. We use three pointers: prev, current, and next.

The idea is to iterate through the list and reverse the next pointer of each node so that it points to the previous node.

The steps are as follows:

- Initialize `prev` to `null` and `current` to `head`.

- As we traverse the list, we store the `next` node (*next = current.next*), then reverse the `next` pointer of the `current` node (*current.next = prev*).
- Move `prev` and `current` one step forward (*prev = current, current = next*) until `current` becomes `null`.

At the end of the process, `prev` will point to the *new head* of the reversed list.

Code Solution

Here is how I would implement this in Java:

```
public class ReverseLinkedList {
   public static class ListNode {
        int val;
        ListNode next;

        ListNode(int x) {
            val = x;
        }
   }

   public ListNode reverseList(ListNode head) {
        ListNode prev = null;      // Initialize previous pointer to
null
        ListNode current = head;  // Start with the head of the list

        // Traverse the list and reverse the pointers
        while (current != null) {
            ListNode next = current.next;  // Store the next node
            current.next = prev;           // Reverse the current
node's pointer
            prev = current;                // Move prev one step
forward
            current = next;                // Move current one step
forward
        }

        // At the end, prev will be the new head of the reversed
list
        return prev;
   }

   public static void main(String[] args) {
        // Test case: Create a linked list [1, 2, 3, 4, 5]
        ListNode head = new ListNode(1);
        head.next = new ListNode(2);
        head.next.next = new ListNode(3);
        head.next.next.next = new ListNode(4);
        head.next.next.next.next = new ListNode(5);

        ReverseLinkedList solver = new ReverseLinkedList();
        ListNode reversedHead = solver.reverseList(head);
```

```
        // Print the reversed list: Expected [5, 4, 3, 2, 1]
        while (reversedHead != null) {
            System.out.print(reversedHead.val + " ");
            reversedHead = reversedHead.next;
        }
    }
}
```

Time and Space Complexity

- The time complexity is O(n), where n is the number of nodes in the linked list. We traverse the entire list once.
- The space complexity is O(1), as we only use a few extra pointers and reverse the list in place.

Problem 4: Group Odd Even Nodes in Linked List

Problem Statement

You are given the head of a singly linked list. Your task is to group all nodes with odd indices together, followed by all nodes with even indices, and return the reordered list.

The first node is considered odd, the second node is even, and so on. The relative order of nodes within the odd and even groups should be preserved.

Solution

Let's follow the structured approach to solve this problem.

Clarifying Questions

Candidate: I'd like to clarify a few points before starting.
Interviewer: Sure, go ahead.

Candidate: Should I assume that the list contains at least one node?
Interviewer: Yes, you can assume that the list contains at least one node.

Candidate: Got it. Also, should the order within the odd-indexed and even-indexed nodes be maintained?
Interviewer: Yes, the order of nodes within the odd and even groups should be preserved.

Candidate: Lastly, should I aim for an in-place solution?
Interviewer: Yes, the solution should be in-place.

Candidate: Understood. I have all the information I need to proceed.

Example

Let's consider an example:

- Input: `head = [1, 2, 3, 4, 5]`
- Expected Output: `[1, 3, 5, 2, 4]`

Here, the nodes with odd indices (1, 3, 5) are grouped first, followed by the nodes with even indices (2, 4).

Brute Force Approach

A brute force approach would involve traversing the list twice:

- First, we could collect all the odd-indexed nodes.
- Then, we traverse the list again to collect all the even-indexed nodes.
- Finally, we concatenate the odd-indexed nodes with the even-indexed ones.

However, this would require two passes through the list and would involve extra space to store the nodes temporarily.

Optimal Approach

We can solve this problem in one pass using two pointers: odd and even.

The odd pointer will track the current odd-indexed node. The even pointer will track the current even-indexed node, and we'll also store a pointer to the head of the even nodes (evenHead) to append it at the end of the odd list.
Here are the steps:

- Step 1: Initialize the odd pointer to point to the first node and the even pointer to point to the second node.
- Step 2: Traverse the list, alternating between odd and even nodes. Connect each odd node to the next odd node and each even node to the next even node.
- Step 3: At the end of the traversal, connect the last odd node to the head of the even nodes.

This ensures that the odd and even groups are constructed in place, and the relative order is preserved.

Code Solution

Here is the implementation:

```
public class OddEvenLinkedList {
   public static class ListNode {
       int val;
       ListNode next;

       ListNode(int x) {
           val = x;
       }
   }
```

```
    public ListNode oddEvenList(ListNode head) {
        if (head == null || head.next == null) {
            return head;  // If the list is empty or has only one
node, no reordering is needed
        }

        // Initialize pointers
        ListNode odd = head;
        ListNode even = head.next;
        ListNode evenHead = even;  // Store the head of the even
nodes

        // Traverse the list while there are still even and odd
nodes to process
        while (even != null && even.next != null) {
            odd.next = even.next;  // Connect the odd node to the
next odd node
            odd = odd.next;          // Move the odd pointer forward

            even.next = odd.next;  // Connect the even node to the
next even node
            even = even.next;        // Move the even pointer forward
        }

        // After the traversal, connect the odd list to the even
list
        odd.next = evenHead;

        return head;  // Return the head of the reordered list
    }

    public static void main(String[] args) {
        // Test case: Create a linked list [1, 2, 3, 4, 5]
        ListNode head = new ListNode(1);
        head.next = new ListNode(2);
        head.next.next = new ListNode(3);
        head.next.next.next = new ListNode(4);
        head.next.next.next.next = new ListNode(5);

        OddEvenLinkedList solver = new OddEvenLinkedList();
        ListNode reorderedHead = solver.oddEvenList(head);

        // Print the reordered list: Expected [1, 3, 5, 2, 4]
        while (reorderedHead != null) {
            System.out.print(reorderedHead.val + " ");
            reorderedHead = reorderedHead.next;
        }
    }
}
```

Time and Space Complexity

- The time complexity is O(n), where n is the number of nodes in the linked list. We traverse the list once to reorder the nodes.
- The space complexity is O(1), as we are only using a few extra pointers and modifying the list in place.

Problem 5: Insert into a Sorted Circular Linked List

Problem Statement

You are given a node from a circular linked list that is sorted in non-descending order. Your task is to insert a new value `insertVal` into the list such that it remains sorted.

The list is circular, and you are provided a reference to any node in the list, which may not necessarily be the node with the smallest value.

Solution

Let's follow the structured approach to solve this problem.

Clarifying Questions

Candidate: I'd like to clarify a few points before starting the implementation.
Interviewer: Sure, go ahead.

Candidate: Should I assume that the circular list is always sorted in non-descending order?
Interviewer: Yes, the list is guaranteed to be sorted in non-descending order.

Candidate: Got it. Should I handle the case when the list is empty by creating a new circular list?
Interviewer: Yes, if the list is empty, create a new node that points to itself and return
it.

Candidate: Lastly, if there are multiple valid positions for insertion, should I be concerned about where exactly the value is inserted, or is any valid position fine?
Interviewer: Any valid position that keeps the list sorted is acceptable.

Candidate: Understood. I have everything I need to proceed.

Example

Let's consider an example to clarify:

- Input: `node = [3, 4, 1], insertVal = 2`
- Expected Output: The circular list becomes `[3, 4, 1, 2]`.

In this example, we insert 2 between 1 and 3, keeping the circular list sorted.

Optimal Approach

We can solve this problem in one pass through the circular linked list by traversing the list and checking the following conditions:

- If `current.val <= insertVal <= current.next.val`, insert between `current` and `current.next`.
- If `current.val > current.next.val` (which indicates the transition between the largest and smallest values), we check if `insertVal` is either larger than the largest value or smaller than the smallest value, and insert accordingly.
- If no condition is satisfied after *one full pass*, the new value can be inserted anywhere, meaning we can *insert it after any node.*

Code Solution

Here is the implementation in Java:

```
public class InsertIntoSortedCircularList {
    public static class ListNode {
        int val;
        ListNode next;

        ListNode(int val) {
            this.val = val;
            this.next = null;
        }
    }

    public ListNode insert(ListNode node, int insertVal) {
        // Case 1: Empty list, create a new single circular list
        if (node == null) {
            ListNode newNode = new ListNode(insertVal);
            newNode.next = newNode;
            return newNode;
        }

        ListNode current = node;
        while (true) {
            // Case 2: Inserting the value between two nodes
            if (current.val <= insertVal && insertVal <=
current.next.val) {
                break;
            }

            // Case 3: Inserting at the end of the circular list
(handling the transition between max and min)
            if (current.val > current.next.val) {
                if (insertVal >= current.val || insertVal <=
current.next.val) {
                    break;
                }
            }
```

```
            // Move to the next node
            current = current.next;

            // Case 4: Full pass completed, insert after any node
            if (current == node) {
                break;
            }
        }

        // Insert the new node
        ListNode newNode = new ListNode(insertVal);
        newNode.next = current.next;
        current.next = newNode;

        // Return the original node
        return node;
    }

    public static void main(String[] args) {
        // Create a circular linked list: [3, 4, 1]
        ListNode node1 = new ListNode(3);
        ListNode node2 = new ListNode(4);
        ListNode node3 = new ListNode(1);
        node1.next = node2;
        node2.next = node3;
        node3.next = node1;

        // Test case: insert 2 into the circular list
        InsertIntoSortedCircularList solver = new
InsertIntoSortedCircularList();
        ListNode newHead = solver.insert(node1, 2);

        // Print the new circular linked list starting from the new
head (one full loop)
        ListNode current = newHead;
        do {
            System.out.print(current.val + " ");
            current = current.next;
        } while (current != newHead);  // Stop when we complete a
full circle
    }
}
```

Time and Space Complexity

- The time complexity is O(n), where n is the number of nodes in the circular linked list. In the worst case, we traverse the list once to find the insertion point.
- The space complexity is O(1), as we are only using a few pointers and modifying the list in place.

Problem 6: Plus One Linked List

Problem Statement

You are given a non-negative integer represented as a singly linked list where each node contains a single digit.

The digits are stored such that the most significant digit is at the head of the list. Your task is to add 1 to this integer and return the updated linked list.

Solution

Let's follow the structured approach to solve this problem.

Clarifying Questions

Candidate: I'd like to clarify a few points before starting.
Interviewer: Sure, go ahead.

Candidate: Got it. Should I handle the case where adding one causes a carry, and should that propagate through the list (e.g., 999 + 1 becomes 1000)?
Interviewer: Yes, if there's a carry, it should propagate through the list as needed.

Candidate: Lastly, do I need to account for edge cases such as an empty list?
Interviewer: You can assume that the list always represents a valid non-negative integer, so no empty list cases.

Candidate: Understood. I have all the information I need to proceed.

Example

Let's consider an example:

- Input: `head = [1, 2, 3]`
- Expected Output: `[1, 2, 4]`

Here, the integer is 123, and adding one results in 124.

Optimal Approach

We can solve this problem using the reverse-then-add approach to handle the addition and carry efficiently.

- Step 1: Reverse the linked list so that the least significant digit is at the head.
- Step 2: Add 1 to the first node of the reversed list and propagate any carry through the list.
- Step 3: Reverse the list again to restore the original order and return the head of the updated list.

Code Solution

Here's how I would implement it in Java:

```
public class AddOneToLinkedList {

   static class ListNode {
       int val;
       ListNode next;

       ListNode(int x) {
           val = x;
       }
   }

   // Helper function to reverse the linked list
   private ListNode reverse(ListNode head) {
       ListNode prev = null;
       ListNode current = head;

       while (current != null) {
           ListNode next = current.next;
           current.next = prev;
           prev = current;
           current = next;
       }

       return prev;  // New head after reversing
   }

   public ListNode plusOne(ListNode head) {
       // Step 1: Reverse the linked list
       head = reverse(head);

       // Step 2: Add one to the least significant digit and handle
the carry
       ListNode current = head;
       int carry = 1;

       while (current != null) {
           int sum = current.val + carry;
           current.val = sum % 10;
           carry = sum / 10;

           // If no carry remains, we can stop early
           if (carry == 0) {
               break;
           }

           // Move to the next node
           if (current.next == null && carry > 0) {
               // If we're at the last node and there's still a
carry, create a new node
                current.next = new ListNode(1);
               carry = 0;
           }
```

```
            current = current.next;
        }

        // Step 3: Reverse the list back to its original order
        return reverse(head);
    }

    public static void main(String[] args) {
        // Test case: Create a linked list [1, 2, 3]
        ListNode head = new ListNode(1);
        head.next = new ListNode(2);
        head.next.next = new ListNode(3);

        AddOneToLinkedList solver = new AddOneToLinkedList();
        ListNode updatedHead = solver.plusOne(head);

        // Print the updated list: Expected [1, 2, 4]
        while (updatedHead != null) {
            System.out.print(updatedHead.val + " ");
            updatedHead = updatedHead.next;
        }
    }
}
```

Time and Space Complexity

- The time complexity is `O(n)`, where `n` is the number of nodes in the linked list. We reverse the list twice and make a single pass to add `1`.
- The space complexity is `O(1)`, as we are only using a few pointers and modifying the list in place.

Chapter 9: Stacks

Introduction

Understanding how stacks work, when to use them, and how to implement them efficiently can make a significant difference in your problem-solving approach.

> A **stack** is a linear data structure that follows the **Last In, First Out (LIFO)** principle.

This means that the *last element added* to the stack will be the *first one to be removed.*

Imagine a stack of plates; you add plates to the top and remove them from the top.

Key Operations

- **Push**: Add an element to the top of the stack.
- **Pop**: Remove the top element from the stack.
- **Peek/Top**: Retrieve the top element without removing it.
- **isEmpty**: Check if the stack is empty.

When to Use a Stack

Stacks are particularly useful in scenarios where you need to:

- **Reverse elements**: Since the last added element is the first to be removed, stacks are ideal for reversing orders, such as characters in a string.
- **Undo operations**: Many applications use stacks to implement undo functionality, where the last action is undone first.
- **Balanced parentheses and syntax validation**: Stacks are essential in validating expressions involving parentheses, brackets, or braces.
- **Depth-First Search (DFS)**: DFS traversal in graphs or trees can be efficiently implemented using stacks.
- **Backtracking problems**: Problems like generating permutations or solving mazes often use stacks to track choices and backtrack when necessary.
- **Expression evaluation**: Stacks are used to evaluate postfix (Reverse Polish notation) expressions or to convert infix expressions to postfix.

Popular Interview Questions on Stacks

In this section, we will go over the most popular Stack based questions and the approach to efficiently solve them.

Problem 1: Implement the Basic Calculator

Problem Statement

You are given a string s representing a valid arithmetic expression that may contain numbers, +, -, and parentheses (and).

Your task is to implement a basic calculator to evaluate the expression and return the result.

Solution

Let's follow the structured approach to solve the problem.

Clarifying Questions

Candidate: I'd like to clarify a few points before starting the implementation.
Interviewer: Sure, go ahead.

Candidate: Should I handle only + and - operators, or should I also handle multiplication and division?
Interviewer: You only need to handle +, -, and parentheses for this question. You don't need to handle multiplication or division.

Candidate: Got it. Should I assume that the input string is always valid, meaning it has balanced parentheses and no invalid characters?
Interviewer: Yes, the input string is guaranteed to be valid.

Candidate: Lastly, should I worry about spaces in the input string, or can I ignore them?
Interviewer: You can assume that the string may contain spaces, but they should be ignored.

Candidate: Understood. I have all the information I need to proceed.

Example

Let's consider an example to clarify:

- Input: `s = "(1 + (4 + 5 + 2) - 3) + (6 + 8)"`
- Expected Output: `23`

Here, the expression evaluates to 23 after following the order of operations and handling parentheses correctly.

Approach

The problem involves evaluating an expression with +, -, and parentheses. *We can use a **stack** to handle the parentheses and keep track of intermediate results.*

Here's how the approach works:

1. Since spaces don't affect the result, we can skip them.
2. The stack will be used to store intermediate results and signs. We will push the current result and sign when encountering an opening parenthesis (, and we will pop the stack when encountering a closing parenthesis).
3. We will process the string one character at a time:
    - If we encounter a number, we form the entire number and add or subtract it based on the current sign.
    - If we encounter +, we set the current sign to +.
    - If we encounter -, we set the current sign to -.
    - If we encounter (, we push the current result and sign onto the stack and reset the result for the new sub-expression.
    - If we encounter), we pop the stack to get the previous result and add/subtract the current result to it.

Code Solution

Here is how I would implement this in Java:

```
import java.util.Stack;

public class BasicCalculator {

   public int calculate(String s) {
        Stack<Integer> stack = new Stack<>();
        int result = 0;
        int sign = 1; // 1 means positive, -1 means negative
        int i = 0;

        while (i < s.length()) {
            char ch = s.charAt(i);

            // Case 1: If it's a digit, form the full number and
add/subtract it to the result
            if (Character.isDigit(ch)) {
                int num = 0;
                while (i < s.length() &&
Character.isDigit(s.charAt(i))) {
                    num = num * 10 + (s.charAt(i) - '0');
                    i++;
                }
                result += sign * num;
                continue;  // Move to the next iteration since we
already advanced `i`
            }

            // Case 2: If it's a plus sign, set the sign to positive
            if (ch == '+') {
```

```
                sign = 1;
            }

            // Case 3: If it's a minus sign, set the sign to
negative
            if (ch == '-') {
                sign = -1;
            }

            // Case 4: If it's an opening parenthesis, push the
current result and sign to the stack
            if (ch == '(') {
                stack.push(result);
                stack.push(sign);
                result = 0; // Reset result for the sub-expression
inside the parentheses
                sign = 1;   // Reset sign
            }

            // Case 5: If it's a closing parenthesis, pop the stack
and combine the result
            if (ch == ')') {
                result = result * stack.pop() + stack.pop();
            }

            // Move to the next character
            i++;
        }

        return result;
    }

    public static void main(String[] args) {
        BasicCalculator solver = new BasicCalculator();

        // Test cases
        String expression1 = "(1 + (4 + 5 + 2) - 3) + (6 + 8)";
        System.out.println("Result: " +
solver.calculate(expression1));  // Expected: 23

        String expression2 = "2 - (1 + 2)";
        System.out.println("Result: " +
solver.calculate(expression2));  // Expected: -1

        String expression3 = "1 + 1";
        System.out.println("Result: " +
solver.calculate(expression3));  // Expected: 2

        String expression4 = "(1 + (2 - 3))";
        System.out.println("Result: " +
solver.calculate(expression4));  // Expected: 0
    }
}
```

Time and Space Complexity

- The time complexity is `O(n)`, where `n` is the length of the string. We process each character in the string once.
- The space complexity is `O(n)` due to the stack, which stores intermediate results and signs.

Problem 2: Next Greater Element in An Array

Problem Statement

You are given an array of integers. For each element in the array, find the next greater element to its right.

The next greater element of a number `x` is the first number to the right of `x` that is greater than `x`. If no such number exists, return `-1` for that element.

Solution

Let's follow the structured approach to solve this problem.

Clarifying Questions

Candidate: I'd like to clarify a few points before starting the implementation.
Interviewer: Sure, go ahead.

Candidate: Got it. Should I handle arrays with negative numbers, or can the elements only be positive?
Interviewer: The array can contain both positive and negative integers.

Candidate: Understood. I have all the information I need to proceed.

Example

Let's consider an example to clarify:

- Input: `nums = [2, 1, 2, 4, 3]`
- Expected Output: `[4, 2, 4, -1, -1]`

Here, for each element:

- 2 → the next greater element is 4
- 1 → the next greater element is 2
- 2 → the next greater element is 4
- 4 → there is no greater element, so -1
- 3 → there is no greater element, so -1

Brute Force Approach

A brute force approach would involve iterating over each element in the array and, for each element, scanning the rest of the array to find the next greater element. This would take $O(n^2)$ time.

Optimal Approach

We can solve this problem more efficiently using a stack.

The idea is to use a stack to keep track of elements for which we haven't yet found the next greater element.

We iterate through the array from left to right, and for each element, we check whether it is greater than the element at the top of the stack:

- If the current element is greater, it becomes the next greater element for the element on the top of the stack, and we pop the stack.
- We continue this process until the stack is empty or the current element is not greater than the top of the stack.
- Finally, we push the current element onto the stack.

By the time we finish the iteration, all elements for which we haven't found a greater element will remain in the stack, and we can set their result to -1.

Code Solution

Here is the implementation in Java:

```
import java.util.Stack;

public class NextGreaterElement {

   public int[] nextGreaterElements(int[] nums) {
        int[] result = new int[nums.length];
        Stack<Integer> stack = new Stack<>();  // Stack to store
indices of elements

        // Initialize the result array with -1
        for (int i = 0; i < nums.length; i++) {
            result[i] = -1;
        }

        // Iterate through the array
        for (int i = 0; i < nums.length; i++) {
            // While the current element is greater than the element
at the top of the stack
            while (!stack.isEmpty() && nums[i] > nums[stack.peek()])
{
                int index = stack.pop();
                result[index] = nums[i];  // Set the next greater
element for the popped index
            }
            // Push the current index onto the stack
```

```
            stack.push(i);
        }

        return result;
    }

    public static void main(String[] args) {
        NextGreaterElement solver = new NextGreaterElement();

        // Test case 1
        int[] nums1 = {2, 1, 2, 4, 3};
        int[] result1 = solver.nextGreaterElements(nums1);
        System.out.println("Next Greater Elements: " +
java.util.Arrays.toString(result1));
        // Expected output: [4, 2, 4, -1, -1]

        // Test case 2
        int[] nums2 = {1, 3, 4, 2};
        int[] result2 = solver.nextGreaterElements(nums2);
        System.out.println("Next Greater Elements: " +
java.util.Arrays.toString(result2));
        // Expected output: [3, 4, -1, -1]
    }
}
```

Time and Space Complexity

- The time complexity is `O(n)`, where `n` is the length of the array. Each element is pushed and popped from the stack at most once.
- The space complexity is `O(n)` due to the stack, which stores the indices of elements.

Problem 3: Next Greater Element in a Circular Array

Problem Statement

You are given a circular integer array `nums`. Your task is to return the next greater number for every element in `nums`.

The next greater number of an element `x` is the first number that is greater than `x` when traversing circularly through the array. If no greater number exists, return `-1` for that element.

Solution

Let's follow the structured approach to solve this problem.

Clarifying Questions

Candidate: As the array is circular, we have to wrap around after the last element to continue checking from the start of the array for the next greater element, right?
Interviewer: Yes, that's correct.

Candidate: Understood. I have all the information I need to proceed.

Example

Let's consider an example:

- Input: `nums = [1, 2, 1]`
- Expected Output: `[2, -1, 2]`

Here, the circular array allows wrapping around:

- For the first element 1, the next greater number is 2.
- For the second element 2, there is no greater number in the array, so return -1.
- For the third element 1, the next greater number (after wrapping around) is 2.

Brute Force Approach

A brute force approach would involve iterating over each element in the array, and for each element, scanning the remaining elements (circularly) to find the next greater number. This would result in $O(n^2)$ time complexity, hence not very efficient.

Optimal Approach

We can solve this problem more efficiently using a stack combined with the concept of iterating over the array twice (to handle the circular nature).

The idea is to simulate the circular nature of the array by iterating over it twice. We use a stack to keep track of indices of elements for which we haven't found the next greater element.

The stack stores the indices of elements in decreasing order of their values:

- As we iterate through the array, if the current element is greater than the element at the top of the stack, it becomes the next greater element for the element at the top of the stack.
- To handle the circular nature, we iterate over the array twice by using `i % n` to wrap around.

Code Solution

Here's how I would implement this in Java:

```
import java.util.Stack;

public class NextGreaterElementCircular {
```

```
    public int[] nextGreaterElements(int[] nums) {
        int n = nums.length;
        int[] result = new int[n];
        Stack<Integer> stack = new Stack<>();

        // Initialize the result array with -1
        for (int i = 0; i < n; i++) {
            result[i] = -1;
        }

        // Iterate through the array twice to simulate the circular
nature
        for (int i = 0; i < 2 * n; i++) {
            // Wrap around using i % n
            while (!stack.isEmpty() && nums[i % n] >
nums[stack.peek()]) {
                result[stack.pop()] = nums[i % n];
            }
            // Push the index to the stack only for the first pass
(i < n)
            if (i < n) {
                stack.push(i);
            }
        }

        return result;
    }

    public static void main(String[] args) {
        NextGreaterElementCircular solver = new
NextGreaterElementCircular();

        // Test case 1
        int[] nums1 = {1, 2, 1};
        int[] result1 = solver.nextGreaterElements(nums1);
        System.out.println("Next Greater Elements: " +
java.util.Arrays.toString(result1));
        // Expected output: [2, -1, 2]

        // Test case 2
        int[] nums2 = {3, 8, 4, 1, 2};
        int[] result2 = solver.nextGreaterElements(nums2);
        System.out.println("Next Greater Elements: " +
java.util.Arrays.toString(result2));
        // Expected output: [8, -1, 8, 2, 3]
    }
}
```

Time and Space Complexity

- The time complexity is `O(n)`, where `n` is the length of the array. Each element is pushed and popped from the stack at most once.
- The space complexity is `O(n)` due to the stack, which stores the indices of elements.

Problem 4: Remove Stars from a String

Problem Statement

You are given a string s that contains stars (*). Each star in the string represents an operation where you remove the closest non-star character to its left and remove the star itself.
Your task is to return the string after all stars and their corresponding closest left characters have been removed.

Solution

Let's follow the structured approach to solve this problem.

Clarifying Questions

Candidate: Should I assume that every star will have a non-star character to its left to remove?
Interviewer: Yes, for the purpose of this question, you can assume that every star will have a valid non-star character to its left.

Candidate: Understood. I have all the information I need to proceed.

Example

Let's consider an example:

- Input: `s = "ab*c*d*"`
- Expected Output: `"a"`

In this example:

- The first * removes b and itself, leaving "a*c*d*".
- The second * removes c and itself, leaving "a*d*".
- The third * removes d and itself, leaving "a".

Optimal Approach

We can solve this problem in one pass using a stack to handle the removal efficiently.

Here's the approach:

- Traverse through the string character by character.
- If the character is not a star, push it onto the stack.
- If the character is a star, pop the top of the stack to remove the closest non-star character.
- After the traversal, the stack will contain the remaining characters, which can be joined to form the result.

Code Solution

Here's how I would implement in Java:

```
import java.util.Stack;

public class RemoveStars {

    public String removeStars(String s) {
        Stack<Character> stack = new Stack<>();

        // Traverse through the string
        for (char ch : s.toCharArray()) {
            if (ch == '*') {
                // Pop the stack to remove the closest non-star
character
                if (!stack.isEmpty()) {
                    stack.pop();
                }
            } else {
                // Push the non-star character onto the stack
                stack.push(ch);
            }
        }

        // Convert the stack to a string
        StringBuilder result = new StringBuilder();
        for (char ch : stack) {
            result.append(ch);
        }

        return result.toString();
    }

    public static void main(String[] args) {
        RemoveStars solver = new RemoveStars();

        // Test cases
        String s1 = "ab*c*d*";
        System.out.println("Result: " + solver.removeStars(s1));   //
Expected: "a"

        String s2 = "code**fun*!";
        System.out.println("Result: " + solver.removeStars(s2));   //
Expected: "cofu!"

        String s3 = "delete*****";
        System.out.println("Result: " + solver.removeStars(s3));   //
Expected: ""
    }
}
```

Time and Space Complexity

- The time complexity is `O(n)`, where `n` is the length of the string. We process each character once.
- The space complexity is `O(n)` in the worst case, as we may store up to all non-star characters in the stack.

Problem 5: Asteroid Collision

Problem Statement

You are given an array called `asteroids` of integers, where the absolute value represents the size of the asteroid and the sign represents its direction (positive for right and negative for left).

All asteroids move at the same speed. If two asteroids meet, the smaller one will explode, and if both are the same size, both will explode. Asteroids moving in the same direction will never meet.

Your task is to find the final state of the asteroids after all collisions.

Solution

Let's follow the structured approach to solve this problem.

Clarifying Questions

Candidate: Just to clarify, asteroids moving in the same direction, whether both to the right or both to the left, will never collide?
Interviewer: Yes, asteroids moving in the same direction will never meet or collide.

Candidate: Should I return the final state of the asteroids after all collisions, and should the order be preserved for any surviving asteroids?
Interviewer: Yes, return the final state, and the order of surviving asteroids should be preserved.

Candidate: Understood. I have all the information I need to proceed.

Example

Let's consider an example to clarify:

- Input: asteroids = [5, 10, -5]
- Expected Output: [5, 10]

In this case:

- 5 and 10 are moving to the right.
- -5 is moving to the left and collides with 10. Since 10 is larger, -5 explodes.
- The final state is [5, 10].

Optimal Approach (Using a Stack)

We can solve this problem efficiently using a stack to simulate asteroid collisions:

- Step 1: Traverse the array of asteroids.
- Step 2: If the asteroid is positive (moving right), we push it onto the stack.
- Step 3: If the asteroid is negative (moving left), we check for collisions:
    - If the top of the stack is a positive asteroid, compare their sizes:
        - If the positive asteroid is larger, the negative asteroid explodes.
        - If the negative asteroid is larger, the positive asteroid explodes.
        - If they are the same size, both explode.
    - Repeat this process until the collisions are resolved.
- Step 4: Return the stack as the final state of the asteroids.

Code Solution

Here's how I would implement this in Java:

```
import java.util.Stack;

public class AsteroidCollision {

   public int[] asteroidCollision(int[] asteroids) {
        Stack<Integer> stack = new Stack<>();

        for (int asteroid : asteroids) {
            // Handle collisions with the stack top
            boolean exploded = false;
            while (!stack.isEmpty() && asteroid < 0 && stack.peek() >
0) {
                if (Math.abs(asteroid) > stack.peek()) {
                    stack.pop();  // The right-moving asteroid
explodes
                } else if (Math.abs(asteroid) == stack.peek()) {
                    stack.pop();  // Both asteroids explode
                    exploded = true;
                    break;
                } else {
                    exploded = true;  // The left-moving asteroid
explodes
                    break;
                }
            }

            // If the asteroid didn't explode, add it to the stack
            if (!exploded) {
                stack.push(asteroid);
            }
        }

        // Convert stack to array
        int[] result = new int[stack.size()];
        for (int i = result.length - 1; i >= 0; i--) {
            result[i] = stack.pop();
```

```
        }

        return result;
    }

    public static void main(String[] args) {
        AsteroidCollision solver = new AsteroidCollision();

        // Test case 1
        int[] asteroids1 = {5, 10, -5};
        int[] result1 = solver.asteroidCollision(asteroids1);
        System.out.println("Final State: " +
java.util.Arrays.toString(result1));  // Expected: [5, 10]

        // Test case 2
        int[] asteroids2 = {8, -8};
        int[] result2 = solver.asteroidCollision(asteroids2);
        System.out.println("Final State: " +
java.util.Arrays.toString(result2));  // Expected: []

        // Test case 3
        int[] asteroids3 = {10, 2, -5};
        int[] result3 = solver.asteroidCollision(asteroids3);
        System.out.println("Final State: " +
java.util.Arrays.toString(result3));  // Expected: [10]
    }
}
```

Time and Space Complexity

- The time complexity is `O(n)`, where `n` is the number of asteroids. Each asteroid is pushed and popped from the stack at most once.
- The space complexity is `O(n)` due to the stack, which stores the asteroids that survive the collisions.

Problem 6: Decode String

Problem Statement

You are given an encoded string where the format is `k[encoded_string]`. The encoding rule is that the `encoded_string` inside the square brackets is repeated exactly `k` times.

Your task is to decode the string and return the decoded result.

Solution

Let's follow the structured approach to solve this problem.

Clarifying Questions

Candidate: Should I assume that there will always be a positive integer k before each [and that the brackets are always properly closed?
Interviewer: Yes, the format is always valid, and k will always be a positive integer.

Candidate: Got it. Should I handle nested encodings, such as 3[a2[bc]]?
Interviewer: Yes, you should be able to handle nested encodings like that.

Candidate: Lastly, should I assume that the decoded string only contains lowercase English letters?
Interviewer: Yes, you can assume that.

Candidate: Understood. I have all the information I need to proceed.

Example

Let's consider an example:

- Input: `s = "3[a]2[bc]"`
- Expected Output: `"aaabcbc"`

Explanation:

- 3[a] decodes to aaa.
- 2[bc] decodes to bcbc.
- The final result is aaabcbc.

Optimal Approach

The problem involves decoding strings with repeated patterns and handling nested encodings.

We can use two stacks to solve the problem optimally:

1. **Stack for Numbers:** This will store the repeat count before each [(e.g., 3 for 3[a]).
2. **Stack for Strings:** This will store the current decoded string before each [so we can build the decoded string as we process the input.

Here's how the approach works:

- Traverse the string character by character.
- If we encounter a number, we extract the full number and push it onto the number stack.
- If we encounter [, it means we have encountered the start of an encoded string, so we push the current decoded string onto the string stack and reset the current string.
- If we encounter], we pop from both stacks (the number and the string) and use the popped number to repeat the current string the required number of times, then append it to the string from the string stack.
- If we encounter a letter, we simply append it to the current string.

Code Solution

Here's how I would implement it in Java:

```
import java.util.Stack;

public class DecodeString {

    public String decodeString(String s) {
        Stack<Integer> countStack = new Stack<>();
        Stack<StringBuilder> stringStack = new Stack<>();
        StringBuilder currentString = new StringBuilder();
        int k = 0;

        for (char ch : s.toCharArray()) {
            if (Character.isDigit(ch)) {
                // If it's a digit, form the full number (handles
multiple-digit numbers)
                k = k * 10 + (ch - '0');
            } else if (ch == '[') {
                // Push the current count and current string onto
their respective stacks
                countStack.push(k);
                stringStack.push(currentString);
                // Reset for the next encoded string
                currentString = new StringBuilder();
                k = 0;
            } else if (ch == ']') {
                // Pop the number of repetitions and the previous
string from the stack
                int repeatCount = countStack.pop();
                StringBuilder decodedString = stringStack.pop();
                // Append the repeated current string to the
previous string
                for (int i = 0; i < repeatCount; i++) {
                    decodedString.append(currentString);
                }
                // Update the current string to the decoded one
                currentString = decodedString;
            } else {
                // Append the current character to the current
string
                currentString.append(ch);
            }
        }

        return currentString.toString();
    }

    public static void main(String[] args) {
        DecodeString solver = new DecodeString();

        // Test case 1
        String s1 = "3[a]2[bc]";
        System.out.println("Decoded String: " +
solver.decodeString(s1));  // Expected: "aaabcbc"

        // Test case 2
```

```
        String s2 = "3[a2[c]]";
        System.out.println("Decoded String: " +
solver.decodeString(s2)); // Expected: "accaccacc"

        // Test case 3
        String s3 = "2[abc]3[cd]ef";
        System.out.println("Decoded String: " +
solver.decodeString(s3)); // Expected: "abcabccdcdcdef"
    }
}
```

Time and Space Complexity

- The time complexity is `O(n)`, where `n` is the length of the string. We process each character once.
- The space complexity is `O(n)` due to the use of two stacks for numbers and strings.

Chapter 10: Queues

A Queue is a linear data structure that follows the *First-In-First-Out (FIFO)* principle.

This means that the first element added to the queue will be the first one to be removed.

Queues are analogous to lines of people waiting for a service, where the first person in line is served first.

Core Concepts

1. **Basic Operations**
   - **Enqueue**: Adding an element to the end of the queue.
   - **Dequeue**: Removing the element from the front of the queue.
   - **Peek/Front**: Accessing the element at the front without removing it.
   - **IsEmpty**: Checking if the queue is empty.
   - **Size**: Determining the number of elements in the queue.

2. **Types of Queues**
   - **Simple Queue**: A basic FIFO queue.
   - **Circular Queue**: A queue where the last position is connected back to the first position, forming a circle. This avoids the problem of unused space in a simple queue.
   - **Priority Queue**: A queue where each element has a priority. Elements with higher priority are dequeued before elements with lower priority.
   - **Deque (Double-Ended Queue)**: A queue where elements can be added or removed from both ends.

3. **Implementation**
   - **Array-Based Implementation**: Easy to implement but can lead to space wastage if not managed properly (circular queues mitigate this).
   - **Linked List-Based Implementation**: Efficient in terms of space usage, especially when the size of the queue is not known beforehand.
   - **Built-In Queue Classes**: Most programming languages offer built-in queue implementations, which are optimized and easy to use (e.g., Queue in Java's *java.util* package).

Applications of Queues

Queues are widely used in various real-world applications where *order and sequential processing* are crucial. Queues provide a simple yet powerful mechanism to manage *sequential data processing.*

Key applications include:

1. **Task Scheduling**: Queues are essential in scheduling tasks in operating systems, where processes are managed in a queue to ensure fair CPU time distribution.

2. **Breadth-First Search (BFS)**: In graph traversal, queues are used to explore nodes level by level, making BFS ideal for finding the shortest path or exploring all nodes in a layer.

3. **Resource Management**: In systems like print servers or customer service centers, queues manage requests to ensure that resources are allocated in the order they are received.

4. **Data Streaming**: Queues are used to maintain and process data streams in real-time, such as calculating moving averages or handling incoming network packets.

5. **Buffering**: Queues act as buffers in data transmission, ensuring smooth and orderly data flow, especially in situations where data is produced and consumed at different rates.

Queue Implementations

Implementing a Queue Using Arrays

Here is a java code which implements Queue using array:

```
public class MyQueue {
   private int front, rear, size;
   private final int capacity;
   private final int[] queue;

   public MyQueue(int capacity) {
       this.capacity = capacity;
       front = this.size = 0;
       rear = capacity - 1;
       queue = new int[this.capacity];
   }

   // Enqueue an element
   void enqueue(int item) throws Exception {
       if (size == capacity) {
           throw new Exception("Queue is full. Cannot enqueue
element " + item);
       }
       rear = (rear + 1) % capacity;
       queue[rear] = item;
       size++;
```

```
    }

    // Dequeue an element
    int dequeue() throws Exception {
        if (size == 0) {
            throw new Exception("Queue is empty. Cannot dequeue
element.");
        }
        int item = queue[front];
        front = (front + 1) % capacity;
        size--;
        return item;
    }

    // Peek the front element
    int front() throws Exception {
        if (size == 0) {
            throw new Exception("Queue is empty. Cannot peek
element.");
        }
        return queue[front];
    }

    // Check if the queue is empty
    boolean isEmpty() {
        return size == 0;
    }

    // Return the size of the queue
    int size() {
        return size;
    }

    public static void main(String[] args) {
        try {
            // Create a queue of capacity 5
            MyQueue queue = new MyQueue(5);

            // Test enqueue operation
            queue.enqueue(10);
            queue.enqueue(20);
            queue.enqueue(30);
            queue.enqueue(40);
            queue.enqueue(50);
            // Trying to enqueue in a full queue
            queue.enqueue(60); // This will throw an exception

        } catch (Exception e) {
            System.out.println(e.getMessage());
        }

        try {
            // Create a queue of capacity 5
            MyQueue queue = new MyQueue(5);
```

```
            // Test front operation
            System.out.println("Front element is: " + queue.front());
// This will throw an exception

        } catch (Exception e) {
            System.out.println(e.getMessage());
        }

        try {
            // Create a queue of capacity 5
            MyQueue queue = new MyQueue(5);

            // Enqueue some elements
            queue.enqueue(10);
            queue.enqueue(20);

            // Test dequeue operation
            System.out.println("Dequeued element is: " +
queue.dequeue()); // Should print 10
            System.out.println("Dequeued element is: " +
queue.dequeue()); // Should print 20

            // Test dequeue from an empty queue
            System.out.println("Dequeued element is: " +
queue.dequeue()); // This will throw an exception

        } catch (Exception e) {
            System.out.println(e.getMessage());
        }

        try {
            // Create a queue of capacity 5
            MyQueue queue = new MyQueue(5);

            // Test enqueue operation after dequeue
            queue.enqueue(10);
            queue.enqueue(20);
            queue.enqueue(30);
            queue.enqueue(40);
            queue.enqueue(50);
            queue.dequeue();
            queue.dequeue();
            queue.enqueue(60);
            queue.enqueue(70); // This should work since two elements
were dequeued earlier

            // Test the size of the queue
            System.out.println("Queue size is: " + queue.size()); //
Should print 5

            // Test dequeue all elements
            while (!queue.isEmpty()) {
                System.out.println("Dequeued element is: " +
```

```
queue.dequeue());
            }

        } catch (Exception e) {
            System.out.println(e.getMessage());
        }
    }
}
```

Implementing a Queue Using Linked List

Here's a code to implement a queue using Linked List:

```
class MyLinkedListQueue {

    // Node class representing each element in the linked list
    static class Node {
        int data;
        Node next;

        // Constructor
        Node(int data) {
            this.data = data;
            this.next = null;
        }
    }

    private Node front, rear; // Pointers to the front and rear of
the queue
    private int size;         // To keep track of the size of the
queue

    // Constructor
    public MyLinkedListQueue() {
        this.front = this.rear = null;
        this.size = 0;
    }

    // Enqueue an element at the rear of the queue
    public void enqueue(int item) {
        Node newNode = new Node(item);

        // If the queue is empty, then both front and rear will
point to the new node
        if (this.rear == null) {
            this.front = this.rear = newNode;
        } else {
            // Add the new node at the end of the queue and change
the rear pointer
            this.rear.next = newNode;
            this.rear = newNode;
        }
        size++;
```

```
    }

    // Dequeue an element from the front of the queue
    public int dequeue() throws Exception {
        if (this.front == null) {
            throw new Exception("Queue is empty. Cannot dequeue 
element.");
        }

        int item = this.front.data; // Get the front data
        this.front = this.front.next; // Move the front pointer to 
the next node

        // If the front becomes null, then set rear to null as well 
(queue becomes empty)
        if (this.front == null) {
            this.rear = null;
        }
        size--;
        return item;
    }

    // Peek the front element without removing it
    public int front() throws Exception {
        if (this.front == null) {
            throw new Exception("Queue is empty. Cannot peek 
element.");
        }
        return this.front.data;
    }

    // Check if the queue is empty
    public boolean isEmpty() {
        return front == null;
    }

    // Get the size of the queue
    public int size() {
        return size;
    }

    public static void main(String[] args) {
        try {
            // Create a queue
            MyLinkedListQueue queue = new MyLinkedListQueue();

            // Test enqueue operation
            queue.enqueue(10);
            queue.enqueue(20);
            queue.enqueue(30);
            queue.enqueue(40);

            // Test front operation
            System.out.println("Front element is: " + queue.front());
```

```
// Should print 10

            // Test dequeue operation
            System.out.println("Dequeued element is: " +
queue.dequeue()); // Should print 10
            System.out.println("Dequeued element is: " +
queue.dequeue()); // Should print 20

            // Test front operation after dequeue
            System.out.println("Front element is: " + queue.front());
// Should print 30

            // Test the size of the queue
            System.out.println("Queue size is: " + queue.size()); //
Should print 2

            // Test dequeue all elements
            while (!queue.isEmpty()) {
                System.out.println("Dequeued element is: " +
queue.dequeue());
            }

            // Test dequeue from an empty queue
            System.out.println("Dequeued element is: " +
queue.dequeue()); // This will throw an exception

        } catch (Exception e) {
            System.out.println(e.getMessage());
        }
    }
}
```

Implementing a Circular Queue

Here's a java code to implement circular queue on your own:

```
class MyCircularQueue {
   private final int[] queue;
   private int front;
   private int rear;
   private int size;
   private final int capacity;

   // Constructor to initialize the circular queue with a given
capacity
   public MyCircularQueue(int capacity) {
        this.capacity = capacity;
        this.queue = new int[capacity];
        this.front = 0;
        this.rear = -1;
        this.size = 0;
   }
```

```
    // Enqueue an element into the circular queue
    public boolean enqueue(int item) {
        if (isFull()) {
            System.out.println("Queue is full. Cannot enqueue element
" + item);
            return false;
        }
        rear = (rear + 1) % capacity; // Circular increment
        queue[rear] = item;
        size++;
        return true;
    }

    // Dequeue an element from the circular queue
    public int dequeue() throws Exception {
        if (isEmpty()) {
            throw new Exception("Queue is empty. Cannot dequeue
element.");
        }
        int item = queue[front];
        front = (front + 1) % capacity; // Circular increment
        size--;
        return item;
    }

    // Peek the front element of the circular queue without removing
it
    public int front() throws Exception {
        if (isEmpty()) {
            throw new Exception("Queue is empty. Cannot peek
element.");
        }
        return queue[front];
    }

    // Peek the rear element of the circular queue without removing
it
    public int rear() throws Exception {
        if (isEmpty()) {
            throw new Exception("Queue is empty. Cannot peek
element.");
        }
        return queue[rear];
    }

    // Check if the circular queue is empty
    public boolean isEmpty() {
        return size == 0;
    }

    // Check if the circular queue is full
    public boolean isFull() {
        return size == capacity;
```

```
    }

    // Get the size of the circular queue
    public int size() {
        return size;
    }

    public static void main(String[] args) {
        try {
            // Create a circular queue of capacity 5
            MyCircularQueue queue = new MyCircularQueue(5);

            // Test enqueue operation
            queue.enqueue(10);
            queue.enqueue(20);
            queue.enqueue(30);
            queue.enqueue(40);
            queue.enqueue(50);

            // Test isFull operation
            System.out.println("Is the queue full? " +
queue.isFull()); // Should print true

            // Trying to enqueue in a full queue
            queue.enqueue(60); // Should print "Queue is full"

            // Test front operation
            System.out.println("Front element is: " + queue.front());
// Should print 10

            // Test rear operation
            System.out.println("Rear element is: " + queue.rear());
// Should print 50

            // Test dequeue operation
            System.out.println("Dequeued element is: " +
queue.dequeue()); // Should print 10
            System.out.println("Dequeued element is: " +
queue.dequeue()); // Should print 20

            // Test front and rear after dequeue
            System.out.println("Front element is: " + queue.front());
// Should print 30
            System.out.println("Rear element is: " + queue.rear());
// Should print 50

            // Test enqueue after dequeue (circular nature)
            queue.enqueue(60);
            queue.enqueue(70); // These should succeed due to the
circular nature

            // Check the state of the queue
            System.out.println("Is the queue full? " +
queue.isFull()); // Should print true
```

```
            System.out.println("Front element is: " + queue.front());
// Should print 30
            System.out.println("Rear element is: " + queue.rear());
// Should print 70

            // Dequeue all elements
            while (!queue.isEmpty()) {
                System.out.println("Dequeued element is: " +
queue.dequeue());
            }

            // Test dequeue from an empty queue
            System.out.println("Dequeued element is: " +
queue.dequeue()); // This will throw an exception

        } catch (Exception e) {
            System.out.println(e.getMessage());
        }
    }
}
```

Most Popular Questions on Queues

In this section, we will look at the most popular queue based questions asked in coding interviews.

Problem 1: Moving Average from Data Stream

Problem Statement

You are given a stream of integers and a fixed window size. Your task is to calculate the moving average of all integers within a sliding window as new integers arrive.

You need to implement a `MovingAverage` class with two methods:

- `MovingAverage(int size)`: Initializes the object with the given window size.
- `double next(int val)`: Returns the moving average of the last size values of the stream, including the most recent integer.

Solution

Let's follow the structured method to solve this problem.

Clarifying Questions

Candidate: Should I assume that the stream of integers is continuous, and I need to calculate the moving average dynamically as new integers arrive?

Interviewer: Yes, you will receive new integers one at a time, and you need to update the moving average as each integer arrives.

Candidate: Got it. Should I handle cases where the number of integers processed is less than the window size, meaning I haven't received enough integers to fill the window yet?
Interviewer: Yes, if the number of integers is less than the window size, calculate the average of the available integers.

Candidate: Understood. I have all the information I need to proceed.

Example

Let's consider an example to clarify:

Input:

```
MovingAverage m = new MovingAverage(3);
m.next(1); // returns 1.0
m.next(10); // returns 5.5
m.next(3); // returns 4.67
m.next(5); // returns 6.0
```

In this case, the moving average is calculated as follows:

- After receiving `1`, the average is `1.0`.
- After receiving `10`, the average of `[1, 10]` is `5.5`.
- After receiving `3`, the average of `[1, 10, 3]` is `4.67`.
- After receiving `5`, the average of `[10, 3, 5]` is `6.0` (since the window size is `3`).

Optimal Approach

To solve this problem efficiently, we can use a *queue* to keep track of the integers within the current window.

The steps are as follows:

1. Initialize the object with a fixed window size.
2. For each new integer:
    - Add the integer to the queue.
    - If the queue size exceeds the window size, remove the oldest integer.
    - Calculate the average of the integers in the queue.

The queue helps maintain the order of the elements, and we can efficiently add and remove elements from the window.

Code Solution

Here's the code for this approach:

```
import java.util.LinkedList;
import java.util.Queue;
```

```
public class MovingAverage {

   private final Queue<Integer> window;
   private final int maxSize;
   private double sum;  // To keep track of the sum of elements in
the window

   public MovingAverage(int size) {
       this.maxSize = size;
       this.window = new LinkedList<>();
       this.sum = 0;
   }

   public double next(int val) {
       // Add the new value to the window
       window.add(val);
       sum += val;

       // If the window exceeds the allowed size, remove the oldest
element
       if (window.size() > maxSize) {
           sum -= window.poll();  // Remove the oldest element and
subtract its value from the sum
       }

       // Return the moving average
       return sum / window.size();
   }

   public static void main(String[] args) {
       // Test case
       MovingAverage m = new MovingAverage(3);
       System.out.println(m.next(1));   // Expected output: 1.0
       System.out.println(m.next(10)); // Expected output: 5.5
       System.out.println(m.next(3));   // Expected output: 4.67
       System.out.println(m.next(5));   // Expected output: 6.0
   }
}
```

Time and Space Complexity

- Time Complexity: Each call to `next()` takes `O(1)` to enqueue the new element, possibly dequeue the oldest element, and compute the moving average.
- The space complexity is `O(size)`, where `size` is the window size, because we store up to `size` elements in the queue.

Problem 2: First Unique Number

Problem Statement

You are given a queue of integers. Your task is to retrieve the first unique integer in the queue.

You need to implement the `FirstUnique` class with the following methods:

- `FirstUnique(int[] nums)`: Initializes the object with the numbers in the queue.
- `int showFirstUnique()`: Returns the value of the first unique integer in the queue, or returns -1 if there is no unique integer.
- `void add(int value)`: Inserts the given value into the queue.

Solution

Let's follow the structured approach to solve this problem.

Clarifying Questions

Candidate: Should I assume that the queue can contain duplicate numbers, and I need to track which numbers have already appeared?
Interviewer: Yes, the queue can contain duplicate numbers, and you need to track the uniqueness of the numbers.

Candidate: Just to confirm, should I return -1 when there is no unique number left in the queue?
Interviewer: Yes, if no unique numbers remain, return -1.

Candidate: Understood. I have all the information I need to proceed.

Example

Let's consider an example:

Input:

```
FirstUnique firstUnique = new FirstUnique(new int[]{2, 3, 5});
firstUnique.showFirstUnique(); // returns 2
firstUnique.add(5); // adds 5 to the queue
firstUnique.showFirstUnique(); // returns 2
firstUnique.add(2); // adds 2 to the queue
firstUnique.showFirstUnique(); // returns 3
firstUnique.add(3); // adds 3 to the queue
firstUnique.showFirstUnique(); // returns -1
```

Explanation:

- Initially, the unique numbers are 2, 3, and 5, so 2 is the first unique.
- After adding 5, 2 is still the first unique.
- After adding 2, 3 becomes the first unique.
- After adding 3, no unique numbers remain, so the result is -1.

Optimal Approach

We can use a *queue* to keep track of the numbers in the order they were added, and a *hashmap* to keep track of the frequency of each number.

Here's is how it works:

1. When the class is initialized, process the given numbers by adding them to the queue and updating the frequency map.
2. `showFirstUnique` method: The first element in the queue that has a frequency of 1 is the first unique number. If no such element exists, return `-1`.
3. `add` method: Add the new value to the queue and update its frequency in the hash map. If it is no longer unique, it will eventually be removed from the front of the queue.

Code Solution

The implementation in Java is as follows:

```
import java.util.HashMap;
import java.util.LinkedList;
import java.util.Queue;

public class FirstUnique {

   private final Queue<Integer> queue;
   private final HashMap<Integer, Integer> countMap;

   public FirstUnique(int[] nums) {
       this.queue = new LinkedList<>();
       this.countMap = new HashMap<>();

       // Add the initial numbers to the queue and map
       for (int num : nums) {
           add(num);
       }
   }

   public int showFirstUnique() {
       // Remove non-unique numbers from the front of the queue
       while (!queue.isEmpty() && countMap.get(queue.peek()) > 1) {
           queue.poll();
       }

       // Return the first unique number or -1 if none exist
       if (!queue.isEmpty()) {
           return queue.peek();
       } else {
           return -1;
       }
   }

   public void add(int value) {
```

```
        // Add the number to the queue
        queue.add(value);

        // Update its count in the map
        countMap.put(value, countMap.getOrDefault(value, 0) + 1);
    }

    public static void main(String[] args) {
        // Test case
        FirstUnique firstUnique = new FirstUnique(new int[]{2, 3, 5});
        System.out.println(firstUnique.showFirstUnique()); // Expected: 2
        firstUnique.add(5); // Add 5
        System.out.println(firstUnique.showFirstUnique()); // Expected: 2
        firstUnique.add(2); // Add 2
        System.out.println(firstUnique.showFirstUnique()); // Expected: 3
        firstUnique.add(3); // Add 3
        System.out.println(firstUnique.showFirstUnique()); // Expected: -1
    }
}
```

Time and Space Complexity

- Time Complexity:
  - The `add()` method takes `O(1)`, as updating the hash map and adding to the queue are constant-time operations.
  - The `showFirstUnique()` method may require removing non-unique elements from the front of the queue, but each element is added and removed at most once, making it `O(1)` on average.
- Space Complexity: The space complexity is `O(n)`, where `n` is the number of elements processed, as we store the elements in both the queue and the hash map.

Problem 3: Implement a Stack using Queues

Problem Statement

You are tasked with implementing a stack using two queues.

The stack should support the following operations:
- `push(int x)`: Pushes element `x` onto the stack.
- `pop()`: Removes the element on top of the stack.
- `top()`: Returns the element on top of the stack.
- `empty()`: Returns whether the stack is empty.

Solution

Let's follow the structured method to solve this problem.

Clarifying Questions

Candidate: Should I implement the stack operations in a way that mimics the behavior of a normal stack (*LIFO – last-in, first-out*)?
Interviewer: Yes, you should mimic the exact behavior of a stack, with the operations following the LIFO principle.

Candidate: Got it. Should the solution prioritize efficiency for certain operations, like *push()* or *pop()*?
Interviewer: You can make that trade off between *push* and *pop* method implementations.

Candidate: Understood. I have all the information I need to proceed.

Example

Let's consider an example:

Input:
```
MyStack stack = new MyStack();
stack.push(1);
stack.push(2);
stack.top();     // returns 2
stack.pop();     // returns 2
stack.empty();   // returns false
```

Explanation:

- `stack.push(1)` pushes 1 onto the stack.
- `stack.push(2)` pushes 2 onto the stack.
- `stack.top()` returns the top element, which is 2.
- `stack.pop()` removes and returns the top element, which is 2.
- `stack.empty()` checks if the stack is empty and returns `false`.

Approach

To implement a stack using two queues, the challenge is that the queue operations follow FIFO (first-in, first-out) order, while a stack follows LIFO (last-in, first-out) order. The goal is to simulate the stack behavior using two queues.

Here's the strategy for implementation:

1. **Push Operation**: Add the new element to q2. Then, transfer all elements from q1 to q2. After that, swap q1 and q2 so that q1 always contains the elements in the correct order for popping.
2. **Pop Operation**: Simply remove the front element from q1, which represents the top of the stack.
3. **Top Operation**: Return the front element of q1, which represents the top of the stack.
4. **Empty Operation**: Check if q1 is empty.

Code Solution

Here is the implementation:

```
import java.util.LinkedList;
import java.util.Queue;

public class MyStack {

   private Queue<Integer> q1;
   private Queue<Integer> q2;

   public MyStack() {
       q1 = new LinkedList<>();
       q2 = new LinkedList<>();
   }

   // Pushes element x onto the stack
   public void push(int x) {
       // Add the new element to q2
       q2.add(x);

       // Transfer all elements from q1 to q2
       while (!q1.isEmpty()) {
           q2.add(q1.poll());
       }

       // Swap q1 and q2 to maintain order
       Queue<Integer> temp = q1;
       q1 = q2;
       q2 = temp;
   }

   // Removes the element on top of the stack and returns it
   public int pop() {
       if (!q1.isEmpty()) {
           return q1.poll();
       }
       return -1;  // Should not happen in a normal scenario
   }

   // Returns the element on top of the stack without removing it
   public int top() {
       if (!q1.isEmpty()) {
           return q1.peek();
       }
       return -1;  // Should not happen in a normal scenario
   }

   // Returns whether the stack is empty
   public boolean empty() {
       return q1.isEmpty();
   }
```

```
    public static void main(String[] args) {
        // Test case
        MyStack stack = new MyStack();
        stack.push(1);
        stack.push(2);
        System.out.println("Top: " + stack.top());     // Expected: 2
        System.out.println("Pop: " + stack.pop());     // Expected: 2
        System.out.println("Empty: " + stack.empty()); // Expected:
false
        System.out.println("Pop: " + stack.pop());     // Expected: 1
        System.out.println("Empty: " + stack.empty()); // Expected:
true
    }
}
```

Time and Space Complexity

- Time Complexity:
    - *Push*: The `push()` operation takes `O(n)` time, where `n` is the number of elements in the stack, due to the need to transfer elements between q1 and q2.
    - *Pop, Top, and Empty*: These operations take `O(1)` time, as they involve simple operations on the queue.
- Space Complexity: The space complexity is `O(n)`, where `n` is the number of elements in the stack, since we are using two queues to store the elements.

Chapter 11: HashMap & HashSet

In this chapter, we will go over basics of *HashMap* and *HashSet* data structures, their use cases and most commonly asked questions based on these data structures. These data structures are very fundamental and are commonly used in various patterns to solve coding problems.

HashMap

A HashMap is a data structure that stores *key-value* pairs, allowing *efficient retrieval of values based on their keys.*

It uses a *hashing mechanism* to map keys to indices in an internal array, making most operations, such as *insertion*, *deletion*, and *lookup*, on average `O(1)` time.

HashSet

A HashSet is a collection that stores *unique elements* and provides efficient insertion, deletion, and lookup operations, similar to a HashMap but without key-value pairs.

It is used when you need to store unique elements (no duplicates).

Key Operations and Their Complexities

- HashMap:
  - `put(K key, V value)`: Inserts a key-value pair. `O(1)` on average.
  - `get(Object key)`: Retrieves the value for the given key. `O(1)` on average.
  - `remove(Object key)`: Removes the key-value pair. `O(1)` on average.
  - `containsKey(Object key)`: Checks if the map contains the specified key. `O(1)` on average.
  - `size()`: Returns the number of key-value pairs. `O(1)`.
- HashSet:
  - `add(E element)`: Adds the element if it is not already present. `O(1)` on average.
  - `remove(Object element)`: Removes the element if it is present. `O(1)` on average.
  - `contains(Object element)`: Checks if the set contains the specified element. `O(1)` on average.
  - `size()`: Returns the number of elements in the set. `O(1)`.

Use Cases

1. Use *HashMap* when *key-value associations* are required.
2. Use *HashSet* when you only need to track *unique elements.*

Popular Questions on HashMap & HashSet

We have already seen a few problems which can be effectively solved using HashMap in Arrays, Strings and Sliding Window chapters.

Let's dive into a few more popular problems based on HashMap and/or HashSet.

Problem 1: Implement Your Own HashMap

Problem Statement

You are tasked with implementing a simplified version of a HashMap from scratch, which should support the following operations:

- `put(key, value)`: Inserts the key-value pair into the HashMap. If the key already exists, update the value.
- `get(key)`: Returns the value associated with the key. If the key does not exist, return `-1`.
- `remove(key)`: Removes the key-value pair from the HashMap if it exists.

Solution

Let's follow the structured method to solve this problem.

Clarifying Questions

Candidate: I'd like to ask a few clarifying questions. Is that ok?
Interviewer: Absolutely. Go ahead.

Candidate: Should I assume that both keys and values are integers, as in a basic integer HashMap?
Interviewer: Yes, for simplicity, both keys and values will be integers.

Candidate: Got it. Should I handle collisions using a specific technique, like chaining or open addressing?
Interviewer: You can use chaining to handle collisions.

Candidate: Understood. I have all the information I need to proceed.

Approach

To implement a basic HashMap, I will use:

1. **Array of Buckets:** The underlying data structure will be an array where each index stores a linked list of key-value pairs (buckets).
2. **Hash Function:** The hash function will map the key to an index in the array. A simple *modulo* operation (`key % array_size`) will map keys to indices in the array.

3. **Collision Handling**: If multiple keys hash to the same index (collision), they will be stored in a linked list at that index, which is called *chaining* technique.

This is how various operations would work:

- **Put Operation:** Compute the hash, check if the key already exists in the linked list at that index, and either update the value or add a new node.
- **Get Operation:** Use the hash to locate the linked list and search for the key.
- **Remove Operation:** Use the hash to find the key and remove the corresponding node.

Code Solution

Here is the implementation in Java:

```
public class MyHashMap {

    // Node class to represent key-value pairs
    private static class Node {
        int key, value;
        Node next;

        Node(int key, int value) {
            this.key = key;
            this.value = value;
            this.next = null;
        }
    }

    // The size of the underlying array (bucket array)
    private final int SIZE = 1000;
    private final Node[] bucketArray;

    // Constructor: Initializes the HashMap
    public MyHashMap() {
        bucketArray = new Node[SIZE];
    }

    // Hash function: Computes the index in the array for a given
key
    private int getHash(int key) {
        return key % SIZE;
    }

    // Put method: Inserts a key-value pair or updates the value if
the key already exists
    public void put(int key, int value) {
        int hashIndex = getHash(key);
        Node head = bucketArray[hashIndex];

        // If no nodes are present at the hashIndex, create a new
node
        if (head == null) {
            bucketArray[hashIndex] = new Node(key, value);
```

```
            return;
        }

        // Traverse the linked list to find if the key already
exists
        Node current = head;
        while (current != null) {
            if (current.key == key) {
                // Key found, update its value
                current.value = value;
                return;
            }
            if (current.next == null) break;  // End of list
            current = current.next;
        }

        // Key not found, insert new node at the end of the list
        current.next = new Node(key, value);
    }

    // Get method: Returns the value associated with the key, or -1
if the key doesn't exist
    public int get(int key) {
        int hashIndex = getHash(key);
        Node head = bucketArray[hashIndex];

        // Traverse the linked list at the hashIndex to find the key
        Node current = head;
        while (current != null) {
            if (current.key == key) {
                return current.value;  // Key found
            }
            current = current.next;
        }

        // Key not found, return -1
        return -1;
    }

    // Remove method: Removes the key-value pair if it exists
    public void remove(int key) {
        int hashIndex = getHash(key);
        Node head = bucketArray[hashIndex];

        // If the bucket is empty, do nothing
        if (head == null) {
            return;
        }

        // If the key is in the first node of the list
        if (head.key == key) {
            bucketArray[hashIndex] = head.next;
            return;
        }
```

```
        // Traverse the list to find the key and remove it
        Node prev = head;
        Node current = head.next;
        while (current != null) {
            if (current.key == key) {
                prev.next = current.next;  // Bypass the node to
remove it
                return;
            }
            prev = current;
            current = current.next;
        }
    }

    public static void main(String[] args) {
        MyHashMap hashMap = new MyHashMap();
        hashMap.put(1, 10);
        hashMap.put(2, 20);
        System.out.println("Get key 1: " + hashMap.get(1));  //
Expected: 10
        System.out.println("Get key 2: " + hashMap.get(2));  //
Expected: 20
        System.out.println("Get key 3: " + hashMap.get(3));  //
Expected: -1 (key not found)

        hashMap.put(1, 15);  // Update key 1 with a new value
        System.out.println("Get updated key 1: " + hashMap.get(1));
// Expected: 15

        hashMap.remove(2);  // Remove key 2
        System.out.println("Get removed key 2: " + hashMap.get(2));
// Expected: -1 (key not found)
    }
}
```

Time and Space Complexity

- Time Complexity:
    - `Put`, `Get`, and `Remove`: In the average case, these operations take `O(1)` time. However, in the worst case (when many keys hash to the same index), the operations could take `O(n)` time, where `n` is the number of elements in the bucket.
- Space Complexity: The space complexity is `O(n)`, where `n` is the number of elements stored in the HashMap.

Problem 2: Implement HashSet

Problem Statement

You are tasked with implementing a simplified version of a `HashSet` from scratch, which should support the following operations:

- `add(value)`: Inserts the value into the set. If the value already exists, do nothing.
- `contains(value)`: Returns `true` if the value exists in the set, `false` otherwise.
- `remove(value)`: Removes the value from the set if it exists.

Solution

Let's follow the structured method to solve this problem.

Clarifying Questions

Candidate: I'd like to clarify a few points before starting the implementation.
Interviewer: Sure, go ahead.

Candidate: Should I assume that the HashSet only needs to store integers?
Interviewer: Yes, for simplicity, the HashSet will only store integer values.

Candidate: Understood. I have all the information I need to proceed.

Approach

To implement a basic HashSet, I will use:

1. **Array of Buckets:** Similar to a HashMap, I will use an array of linked lists to handle collisions. Each index in the array (bucket) will store a linked list of integers.
2. **Hash Function:** A simple hash function using the modulo operation (`value % array_size`) will map values to indices in the array.
3. **Chaining for Collision Handling**: If multiple values hash to the same index, they will be stored in a linked list at that index.

The key operation will work as follows:

- **Add Operation:** Use the hash to locate the bucket. If the value is not already in the linked list at that index, add it.
- **Contains Operation:** Use the hash to find the bucket and check if the value exists.
- **Remove Operation:** Use the hash to find the value and remove it from the linked list.

Code Solution

Here's the implementation in Java:

```
public class MyHashSet {

   // Node class to represent values in the HashSet
   private static class Node {
       int value;
       Node next;

       Node(int value) {
           this.value = value;
           this.next = null;
       }
   }

   // The size of the underlying array (bucket array)
   private final int SIZE = 1000;
   private final Node[] bucketArray;

   // Constructor: Initializes the HashSet
   public MyHashSet() {
       bucketArray = new Node[SIZE];
   }

   // Hash function: Computes the index in the array for a given
value
   private int getHash(int value) {
       return value % SIZE;
   }

   // Add method: Inserts a value into the set
   public void add(int value) {
       int hashIndex = getHash(value);
       Node head = bucketArray[hashIndex];

       // If no nodes are present at the hashIndex, create a new
node
       if (head == null) {
           bucketArray[hashIndex] = new Node(value);
           return;
       }

       // Traverse the linked list to see if the value already
exists
       Node current = head;
       while (current != null) {
           if (current.value == value) {
               // Value already exists, do nothing
               return;
           }
           if (current.next == null) break;  // End of list
           current = current.next;
       }

       // Value not found, insert new node at the end of the list
       current.next = new Node(value);
```

```
    }

    // Contains method: Returns true if the value exists in the set,
false otherwise
    public boolean contains(int value) {
        int hashIndex = getHash(value);
        Node head = bucketArray[hashIndex];

        // Traverse the linked list at the hashIndex to find the
value
        Node current = head;
        while (current != null) {
            if (current.value == value) {
                return true;  // Value found
            }
            current = current.next;
        }

        // Value not found, return false
        return false;
    }

    // Remove method: Removes the value from the set if it exists
    public void remove(int value) {
        int hashIndex = getHash(value);
        Node head = bucketArray[hashIndex];

        // If the bucket is empty, do nothing
        if (head == null) {
            return;
        }

        // If the value is in the first node of the list
        if (head.value == value) {
            bucketArray[hashIndex] = head.next;
            return;
        }

        // Traverse the list to find the value and remove it
        Node prev = head;
        Node current = head.next;
        while (current != null) {
            if (current.value == value) {
                prev.next = current.next;  // Bypass the node to
remove it
                return;
            }
            prev = current;
            current = current.next;
        }
    }

    public static void main(String[] args) {
        MyHashSet hashSet = new MyHashSet();
```

```
        hashSet.add(1);             // Add 1
        hashSet.add(2);             // Add 2
        System.out.println("Contains 1: " + hashSet.contains(1)); //
Expected: true
        System.out.println("Contains 3: " + hashSet.contains(3)); //
Expected: false
        hashSet.add(2);             // Add 2 (already exists, do
nothing)
        System.out.println("Contains 2: " + hashSet.contains(2)); //
Expected: true
        hashSet.remove(2);          // Remove 2
        System.out.println("Contains 2 after removal: " +
hashSet.contains(2)); // Expected: false
    }
}
```

Time and Space Complexity

- **Time Complexity:**
    - Add, Contains, and Remove: These operations take `O(1)` on average due to the hash function. However, in the worst case (when multiple values hash to the same index), they may take `O(n)` time, where `n` is the number of elements in the bucket.
- **Space Complexity:** The space complexity is `O(n)`, where `n` is the number of elements stored in the HashSet, because we are using an array and linked lists to store values.

Problem 3: Ransom Note

Problem Statement

You are given two strings, `ransomNote` and `magazine`.

Your task is to determine whether the `ransomNote` can be constructed using the letters from `magazine`. Each letter in `magazine` can only be used once.

Return `true` if `ransomNote`can be constructed, otherwise return `false`.

Solution

Let's follow the structured approach to solve this problem.

Clarifying Questions

Candidate: Should I consider both strings to contain only lowercase English letters?
Interviewer: Yes, both ransomNote and magazine will only contain lowercase English letters.

Candidate: Understood. I think I have all the information I need to proceed.

Example

Let's consider an example:

```
Input:
      ransomNote = "aabb"
      magazine = "baba"
Output: true
```

In this case, the ransomNote "*aabb*" can be constructed using the letters from the magazine "*baba*", because the number of occurrences of each letter in `ransomNote` does not exceed its count in `magazine`.

Approach

To solve this problem, we can:

1. Count the frequency of letters in both *ransomNote* and *magazine*.
2. Check if `magazine` contains enough occurrences of each letter required by `ransomNote`. If any letter is missing or insufficient in `magazine`, return false.

Code Solution

Here is the implementation:

```
import java.util.HashMap;

public class RansomNote {

   public boolean canConstruct(String ransomNote, String magazine) {
        // Create a HashMap to count the frequency of each letter in
the magazine
        HashMap<Character, Integer> letterCount = new HashMap<>();

        // Count each letter in the magazine
        for (char ch : magazine.toCharArray()) {
            letterCount.put(ch, letterCount.getOrDefault(ch, 0) + 1);
        }

        // Check if ransomNote can be constructed using magazine's
letters
        for (char ch : ransomNote.toCharArray()) {
            // If any letter is unavailable or insufficient, return
false
            if (!letterCount.containsKey(ch) || letterCount.get(ch)
== 0) {
                return false;
            }
            letterCount.put(ch, letterCount.get(ch) - 1);  // Use one
occurrence of the letter
        }
```

```
        // If all letters are available, return true
        return true;
    }

    public static void main(String[] args) {
        RansomNote solver = new RansomNote();

        // Test case 1: True case
        String ransomNote1 = "aabb";
        String magazine1 = "baba";
        System.out.println("Can construct ransom note: " +
solver.canConstruct(ransomNote1, magazine1));   // Expected: true

        // Test case 2: False case
        String ransomNote2 = "aabbcc";
        String magazine2 = "aabb";
        System.out.println("Can construct ransom note: " +
solver.canConstruct(ransomNote2, magazine2));   // Expected: false
    }
}
```

Time and Space Complexity

- The time complexity is `O(mn)`, where `m` is the length of `magazine` and `n` is the length of ransomNote. We traverse both strings once.
- The space complexity is `O(k)`, where `k` is the number of distinct characters in the magazine (since we store character counts in the HashMap).

Problem 4: Isomorphic Strings

Problem Statement

You are given two strings `s` and `t`. Your task is to determine whether they are ***isomorphic***.

Two strings are considered isomorphic if the characters in `s` can be replaced to get `t`, with the following conditions:

- All occurrences of a character in `s` must be replaced by the same character in `t` (preserving the order of characters).
- No two characters in `s` may map to the same character in `t`.
- A character can map to itself.

Return `true` if `s` and `t` are isomorphic, otherwise return `false`.

Solution

Let's follow our structured approach to solve this problem.

Clarifying Questions

Candidate: Should I assume that the strings s and t are of the same length?
Interviewer: Yes, you can assume that the strings are of the same length.

Candidate: Got it. Should I handle both lowercase and uppercase letters, or just lowercase?
Interviewer: You can assume the strings will only contain lowercase letters.

Candidate: Understood. I have all the information I need to proceed.

Example

Let's consider an example:

- Input: `s = "egg", t = "add"`
- Output: `true`

Explanation: The characters in s can be mapped to t as follows:

- `'e' → 'a'`
- `'g' → 'd'`

Approach

To solve this problem, we need to track the character mappings between s and t while ensuring:

1. Each character in s maps to only one character in t.
2. No two different characters in s map to the same character in t.

We can use two hash maps:

1. Map1: Maps characters from s to t.
2. Map2: Maps characters from t to s (to ensure no two characters from s map to the same character in t).

As we traverse the strings s and t:

- For each character pair (`s[i], t[i]`), check the mappings:
    - If `s[i]` is already mapped to a character in t, ensure it maps to `t[i]`.
    - If `t[i]` is already mapped to a character in s, ensure it maps to `s[i]`.
- If any inconsistency is found, return `false`.
- If the mapping is valid throughout, return `true`.

Code Solution

Here is the implementation in Java:

```
import java.util.HashMap;

public class IsomorphicStrings {

    public boolean isIsomorphic(String s, String t) {
        // Edge case: if lengths don't match, they can't be
isomorphic
```

```
        if (s.length() != t.length()) {
            return false;
        }

        // Create two HashMaps to store mappings from s -> t and t
-> s
        HashMap<Character, Character> mapS2T = new HashMap<>();
        HashMap<Character, Character> mapT2S = new HashMap<>();

        // Traverse both strings simultaneously
        for (int i = 0; i < s.length(); i++) {
            char sChar = s.charAt(i);
            char tChar = t.charAt(i);

            // Check if there's a mapping from sChar -> tChar in
mapS2T
            if (mapS2T.containsKey(sChar)) {
                // If there's already a mapping, it must match tChar
                if (mapS2T.get(sChar) != tChar) {
                    return false;
                }
            } else {
                // Create a new mapping from sChar -> tChar
                mapS2T.put(sChar, tChar);
            }

            // Check if there's a mapping from tChar -> sChar in
mapT2S
            if (mapT2S.containsKey(tChar)) {
                // If there's already a mapping, it must match sChar
                if (mapT2S.get(tChar) != sChar) {
                    return false;
                }
            } else {
                // Create a new mapping from tChar -> sChar
                mapT2S.put(tChar, sChar);
            }
        }

        // If all mappings are consistent, the strings are
isomorphic
        return true;
    }

    public static void main(String[] args) {
        IsomorphicStrings solver = new IsomorphicStrings();

        // Test case 1: Isomorphic strings
        String s1 = "egg";
        String t1 = "add";
        System.out.println("Is isomorphic: " +
solver.isIsomorphic(s1, t1));  // Expected: true

        // Test case 2: Non-isomorphic strings
```

```
        String s2 = "foo";
        String t2 = "bar";
        System.out.println("Is isomorphic: " +
solver.isIsomorphic(s2, t2));  // Expected: false

        // Test case 3: Isomorphic strings
        String s3 = "paper";
        String t3 = "title";
        System.out.println("Is isomorphic: " +
solver.isIsomorphic(s3, t3));  // Expected: true

        // Test case 4: Non-isomorphic strings (same length,
different mapping)
        String s4 = "ab";
        String t4 = "aa";
        System.out.println("Is isomorphic: " +
solver.isIsomorphic(s4, t4));  // Expected: false
    }
}
```

Time and Space Complexity

- The time complexity is `O(n)`, where `n` is the length of the strings `s` and `t`. We iterate over each character once.
- The space complexity is `O(n)`, since we are using two hashmaps to store the mappings between characters.

Problem 5: Check for Duplicates in an Array

Problem Statement

You are given an integer array `nums`. Your task is to determine whether any value appears at least twice in the array.

Return `true` if any value appears at least twice, and `false` if every element is distinct.

Solution

Note: *This problem is chosen for completeness of the topic, so that we cover at least one question based specifically on HashSet. This might be one of the easiest problems to solve!*

Let's follow our structured method to solve the problem.

Clarifying Questions

Candidate: Just to confirm, we are given an array of integers as input and asked to find if any number appears more than once, is that correct?
Interviewer: Yes, that's correct.

Candidate: Understood. I think I have all the information I need to proceed.

Example

Let's consider an example:

- Input: `nums = [1, 2, 3, 1]`
- Output: `true`

Explanation: The number 1 appears twice in the array, so we return true.

Approach

A straightforward approach is to use a HashSet to track the elements we've encountered:

1. Traverse through the array.
2. For each element:
   - If the element is already in the set, return true.
   - If it's not in the set, add it to the set.
3. If we finish traversing the array without finding any duplicates, return false.

Code Solution

Here is the implementation in Java:

```
import java.util.HashSet;

public class ContainsDuplicate {

   public boolean containsDuplicate(int[] nums) {
       // Create a HashSet to track the elements we've encountered
       HashSet<Integer> seen = new HashSet<>();

       // Traverse through the array
       for (int num : nums) {
           // If the element is already in the set, return true
(duplicate found)
           if (seen.contains(num)) {
               return true;
           }
           // Otherwise, add the element to the set
           seen.add(num);
       }

       // If no duplicates were found, return false
       return false;
   }

   public static void main(String[] args) {
       ContainsDuplicate solver = new ContainsDuplicate();

       // Test case 1: Array with duplicates
       int[] nums1 = {1, 2, 3, 1};
       System.out.println("Contains duplicate: " +
```

```
solver.containsDuplicate(nums1));  // Expected: true

        // Test case 2: Array with distinct elements
        int[] nums2 = {1, 2, 3, 4};
        System.out.println("Contains duplicate: " +
solver.containsDuplicate(nums2));  // Expected: false

        // Test case 3: Empty array
        int[] nums3 = {};
        System.out.println("Contains duplicate: " +
solver.containsDuplicate(nums3));  // Expected: false

        // Test case 4: Array with one element
        int[] nums4 = {1};
        System.out.println("Contains duplicate: " +
solver.containsDuplicate(nums4));  // Expected: false

        // Test case 5: Array with negative numbers
        int[] nums5 = {-1, -2, -3, -1};
        System.out.println("Contains duplicate: " +
solver.containsDuplicate(nums5));  // Expected: true
    }
}
```

Time and Space Complexity

- The time complexity is `O(n)`, where `n` is the number of elements in the array. Each insertion and lookup operation in the HashSet takes `O(1)` on average.
- The space complexity is `O(n)`, since we store up to `n` unique elements in the HashSet.

Chapter 12: Recursion

In this chapter, we'll explore the concept of recursion, identify when and how to apply it, discuss common pitfalls, and provide tips and tricks to master recursion for coding interviews.

What is Recursion?

Simply put, recursion is when a *function calls itself to solve a smaller version of its problem*. This keeps happening *until the problem can't be made any smaller*, which is when we stop calling the function again. This stopping point is known as the "*base case*".

In essence, recursion is a strategy for solving problems by defining the problem in terms of smaller versions of itself.

It involves a function calling itself until it reaches a condition known as the base case that halts further recursion. A function that incorporates such self-references is called a recursive function.

Here's a simple analogy to understand recursion:

"Imagine you're standing in a long line of people, and you want to know what position you're in. You could count every person in front of you, but that would be time-consuming. Instead, you ask the person in front of you what their position is. They don't know, so they ask the person in front of them, and so forth. When the request reaches the front of the line, that person can confidently say, "I'm number 1!" Each person then adds one before replying to the person behind them. By the time this information reaches you, you've effectively counted your position in the line without having to count each individual ahead of you. This is the concept of recursion".

There are ***two main parts*** to a recursive function:

1. **Base Case:** This is the simplest form of the problem, one that can be solved directly. In our line example, this is the person at the front of the line who knows they are number 1.
2. **Recursive Step:** This breaks down larger problems into a smaller problem that is a step closer to the base case. In our example, this would be each person asking the person in front of them for their position number.

It's crucial to define the base case and ***make sure each recursive step progresses towards reaching that base case***, otherwise, the recursion could go on infinitely.

Example: Factorial Calculation

```
public class Factorial {
    public static int factorial(int n) {
```

```
        // Base case: factorial of 0 or 1 is 1
        if (n == 0 || n == 1) {
            return 1;
        }
        // Recursive case: n * factorial of (n-1)
        return n * factorial(n - 1);
    }

    public static void main(String[] args) {
        System.out.println(factorial(5));
    }
}
```

Key to understanding recursion: Trust the process

The key to understanding recursion is to ***trust the process*** and understand that:

- Each recursive call is a self-contained invocation of the function, with its own inputs and output.
- Each recursive call is independent and doesn't "know" about the others, just like how a for-loop's current iteration doesn't "know" about other iterations.
- Each recursive call continues until it hits a base case, at which point it starts returning and "unwinding" the recursion.

Once you understand and trust these principles, you can focus on understanding how recursion is used in each specific problem, instead of getting lost in trying to mentally visualize or trace the recursive process.

Identifying Problems Suitable for Recursion

Recursion is particularly effective for problems that exhibit the following characteristics:

- **Divide and Conquer**: Problems that can be divided into smaller, similar subproblems.
- **Tree Structures**: Traversing or manipulating trees (e.g., binary trees) often requires recursion.
- **Backtracking**: Problems that require exploring multiple possibilities, such as combinatorial problems or puzzles.
- **Dynamic Programming**: Certain dynamic programming problems, especially those that can be solved using memoization, start with a recursive solution.

Tips for Writing Recursive Solutions

- **Understand the Problem**: Clearly identify the problem and understand how it can be broken down into smaller subproblems.

- **Define the Base Case**: Ensure that your recursive function has a clear and correct base case to prevent infinite recursion.
- **Think about the Recursive Case**: Carefully define how the problem reduces to smaller instances and how these smaller instances contribute to the overall solution.
- **Test with Simple Inputs**: Start by testing your recursive function with simple inputs to ensure that the base case and recursive steps work correctly.
- **Consider Stack Overflow**: Be cautious with problems that have deep recursion, as they can lead to stack overflow. Tail recursion or iterative solutions might be needed in such cases.

Common Pitfalls and How to Avoid Them

- **Missing Base Case**: Always ensure that the base case is well-defined. A missing or incorrect base case will cause the function to recurse indefinitely.
- **Excessive Memory Usage**: Recursive calls consume stack space. For problems with large input sizes, consider converting the recursion to iteration if feasible.
- **Integer Overflow**: Be mindful of integer overflow in languages like Java. Use appropriate data types or check for overflow conditions.

Recursion vs. Iteration

While recursion is elegant and often easier to implement for certain problems, it's important to know when to use iteration instead:

- **Iteration** is generally more memory-efficient because it doesn't consume stack space.
- **Recursion** is often more intuitive and simpler to write for problems like tree traversal or backtracking.

Example: Iterative vs. Recursive Fibonacci

```
public class Fibonacci {
    // Iterative
    public static int fibonacciIterative(int n) {
        if (n == 0 || n == 1) return n;
        int a = 0, b = 1, c;
        for (int i = 2; i <= n; i++) {
            c = a + b;
            a = b;
            b = c;
        }
        return b;
    }

    // Recursive
    public static int fibonacciRecursive(int n) {
```

```
        if (n == 0 || n == 1) return n;
        return fibonacciRecursive(n - 1) + fibonacciRecursive(n - 2);
    }

    public static void main(String[] args) {
        System.out.println("Iterative method: " +
fibonacciIterative(10));
        System.out.println("Recursive method: " +
fibonacciRecursive(10));
    }
}
```

Key Takeaways

- Always define a clear base case to avoid infinite recursion.
- Use recursion for problems with natural recursive structures, like trees and combinatorial problems.
- Be aware of stack space limitations and consider iteration for large inputs.
- Practice writing recursive solutions and converting them to iterative ones when necessary.

Most popular Recursion Questions

In this section, we will go over some of the coding interview questions which can be solved using recursion. Note that recursion is the basis for the many algorithms and problem solving techniques such depth first search, backtracking, top down dynamic programming etc.

Problem 1: Integer to English Words

Problem Statement

Convert a non-negative integer num to its English words representation.

Solution

Let's follow the structured approach to solve this problem.

Clarifying Questions

Candidate: What is the range of the input num? Are there any upper limits on the value of the integer?
Interviewer: The input num will be a non-negative integer, and it can range up to 2^{31} - 1 (i.e., num can be as large as 2,147,483,647).

Candidate: Should the output string have any specific formatting, such as capitalization of the first letter, or should it all be in lowercase?

Interviewer: Capitalize the first letter of every word, and there should be a single space between words.

Candidate: How should we handle the input `0`? Should it simply return "*zero*"?
Interviewer: Yes, if the input is 0, the output should be "zero".

Brute Force Approach

We can hard code the English word equivalents for all numbers. We could create a large mapping for every possible number up to the maximum input and directly return the result from this mapping. However, this would be highly inefficient in terms of both time and space.

Optimal Approach

A more optimal approach is to break down the problem by converting each segment of the number into words.

We can break the number into *billions*, *millions*, *thousands*, and *units*, and then *recursively convert each part into its English representation.*

Code Solution

```
public class NumberToWords {

   private static final String[] LESS_THAN_20 = {
           "", "One", "Two", "Three", "Four", "Five", "Six",
"Seven", "Eight", "Nine", "Ten",
           "Eleven", "Twelve", "Thirteen", "Fourteen", "Fifteen",
"Sixteen", "Seventeen", "Eighteen", "Nineteen"
   };

   private static final String[] TENS = {
           "", "", "Twenty", "Thirty", "Forty", "Fifty", "Sixty",
"Seventy", "Eighty", "Ninety"
   };

   private static final String[] THOUSANDS = {
           "", "Thousand", "Million", "Billion"
   };

   public String numberToWords(int num) {
       if (num == 0) return "Zero";

       int i = 0;
       String words = "";

       while (num > 0) {
           if (num % 1000 != 0) {
               words = helper(num % 1000) + THOUSANDS[i] + " " +
words;
           }
```

```
            num /= 1000;
            i++;
        }

        return words.trim();
    }

    private String helper(int num) {
        if (num == 0) {
            return "";
        } else if (num < 20) {
            return LESS_THAN_20[num] + " ";
        } else if (num < 100) {
            return TENS[num / 10] + " " + helper(num % 10);
        } else {
            return LESS_THAN_20[num / 100] + " Hundred " + helper(num
% 100);
        }
    }

    public static void main(String[] args) {
        NumberToWords converter = new NumberToWords();

        // Test cases
        System.out.println(converter.numberToWords(0));         //
"Zero"
        System.out.println(converter.numberToWords(13));        //
"Thirteen"
        System.out.println(converter.numberToWords(123));       //
"One Hundred Twenty Three"
        System.out.println(converter.numberToWords(12345));     //
"Twelve Thousand Three Hundred Forty Five"
        System.out.println(converter.numberToWords(1234567));   //
"One Million Two Hundred Thirty Four Thousand Five Hundred Sixty
Seven"
        System.out.println(converter.numberToWords(1000000));   //
"One Million"
        System.out.println(converter.numberToWords(1000010));   //
"One Million Ten"
        System.out.println(converter.numberToWords(1000000000));//
"One Billion"
    }
}
```

Time and Space Complexity

- The time complexity of the solution is O(n), where n is the number of digits in the input number. This is because we process each digit or group of digits a constant number of times.
- The space complexity is O(1) in terms of auxiliary space. We are using a constant amount of extra space for storing the mappings and intermediate strings.

Problem 2: pow(x, n)

Problem Statement

Implement `pow(x, n)`, which calculates x raised to the power n (i.e., x^n).

Solution

Let's approach the problem in a structured manner.

Clarifying Questions

Candidate: What are the constraints on the inputs x and n? Specifically, can n be negative, and what range of values should x support?
Interviewer: Yes, n can be negative, zero, or positive. The value of x can be any real number.

Candidate: How should we handle edge cases such as `x = 0` and `n = 0`? Should the function return 1 in this case?
Interviewer: Yes, by convention, 0^0 should return 1. Also, when n is 0 for any other x, the function should return 1.

Candidate: Should the output be a floating-point number, or should it be rounded to an integer?
Interviewer: The output should be a floating-point number.

Candidate: Is there any specific time or space complexity you expect the solution to meet?
Interviewer: We expect the solution to be efficient, ideally logarithmic in time complexity.

Brute Force Approach

A brute force approach to calculate `pow(x, n)` could be multiplying x by itself n times if n is positive, or 1/x by itself n times if n is negative.

However, this approach would be inefficient, especially for large values of n, as it would have a time complexity of O(n).

Optimal Approach

A more optimal approach is to use the ***Exponentiation by Squaring*** technique.

The idea is to *reduce the problem size by half* at each step:

- If n is *even*, we can reduce x^n to $(x^{n/2})^2$.
- If n is *odd*, we can reduce x^n to $x * x^{n-1}$ and then apply the previous rule.
- For negative n, we can calculate the power for n and take its reciprocal.

This approach will reduce the time complexity to `O(log n)`, which is much more efficient for large values of `n`.

Code Solution

```
public class PowerFunction {

    public double myPow(double x, int n) {
        // Handle the base case where n is 0
        if (n == 0) return 1.0;

        // Handle the case where n is negative
        long N = n;
        if (N < 0) {
            x = 1 / x;
            N = -N; // Convert n to positive to simplify the process
        }

        return power(x, N);
    }

    private double power(double x, long n) {
        // Base case: if n is 0, return 1 (x^0 = 1)
        if (n == 0) return 1.0;

        // Recursively compute power
        double half = power(x, n / 2);

        // If n is even, the result is half * half
        if (n % 2 == 0) {
            return half * half;
        } else {
            // If n is odd, multiply the base once more
            return half * half * x;
        }
    }

    public static void main(String[] args) {
        PowerFunction calculator = new PowerFunction();

        // Test cases
        System.out.println(calculator.myPow(2.0, 10));   // 1024.0
        System.out.println(calculator.myPow(2.1, 3));    // 9.261
        System.out.println(calculator.myPow(2.0, -2));   // 0.25
        System.out.println(calculator.myPow(0.0, 0));    // 1.0 (edge
case)
        System.out.println(calculator.myPow(-2.0, 3));   // -8.0
        System.out.println(calculator.myPow(1.0, Integer.MAX_VALUE));
// 1.0 (large n edge case)
        System.out.println(calculator.myPow(1.0, Integer.MIN_VALUE));
// 1.0 (large negative n edge case)
    }
}
```

Time and Space Complexity

- The time complexity of this solution is `O(log n)`, where `n` is the absolute value of `n`. This is because we're reducing the problem size by half at each step.
- The space complexity is `O(log n)` due to the recursive call stack.

Problem 3: Maximum Depth of a Binary Tree

Problem Statement

Given the root of a binary tree, return its maximum depth.

Solution

Let's follow the structured approach to solve this problem.

Clarifying Questions

Candidate: Just to clarify, by "maximum depth," do we mean *the number of nodes along the longest path from the root node down to the farthest leaf node*?
Interviewer: Yes, that's correct. The depth is the number of nodes along the longest path from the root to a leaf.

Candidate: Can the tree be empty? If the root is null, should we return 0 as the depth?
Interviewer: Yes, if the tree is empty, the depth should be 0.

Candidate: Do the values of the nodes affect the calculation of depth, or should we consider only the structure of the tree?
Interviewer: Only the structure of the tree matters. The node values do not affect the depth calculation.

Optimal Approach

We can implement this using a *recursive Depth-First Search (DFS)* strategy:

1. Base Case: If the node is *null*, return 0 (indicating that there's no depth below this node).
2. Recursive Case: Calculate the depth of the left and right subtrees and return the maximum of these two depths plus one.

Code Solution

```
public class BinaryTreeMaximumDepth {

    // Definition for a binary tree node.
    public static class TreeNode {
        int val;
        TreeNode left;
        TreeNode right;
```

```
        TreeNode(int x) {
            val = x;
        }
    }

    public int maxDepth(TreeNode root) {
        if (root == null) {
            return 0;
        }
        int leftDepth = maxDepth(root.left);
        int rightDepth = maxDepth(root.right);
        return Math.max(leftDepth, rightDepth) + 1;
    }

    public static void main(String[] args) {
        BinaryTreeMaximumDepth solution = new
BinaryTreeMaximumDepth();

        // Example tree:
        //       3
        //      / \
        //     9  20
        //        /  \
        //       15   7

        TreeNode root = new TreeNode(3);
        root.left = new TreeNode(9);
        root.right = new TreeNode(20);
        root.right.left = new TreeNode(15);
        root.right.right = new TreeNode(7);

        // Test case
        System.out.println(solution.maxDepth(root));  // Output: 3
    }
}
```

Time and Space Complexity

- The time complexity is `O(n)`, where `n` is the number of nodes in the tree. This is because we need to visit each node exactly once.
- The space complexity is `O(n)` in the worst case (for a completely unbalanced tree), due to the recursion stack.

Problem 4: Swap Nodes in Pairs

Problem Statement

Given a linked list, swap every two adjacent nodes and return its head. You must solve the problem without modifying the values in the list's nodes (i.e., only nodes themselves may be changed.)

Solution

Let's follow the structured approach to solve the problem.

Clarifying Questions

Candidate: Is there any restriction on the length of the linked list? Specifically, should we consider cases where the list length is *odd or even*?
Interviewer: The length of the list can be any non-negative integer, including zero. You should handle both odd and even lengths appropriately.

Candidate: Can we assume that the input linked list will not contain any *cycles*?
Interviewer: Yes, you can assume the linked list is well-formed and does not contain any cycles.

Candidate: How should we handle a list with a single node? Should the list remain unchanged in this case?
Interviewer: Yes, if there's only one node, the list should remain unchanged.

Optimal Approach

Since we are required to swap the nodes themselves and not just their values, we need to carefully adjust the pointers of the linked list to perform the swaps.

We can solve this problem using recursion. The idea is to swap the first two nodes and then recursively call the function for the rest of the list.

Code Solution

```
public class SwapNodesInPairs {

    // Definition for singly-linked list.
    public static class ListNode {
        int val;
        ListNode next;

        ListNode(int val) {
            this.val = val;
        }
    }

    public ListNode swapPairs(ListNode head) {
        // Base case: if there are fewer than 2 nodes left, return
the head
        if (head == null || head.next == null) {
            return head;
        }

        // Nodes to be swapped
        ListNode first = head;
        ListNode second = head.next;

        // Perform the swap
```

```
        first.next = swapPairs(second.next);
        second.next = first;

        // Return the new head
        return second;
    }

    public static void main(String[] args) {
        SwapNodesInPairs solution = new SwapNodesInPairs();

        // Example: 1 -> 2 -> 3 -> 4
        ListNode head = new ListNode(1);
        head.next = new ListNode(2);
        head.next.next = new ListNode(3);
        head.next.next.next = new ListNode(4);

        // Swapping pairs
        ListNode newHead = solution.swapPairs(head);

        // Printing the swapped list: should print 2 -> 1 -> 4 -> 3
        ListNode current = newHead;
        while (current != null) {
            System.out.print(current.val + " ");
            current = current.next;
        }
    }
}
```

Time and Space Complexity

- The time complexity is `O(n)`, where `n` is the number of nodes in the linked list. This is because each node is visited and processed exactly once.
- The space complexity is `O(n)` due to the *recursion stack*, which will store one call for each pair of nodes being swapped.

Chapter 13: Backtracking

Introduction

Backtracking is a powerful algorithmic technique used to solve problems incrementally, ***trying out possible solutions and discarding those that fail to satisfy the problem constraints***.

This approach is particularly useful for problems involving ***combinatorial search spaces***, such as generating permutations, combinations, and solving constraint satisfaction problems like Sudoku, N-Queens, and others.

The essence of backtracking lies in its ***systematic exploration of all potential candidates for a solution***. It constructs a solution incrementally, abandoning a candidate ("backtracking") as soon as it determines that this candidate cannot possibly lead to a valid solution.

In this chapter, we will cover the key concepts, common patterns, and frequently asked coding interview questions that involve backtracking, along with solutions in Java.

Key Concepts

1. **Recursive Exploration:**
   - Backtracking relies heavily on *recursion*. Each recursive call represents a decision point, where the algorithm chooses one of several options. If a chosen path leads to a dead end (i.e., a solution is not possible), the algorithm backtracks to the previous decision point and tries another option.
2. **State Space Tree:**
   - *The problem is represented as a tree where each node corresponds to a state of the problem.* The tree is explored depth-first, with backtracking occurring when a node's state is determined to be invalid or complete.
3. **Pruning:**
   - *Pruning is a key optimization technique in backtracking.* It involves *cutting off paths* that cannot possibly lead to a solution early in the search process. Effective pruning reduces the number of states to explore, thereby improving the algorithm's efficiency.
4. **Base Case:**
   - Each backtracking algorithm has a base case, which is a condition that determines when the *solution has been found or when no further exploration is needed.*
5. **Backtracking vs. Brute Force:**
   - While brute force explores all possible combinations indiscriminately, backtracking intelligently cuts off paths that are guaranteed to fail, thus reducing unnecessary computations.

Common Backtracking Patterns

1. **Subset Generation:**
   - Problems that require generating all possible subsets of a set, such as finding all subsets that sum to a specific value.
2. **Permutations and Combinations:**
   - Problems that involve generating all permutations or combinations of a set of elements.
3. **Constraint Satisfaction Problems:**
   - Problems like the N-Queens problem, where the goal is to place elements on a board such that no two elements violate a given constraint.
4. **Grid-Based Problems:**
   - Problems like solving mazes, Sudoku, or word search puzzles that require moving through a grid while satisfying certain conditions.
5. **Partitioning Problems:**
   - Problems that involve dividing a set into multiple parts, such as partitioning a set into two subsets with equal sums.

Steps to Solve Backtracking Problems

1. **Identify the Decision Points:**
   - Determine the *choices available at each step* of the problem. These choices will form the basis of your recursive calls.
2. **Define the State:**
   - Clearly *define the state of the problem* at each recursive call. This often involves *passing parameters that represent the current state.*
3. **Implement the Base Case:**
   - Identify when a *solution is complete or when further exploration is unnecessary*, and implement this as the base case in your recursive function.
4. **Explore All Possibilities:**
   - Use recursion to *explore all possible choices at each decision point.* If a choice leads to an invalid state, backtrack by returning from the recursive call.
5. **Prune Unnecessary Paths:**
   - *Incorporate checks to eliminate paths that cannot lead to a valid solution*, thus reducing the search space and improving efficiency.

Most Popular Questions on Backtracking

Problem 1: Generate Parentheses

Problem statement

Given n pairs of parentheses, write a function to *generate all combinations of well-formed parentheses.*

Solution

Let's dive into it as if we're in a real life interview setting.

Clarifying Questions

Candidate: By *well-formed*, I assume you mean that the parentheses combinations should be *balanced*. For example, with `n = 3`, the combinations would include something like `((()))` or `(()())`, but not `(()))(`, since that would be unbalanced. Is that right?
Interviewer: Exactly. The parentheses need to be properly matched and nested.

Candidate: Understood. Also to confirm, if `n = 3`, we should return combinations that have `3 opening` and `3 closing` parentheses?
Interviewer: Yes, that's correct.

Candidate: Perfect. Before I dive into the solution, let me walk you through my thought process. First, I'll explain the brute force approach, and then I'll move on to a more optimal solution. Does that sound good?
Interviewer: Sounds good. Go ahead.

Brute Force Approach

For the brute force approach, we could generate all possible combinations of n pairs of parentheses and then ***filter out the ones that are not well-formed***.

However, generating all possible combinations would involve generating strings of length 2n, where each position in the string can either be an opening or a closing parenthesis. The total number of such combinations would be 2^{2n}.

After generating these combinations, we would check each one for validity. The check would involve ensuring that the number of opening parentheses never falls below the number of closing ones at any point in the string.

This brute force approach, while straightforward, would be inefficient *because it generates many invalid combinations that we would discard later*.

Optimal Approach

Optimal approach to solve this problem would be using backtracking.

The key observation here is that at any point in constructing the string:

1. We can only add an opening parenthesis *if we still have one available*.
2. We can only add a closing parenthesis if it would not unbalance the string, meaning the *number of closing parentheses used should not exceed the number of opening parentheses used*.

This backtracking approach will help us efficiently *generate only valid combinations* without needing to filter out invalid ones later.

Candidate: Would you like me to proceed with the implementation of this approach in Java?
Interviewer: Yes, that sounds good. Please go ahead with the implementation.

Code Solution

```
import java.util.ArrayList;
import java.util.List;

public class GenerateParentheses {

   public static List<String> generateParenthesis(int n) {
       List<String> result = new ArrayList<>();
       backtrack(result, "", 0, 0, n);
       return result;
   }

   private static void backtrack(List<String> result, String
current, int open, int close, int max) {
       // Base case: If the current string's length is equal to 2 *
n, it's a valid combination
       if (current.length() == max * 2) {
           result.add(current);
           return;
       }

       // If we can still add an opening parenthesis, do so
       if (open < max) {
           backtrack(result, current + "(", open + 1, close, max);
       }

       // If we can still add a closing parenthesis without
violating the rules, do so
       if (close < open) {
           backtrack(result, current + ")", open, close + 1, max);
       }
   }

   public static void main(String[] args) {
       // Test cases
       System.out.println("n = 3: " + generateParenthesis(3));
       System.out.println("n = 2: " + generateParenthesis(2));
       System.out.println("n = 1: " + generateParenthesis(1));
       System.out.println("n = 4: " + generateParenthesis(4));
   }
}
```

Time and Space Complexity

- The time complexity of this approach is $O(4^n/\sqrt{n})$. This is the number of valid parentheses combinations, which is given by the ***Catalan number*** C_n. For the purpose of the interview, just know that Catalan numbers are a sequence of positive integers, where the nth term in the sequence, denoted by C_n, is calculated using the formula: `(2n)! / ((n + 1)! n!)`. As we have to generate valid parentheses for n pairs, it is in the order of the nth Catalan number.

- The space complexity is `O(n)` due to the depth of the recursion tree, which can go as deep as `2n`.

Problem 2: Letter Combinations of a Phone Number

Problem Statement

Given a string containing digits from `2-9` inclusive, return *all possible letter combinations* that the number could represent on the Phone keypad.

Mapping of the numbers to the letters is shown below:

Solution

Let's follow our structured approach to tackle this problem.

Clarifying Questions

Candidate: To clarify, if the input is something like `23`, we would return combinations like "ad", "ae", "af", "bd", "be", "bf", "cd", "ce", and "cf", correct?
Interviewer: That's correct.

Candidate: Great! Let me explain my thought process to approach this problem before writing the code. Does that sound good?
Interviewer: Yes, that sounds good.

Brute Force Approach

For the brute force approach, we could generate all possible combinations of letters for each digit and then combine them.

For example, for "23", we'd first get all combinations for 2 ("a", "b", "c") and then combine each of these with all combinations for 3 ("d", "e", "f").

This approach involves building a tree where *each level corresponds to a digit* and *each branch represents a letter.*

However, this isn't the most efficient way because it doesn't leverage the problem's structure to minimize redundant computations.

Optimal Approach

The more efficient approach is to use backtracking. ***The idea is to build the combinations by adding one letter at a time and backtracking when we reach the desired combination length.*** This approach is efficient because it systematically explores all possibilities without redundant operations.

For each digit in the input string, we'll add a corresponding letter to our current combination and proceed to the next digit. If we reach the end of the string, we add the current combination to our results.

Candidate: Would you like me to proceed with the implementation of this approach in Java?
Interviewer: Yes, please go ahead with the implementation.

Code Solution

```
import java.util.ArrayList;
import java.util.HashMap;
import java.util.List;
import java.util.Map;

public class LetterCombinationsOfPhoneNumber {

    // Mapping from digit to corresponding letters
    private static final Map<Character, String> phoneMap = new
HashMap<>() {{
        put('2', "abc");
        put('3', "def");
        put('4', "ghi");
        put('5', "jkl");
        put('6', "mno");
        put('7', "pqrs");
        put('8', "tuv");
        put('9', "wxyz");
    }};

    public static List<String> letterCombinations(String digits) {
        List<String> result = new ArrayList<>();
        if (digits == null || digits.isEmpty()) {
            return result; // Return empty list for empty input
        }
        backtrack(result, new StringBuilder(), digits, 0);
        return result;
    }
```

```
    private static void backtrack(List<String> result, StringBuilder
current, String digits, int index) {
        // Base case: If we've processed all the digits, add the
current combination to the result
        if (index == digits.length()) {
            result.add(current.toString());
            return;
        }

        // Get the letters that the current digit maps to
        String letters = phoneMap.get(digits.charAt(index));

        // Iterate over each letter and recursively build the
combination
        for (char letter : letters.toCharArray()) {
            current.append(letter);  // Add the letter to the current
combination
            backtrack(result, current, digits, index + 1);  //
Recurse for the next digit
            current.deleteCharAt(current.length() - 1);  // Remove
the last added letter (backtrack)
        }
    }

    public static void main(String[] args) {
        // Test cases
        System.out.println("Input: '23' => " +
letterCombinations("23"));
        System.out.println("Input: '2' => " +
letterCombinations("2"));
        System.out.println("Input: '' => " + letterCombinations(""));
        System.out.println("Input: '234' => " +
letterCombinations("234"));
    }
}
```

Time and Space Complexity

The *time* and *space* complexity for this solution is $O(4^n)$, where n is the number of digits. This is because in the worst case, each digit will be 7 or 9, which has 4 *possible letters*, and we generate combinations for each. Therefore, the complexity is exponential in the size of the input.

Problem 3: Subsets

Problem Statement

Given an integer array *nums* of unique elements, return all possible subsets (the power set). The solution set must not contain duplicate subsets.

Solution

Let's tackle this problem as if we're in a coding interview setting.

Clarifying Questions

Candidate: Before I jump into solving the problem, I'd like to ask a few clarifying questions to ensure we're on the same page.
Candidate: What should be the order of the subsets in the output? Should they be in any specific order, like lexicographical?
Interviewer: The order of the subsets in the output doesn't matter. You can return them in any order.

Candidate: Are there any constraints on the size of the array? For instance, can it be very large?
Interviewer: You can assume that the size of the array will be reasonable, say up to 10-15 elements, so efficiency is important but we don't need to optimize for extremely large inputs.

Candidate: Great! I'll first walk through an example to make sure we're on the same page about the expected output.

Example
Let's say the input array is `nums = [1, 2, 3]`.

The possible subsets for this input would be:

- `[]`
- `[1]`
- `[2]`
- `[3]`
- `[1, 2]`
- `[1, 3]`
- `[2, 3]`
- `[1, 2, 3]`

So, the expected output would be something like `[[], [1], [2], [3], [1, 2], [1, 3], [2, 3], [1, 2, 3]]`.

Brute Force Approach

As we need to generate all possible subsets for a given input, there is no scope for optimization in it. Hence, the brute force approach is essentially the same as the optimal approach in this case.

Optimal Approach

We can use backtracking to generate all possible subsets. The idea is to build subsets incrementally and explore each possibility by *either including or excluding each element* in the array.

Here's the outline of the approach:

1. Start with an empty subset.
2. For each element in nums, you have two choices:
    - Include the element in the current subset.
    - Exclude the element and move to the next one.
3. This process is repeated *recursively* until all subsets are generated.

Code Solution

Let me implement this approach in Java.

```
import java.util.ArrayList;
import java.util.List;

public class SubsetGenerator {

   // Method to generate all subsets
   public List<List<Integer>> subsets(int[] nums) {
       List<List<Integer>> result = new ArrayList<>();
       backtrack(0, nums, new ArrayList<>(), result);
       return result;
   }

   // Helper method to perform backtracking
   private void backtrack(int start, int[] nums, List<Integer>
currentSubset, List<List<Integer>> result) {
       // Add the current subset to the result list
       result.add(new ArrayList<>(currentSubset));

       // Explore further elements to add to the subset
       for (int i = start; i < nums.length; i++) {
           // Include nums[i] in the current subset
           currentSubset.add(nums[i]);

           // Recurse with the next element
           backtrack(i + 1, nums, currentSubset, result);

           // Backtrack by removing the last added element
           currentSubset.remove(currentSubset.size() - 1);
       }
   }

   // Main method to test the subsets method
   public static void main(String[] args) {
       SubsetGenerator generator = new SubsetGenerator();

       int[] nums1 = {1, 2, 3};
       System.out.println("Subsets of [1, 2, 3]: " +
generator.subsets(nums1));

       int[] nums2 = {0};
       System.out.println("Subsets of [0]: " +
generator.subsets(nums2));

       int[] nums3 = {};
```

```
        System.out.println("Subsets of []: " +
generator.subsets(nums3));
    }
}
```

The backtrack method is the core of this solution. It explores each subset possibility by either including or excluding each element in the given input.

Time and Space Complexity

- Time Complexity: $O(2^n)$, where n is the number of elements in the input array. This is because there are 2^n possible subsets for an array of length n.
- Space Complexity: O(n) for the recursion stack, where n is the depth of the recursion tree (which in the worst case is equal to the number of elements in the input array).

Problem 4: Permutations

Problem Statement

Given an array *nums* of distinct integers, return all the possible permutations.

Solution

Let's tackle this problem as if we're in a coding interview setting.

Clarifying Questions

Candidate: Before I start, I'd like to ask a few clarifying questions to ensure we're on the same page.

Candidate: Is there any specific order in which you would like the permutations to be returned, or is any order acceptable?
Interviewer: Any order is fine. The focus is on generating all possible permutations.

Candidate: Let me walk through an example to make sure we're aligned on the expected output.

Example
Let's take an example where `nums = [1, 2, 3]`.

The possible permutations would be:

- [1, 2, 3]
- [1, 3, 2]
- [2, 1, 3]
- [2, 3, 1]
- [3, 1, 2]
- [3, 2, 1]

So, the expected output should be something like `[[1, 2, 3], [1, 3, 2], [2, 1, 3], [2, 3, 1], [3, 1, 2], [3, 2, 1]]`.

Brute Force Approach

A brute force approach would involve generating all possible sequences of the array and checking if each sequence is a valid permutation (i.e., contains every element exactly once). However, this approach is inefficient and redundant since it doesn't leverage the distinct nature of the elements in nums.

Optimal Approach

Given the distinct nature of the elements, we can directly generate all permutations without redundancy by using a backtracking approach.

The backtracking approach works as follows:

1. We generate permutations by swapping elements in the array.
2. We start with an empty permutation and add elements one by one while swapping to generate new permutations.
3. Backtracking helps us explore all possible permutations by recursively swapping elements and then undoing the swap (backtracking) to explore other permutations.

Code Solution

Here's how I would implement this approach in Java:

```
import java.util.ArrayList;
import java.util.List;

public class PermutationGenerator {

    // Method to generate all permutations
    public List<List<Integer>> permute(int[] nums) {
        List<List<Integer>> result = new ArrayList<>();
        backtrack(nums, new ArrayList<>(), result);
        return result;
    }

    // Helper method to perform backtracking
    private void backtrack(int[] nums, List<Integer>
currentPermutation, List<List<Integer>> result) {
        // Base case: if the current permutation is of the same
length as nums, add it to the result
        if (currentPermutation.size() == nums.length) {
            result.add(new ArrayList<>(currentPermutation));
            return;
        }

        // Explore each element for the next position in the
permutation
        for (int i = 0; i < nums.length; i++) {
            // Skip if the element is already in the current
```

```
permutation
            if (currentPermutation.contains(nums[i])) continue;

            // Add the element to the current permutation
            currentPermutation.add(nums[i]);

            // Recurse to build the permutation further
            backtrack(nums, currentPermutation, result);

            // Backtrack by removing the last added element
            currentPermutation.remove(currentPermutation.size() - 1);
        }
    }

    // Main method to test the permute method
    public static void main(String[] args) {
        PermutationGenerator generator = new PermutationGenerator();

        int[] nums1 = {1, 2, 3};
        System.out.println("Permutations of [1, 2, 3]: " +
generator.permute(nums1));

        int[] nums2 = {0, 1};
        System.out.println("Permutations of [0, 1]: " +
generator.permute(nums2));

        int[] nums3 = {1};
        System.out.println("Permutations of [1]: " +
generator.permute(nums3));
    }
}
```

The `currentPermutation.contains(nums[i])` check ensures that we don't include an element more than once in any given permutation.

Time and Space Complexity

- Time Complexity: `O(n × n!)`. It is because we have `n!` permutations, and generating each permutation involves `O(n)` *operations* to build the permutation.
- Space Complexity: `O(n!)` for storing all the permutations plus `O(n)` for the recursion stack.

Problem 5: Combinations

Problem Statement

Given two integers `n` and `k`, return all possible combinations of `k` numbers chosen from the range `[1, n]`.

Solution

Let's dive into this problem as if we're in a coding interview setting.

Clarifying Questions

Candidate: Before I start with the solution, I'd like to ask a few clarifying questions to make sure I fully understand the problem.

Candidate: Should we assume that k ≤ n?
Interviewer: Yes, you can assume that k ≤ n.

Candidate: Should the combinations be unique, and is the order within each combination important?
Interviewer: Yes, each combination should be unique, and the order ***within each combination*** does not matter.

Candidate: Understood. Is there any specific order you would like the combinations to be returned in, or is any order acceptable?
Interviewer: The order of the combinations in the output does not matter.

Candidate: Great, thanks for the clarifications! Let's go through an example to make sure I understand what the output should look like.

Example
Let's consider `n = 4` and `k = 2`.

The possible combinations of 2 ***numbers chosen from the range [1, 4]*** would be:

- `[1, 2]`
- `[1, 3]`
- `[1, 4]`
- `[2, 3]`
- `[2, 4]`
- `[3, 4]`

So, the expected output should be something like `[[1, 2], [1, 3], [1, 4], [2, 3], [2, 4], [3, 4]]`.

Brute Force Approach

One approach would be to generate all possible subsets of the numbers from 1 to n and then filter out those subsets that have exactly k elements. However, this approach would be inefficient because it would involve generating many unnecessary subsets.

Optimal Approach

Given the constraints, a more efficient approach would involve using backtracking to directly *generate only the combinations of k elements.*

Here's the idea:

1. We start with an empty combination and add elements one by one, always ensuring that the combination contains exactly k elements.
2. Once a combination is complete (i.e., has k elements), we add it to the result list.
3. We recursively explore all possibilities by including or excluding each element in the range [1, n].

Code Solution

Here's how I would implement this approach in Java:

```
import java.util.ArrayList;
import java.util.List;

public class CombinationGenerator {

    // Method to generate all combinations
    public List<List<Integer>> combine(int n, int k) {
        List<List<Integer>> result = new ArrayList<>();
        backtrack(1, n, k, new ArrayList<>(), result);
        return result;
    }

    // Helper method to perform backtracking
    private void backtrack(int start, int n, int k, List<Integer>
currentCombination, List<List<Integer>> result) {
        // Base case: if the current combination has k elements, add
it to the result
        if (currentCombination.size() == k) {
            result.add(new ArrayList<>(currentCombination));
            return;
        }

        // Explore further elements to add to the combination
        for (int i = start; i <= n; i++) {
            // Add the element to the current combination
            currentCombination.add(i);

            // Recurse with the next element
            backtrack(i + 1, n, k, currentCombination, result);

            // Backtrack by removing the last added element
            currentCombination.remove(currentCombination.size() - 1);
        }
    }

    // Main method to test the combine method
    public static void main(String[] args) {
        CombinationGenerator generator = new CombinationGenerator();

        int n1 = 4, k1 = 2;
        System.out.println("Combinations of 2 numbers from [1, 4]: "
```

```
+ generator.combine(n1, k1));

        int n2 = 5, k2 = 3;
        System.out.println("Combinations of 3 numbers from [1, 5]: "
+ generator.combine(n2, k2));

        int n3 = 3, k3 = 1;
        System.out.println("Combinations of 1 number from [1, 3]: " +
generator.combine(n3, k3));
    }
}
```

Candidate: Let me explain what's happening in this code:

- The *combine* method is our main function that generates all combinations of k elements from the range [1, n].
- The *backtrack* method is used to recursively build up combinations.
- We start from `start = 1` and explore adding each element up to `n` to the current combination.
- If the *currentCombination* has exactly `k` elements, it's added to the result list.
- After exploring each possibility, we *backtrack by removing the last added element to explore other combinations.*

Time and Space Complexity

- Time Complexity: `O(n! / (k - 1)! . (n - k)!)`. This is a standard combinatorics problem where we generate "*n choose k*" combinations, and generating each combination involves `O(k)` *operations* to build the combination.
- Space Complexity: `O(k)` for the recursion stack.

Problem 6: Combination Sum

Problem Statement

Given an array of distinct integers called *candidates* and a target integer *target*, return a list of all unique combinations of candidates *where the chosen numbers sum to target.*

You may return the combinations in any order.

The same number may be chosen from candidates an unlimited number of times. Two combinations are unique if the frequency of at least one of the chosen numbers is different.

Solution

Let's work through this problem as if we're in a coding interview setting.

Clarifying Questions

Candidate: Before I start with the solution, I'd like to ask a few clarifying questions to ensure I fully understand the problem.

Candidate: The array candidates contains distinct integers, and the same number can be chosen multiple times in the combinations. Can I assume that all numbers are positive, and the target is a positive integer as well?
Interviewer: Yes, you can assume that all numbers in candidates are positive integers, and the target is also a positive integer.

Candidate: Should I account for cases where it's impossible to reach the target with the given candidates, and if so, should I return an empty list in those cases?
Interviewer: Yes, if there's no valid combination that sums to the target, you should return an empty list.

Candidate: Understood. Is there any specific order in which you would like the combinations to be returned, or is any order acceptable?
Interviewer: Any order is fine. The focus is on generating all unique combinations.

Candidate: Thanks for the clarifications! Let's go through an example to make sure I understand what the output should look like.

Example
Let's consider `candidates = [2, 3, 6, 7]` and `target = 7`.

The possible combinations that sum to 7 would be:

- `[2, 2, 3] (since 2 + 2 + 3 = 7)`
- `[7] (since 7 = 7)`

So, the expected output should be something like `[[2, 2, 3], [7]]`.

Candidate: Now that we've clarified the problem, let me go over the approaches on how to solve it.

Brute Force Approach

A brute force approach would involve generating all possible combinations of the numbers in candidates and then checking if any of those combinations sum to the target.

However, this would be highly inefficient, especially given that the same number can be used multiple times, leading to many redundant combinations.

Optimal Approach

*Given the constraints, a more efficient approach would involve using **backtracking** to explore combinations that sum to the target.*

The backtracking approach works as follows:

1. We start with an empty combination and try adding each candidate to it, one by one.
2. If the sum of the current combination exceeds the target, ***we stop exploring that path (pruning the search)***.
3. If the sum matches the target, we add the combination to our result list.
4. We allow the same candidate to be used multiple times by not incrementing the index in the recursive call.

Code Solution

Here's how I would implement this approach in Java:

```
import java.util.ArrayList;
import java.util.List;

public class CombinationSum {

   // Method to generate all combinations that sum to the target
   public List<List<Integer>> combinationSum(int[] candidates, int
target) {
       List<List<Integer>> result = new ArrayList<>();
       backtrack(candidates, target, 0, new ArrayList<>(), result);
       return result;
   }

   // Helper method to perform backtracking
   private void backtrack(int[] candidates, int target, int start,
List<Integer> currentCombination, List<List<Integer>> result) {
       // Base case: if the target becomes 0, add the current
combination to the result
       if (target == 0) {
           result.add(new ArrayList<>(currentCombination));
           return;
       }

       // Explore further elements to add to the combination
       for (int i = start; i < candidates.length; i++) {
           // If the current candidate exceeds the target, skip it
(pruning)
           if (candidates[i] > target) continue;

           // Add the candidate to the current combination
           currentCombination.add(candidates[i]);

           // Recurse with the reduced target and allow the same
element to be chosen again
           backtrack(candidates, target - candidates[i], i,
currentCombination, result);

           // Backtrack by removing the last added element
           currentCombination.remove(currentCombination.size() - 1);
       }
   }
```

```
    // Main method to test the combinationSum method
    public static void main(String[] args) {
        CombinationSum cs = new CombinationSum();

        int[] candidates1 = {2, 3, 6, 7};
        int target1 = 7;
        System.out.println("Combinations summing to 7: " +
cs.combinationSum(candidates1, target1));

        int[] candidates2 = {2, 3, 5};
        int target2 = 8;
        System.out.println("Combinations summing to 8: " +
cs.combinationSum(candidates2, target2));

        int[] candidates3 = {2};
        int target3 = 1;
        System.out.println("Combinations summing to 1: " +
cs.combinationSum(candidates3, target3));
    }
}
```

Candidate: Let me walk you through what's happening in this code:

- The *combinationSum* method is our main function that generates all unique combinations that sum to the target.
- The *backtrack* method is the core of our backtracking approach. It recursively builds combinations by adding candidates while ensuring the sum of the combination doesn't exceed the target.
- We start from index `start = 0` to ensure that we can use the same element multiple times (this is key to allowing repeated elements).
- If at any point, the sum of the current combination equals the target (i.e., *target == 0*), we add that combination to the result list.
- We *prune unnecessary exploration by skipping candidates* that exceed the current target.

Time and Space Complexity

- The time complexity is a bit tricky to calculate exactly *due to the nature of backtracking*. However, ***in the worst case***, we explore all possible combinations, which could be ***exponential in the size of the input***. The approximate time complexity is $O(2^n)$, where n is the number of elements in candidates. However, this depends on the values and target.
- Space Complexity: `O(target)`, which is the depth of the recursion tree. This corresponds to the maximum length of the current combination (since we can only add up to target).

Problem 7: Word Search

Problem Statement

Given an `m x n` grid of characters called *board* and a string called *word*, return *true* if *word* exists in the grid.

The word can be constructed from letters of sequentially adjacent cells, where adjacent cells are *horizontally or vertically neighboring*. The same letter cell may not be used more than once.

Solution

Let's tackle this problem as if we're in a coding interview setting.

[**Note**: This is also a graph based problem, as it is related to ***backtracking*** technique, this is covered here. Refer to the *Graph* chapter for more context on Graph based questions.]

Clarifying Questions

Candidate: Before diving into the solution, I'd like to ask a few clarifying questions to make sure I fully understand the problem.

Candidate: You mentioned that the word must be constructed from sequentially adjacent cells. Just to confirm, diagonal cells do not count as adjacent, correct?
Interviewer: That's correct. Only horizontal and vertical neighbors are considered adjacent.

Candidate: Can the grid contain any characters, and is the word guaranteed to be non-empty?
Interviewer: Yes, the grid can contain any characters, and the word is guaranteed to be non-empty.

Candidate: What should be the return value if the grid is empty or if the word cannot be found in the grid?
Interviewer: If the grid is empty or if the word cannot be found in the grid, the function should return false.

Candidate: Great, thanks for the clarifications! Let's go through an example for more concrete understanding.

Example
Let's say the *board* is:
```
[   ['A', 'B', 'C', 'E'],
    ['S', 'F', 'C', 'S'],
    ['A', 'D', 'E', 'E']
]
```
And the *word* is "`ABCCED`".

The word ABCCED can be constructed as follows:

- `Start at board[0][0] = 'A'`
- `Move right to board[0][1] = 'B'`
- `Move right to board[0][2] = 'C'`
- `Move down to board[1][2] = 'C'`
- `Move down to board[2][2] = 'E'`
- `Move left to board[2][1] = 'D'`

So, the expected output should be *true*.

Approach

Candidate: Now that we've clarified the problem, let me discuss the approach to solve it.

We can use a *depth first search with a backtracking* approach to explore all possible paths in the grid that could form the given word.

The idea is to start from each cell in the grid and try to match the word one character at a time by *moving to adjacent cells.*

Steps to Solve the Problem:

1. **Starting Point**: For each cell in the grid, check if we can start forming the word from that cell.
2. **Depth First Search**: Recursively explore all four possible directions (*up, down, left, right*) to match the next character in the word.
3. **Backtracking**: If we've matched all characters in the word, return true. ***If a path doesn't lead to a solution, backtrack by undoing the last move*** and continue exploring other possibilities.
4. **Marking Visited Cells**: To ensure we don't reuse the same cell more than once, temporarily mark cells as visited while exploring that path and then revert them back during backtracking.

Code Solution

Here's how I would implement this approach in Java:

```
public class WordSearch {

    // Main method to check if the word exists in the board
    public boolean exist(char[][] board, String word) {
        int m = board.length;
        int n = board[0].length;

        for (int i = 0; i < m; i++) {
            for (int j = 0; j < n; j++) {
                if (backtrack(board, word, i, j, 0)) {
                    return true;
                }
            }
        }
        return false;
    }
```

```
    // Helper method to perform backtracking
    private boolean backtrack(char[][] board, String word, int i, int
j, int index) {
        // Base case: if the entire word is found, return true
        if (index == word.length()) {
            return true;
        }

        // If out of bounds or the current cell doesn't match the
current character, return false
        if (i < 0 || i >= board.length || j < 0 || j >=
board[0].length || board[i][j] != word.charAt(index)) {
            return false;
        }

        // Mark the cell as visited by temporarily changing the
character
        char temp = board[i][j];
        board[i][j] = '#';

        // Explore all four directions (up, down, left, right)
        boolean found = backtrack(board, word, i + 1, j, index + 1)
||
                backtrack(board, word, i - 1, j, index + 1) ||
                backtrack(board, word, i, j + 1, index + 1) ||
                backtrack(board, word, i, j - 1, index + 1);

        // Backtrack by reverting the change
        board[i][j] = temp;

        return found;
    }

    // Main method to test the exist method
    public static void main(String[] args) {
        WordSearch ws = new WordSearch();

        char[][] board1 = {
                {'A', 'B', 'C', 'E'},
                {'S', 'F', 'C', 'S'},
                {'A', 'D', 'E', 'E'}
        };
        String word1 = "ABCCED";
        System.out.println("Word ABCCED exists: " + ws.exist(board1,
word1));  // true

        String word2 = "SEE";
        System.out.println("Word SEE exists: " + ws.exist(board1,
word2));  // true

        String word3 = "ABCB";
        System.out.println("Word ABCB exists: " + ws.exist(board1,
word3));  // false
```

```
    }
}
```

Candidate: Now, Let me explain what's happening in this code:

- The *exist* method is the main function that checks if the word exists in the board. It iterates over each cell in the grid, treating it as a *potential starting point* for the word.
- The *backtrack* method is where the core logic happens. It recursively tries to match the characters of the word by exploring all four possible directions from each cell.
- We mark the cell as *visited* by temporarily changing its value to # and then revert it after exploring all possibilities from that cell.
- If at any point we match all characters of the word (`index == word.length()`), we return `true`.

Time and Space Complexity

- The time complexity is $O(m \times n \times 4^L)$, where `m` is the number of rows, `n` is the number of columns, and `L` is the length of the word. This is because for each cell, we potentially explore `4 directions` and continue this exploration up to the length of the word.
- Space Complexity: `O(L)` is the space complexity due to the recursion stack, where `L` is the length of the word.

Problem 8: Word Break II

Problem Statement

Given a string `s` and a dictionary of strings `wordDict`, add spaces in `s` to construct a sentence where each word is a valid dictionary word.

Return all such possible sentences in any order.

Note that the same word in the dictionary may be reused multiple times in the segmentation.

Solution

Let's approach this problem as if we're in a coding interview setting.

Clarifying Questions

Candidate: Before jumping into the solution, I'd like to ask a few clarifying questions to make sure I fully understand the problem.

Candidate: Is there any limit on the length of `s` or the size of `wordDict`? Should we assume reasonable constraints?
Interviewer: Yes, you can assume reasonable constraints, such as `s` being of

moderate length (e.g., a few hundred characters) and `wordDict` containing a manageable number of words.

Candidate: Are there any specific requirements for the output order of the sentences, or is any order acceptable?
Interviewer: Any order is fine. The focus is on generating all possible valid sentences.

Candidate: Great! Let me take an example for concrete understanding of the expected input and output.

Example
Let's consider the string `s = "catsanddog"` and the dictionary `wordDict = ["cat", "cats", "and", "sand", "dog"]`.

Possible sentences that can be constructed are:

- `"cat sand dog"`
- `"cats and dog"`

So, the expected output would be `["cat sand dog", "cats and dog"]`.

Approach

The problem essentially requires us to explore all possible ways to break down the string s into valid words from `wordDict`. This is a ***typical backtracking problem*** where we explore *all possible word breaks* and backtrack when necessary.

Steps to Solve the Problem:

1. **Backtracking**: We start from the beginning of the string s and try to match each *prefix* of s with a *word* in `wordDict`. If a match is found, we recursively attempt to break the *remaining part of the string.*
2. **Memoization**: Since the problem has overlapping subproblems (i.e., *different paths in the recursion tree might end up solving the same subproblem*), we can use memoization to store and reuse results of subproblems to optimize the solution (memoization is a dynamic programming technique to cache the intermediate results of the computation in order to avoid same computations again and again, refer to Dynamic Programming chapter for more details).

Code Solution

Here's how I would implement this approach in Java:

```
import java.util.ArrayList;
import java.util.HashMap;
import java.util.List;
import java.util.Map;

public class WordBreakII {

    // Main method to return all possible sentences
```

```
    public List<String> wordBreak(String s, List<String> wordDict) {
        Map<String, List<String>> memo = new HashMap<>();
        return backtrack(s, wordDict, memo);
    }

    // Helper method to perform backtracking with memoization
    private List<String> backtrack(String s, List<String> wordDict,
Map<String, List<String>> memo) {
        // If we have already computed the result for this
substring, return it
        if (memo.containsKey(s)) {
            return memo.get(s);
        }

        List<String> result = new ArrayList<>();

        // If the entire string is in the dictionary, add it as a
valid sentence
        if (wordDict.contains(s)) {
            result.add(s);
        }

        // Explore all possible breaks in the string
        for (int i = 1; i < s.length(); i++) {
            String prefix = s.substring(0, i);
            if (wordDict.contains(prefix)) {
                String suffix = s.substring(i);
                List<String> suffixBreaks = backtrack(suffix,
wordDict, memo);
                for (String sentence : suffixBreaks) {
                    result.add(prefix + " " + sentence);
                }
            }
        }

        // Memoize the result for this substring
        memo.put(s, result);
        return result;
    }

    // Main method to test the wordBreak method
    public static void main(String[] args) {
        WordBreakII wb = new WordBreakII();

        String s1 = "catsanddog";
        List<String> wordDict1 = List.of("cat", "cats", "and",
"sand", "dog");
        System.out.println("Possible sentences: " + wb.wordBreak(s1,
wordDict1));

        String s2 = "pineapplepenapple";
        List<String> wordDict2 = List.of("apple", "pen", "applepen",
"pine", "pineapple");
        System.out.println("Possible sentences: " + wb.wordBreak(s2,
```

```
wordDict2));

        String s3 = "catsandog";
        List<String> wordDict3 = List.of("cats", "dog", "sand",
"and", "cat");
        System.out.println("Possible sentences: " + wb.wordBreak(s3,
wordDict3));
    }
}
```

Time and Space Complexity

- The time complexity, in the worst case, could be exponential in the length of s due to the vast number of possible splits. Memoization helps reduce the complexity by avoiding redundant calculations, making it more efficient in practice.
- The space complexity is primarily driven by the *recursion stack* and the memoization map, which can store results for up to n substrings, where n is the length of s. Thus, the space complexity is $O(n^2)$, considering the storage of all substrings in the *memo* map.

Problem 9: Palindrome Partitioning

Problem Statement

Given a string s, partition s such that *every substring of the partition is a palindrome.* Return all possible palindrome partitioning of s.

Solution

Let's tackle this problem step by step as if we're in a coding interview setting.

Clarifying Questions

Candidate: Before I start with the solution, I'd like to ask a few clarifying questions to ensure I fully understand the problem.

Candidate: You mentioned that every substring of the partition should be a palindrome. Just to confirm, the output should include all possible ways to partition the string such that each substring in the partition is a palindrome, correct?
Interviewer: Yes, that's correct. You need to return all possible partitions where each substring is a palindrome.

Candidate: Is there any specific order required for the output, or can the partitions be returned in any order?
Interviewer: The order of the partitions doesn't matter. You can return them in any order.

Candidate: Finally, is there a constraint on the length of the string s?
Interviewer: You can assume that the length of s is reasonable, typically up to a few hundred characters.

Candidate: Great! Let's go through an example to ensure we're aligned on what the expected output should look like.

Example
Let's consider the string s = "aab".

The possible palindromic partitions are:

- ["a", "a", "b"] (where "a", "a" and "b" are palindromes)
- ["aa", "b"] (where "aa" and "b" are palindromes)

So, the expected output would be something like [["a", "a", "b"], ["aa", "b"]].

Approach

This problem can be efficiently solved using a backtracking approach.

We can *recursively explore* all possible partitions of the string and check if each substring is a palindrome. As we generate substrings, we check if they are palindromes.

If they are, we continue to partition the remaining string, otherwise backtrack. If we reach the end of the string with all valid palindromes, we add the current partition to the result.

Code Solution

Here's how I would implement this approach in Java:

```
import java.util.ArrayList;
import java.util.List;

public class PalindromePartitioning {

    // Main method to return all possible palindrome partitions
    public List<List<String>> partition(String s) {
        List<List<String>> result = new ArrayList<>();
        backtrack(s, 0, new ArrayList<>(), result);
        return result;
    }

    // Helper method to perform backtracking
    private void backtrack(String s, int start, List<String>
currentPartition, List<List<String>> result) {
        // Base case: if we've reached the end of the string, add
the current partition to the result
        if (start == s.length()) {
            result.add(new ArrayList<>(currentPartition));
```

```
            return;
        }

        // Explore all possible partitions starting from the current
position
        for (int end = start; end < s.length(); end++) {
            if (isPalindrome(s, start, end)) {
                // If the substring s[start:end+1] is a palindrome,
add it to the current partition
                currentPartition.add(s.substring(start, end + 1));

                // Recurse to partition the remaining string
                backtrack(s, end + 1, currentPartition, result);

                // Backtrack by removing the last added substring
                currentPartition.remove(currentPartition.size() - 1);
            }
        }
    }

    // Helper method to check if a substring is a palindrome
    private boolean isPalindrome(String s, int left, int right) {
        while (left < right) {
            if (s.charAt(left) != s.charAt(right)) {
                return false;
            }
            left++;
            right--;
        }
        return true;
    }

    // Main method to test the partition method
    public static void main(String[] args) {
        PalindromePartitioning pp = new PalindromePartitioning();

        String s1 = "aab";
        System.out.println("Palindrome partitions of 'aab': " +
pp.partition(s1));  // [["a","a","b"],["aa","b"]]

        String s2 = "a";
        System.out.println("Palindrome partitions of 'a': " +
pp.partition(s2));  // [["a"]]

        String s3 = "abc";
        System.out.println("Palindrome partitions of 'abc': " +
pp.partition(s3));  // [["a","b","c"]]
    }
}
```

Let review what's happening in this code:

- The *partition* method is the main function that initializes the backtracking process and returns all possible palindromic partitions.

- The *backtrack* method recursively explores all possible partitions starting from the current position in the string. If a valid palindrome substring is found, it is added to the current partition, and the process continues for the remaining substring.
- The *isPalindrome* helper method checks if a given substring is a palindrome by comparing characters from both ends toward the center.

Time and Space Complexity

- The time complexity is `O(n × 2ⁿ)`, where `n` is the length of the string. This is because in the worst case, there are 2^n possible substrings, and for each substring, we might need `O(n)` time to check if it is a palindrome.
- The space complexity is `O(n)` due to the recursion stack and the space required to store the current partition.

Problem 10: Optimal Account Balancing

Problem Statement

You are given an array of transactions called *transactions* where `transactions[i]` = $[from_i, to_i, amount_i]$ indicates that the person with `ID` = $from_i$ gave $amount_i$ $ to the person with `ID` = to_i.

Return the minimum number of transactions required to ***settle the debt***.

Solution

Candidate: Thanks for the question! I'd like to make sure I understand the problem correctly before proceeding. May I ask a few clarifying questions?
Interviewer: Of course, go ahead.

Candidate: Are the person IDs arbitrary integers, or do they range from 0 to some maximum value without gaps?
Interviewer: The person IDs are arbitrary integers and can be any integer values.

Candidate: Can there be multiple transactions between the same pair of people?
Interviewer: Yes, there can be multiple transactions between the same pair of people.

Candidate: Is it possible for a person to both give and receive money in different transactions?
Interviewer: Yes, a person can both give and receive money across different transactions.

Candidate: What exactly do we mean by "settling the debt"? Is the goal to have everyone's net balance equal to zero using the minimal number of transactions?
Interviewer: Exactly. You need to find the minimal number of transactions required so that everyone's net balance becomes zero.

Candidate: Are we allowed to have transactions between any two people, or only between those who had transactions initially?
Interviewer: You can have transactions between any two people to settle the debts.

Candidate: Understood. So, given all that, if we can *redistribute the debts* such that the net balances become zero with the fewest number of transactions, that would be our optimal solution.
Interviewer: That's correct.

Candidate: Let me take an example to illustrate the Problem

Example:
Input: `transactions = [[0,1,10], [2,0,5]]`

Explanation:

- Person `0` gives $`10` to person `1`.
- Person 2 gives $5 to person `0`.

We want to settle these debts with the minimum number of transactions.

Possible Solution:

- Person `1` gives $5 to person 2. This single transaction settles all debts. So, the minimum number of transactions required is `1`.

Approach

We can use a backtracking technique to efficiently find the minimal number of transactions.

Outline of the approach is:

1. **Calculate Net Balances:**
   - First, calculate each person's net balance. *Positive balance means they should receive money, negative means they owe money.*
2. **Backtracking to Settle Debts:**
   - We try to settle one person's debt with another's credit recursively.
   - At each step, we attempt to offset a debtor's balance with a creditor's balance.
   - We *skip zero balances* to optimize the process.
   - We keep *track of the minimal number of transactions* needed.

Why Backtracking?

- It systematically ***explores all possible settlements but prunes unnecessary paths*** by skipping invalid or redundant states.
- It efficiently reaches the optimal solution by minimizing transactions.

Code Solution

```
import java.util.ArrayList;
import java.util.HashMap;
```

```
import java.util.List;
import java.util.Map;

public class OptimalAccountBalancing {

   public static int minTransfers(int[][] transactions) {
        // Step 1: Calculate net balances
        Map<Integer, Integer> balanceMap = new HashMap<>();
        for (int[] transaction : transactions) {
            int from = transaction[0];
            int to = transaction[1];
            int amount = transaction[2];

            balanceMap.put(from, balanceMap.getOrDefault(from, 0) -
amount);
            balanceMap.put(to, balanceMap.getOrDefault(to, 0) +
amount);
        }

        // Filter out zero balances
        List<Integer> balances = new ArrayList<>();
        for (int amount : balanceMap.values()) {
            if (amount != 0) {
                balances.add(amount);
            }
        }

        return settleDebt(balances, 0);
   }

   private static int settleDebt(List<Integer> balances, int start)
{
        // Skip settled debts
        while (start < balances.size() && balances.get(start) == 0) {
            start++;
        }

        // If all debts are settled
        if (start == balances.size()) {
            return 0;
        }

        int minTransactions = Integer.MAX_VALUE;
        int currentDebt = balances.get(start);

        for (int i = start + 1; i < balances.size(); i++) {
            int nextDebt = balances.get(i);
            // If debts can be settled
            if (currentDebt * nextDebt < 0) {
                // Settle debts
                balances.set(i, currentDebt + nextDebt);

                int transactions = 1 + settleDebt(balances, start +
1);
```

```
                minTransactions = Math.min(minTransactions,
transactions);

                // Backtrack
                balances.set(i, nextDebt);

                // Optimization: if debts are completely settled,
break early
                if (currentDebt + nextDebt == 0) {
                    break;
                }
            }
        }

        return minTransactions;
    }

    public static void main(String[] args) {
        // Test case 1
        int[][] transactions1 = {{0, 1, 10}, {2, 0, 5}};
        System.out.println("Minimum transactions required: " +
minTransfers(transactions1));
        // Expected output: 1

        // Test case 2
        int[][] transactions2 = {{0, 1, 10}, {1, 0, 1}, {1, 2, 5},
{2, 0, 5}};
        System.out.println("Minimum transactions required: " +
minTransfers(transactions2));
        // Expected output: 2

        // Test case 3
        int[][] transactions3 = {{0, 1, 5}, {0, 2, 10}, {1, 2, 5}};
        System.out.println("Minimum transactions required: " +
minTransfers(transactions3));
        // Expected output: 2

        // Test case 4
        int[][] transactions4 = {};
        System.out.println("Minimum transactions required: " +
minTransfers(transactions4));
        // Expected output: 0

        // Test case 5
        int[][] transactions5 = {{0, 1, 5}, {1, 2, 5}, {2, 0, 5}};
        System.out.println("Minimum transactions required: " +
minTransfers(transactions5));
        // Expected output: 0
    }
}
```

Time and Space Complexity

Time Complexity:

- The worst-case time complexity is `O(n!)`, where `n` is the number of people with non-zero balances.
- This is because, in the worst case, we might need to explore all permutations to find the minimal transactions.
- However, practical performance is acceptable for reasonable values of `n` (up to around 20), thanks to optimizations like skipping zeros and early termination.

Space Complexity:

- The space complexity is `O(n)`:
    - We store the balances in a list of size `n`.
    - The recursion stack can go up to depth `n`.

Chapter 14: Trees

Introduction to Trees

A tree is a *hierarchical* data structure consisting of *nodes* connected by *edges.*

Each tree has a *single root* node, and *every node*, except the root, has *exactly one parent.*

Nodes without children are called *leaf nodes.*

Trees are used to represent hierarchical relationships, making them ideal for organizing data such as *file systems*, *organizational structures* etc.

Types of Trees

Understanding different types of trees is essential for solving a wide range of problems.

Here are the most common types:

- **Binary Tree**: A tree in which each node has *at most two children*, referred to as the *left child* and the *right child.*

- **Binary Search Tree (BST)**: A binary tree where the *left subtree* of a node contains only nodes with values less than the node's value, and the *right subtree* contains only nodes with values greater than the node's value.

- **Balanced Trees**: It is a type of binary tree in which the difference between the height of the left and the right subtree for each node is either `0` or `1`.

- **Full Binary Tree**: A binary tree in which every node has `0` or `2` children.

- **Complete Binary Tree**: A binary tree in which *all levels are completely filled except possibly the last*, which is filled from left to right.

- **Perfect Binary Tree**: A binary tree in which all internal nodes have exactly two children and all leaf nodes are at the same level.

- **N-ary Tree**: A tree in which each node can have up to N children.

Tree Traversals

Tree traversal is a way of visiting all the nodes in a tree.

There are several methods of tree traversal:

- **Preorder Traversal (Root, Left, Right)**: Visit the root node first, then recursively visit the left subtree, followed by the right subtree.

- **Inorder Traversal (Left, Root, Right)**: Recursively visit the left subtree, visit the root node, and finally visit the right subtree. This traversal is particularly important for BSTs as it returns the nodes in sorted order.

- **Postorder Traversal (Left, Right, Root)**: Recursively visit the left subtree, then the right subtree, and finally visit the root node.

- **Level Order Traversal**: Visit nodes level by level from left to right.

Tree Operations

Here are some fundamental operations on trees:

- **Insertion**: Adding a node to the tree while maintaining its properties (e.g., in BST).
- **Deletion**: Removing a node from the tree, requiring adjustments to maintain tree properties.
- **Searching**: Finding a node in the tree, particularly efficient in BSTs.
- **Finding Minimum/Maximum**: In a BST, the minimum value is the leftmost node, and the maximum is the rightmost node.
- **Height/Depth Calculation**: The height of a tree is the length of the longest path from the root to a leaf.

DFS & BFS on Trees

Understanding tree traversal techniques like Depth-First Search (DFS) and Breadth-First Search (BFS) is crucial from a coding interview point of view. These fundamental algorithms are commonly used to *explore or search through tree* data structures.

Let's look into the key concepts, typical use cases, and example implementations of DFS and BFS in the context of tree-based coding interview problems.

Depth-First Search (DFS) on Trees

DFS explores as far as possible along each branch before backtracking, effectively diving deep into one branch of the tree before moving to another.

This approach can be implemented using either recursion (which implicitly uses the call stack) or an explicit stack data structure.

Common Use Cases in Interviews

- Finding paths between nodes
- Checking for the existence of a path that satisfies certain conditions (e.g., path sum problems)
- Determining tree depth (maximum depth of any leaf node)

- Identifying cycles in graphs (though less common in trees)

Implementation in Java

Here's how you can implement DFS recursively for a binary tree:

```
class TreeNode {
    int val;
    TreeNode left, right;

    TreeNode(int x) {
        val = x;
    }
}

public class DFSTreeTraversal {
    public void dfs(TreeNode node) {
        if (node == null) return;

        // Process the current node (Preorder)
        System.out.print(node.val + " ");

        // Traverse left subtree
        dfs(node.left);

        // Traverse right subtree
        dfs(node.right);
    }

    public static void main(String[] args) {
        // Constructing the binary tree
        TreeNode root = new TreeNode(1);
        root.left = new TreeNode(2);
        root.right = new TreeNode(3);
        root.left.left = new TreeNode(4);
        root.left.right = new TreeNode(5);
        root.right.left = new TreeNode(6);
        root.right.right = new TreeNode(7);

        // Testing DFS Traversal
        System.out.println("DFS Traversal:");
        DFSTreeTraversal dfsTraversal = new DFSTreeTraversal();
        dfsTraversal.dfs(root);
        System.out.println(); // For better formatting of output\
    }
}
```

DFS Variations

- Preorder DFS: Process node, then left subtree, then right subtree.
- Inorder DFS: Process left subtree, then node, then right subtree.
- Postorder DFS: Process left subtree, then right subtree, then node.

Time and Space Complexity

- Time Complexity: `O(n)`, where `n` is the number of nodes in the tree, since each node is visited once.
- Space Complexity: `O(h)`, where `h` is the height of the tree (due to the recursive call stack or explicit stack). In the worst case, `h` can be `n` (for a skewed tree).

Breadth-First Search (BFS) on Trees

BFS explores nodes level by level, starting from the root and moving outward.

This algorithm is implemented using a queue, ensuring that nodes at the current level are fully explored before moving on to nodes at the next level.

Common Use Cases in Interviews

- Finding the shortest path in an unweighted tree or graph
- Level order traversal (often used for binary tree problems)
- Determining the minimum depth of a tree
- Serializing and deserializing binary trees (e.g., converting a tree to/from a string or array representation)

Implementation in Java

Here's how you can implement BFS for a binary tree:

```
import java.util.LinkedList;
import java.util.Queue;

public class BFSTreeTraversal {
   public void bfs(TreeNode root) {
       if (root == null) return;

       Queue<TreeNode> queue = new LinkedList<>();
       queue.offer(root);

       while (!queue.isEmpty()) {
           TreeNode node = queue.poll();

           // Process the current node
           System.out.print(node.val + " ");

           // Add the left and right children to the queue
           if (node.left != null) queue.offer(node.left);
           if (node.right != null) queue.offer(node.right);
       }
   }

   public static void main(String[] args) {
       // Constructing the binary tree
```

```
        TreeNode root = new TreeNode(1);
        root.left = new TreeNode(2);
        root.right = new TreeNode(3);
        root.left.left = new TreeNode(4);
        root.left.right = new TreeNode(5);
        root.right.left = new TreeNode(6);
        root.right.right = new TreeNode(7);

        // Testing BFS Traversal
        System.out.println("BFS Traversal:");
        BFSTreeTraversal bfsTraversal = new BFSTreeTraversal();
        bfsTraversal.bfs(root);
        System.out.println(); // For better formatting of output
    }
}
```

BFS is particularly useful for problems where you need to explore all nodes at a given level before moving deeper.

This method is optimal for finding the shortest path in an unweighted tree because it explores all possibilities level by level.

Time and Space Complexity

- Time Complexity: `O(n)`, where `n` is the number of nodes in the tree, since each node is visited once.
- Space Complexity: `O(n)` in the worst case, which occurs when the tree is a complete binary tree. The queue can hold up to half of the total number of nodes at the last level.

Key Takeaways

- DFS is depth-oriented, diving deep into each branch before backtracking.
- BFS is breadth-oriented, exploring nodes level by level.
- Both DFS and BFS have a time complexity of `O(n)`, but their space complexity varies based on the structure of the tree.

Most Popular Tree Based Questions

In this section we will go over the most popular and frequently asked questions on Trees.

Tree based problems can be broadly divided into following patterns based on the approach we can use to solve those problems:

1. BFS Problems
2. DFS Problems
3. Bottom Up DFS Problems
4. DFS using Stack
5. Tree Construction

We will look at a few problems in each of these categories so that you can be comfortable in solving any Tree based coding interview questions.

Problem 1: Binary Tree Level Order Traversal

Problem Statement

Given the root of a binary tree, return the level order traversal of its nodes' values.

Solution

Let's break down the problem and solve it using our structured approach.

Clarifying Questions

Candidate: Can the tree have duplicate values, and should those be handled in any special way during the level order traversal?
Interviewer: The tree can have duplicate values. The level order traversal should handle them like any other value, maintaining the order they appear in the tree.

Candidate: Should the output be a list of lists, where each inner list represents the values at a specific level of the tree?
Interviewer: Yes, the output should be a list of lists.

Example: Consider the following binary tree:

```
    3
   / \
  9  20
    /  \
   15   7
```

The expected output for the level order traversal of this tree would be a list of lists, where each inner list contains the values of the nodes at each level:

```
[
  [3],
  [9, 20],
  [15, 7]
]
```

Brute Force Approach

The brute force approach would involve recursively traversing the tree to collect nodes at each level, but this would be inefficient and difficult to manage without additional data structures.

Optimal Approach

The optimal approach is to use a queue to facilitate a Breadth-First Search (BFS).

The problem requires us to perform a level order traversal of a binary tree, which means we visit all nodes at each level of the tree from top to bottom, left to right.

A Breadth-First Search (BFS) approach is naturally suited for this problem since it explores nodes level by level.

Code Solution

Here's the Java code implementing the level order traversal using BFS:

```
import java.util.*;

class TreeNode {
    int val;
    TreeNode left;
    TreeNode right;

    TreeNode(int x) {
        val = x;
    }
}

public class BinaryTreeLevelOrderTraversal {

    public List<List<Integer>> levelOrder(TreeNode root) {
        List<List<Integer>> result = new ArrayList<>();

        // Base case: if the tree is empty, return an empty list
        if (root == null) {
            return result;
        }

        // Initialize the queue for BFS
        Queue<TreeNode> queue = new LinkedList<>();
        queue.offer(root);

        // Process the tree level by level
        while (!queue.isEmpty()) {
            int levelSize = queue.size(); // Number of nodes at the
current level
            List<Integer> currentLevel = new ArrayList<>();

            for (int i = 0; i < levelSize; i++) {
                TreeNode currentNode = queue.poll();
                currentLevel.add(currentNode.val);

                // Add the children of the current node to the queue
for the next level
                if (currentNode.left != null) {
                    queue.offer(currentNode.left);
                }
                if (currentNode.right != null) {
                    queue.offer(currentNode.right);
                }
```

```
            }

            // Add the current level to the result
            result.add(currentLevel);
        }

        return result;
    }

    public static void main(String[] args) {
        BinaryTreeLevelOrderTraversal solution = new
BinaryTreeLevelOrderTraversal();

        // Example usage:
        TreeNode root = new TreeNode(3);
        root.left = new TreeNode(9);
        root.right = new TreeNode(20);
        root.right.left = new TreeNode(15);
        root.right.right = new TreeNode(7);

        List<List<Integer>> result = solution.levelOrder(root);
        System.out.println("Level order traversal: " + result);
        // Expected output: [[3], [9, 20], [15, 7]]
    }
}
```

Time and Space Complexity

- The time complexity is `O(n)`, where `n` is the number of nodes in the tree. This is because we visit each node exactly once during the traversal.
- The space complexity is `O(n)` in the worst case, where the queue might store the maximum number of nodes at the widest level of the tree.

Problem 2: Binary Tree Right Side View

Problem Statement

Given the root of a binary tree, imagine yourself standing on the right side of it, return the values of the nodes you can see ordered from top to bottom.

Solution

Let's break down the problem and solve it step by step.

Clarifying Questions

Candidate: Can the tree have duplicate values, and should those be handled in any special way?
Interviewer: Yes, the tree can have duplicate values. Handle them like any other value during the traversal.

Candidate: Should the output be a list of values, ordered from the top to bottom of the tree, representing the right side view?
Interviewer: Yes, the output should be a list of node values that are visible when viewing the tree from the right side, ordered from top to bottom.

Example: Consider the following binary tree:

```
      1
     / \
    2   3
     \   \
      5   4
```

From the right side, the visible nodes are 1, 3, and 4. Hence the expected output is `[1, 3, 4]`

Optimal Approach:

The problem requires us to return the values of the nodes that are visible when viewing the tree from the right side, ordered from top to bottom.

Nodes that are visible on the right side of the tree are the *last nodes* encountered at each level during a *level-order traversal.*

Hence, we can use a Breadth-First Search (BFS) approach, modified to capture the last node at each level.

Code Solution

Here's the Java code implementing the right-side view using BFS:

```
import java.util.*;

class TreeNode {
    int val;
    TreeNode left;
    TreeNode right;

    TreeNode(int x) {
        val = x;
    }
}

public class BinaryTreeRightSideView {

    public List<Integer> rightSideView(TreeNode root) {
        List<Integer> result = new ArrayList<>();

        // Base case: if the tree is empty, return an empty list
        if (root == null) {
            return result;
        }

        // Initialize the queue for BFS
```

```
        Queue<TreeNode> queue = new LinkedList<>();
        queue.offer(root);

        // Process the tree level by level
        while (!queue.isEmpty()) {
            int levelSize = queue.size(); // Number of nodes at the
current level
            TreeNode lastNode = null;

            for (int i = 0; i < levelSize; i++) {
                TreeNode currentNode = queue.poll();
                lastNode = currentNode; // Track the last node at
this level

                // Add the children of the current node to the queue
for the next level
                if (currentNode.left != null) {
                    queue.offer(currentNode.left);
                }
                if (currentNode.right != null) {
                    queue.offer(currentNode.right);
                }
            }

            // The last node at this level is the rightmost node
            if (lastNode != null) {
                result.add(lastNode.val);
            }
        }

        return result;
    }

    public static void main(String[] args) {
        BinaryTreeRightSideView solution = new
BinaryTreeRightSideView();

        // Example usage:
        TreeNode root = new TreeNode(1);
        root.left = new TreeNode(2);
        root.right = new TreeNode(3);
        root.left.right = new TreeNode(5);
        root.right.right = new TreeNode(4);

        List<Integer> result = solution.rightSideView(root);
        System.out.println("Right side view: " + result);
        // Expected output: [1, 3, 4]
    }
}
```

Time and Space Complexity

- The time complexity is `O(n)`, where `n` is the number of nodes in the tree. This is because we visit each node exactly once during the traversal.

- The space complexity is `O(n)` in the worst case, where the queue might store the maximum number of nodes at the widest level of the tree.

Problem 3: Check Completeness of a Binary Tree

Problem Statement

Given the root of a binary tree, determine if it is a complete binary tree.

Solution

Let's break down the problem and solve it by following the structured approach.

Clarifying Questions

Candidate: To clarify, a complete binary tree is a binary tree in which every level, except possibly the last, is completely filled, and all nodes are as far left as possible. Is that correct?
Interviewer: Yes, that is the correct definition.

After clarifying the question with the interviewer, the next step is to take an example and confirm expected input and output.

Example:
Consider the following binary tree:

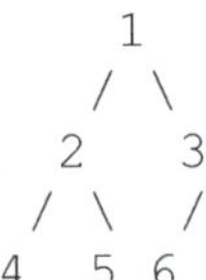

```
      1
     / \
    2   3
   / \  /
  4   5 6
```

The tree is complete because all levels are fully filled except possibly the last, which is filled from left to right. So the expected output is true.

Optimal Approach

The optimal approach is to use Breadth-First Search (BFS) to traverse the tree level by level.
During this traversal:

- We check if we encounter a *null* node.
- If a null node is encountered, *all subsequent nodes in the level-order traversal should also be null*. If we encounter a non-null node after a null node, the tree is not complete.

Code Solution

Here's the Java code implementing the solution using BFS:

```
import java.util.*;
```

```
class TreeNode {
   int val;
   TreeNode left;
   TreeNode right;

   TreeNode(int x) {
       val = x;
   }
}

public class CompleteBinaryTree {

   public boolean isCompleteTree(TreeNode root) {
       if (root == null) {
           return true; // An empty tree is a complete binary tree
       }

       Queue<TreeNode> queue = new LinkedList<>();
       queue.offer(root);
       boolean encounteredNull = false;

       while (!queue.isEmpty()) {
           TreeNode currentNode = queue.poll();

           if (currentNode == null) {
               encounteredNull = true;
           } else {
               if (encounteredNull) {
                   // If we have encountered a null node before,
and now we see a non-null node
                   return false;
               }
               queue.offer(currentNode.left);
               queue.offer(currentNode.right);
           }
       }

       return true; // If we complete the loop, the tree is
complete
   }

   public static void main(String[] args) {
       CompleteBinaryTree solution = new CompleteBinaryTree();

       // Example usage:
       TreeNode root = new TreeNode(1);
       root.left = new TreeNode(2);
       root.right = new TreeNode(3);
       root.left.left = new TreeNode(4);
       root.left.right = new TreeNode(5);
       root.right.left = new TreeNode(6);

       boolean isComplete = solution.isCompleteTree(root);
```

```
        System.out.println("Is the binary tree complete? " +
isComplete); // Expected output: true
    }
}
```

Time and Space Complexity

- The time complexity is `O(n)`, where `n` is the number of nodes in the tree. This is because we need to visit each node exactly once during the traversal.
- The space complexity is `O(n)` due to the queue used to store nodes during the level-order traversal.

Problem 4: Binary Tree Vertical Order Traversal

Problem Statement

Given the `root` of a binary tree, return the ***vertical order traversal*** of its nodes' values. (i.e., from *top to bottom, column by column*).
If two nodes are in the same row and column, the order should be from ***left to right***.

Solution

Before diving into the solution, let's clarify the problem to ensure a full understanding.

Clarifying Questions

Candidate: What is the output format?
Interviewer: The output should be a *list of lists*, where each sublist contains the values of nodes that appear in the same vertical column of the binary tree.

Candidate: Are there any constraints on the size of the tree?
Interviewer: There are no specific constraints mentioned, but we can assume that the tree can be large, so the solution should be efficient.

Candidate: How should we handle cases where the tree is *empty*?
Interviewer: If the tree is empty, the output should be an *empty list*.

Example
Let's consider the following example:

Input:

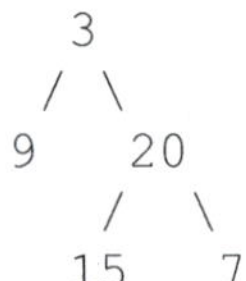

Output:

```
[[9], [3, 15], [20], [7]]
```

Brute Force Approach

Brute force approach could be to:

1. Traverse the tree using a BFS or DFS.
2. For each node, *record its value* along with its *row* and *column indices.*
3. Store the *nodes in a list*, then *sort* this list based on column index, row index, and finally node value.
4. *Group nodes by their column index* to produce the final vertical order traversal.

This approach ensures that nodes are placed in their correct columns and are sorted by their row and order of appearance, providing the correct vertical order traversal.

Efficiency:

- Time Complexity: `O(n log n)`, where `n` is the number of nodes. Sorting is the most expensive operation.
- Space Complexity: `O(n)`, for storing the nodes and their corresponding indices.

Optimal Approach

To improve efficiency, we can use a *BFS approach that directly maps nodes to their corresponding columns during traversal.* This avoids the need for extensive sorting.

Here's the outline of the approach:

1. **BFS Traversal**:
   - We use a queue to perform BFS. Each element in the queue is a pair consisting of a tree node and its corresponding column index.
   - The *root starts at `column 0`*. For each node, its left child is placed in `column - 1`, and its right child is placed in `column + 1`.
2. **Column Table**:
   - We use a hash map (columnTable) to store lists of node values grouped by their *column index.*
   - As we traverse the tree, we *update the minimum and maximum column indices* encountered.
3. Result Construction:
   - After completing the BFS, we construct the output list by iterating through the *column indices from minColumn to maxColumn* and retrieving the corresponding node values from the columnTable.

Code Solution

```
import java.util.*;

class TreeNode {
    int val;
    TreeNode left;
```

```
    TreeNode right;

    TreeNode(int x) {
        val = x;
    }
}

class Pair<U, V> {
    private final U first;  // The first element of the pair
    private final V second; // The second element of the pair

    // Constructor to initialize the pair
    public Pair(U first, V second) {
        this.first = first;
        this.second = second;
    }

    // Getter for the first element of the pair
    public U getKey() {
        return first;
    }

    // Getter for the second element of the pair
    public V getValue() {
        return second;
    }
}

class VerticalOrderTraversal {
    public List<List<Integer>> verticalOrder(TreeNode root) {
        // List to store the result of vertical order traversal
        List<List<Integer>> output = new ArrayList<>();

        // If the root is null, return an empty list
        if (root == null) {
            return output;
        }

        // Map to store the nodes based on their column index
        // Key: column index, Value: list of node values at that
column
        Map<Integer, ArrayList<Integer>> columnTable = new
HashMap<>();

        // Queue for breadth-first search (BFS)
        // Each element in the queue is a pair of a TreeNode and its
corresponding column index
        Queue<Pair<TreeNode, Integer>> queue = new ArrayDeque<>();

        // Start BFS from the root with column index 0
        int column = 0;
        queue.offer(new Pair<>(root, column));

        // Variables to track the minimum and maximum column indices
```

```
encountered
        int minColumn = 0, maxColumn = 0;

        // Perform BFS
        while (!queue.isEmpty()) {
            // Get the front element from the queue
            Pair<TreeNode, Integer> p = queue.poll();
            root = p.getKey();
            column = p.getValue();

            // If the current node is not null
            if (root != null) {
                // If this column is not already in the map,
initialize a list for it
                if (!columnTable.containsKey(column)) {
                    columnTable.put(column, new
ArrayList<Integer>());
                }
                // Add the node's value to the list of the
corresponding column
                columnTable.get(column).add(root.val);

                // Update the minimum and maximum column indices
                minColumn = Math.min(minColumn, column);
                maxColumn = Math.max(maxColumn, column);

                // Add the left child to the queue with the column
index decreased by 1
                queue.offer(new Pair<>(root.left, column - 1));
                // Add the right child to the queue with the column
index increased by 1
                queue.offer(new Pair<>(root.right, column + 1));
            }
        }

        // Collect the results from the columnTable, ordered from
minColumn to maxColumn
        for (int i = minColumn; i < maxColumn + 1; ++i) {
            output.add(columnTable.get(i));
        }

        // Return the final vertical order traversal list
        return output;
    }

    public static void main(String[] args) {
        // Constructing the binary tree
        TreeNode root = new TreeNode(3);
        root.left = new TreeNode(9);
        root.right = new TreeNode(20);
        root.right.left = new TreeNode(15);
        root.right.right = new TreeNode(7);

        // Creating an instance of VerticalOrderTraversal
```

```
        VerticalOrderTraversal traversal = new
VerticalOrderTraversal();

        // Getting the vertical order traversal
        List<List<Integer>> result = traversal.verticalOrder(root);

        // Printing the result
        for (List<Integer> list : result) {
            System.out.println(list);
        }
    }
}
```

Time and Space Complexity

Time Complexity

- BFS Traversal: Each node is visited exactly once, so the time complexity for the BFS traversal itself is `O(n)`, where `n` is the number of nodes in the tree.
- Constructing Output: After BFS, we iterate through the column indices from minColumn to maxColumn, which takes `O(c)`, where `c` is the number of columns. However, since `c ≤ n`, this part is also `O(n)`.
- Overall Time Complexity: The overall time complexity is `O(n)`.

Space Complexity

- Column Table: The space required for the columnTable hash map is `O(n)`, as it stores lists of node values for each column.
- Queue: The queue used for BFS can hold at most `n` elements (in the worst case where the tree is a linked list), so the space complexity is `O(n)`.
- Overall Space Complexity: The overall space complexity is `O(n)`, considering both the columnTable and the queue.

Problem 5: Binary Tree - All Paths

Problem Statement

Given the root of a binary tree, return all root-to-leaf paths in any order.

Solution

Let's follow the structured approach to solve this question.

Clarifying Questions

Candidate: To clarify, a root-to-leaf path is a sequence of nodes in a binary tree starting from the root node and ending at a leaf node. Is that the correct understanding?
Interviewer: Yes, that's correct.

Candidate: What should be the output format?

Interviewer: We should return *a list of all root-to-leaf paths*. Each path should be represented as a *string* with node values separated by "->".

Example:
Consider the following binary tree:

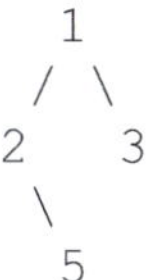

Input: The root of the binary tree.
Expected Output: `["1->2->5", "1->3"]`

Approach

The main idea is to perform a DFS on the binary tree while keeping track of the path from the root to the current node.

When a leaf node is encountered, the path is complete and can be added to the result.

Code Solution

The outline for the code is as follows:

- **DFS Traversal**: Use the helper function *dfs* to recursively traverse the tree. For each node, the *current path* is updated by appending the node's value. If a leaf node is encountered (i.e., both left and right children are null), the *path* is added to the *list of paths*.
- **Path String Construction**: As we traverse, *the path is built as a string*. When we move to a child node, "->" is appended to the path.
- **Leaf Node Check**: When we reach a leaf node, we *add the path to our result list*.

```
import java.util.ArrayList;
import java.util.List;

class TreeNode {
   int val;
   TreeNode left;
   TreeNode right;

   TreeNode(int x) {
       val = x;
   }
}

public class BinaryTreePaths {

   public List<String> binaryTreePaths(TreeNode root) {
       List<String> paths = new ArrayList<>();
       if (root == null) return paths;
```

```
        dfs(root, "", paths);
        return paths;
    }

    private void dfs(TreeNode node, String path, List<String> paths)
{
        // If this is the first node in the path, don't add "->"
        if (node != null) {
            path += Integer.toString(node.val);
            // Check if the current node is a leaf node
            if (node.left == null && node.right == null) {
                // It's a leaf, so add the current path to paths
                paths.add(path);
            } else {
                // Continue to explore the left and right subtree
                path += "->";
                if (node.left != null) dfs(node.left, path, paths);
                if (node.right != null) dfs(node.right, path, paths);
            }
        }
    }

    public static void main(String[] args) {
        BinaryTreePaths solution = new BinaryTreePaths();
        TreeNode root = new TreeNode(1);
        root.left = new TreeNode(2);
        root.right = new TreeNode(3);
        root.left.right = new TreeNode(5);

        List<String> result = solution.binaryTreePaths(root);
        for (String path : result) {
            System.out.println(path);
        }
    }
}
```

Time and Space Complexity:

- Time Complexity: `O(n)`, where `n` is the number of nodes in the tree. We visit each node exactly once.
- Space Complexity: `O(h)`, where `h` is the height of the tree. The space complexity is determined by the recursion stack, which in the worst case (for a skewed tree) can be equal to the height of the tree.

Problem 6: Path Sum

Problem Statement

Given the `root` of a binary tree and an integer `targetSum`, return true if the tree has *a root-to-leaf path* such that adding up all the values along the path *equals targetSum.*

Solution

We can break down the solution as follows:

Clarifying Questions

1. What is a root-to-leaf path?
   A root-to-leaf path is a sequence of nodes in a binary tree starting from the root node and ending at a leaf node (a node with no children).
2. What do we need to determine?
   We need to determine if there exists ***at least one root-to-leaf path*** where the sum of the node values equals `targetSum`.

Example:
Consider the following binary tree:

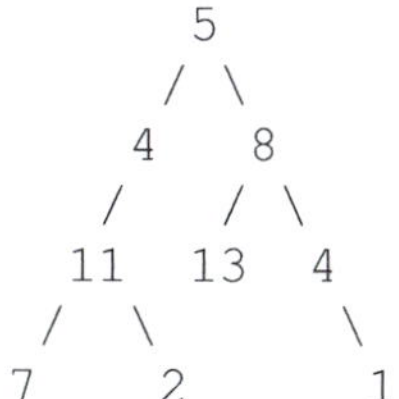

Input: The `root` of the binary tree and `targetSum = 22`.
Output: `true` (because the path 5 -> 4 -> 11 -> 2 equals 22).

Approach

The key idea is to use *DFS* to explore all root-to-leaf paths while *maintaining a running sum* of the node values.

As we traverse the tree, we keep track of the *cumulative sum from the root to the current node*. If we reach a *leaf node and the cumulative sum* equals `targetSum`, we return `true`.

If no such path is found by the time all nodes are visited, we return `false`.

Code Solution

```
class TreeNode {
    int val;
    TreeNode left;
    TreeNode right;

    TreeNode(int x) {
        val = x;
    }
}

public class PathSum {
```

```
    public boolean hasPathSum(TreeNode root, int targetSum) {
        // Base case: if the tree is empty, there is no path to
consider
        if (root == null) return false;

        // If we reach a leaf node, check if the path sum equals
targetSum
        if (root.left == null && root.right == null) {
            return root.val == targetSum;
        }

        // Recur for left and right subtree with the updated
targetSum
        int remainingSum = targetSum - root.val;
        return hasPathSum(root.left, remainingSum) ||
hasPathSum(root.right, remainingSum);
    }

    public static void main(String[] args) {
        PathSum solution = new PathSum();

        TreeNode root = new TreeNode(5);
        root.left = new TreeNode(4);
        root.right = new TreeNode(8);
        root.left.left = new TreeNode(11);
        root.left.left.left = new TreeNode(7);
        root.left.left.right = new TreeNode(2);
        root.right.left = new TreeNode(13);
        root.right.right = new TreeNode(4);
        root.right.right.right = new TreeNode(1);

        int targetSum = 22;
        boolean result = solution.hasPathSum(root, targetSum);
        System.out.println(result);  // Output should be true
    }
}
```

Understanding the code:

- Base Case: If the *tree is empty* (`root == null`), there's no path, so we return `false`.
- Leaf Node Check: If the current node is a leaf node (*both left and right children are* `null`), we check if the *current* path sum equals `targetSum`. If it does, we return `true`.
- Recursive Step: For *non-leaf* nodes, we subtract the *node's value* from `targetSum` and recursively check the left and right subtrees. If *either subtree* has a path that satisfies the condition, the function returns `true`.

Time and Space Complexity:

- Time Complexity: `O(n)`, where n is the number of nodes in the tree. We visit each node exactly once.

- Space Complexity: `O(h)`, where `h` is the height of the tree. The space complexity is determined by the recursion stack, which in the worst case (for a skewed tree) can be equal to the height of the tree.

Problem 7: Path Sum II

Problem statement

Given the root of a binary tree and an integer targetSum, *return all root-to-leaf paths* where the sum of the node values in the path equals targetSum. Each path should be returned as a list of the node values, not node references.

Solution

This is a variation of the previous problem. We can break down the solution as follows:

Clarifying Questions

1. What is a root-to-leaf path?
   A root-to-leaf path is a sequence of nodes in a binary tree starting from the root node and ending at a leaf node.
2. What do we need to return?
   We need to return ***all root-to-leaf paths*** where the sum of the node values equals `targetSum`. Each path should be represented as a list of node values.

Example:
Consider the following binary tree:

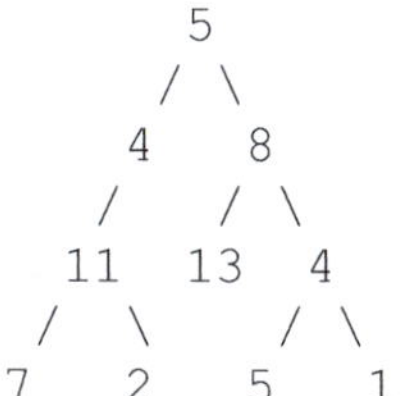

Input: The `root` of the binary tree and `targetSum = 22`.
Output: `[[5, 4, 11, 2], [5, 8, 4, 5]]`

Approach

Similar to the previous problem, the main idea is to use *DFS* to explore all root-to-leaf paths while keeping track of the path from the root to the current node and the running sum. If a path with ***the required sum is found at a leaf node***, ***the path is added to the result.***

Code Solution

```
import java.util.ArrayList;
import java.util.List;

class TreeNode {
   int val;
   TreeNode left;
   TreeNode right;

   TreeNode(int x) {
       val = x;
   }
}

public class PathSumII {

   public List<List<Integer>> pathSum(TreeNode root, int targetSum)
{
       List<List<Integer>> paths = new ArrayList<>();
       if (root == null) return paths;
       dfs(root, targetSum, new ArrayList<>(), paths);
       return paths;
   }

   private void dfs(TreeNode node, int remainingSum, List<Integer>
path, List<List<Integer>> paths) {
       if (node == null) return;

       // Add the current node to the path
       path.add(node.val);

       // Check if we've reached a leaf node and the remaining sum
equals the node's value
       if (node.left == null && node.right == null && remainingSum
== node.val) {
           // Make a copy of the current path and add it to the
paths list
           paths.add(new ArrayList<>(path));
       } else {
           // Continue to explore the left and right subtree with
the updated remaining sum
           dfs(node.left, remainingSum - node.val, path, paths);
           dfs(node.right, remainingSum - node.val, path, paths);
       }

       // Backtrack: remove the current node from the path
       path.remove(path.size() - 1);
   }

   public static void main(String[] args) {
       PathSumII solution = new PathSumII();

       TreeNode root = new TreeNode(5);
```

```
        root.left = new TreeNode(4);
        root.right = new TreeNode(8);
        root.left.left = new TreeNode(11);
        root.left.left.left = new TreeNode(7);
        root.left.left.right = new TreeNode(2);
        root.right.left = new TreeNode(13);
        root.right.right = new TreeNode(4);
        root.right.right.left = new TreeNode(5);
        root.right.right.right = new TreeNode(1);

        int targetSum = 22;
        List<List<Integer>> result = solution.pathSum(root,
targetSum);
        for (List<Integer> path : result) {
            System.out.println(path);
        }
    }
}
```

Understanding the code:

- DFS Traversal: The function `dfs` recursively traverses the tree. For each node, the current path is updated by appending the node's value. If a leaf node is encountered and the remaining sum equals the node's value, the current path is added to the list of paths.
- Path List Management: The path is maintained as a list of integers, and a copy of this list is added to the result list when a valid path is found.
- Backtracking: After exploring a path, the function backtracks by removing the last node from the path list, allowing the function to explore other paths.

Time and Space Complexity

- Time Complexity: `O(n)`, where `n` is the number of nodes in the tree. We visit each node exactly once.
- Space Complexity: `O(H)`, where `h` is the height of the tree. The space complexity is determined by the recursion stack and the space required to store the paths. In the worst case (for a skewed tree), the recursion stack space is equal to the height of the tree.

Problem 8: Path Sum III

Problem Statement

Given the root of a binary tree and an integer targetSum, return the number of paths where the *sum of the values along the path equals targetSum.*

The path does *not need to start or end at the root or a leaf*, but it must go downwards (i.e., traveling only from parent nodes to child nodes).

Solution

Let's follow the structured approach to solve this problem.

Clarifying Questions

1. What is a valid path?
   A valid path is *any sequence of nodes in the tree where the sum of the node values equals* `targetSum`. The path does not need to start at the root or end at a leaf, but it must go downwards.
2. What do we need to return?
   We need to return the *total number of such paths* in the tree.

Example:
Consider the following binary tree:

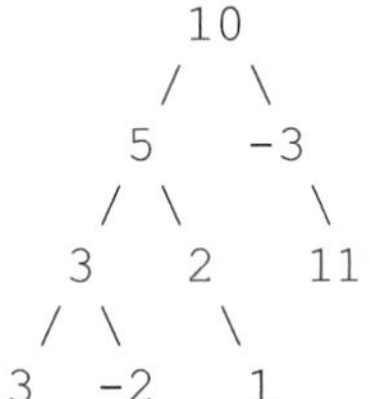

Input: The root of the binary tree and `targetSum = 8`.
Output: 3
The paths that sum to 8 are:

- 5 -> 3
- 5 -> 2 -> 1
- -3 -> 11

Brute Force Approach

A brute force approach would involve checking every possible path in the tree by *starting a new path from every node* and checking if the sum equals `targetSum`. However, this is inefficient and would result in a time complexity of $O(n^2)$.

Optimal Approach

The optimal approach is using DFS combined with a hashmap to keep track of cumulative sums.

As we traverse the tree, we keep track of the sum of all nodes from the root to the current node (`currentSum`).

For each node, we check if there exists a ***prefix sum*** that, *when subtracted from* `currentSum`*, gives us the* `targetSum`. This allows us to efficiently *count the number of valid paths* that end at the current node.

Hashmap stores the cumulative sums and their frequencies as we traverse the tree.

Code Solution

```
import java.util.HashMap;

class TreeNode {
   int val;
   TreeNode left;
   TreeNode right;

   TreeNode(int x) {
       val = x;
   }
}

public class PathSumIII {

   public int pathSum(TreeNode root, int targetSum) {
       HashMap<Long, Integer> prefixSumMap = new HashMap<>();
       prefixSumMap.put(0L, 1); // Initialize with 0 sum having one
count
       return dfs(root, 0L, targetSum, prefixSumMap);
   }

   private int dfs(TreeNode node, long currentSum, int targetSum,
HashMap<Long, Integer> prefixSumMap) {
       if (node == null) {
           return 0;
       }

       // Update the current path sum
       currentSum += node.val;

       // Find the number of valid paths that end at the current
node
       int numPathsToCurr = prefixSumMap.getOrDefault(currentSum -
targetSum, 0);

       // Update the prefix sum map with the current sum
       prefixSumMap.put(currentSum,
prefixSumMap.getOrDefault(currentSum, 0) + 1);

       // Recursively search the left and right subtrees
       int result = numPathsToCurr
               + dfs(node.left, currentSum, targetSum, prefixSumMap)
               + dfs(node.right, currentSum, targetSum,
prefixSumMap);

       // Restore the map, as the recursion goes back up the tree
       prefixSumMap.put(currentSum, prefixSumMap.get(currentSum) -
1);

       return result;
   }
```

```
    public static void main(String[] args) {
        PathSumIII solution = new PathSumIII();

        TreeNode root = new TreeNode(10);
        root.left = new TreeNode(5);
        root.right = new TreeNode(-3);
        root.left.left = new TreeNode(3);
        root.left.right = new TreeNode(2);
        root.right.right = new TreeNode(11);
        root.left.left.left = new TreeNode(3);
        root.left.left.right = new TreeNode(-2);
        root.left.right.right = new TreeNode(1);

        int targetSum = 8;
        int result = solution.pathSum(root, targetSum);
        System.out.println(result);  // Output should be 3

        // for big values
        TreeNode root2 = new TreeNode(1000000000);
        root2.left = new TreeNode(1000000000);
        root2.left.left = new TreeNode(294967296);
        root2.left.left.left = new TreeNode(1000000000);
        root2.left.left.left.left = new TreeNode(1000000000);
        root2.left.left.left.left.left = new TreeNode(1000000000);

        int targetSum2 = 1000000000;
        int result2 = solution.pathSum(root2, targetSum2);
        System.out.println(result2);  // Output should be 5
    }
}
```

Understanding the code:

- DFS Traversal: We traverse the tree using DFS. At each node, we calculate the `currentSum` as the sum of all node values from the root to the current node.
- Prefix Sum Check: We check if there exists a prefix sum (`currentSum - targetSum`) in the hash map. If such a prefix sum exists, it means there's a valid path ending at the current node with a sum equal to `targetSum`.
- HashMap Usage: The hash map (`prefixSumMap`) keeps track of the cumulative sums encountered during the traversal and the number of times each sum has occurred.
- Backtracking: After exploring a node and its children, we backtrack by decrementing the count of the `currentSum` in the hashmap. This ensures that the map reflects only the sums along the current path being explored.

Note:
In Java, the sum of large integers might exceed the maximum value that an int can store, leading to incorrect results. To handle this, we use ***long instead of int*** for the cumulative sums. This will prevent integer overflow and allows the solution to handle large values correctly.

Time and Space Complexity

- Time Complexity: `O(n)`, where `n` is the number of nodes in the tree. Each node is visited exactly once.
- Space Complexity: `O(h)`, where `h` is the height of the tree. This accounts for the recursion stack and the space required by the hash map, which in the worst case (for a skewed tree) can be equal to the height of the tree.

Problem 9: Invert the Binary Tree

Problem Statement

Given the root of a binary tree, invert the tree, and return its root.

Solution

Let's break down the approach step by step.

Clarifying Questions

Candidate: What does it mean to invert a binary tree?
Interviewer: Inverting a binary tree means swapping the left and right children of every node in the tree.
Candidate: What do we need to return?
Interviewer: We need to return the root of the inverted binary tree.

Example:

Original Tree

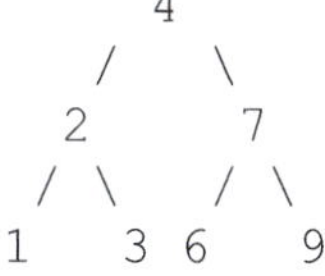

Inverted Tree

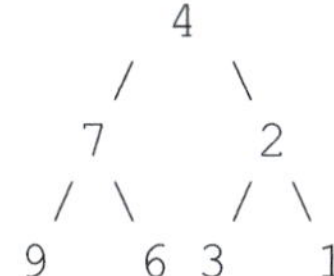

Input: The root of the binary tree.
Output: The root of the inverted binary tree.

Approach

The key idea is to traverse the tree, and at each node, swap its left and right children.

1. **Recursive Approach**: The simplest approach is to use recursion. For each node in the tree, we swap its left and right children and then recursively apply the same operation to its children.
2. **Iterative Approach**: An iterative approach using a *queue* (BFS) or a *stack* (DFS) can also be used to invert the tree. This is particularly useful if you want to avoid deep recursion for very large trees.

Code - Recursive & Iterative Approach

```
import java.util.LinkedList;
import java.util.Queue;

class TreeNode {
    int val;
    TreeNode left;
    TreeNode right;

    TreeNode(int x) {
        val = x;
    }
}

public class InvertBinaryTree {

    public TreeNode invertTree(TreeNode root) {
        if (root == null) {
            return null;
        }

        // Swap the left and right children
        TreeNode temp = root.left;
        root.left = root.right;
        root.right = temp;

        // Recursively invert the left and right subtrees
        invertTree(root.left);
        invertTree(root.right);

        return root;
    }

    public TreeNode invertTreeIterative(TreeNode root) {
        if (root == null) {
            return null;
        }

        Queue<TreeNode> queue = new LinkedList<>();
        queue.add(root);

        while (!queue.isEmpty()) {
            TreeNode current = queue.poll();

            // Swap the left and right children
            TreeNode temp = current.left;
            current.left = current.right;
            current.right = temp;

            // Add children to the queue to process them
            if (current.left != null) {
                queue.add(current.left);
            }
```

```
            if (current.right != null) {
                queue.add(current.right);
            }
        }

        return root;
    }

    private void printTree(TreeNode root) {
        if (root == null) {
            System.out.println("Tree is empty");
            return;
        }

        Queue<TreeNode> queue = new LinkedList<>();
        queue.add(root);

        while (!queue.isEmpty()) {
            int levelSize = queue.size();

            while (levelSize > 0) {
                TreeNode currentNode = queue.poll();
                System.out.print(currentNode.val + " ");

                if (currentNode.left != null) {
                    queue.add(currentNode.left);
                }
                if (currentNode.right != null) {
                    queue.add(currentNode.right);
                }

                levelSize--;
            }
            System.out.println();  // Move to the next level
        }
    }

    public static void main(String[] args) {
        InvertBinaryTree solution = new InvertBinaryTree();

        TreeNode root = new TreeNode(4);
        root.left = new TreeNode(2);
        root.right = new TreeNode(7);
        root.left.left = new TreeNode(1);
        root.left.right = new TreeNode(3);
        root.right.left = new TreeNode(6);
        root.right.right = new TreeNode(9);

        TreeNode invertedRoot = solution.invertTree(root);
        solution.printTree(invertedRoot);

        TreeNode inverted2 =
solution.invertTreeIterative(invertedRoot);
        solution.printTree(inverted2);
```

```
    }
}
```

Understanding the Code:

- Recursive Approach: The function invertTree is called recursively for each node, swapping its left and right children. This continues until all nodes have been processed.
- Iterative Approach (BFS): A queue is used to perform a breadth-first traversal of the tree. For each node, we swap its children and then add the children to the queue for further processing.

Time and Space Complexity

- Time Complexity: `O(n)`, where `n` is the number of nodes in the tree. Every node is visited exactly once.
- Space Complexity:
    - Recursive Approach: `O(h)`, where `h` is the height of the tree. This accounts for the recursion stack.
    - Iterative Approach: `O(n)`, where `n` is the number of nodes in the tree. This accounts for the space used by the queue.

The recursive approach is more intuitive, while the iterative approach avoids deep recursion and can be more suitable for very large trees.

Problem 10: Diameter of Binary Tree

Problem Statement

Given the root of a binary tree, return the length of the diameter of the tree.

Solution

Let's use a structured approach to solve this problem.

Clarifying Questions

Candidate: To Clarify, what is the diameter of a binary tree?
Interviewer: The diameter is the length of the longest path between any two nodes in the tree, measured in the number of edges.

Candidate: What do we need to return?
Interviewer: We need to return the length of this longest path.

Example:
Let's take an example to understand better, consider the following binary tree:

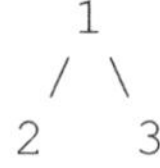

```
    1
   / \
  2   3
```

```
  / \
 4   5
```

Input: The root of the binary tree.
Output: 3
Explanation: The longest path is `[4, 2, 1, 3]` or `[5, 2, 1, 3]`, both with length 3.

Approach

To solve this problem of finding the diameter of a binary tree, we need to determine the longest path between any two nodes in the tree. This path may or may not pass through the root, and the length of the path is measured in terms of the number of edges between the nodes.

We can solve this problem using depth-first search (DFS).

For each node, *we calculate the height of its left and right subtrees.* The potential diameter at that node is the sum of the heights of the left and right subtrees.

We will keep track of the maximum diameter found during the traversal.

Code

```
class TreeNode {
   int val;
   TreeNode left;
   TreeNode right;

   TreeNode(int x) {
       val = x;
   }
}

public class DiameterOfBinaryTree {

   private int diameter;

   public int diameterOfBinaryTree(TreeNode root) {
       diameter = 0;
       height(root);
       return diameter;
   }

   private int height(TreeNode node) {
       if (node == null) {
           return 0;
       }

       // Recursively find the height of the left and right
subtrees
       int leftHeight = height(node.left);
       int rightHeight = height(node.right);
```

```
        // Update the diameter if the path through this node is
larger
        diameter = Math.max(diameter, leftHeight + rightHeight);

        // Return the height of the current node
        return 1 + Math.max(leftHeight, rightHeight);
    }

    public static void main(String[] args) {
        DiameterOfBinaryTree solution = new DiameterOfBinaryTree();

        TreeNode root = new TreeNode(1);
        root.left = new TreeNode(2);
        root.right = new TreeNode(3);
        root.left.left = new TreeNode(4);
        root.left.right = new TreeNode(5);

        int result = solution.diameterOfBinaryTree(root);
        System.out.println(result);  // Output should be 3
    }
}
```

Understanding the code:

- **Recursive DFS**: The `height` function calculates the height of the tree while also updating the diameter. For each node, it calculates the height of its left and right subtrees, and then checks if the sum of these heights is greater than the current maximum diameter.
- **Height Calculation**: The height of a node is `1 + max(leftHeight, rightHeight)`, which accounts for the node itself plus the taller of its two subtrees.
- **Diameter Update**: The `diameter` is updated at each node based on the sum of the heights of the left and right subtrees (`leftHeight + rightHeight`), which represents the longest path passing through that node.

Time and Space Complexity

- Time Complexity: `O(n)`, where `n` is the number of nodes in the tree. Each node is visited exactly once.
- Space Complexity: `O(h)`, where `h` is the height of the tree. The space complexity is determined by the recursion stack, which in the worst case (for a skewed tree) can be equal to the height of the tree.

Problem 11: Lowest Common Ancestor of a Binary Tree

Problem statement

Given a binary tree, find the lowest common ancestor (LCA) of two given nodes in the tree.

Solution

Let's use a structured approach to solve this problem.

Clarifying Questions

Candidate: What is the Lowest Common Ancestor (LCA)?
Interviewer: The LCA of two nodes p and q in a binary tree is the lowest node that has both p and q as ***descendants***. A node can be a descendant of itself.
Candidate: What do we need to return?
Interviewer: We need to return the LCA of the two given nodes.

Example:
Consider the following binary tree:

```
      3
     / \
    5   1
   / \ / \
  6  2 0  8
    / \
   7   4
```

Input:`root = [3,5,1,6,2,0,8,null,null,7,4],p = 5,q = 1`
Output: 3
- Explanation: The LCA of nodes 5 and 1 is 3.

Input: `root = [3,5,1,6,2,0,8,null,null,7,4],p = 5,q = 4`
Output: 5
- Explanation: The LCA of nodes 5 and 4 is 5 since 5 is a direct ancestor of 4.

Approach

We can solve this problem by traversing the tree recursively (depth-first search).

For each node, we check whether it is equal to p, q, or `null`. If it is equal to either p or q, then the current node is the LCA for the nodes p and q.

- If the current node is not p or q, we recursively search the left and right subtrees for p and q.
- If both subtrees return a non-null result, it means that p and ``` are found in different subtrees, and the current node is their LCA.
- If only one subtree returns a non-null result, the non-null result is the LCA.

Code Solution

```
class TreeNode {
    int val;
    TreeNode left;
    TreeNode right;
```

```
    TreeNode(int x) {
        val = x;
    }
}

public class LowestCommonAncestor {

    public TreeNode lowestCommonAncestor(TreeNode root, TreeNode p,
TreeNode q) {
        // Base case: if root is null or equals p or q
        if (root == null || root == p || root == q) {
            return root;
        }

        // Recur for the left and right subtrees
        TreeNode left = lowestCommonAncestor(root.left, p, q);
        TreeNode right = lowestCommonAncestor(root.right, p, q);

        // If both left and right return non-null, this node is the
LCA
        if (left != null && right != null) {
            return root;
        }

        // Otherwise, return the non-null value
        return left != null ? left : right;
    }

    public static void main(String[] args) {
        LowestCommonAncestor solution = new LowestCommonAncestor();

        TreeNode root = new TreeNode(3);
        root.left = new TreeNode(5);
        root.right = new TreeNode(1);
        root.left.left = new TreeNode(6);
        root.left.right = new TreeNode(2);
        root.right.left = new TreeNode(0);
        root.right.right = new TreeNode(8);
        root.left.right.left = new TreeNode(7);
        root.left.right.right = new TreeNode(4);

        TreeNode p = root.left; // Node 5
        TreeNode q = root.right; // Node 1

        TreeNode result = solution.lowestCommonAncestor(root, p, q);
        System.out.println("LCA of 5 and 1 is: " + result.val);  //
Output should be 3

        p = root.left; // Node 5
        q = root.left.right.right; // Node 4

        result = solution.lowestCommonAncestor(root, p, q);
        System.out.println("LCA of 5 and 4 is: " + result.val);  //
Output should be 5
```

```
    }
}
```

Time and Space Complexity

- Time Complexity: `O(n)`, where `n` is the number of nodes in the tree. In the worst case, we might visit every node.
- Space Complexity: `O(h)`, where `h` is the height of the tree. This accounts for the recursion stack. In the worst case (for a skewed tree), the height of the tree could be `O(n)`.

Problem 12: Boundary of a Binary Tree

Problem Statement

The *boundary of a binary tree* is the concatenation of the root, the left boundary, the leaves ordered from left-to-right, and the reverse order of the right boundary.

The left boundary is the set of nodes defined by the following:
- The root node's left child is in the left boundary. If the root does not have a left child, then the left boundary is empty.
- If a node is in the left boundary and has a left child, then the left child is in the left boundary.
- If a node is in the left boundary, has no left child, but has a right child, then the right child is in the left boundary.
- The leftmost leaf is not in the left boundary.

The right boundary is similar to the left boundary, except it is the right side of the root's right subtree. Again, the leaf is not part of the right boundary, and the right boundary is empty if the root does not have a right child.

The leaves are nodes that do not have any children. For this problem, the root is not a leaf.

Given the root of a binary tree, return the values of its boundary.

Solution

Let's go through this coding interview question as if we were in a real-life interview setting.

Clarifying Questions

Candidate:
To clarify the problem, it seems we need to return the boundary of a binary tree. The boundary should include the root, the left boundary (excluding leaves), all the leaf nodes, and the right boundary in reverse order (again, excluding leaves). Is that correct?

Interviewer:
Yes, that's correct.

Candidate:
Great! I have a couple more clarifying questions to ensure we're on the same page:

1. For a tree with only one node (the root), should the boundary be just that single node?
2. If a tree does not have a left or right child, should the corresponding boundary (left or right) be empty?
3. Are there any constraints on the tree's height or the number of nodes?

Interviewer:

1. Yes, if the tree has only one node, the boundary should just be that node.
2. Correct. If there's no left or right child, the boundary on that side would be empty.
3. You can assume the tree height can be arbitrary, and the tree can have up to a few thousand nodes.

Candidate:
Thanks for the clarification! I'll start by discussing a brute force approach and its limitations, then I'll suggest an optimal solution.

Brute Force Approach

The brute force approach involves three separate traversals:

1. Left Boundary: Traverse down the left edge, adding nodes to the boundary list.
2. Leaves: Traverse the entire tree to collect all leaf nodes.
3. Right Boundary: Traverse down the right edge, adding nodes in reverse order to the boundary list.

Efficiency:

- Time Complexity: `O(n + n + n)`, simplifying to `O(3n)` which is `O(n)`, since each node might be visited up to three times.
- Space Complexity: `O(n)` for the list storing boundary nodes.

However, this approach is *not optimal because of redundant traversals.* Let's improve it.

Optimal Approach

We can achieve the desired result by traversing a tree in a structured and efficient manner that reduces overall computational overhead compared to a brute force approach.

Code

```
import java.util.ArrayList;
import java.util.List;

class TreeNode {
    int val;
```

```
    TreeNode left;
    TreeNode right;

    TreeNode(int x) {
        val = x;
    }
}

public class BinaryTreeBoundary {

    public List<Integer> boundaryOfBinaryTree(TreeNode root) {
        List<Integer> boundary = new ArrayList<>();
        if (root == null) return boundary;

        // Add root node first (root itself is part of the boundary)
        boundary.add(root.val);

        // Collect the left boundary (excluding the root and leaves)
        addLeftBoundary(root.left, boundary);

        // Collect all leaf nodes
        addLeaves(root.left, boundary);
        addLeaves(root.right, boundary);

        // Collect the right boundary (excluding the root and
leaves)
        addRightBoundary(root.right, boundary);

        return boundary;
    }

    private void addLeftBoundary(TreeNode node, List<Integer>
boundary) {
        while (node != null) {
            if (!isLeaf(node)) boundary.add(node.val);
            if (node.left != null) node = node.left;
            else node = node.right;
        }
    }

    private void addRightBoundary(TreeNode node, List<Integer>
boundary) {
        List<Integer> temp = new ArrayList<>();
        while (node != null) {
            if (!isLeaf(node)) temp.add(node.val);
            if (node.right != null) node = node.right;
            else node = node.left;
        }
        // Add collected right boundary in reverse order
        for (int i = temp.size() - 1; i >= 0; i--) {
            boundary.add(temp.get(i));
        }
    }
```

```
    private void addLeaves(TreeNode node, List<Integer> boundary) {
        if (node == null) return;
        if (isLeaf(node)) {
            boundary.add(node.val);
        } else {
            addLeaves(node.left, boundary);
            addLeaves(node.right, boundary);
        }
    }

    private boolean isLeaf(TreeNode node) {
        return node.left == null && node.right == null;
    }

    // Main method to test the implementation with multiple test
cases
    public static void main(String[] args) {
        BinaryTreeBoundary treeBoundary = new BinaryTreeBoundary();

        // Test Case 1: A typical binary tree
        TreeNode root1 = new TreeNode(1);
        root1.left = new TreeNode(2);
        root1.right = new TreeNode(3);
        root1.left.left = new TreeNode(4);
        root1.left.right = new TreeNode(5);
        root1.right.left = new TreeNode(6);
        root1.right.right = new TreeNode(7);
        root1.left.left.left = new TreeNode(8);
        root1.left.left.right = new TreeNode(9);
        root1.left.right.left = new TreeNode(10);
        root1.right.left.left = new TreeNode(11);
        root1.right.right.right = new TreeNode(12);

        System.out.println("Boundary of the binary tree (Test Case
1): " + treeBoundary.boundaryOfBinaryTree(root1));

        // Test Case 2: A tree with only one node
        TreeNode root2 = new TreeNode(1);
        System.out.println("Boundary of the binary tree (Test Case
2): " + treeBoundary.boundaryOfBinaryTree(root2));

        // Test Case 3: A left-skewed binary tree
        TreeNode root3 = new TreeNode(1);
        root3.left = new TreeNode(2);
        root3.left.left = new TreeNode(3);
        root3.left.left.left = new TreeNode(4);
        System.out.println("Boundary of the binary tree (Test Case
3): " + treeBoundary.boundaryOfBinaryTree(root3));

        // Test Case 4: A right-skewed binary tree
        TreeNode root4 = new TreeNode(1);
        root4.right = new TreeNode(2);
        root4.right.right = new TreeNode(3);
        root4.right.right.right = new TreeNode(4);
```

```
        System.out.println("Boundary of the binary tree (Test Case
4): " + treeBoundary.boundaryOfBinaryTree(root4));

        // Test Case 5: A tree with no left or right boundary (only
root and leaves)
        TreeNode root5 = new TreeNode(1);
        root5.left = new TreeNode(2);
        root5.right = new TreeNode(3);
        root5.left.right = new TreeNode(4);
        root5.right.left = new TreeNode(5);
        System.out.println("Boundary of the binary tree (Test Case
5): " + treeBoundary.boundaryOfBinaryTree(root5));
    }
}
```

Although some nodes are visited more than once as per the code, the traversal strategy avoids revisiting nodes unnecessarily.

Time and Space Complexity

- Time Complexity: `O(n)`, where `n` is the number of nodes in the tree.
- Space Complexity: `O(n)`, as the boundary nodes are stored in a list, proportional to the number of nodes.

Problem 13: Validate Binary Search Tree

Problem Statement

Given the root of a binary tree, determine if it is a valid binary search tree (BST).

Solution

Let's work through this problem using the structured approach as if we're in a real-life coding interview setting.

Clarifying Questions

Candidate:
Definition of a Valid BST: Just to confirm, a valid Binary Search Tree (BST) is defined as a binary tree in which for every node:

- The value of all nodes in the left subtree is less than the node's value.
- The value of all nodes in the right subtree is greater than the node's value.
- This condition must hold true for every node in the tree. Is that correct?

Interviewer:
Yes, your understanding is correct.

Candidate:
Tree Characteristics: Can the tree contain duplicate values, or should all values be unique?
Interviewer:

The tree should not contain duplicate values. All values must be unique.

Candidate:
Thank you for the clarification! Let's discuss a brute force approach first, and then I'll suggest an optimal approach.

Brute Force Approach

A brute force method would involve *checking each node* to ensure that all values in the left subtree are less than the node's value, and all values in the right subtree are greater. This could be done by recursively validating the entire subtree for each node.
Efficiency:

- Time Complexity: $O(n^2)$ because for each node, we potentially traverse all nodes in its subtree to validate the BST property.
- Space Complexity: `O(h)` where `h` is the height of the tree, due to the recursive stack.

This approach is inefficient because it results in redundant traversals.

Optimal Approach

The optimal solution would be validating the BST properties during ***a single traversal of the tree***.

We can use a recursive function that passes down the *allowable range for each node*:

- For the root node, the allowable range is `(-∞,∞)`.
- For the left child, the range is `(-∞,node.val)`.
- For the right child, the range is `(node.val,∞)`.

This way, each node is checked to see if it falls within its allowable range, ensuring the BST properties are maintained.

Code Solution

```
class TreeNode {
    int val;
    TreeNode left;
    TreeNode right;

    TreeNode(int x) {
        val = x;
    }
}

public class ValidateBinarySearchTree {

    public boolean isValidBST(TreeNode root) {
        return validate(root, null, null);
    }

    private boolean validate(TreeNode node, Integer low, Integer
high) {
```

```
        // Base case: If the node is null, it's a valid BST
        if (node == null) {
            return true;
        }

        // Check if the current node's value is within the valid
range
        if ((low != null && node.val <= low) || (high != null &&
node.val >= high)) {
            return false;
        }

        // Recursively validate the left and right subtrees
        return validate(node.left, low, node.val) &&
validate(node.right, node.val, high);
    }

    // Main method to test the implementation with multiple test
cases
    public static void main(String[] args) {
        ValidateBinarySearchTree validator = new
ValidateBinarySearchTree();

        // Test Case 1: A valid BST
        TreeNode root1 = new TreeNode(2);
        root1.left = new TreeNode(1);
        root1.right = new TreeNode(3);
        System.out.println("Is the tree a valid BST (Test Case 1)? "
+ validator.isValidBST(root1)); // true

        // Test Case 2: An invalid BST
        TreeNode root2 = new TreeNode(5);
        root2.left = new TreeNode(1);
        root2.right = new TreeNode(4);
        root2.right.left = new TreeNode(3);
        root2.right.right = new TreeNode(6);
        System.out.println("Is the tree a valid BST (Test Case 2)? "
+ validator.isValidBST(root2)); // false

        // Test Case 3: A single node tree
        TreeNode root3 = new TreeNode(1);
        System.out.println("Is the tree a valid BST (Test Case 3)? "
+ validator.isValidBST(root3)); // true

        // Test Case 4: A large valid BST
        TreeNode root4 = new TreeNode(10);
        root4.left = new TreeNode(5);
        root4.right = new TreeNode(15);
        root4.right.left = new TreeNode(11);
        root4.right.right = new TreeNode(20);
        System.out.println("Is the tree a valid BST (Test Case 4)? "
+ validator.isValidBST(root4)); // true

        // Test Case 5: A tree with invalid BST properties
```

```
        TreeNode root5 = new TreeNode(10);
        root5.left = new TreeNode(5);
        root5.right = new TreeNode(15);
        root5.left.left = new TreeNode(6); // Invalid, because 6 > 5
but is in the left subtree of 10
        System.out.println("Is the tree a valid BST (Test Case 5)? "
+ validator.isValidBST(root5)); // false
    }
}
```

Time and Space Complexity

- Time Complexity: O(n), where n is the number of nodes in the tree. Each node is visited exactly once during the traversal.
- Space Complexity: O(h), where h is the height of the tree. This is the space used by the recursive call stack. In the worst case, if the tree is skewed, h could be n, making the space complexity O(n).

Problem 14: Kth Smallest Element in BST

Problem Statement

Given the root of a binary search tree, and an integer k, return the kth smallest value (1-indexed) of all the values of the nodes in the tree.

Solution

Let's work through this problem using the structured approach as if we're in a real-life coding interview setting.

Clarifying Questions

Candidate:
Can we assume that the tree is balanced, or do we need to consider both balanced and unbalanced trees?
Interviewer:
Consider both balanced and unbalanced trees.

Candidate:
Should we assume that k is always valid, meaning that 1 <= k <= number of nodes in the tree?
Interviewer:
Yes, you can assume k is always valid.

Candidate:
Thank you for the clarifications! Let's discuss a brute force approach first, and then I'll suggest an optimal approach.

Brute Force Approach

The brute force method would involve performing an in-order traversal of the BST and *storing all node values in a list.*

Since in-order traversal gives us nodes in ascending order, we can directly access the kth smallest element by retrieving the (k-1)th index from the list.

This method is *straightforward* but *not the most space-efficient*, as it requires storing all the node values.

Optimal Approach

We can optimize space usage *by avoiding storing all node values.* Instead, we can perform an in-order traversal and *count the nodes as we go.* Once we reach the ***k***th ***node during traversal, we return*** its value immediately.

This approach leverages the BST property, where in-order traversal naturally gives nodes in ascending order. We simply keep a counter and return the node's value when the counter equals k.

Code Solution

```
class TreeNode {
    int val;
    TreeNode left;
    TreeNode right;

    TreeNode(int x) {
        val = x;
    }
}

public class KthSmallestElementInBST {

    private int count;
    private int result;

    public int kthSmallest(TreeNode root, int k) {
        // Reset count and result before each new search
        count = 0;
        result = -1;

        inOrderTraversal(root, k);
        return result;
    }

    private void inOrderTraversal(TreeNode node, int k) {
        if (node == null) {
            return;
        }

        // Traverse the left subtree
        inOrderTraversal(node.left, k);
```

```
        // Increment the counter when visiting a node
        count++;

        // If the counter equals k, we've found our k-th smallest
element
        if (count == k) {
            result = node.val;
            return;
        }

        // Traverse the right subtree
        inOrderTraversal(node.right, k);
    }

    // Main method to test the implementation with multiple test
cases
    public static void main(String[] args) {
        KthSmallestElementInBST solution = new
KthSmallestElementInBST();

        // Test Case 1: A simple BST
        TreeNode root1 = new TreeNode(3);
        root1.left = new TreeNode(1);
        root1.right = new TreeNode(4);
        root1.left.right = new TreeNode(2);
        System.out.println("The 1st smallest element (Test Case 1): "
+ solution.kthSmallest(root1, 1)); // 1
        System.out.println("The 2nd smallest element (Test Case 1): "
+ solution.kthSmallest(root1, 2)); // 2
        System.out.println("The 3rd smallest element (Test Case 1): "
+ solution.kthSmallest(root1, 3)); // 3

        // Test Case 2: A more complex BST
        TreeNode root2 = new TreeNode(5);
        root2.left = new TreeNode(3);
        root2.right = new TreeNode(6);
        root2.left.left = new TreeNode(2);
        root2.left.right = new TreeNode(4);
        root2.left.left.left = new TreeNode(1);
        System.out.println("The 3rd smallest element (Test Case 2): "
+ solution.kthSmallest(root2, 3)); // 3
        System.out.println("The 4th smallest element (Test Case 2): "
+ solution.kthSmallest(root2, 4)); // 4

        // Test Case 3: A tree with only one node
        TreeNode root3 = new TreeNode(1);
        System.out.println("The 1st smallest element (Test Case 3): "
+ solution.kthSmallest(root3, 1)); // 1

        // Test Case 4: A tree with unbalanced nodes
        TreeNode root4 = new TreeNode(10);
        root4.left = new TreeNode(5);
        root4.left.left = new TreeNode(1);
```

```
        root4.left.left.right = new TreeNode(2);
        root4.left.left.right.right = new TreeNode(3);
        System.out.println("The 3rd smallest element (Test Case 4): "
+ solution.kthSmallest(root4, 3)); // 3
    }
}
```

Time and Space Complexity:

- Time Complexity: `O(n)`, where `n` is the number of nodes in the tree. The in-order traversal visits each node exactly once.
- Space Complexity: `O(h)`, where `h` is the height of the tree, which represents the space used by the recursive call stack. In the worst case, for a completely unbalanced tree, `h` could be `n`, so the space complexity would be `O(n)`. In a balanced tree, the space complexity would be `O(log n)`.

Problem 15: Binary Search Tree Iterator

Problem Statement

Implement the ***BSTIterator*** class that represents an iterator over the in-order traversal of a binary search tree (BST):

- `BSTIterator(TreeNode root)` Initializes an object of the *BSTIterator* class. The root of the BST is given as part of the constructor. The pointer should be initialized to a non-existent number smaller than any element in the BST.
- `boolean hasNext()` Returns true if there exists a number in the traversal to the right of the pointer, otherwise returns false.
- `int next()` Moves the pointer to the right, then returns the number at the pointer.

Notice that by initializing the pointer to a non-existent smallest number, the first call to `next()` will return the smallest element in the BST.

You may assume that `next()` calls will always be valid. That is, there will be at least a next number in the in-order traversal when `next()` is called.

Solution

Let's work through this problem using the structured approach.

Clarifying Questions

Candidate:
The BST structure ensures that an in-order traversal will yield elements in ascending order. Can I assume that this property holds for all input trees?
Interviewer:
Yes, you can assume the BST property holds.

Candidate:

Should the implementation focus on optimizing memory usage, or is a simpler implementation with more memory consumption acceptable?
Interviewer:
Try to balance both memory usage and simplicity. If possible, optimize for memory without sacrificing simplicity.

Candidate:
Should the operations `hasNext()` and `next()` be optimized for time complexity, or is a straightforward approach acceptable?
Interviewer:
The operations should be efficient, preferably `O(1)` time for `hasNext()` and `next()`.

Candidate:
Thank you for the clarifications! Let's proceed with the brute force approach and then optimize it.

Brute Force Approach

A straightforward approach would be to perform an in-order traversal of the BST in the constructor and store the result in a list. The `hasNext()` method would then check if there are more elements in the list, and `next()` would return the next element in the list.
Efficiency:

- Time Complexity:
  - Preprocessing (in-order traversal): `O(n)`
  - `next()`: `O(1)`, since it simply retrieves the next element from the list.
  - `hasNext()`: `O(1)`, since it checks if there are remaining elements.
- Space Complexity: `O(n)` where `n` is the number of nodes, due to storing the entire in-order traversal in a list.

This approach is easy to implement but uses extra space. Let's optimize it.

Optimal Approach

Instead of storing all elements in a list, we can simulate in-order traversal *using an explicit stack*. The stack will store nodes as we traverse left down the tree. The `next()` method will ***pop*** from the stack, process the node, and *then push the right child (and all its left children)* onto the stack if it exists.

This approach uses space proportional to the height of the tree, making it more memory efficient.

Code Solution

```
import java.util.Stack;

class TreeNode {
    int val;
    TreeNode left;
    TreeNode right;
```

```
    TreeNode(int x) {
        val = x;
    }
}

public class BSTIterator {

    private Stack<TreeNode> stack;

    public BSTIterator(TreeNode root) {
        // Initialize the stack and push the leftmost path in the
tree
        stack = new Stack<>();
        pushLeftNodes(root);
    }

    // Push all left nodes of the given node onto the stack
    private void pushLeftNodes(TreeNode node) {
        while (node != null) {
            stack.push(node);
            node = node.left;
        }
    }

    // Return true if there are more nodes to process
    public boolean hasNext() {
        return !stack.isEmpty();
    }

    // Return the next smallest value in the BST
    public int next() {
        // Pop the top node from the stack
        TreeNode nextNode = stack.pop();

        // If the popped node has a right child, push its leftmost
path onto the stack
        if (nextNode.right != null) {
            pushLeftNodes(nextNode.right);
        }

        return nextNode.val;
    }

    // Main method to test the implementation
    public static void main(String[] args) {
        // Test Case 1: A typical BST
        TreeNode root1 = new TreeNode(7);
        root1.left = new TreeNode(3);
        root1.right = new TreeNode(15);
        root1.right.left = new TreeNode(9);
        root1.right.right = new TreeNode(20);

        BSTIterator iterator1 = new BSTIterator(root1);
        System.out.println(iterator1.next());    // Output: 3
```

```
        System.out.println(iterator1.next());     // Output: 7
        System.out.println(iterator1.hasNext()); // Output: true
        System.out.println(iterator1.next());     // Output: 9
        System.out.println(iterator1.hasNext()); // Output: true
        System.out.println(iterator1.next());     // Output: 15
        System.out.println(iterator1.hasNext()); // Output: true
        System.out.println(iterator1.next());     // Output: 20
        System.out.println(iterator1.hasNext()); // Output: false
    }
}
```

Time and Space Complexity

- Time Complexity:
  - `next()`: `O(1)` amortized time complexity. Each element is pushed and popped from the stack exactly once.
  - `hasNext()`: `O(1)` because it simply checks if the stack is non-empty.
- Space Complexity: `O(h)`, where `h` is the height of the tree. This is because the stack contains at most one path from the root to a leaf node.

Chapter 15: Heaps

Introduction to Heaps

Heaps are a fundamental data structure that plays a critical role in many algorithms, especially those that involve *priority queues*, *sorting*, and *graph algorithms*.

A heap is a specialized tree-based data structure that satisfies the *heap property*.

The heap property is divided into two categories:

- **Min-Heap**: The key at the *root* must be the *minimum* among all the keys present in the heap, and the same property must be recursively true for all nodes in the heap.
- **Max-Heap**: The key at the *root* must be the *maximum* among all the keys present in the heap, and the same property must be recursively true for all nodes in the heap.

Heaps are typically implemented as binary trees, where every parent node is greater (in a max-heap) or smaller (in a min-heap) than its children.

They are complete binary trees, meaning all levels of the tree are fully filled except possibly for the last level, which is filled from left to right.

Why Are Heaps Important?

Heaps are used to implement priority queues, which are essential in various algorithms like Dijkstra's shortest path, Huffman coding, and the heap sort algorithm.

The operations on heaps are efficient, with *insertion*, *deletion*, and *access* to the *minimum* or *maximum* element (depending on the type of heap) all operating in ***logarithmic*** time, making them ideal for scenarios where such operations are frequently used.

Key Operations on Heaps

1. **Insertion**: `O(log n)`
   Insert a new element into the heap while maintaining the heap property.

   This operation involves adding the element at the end of the heap and then "*bubbling up*" to restore the heap property.

2. **Deletion (Extract Min/Extract Max)**: `O(log n)`
   Remove the root element (minimum in a min-heap or maximum in a max-heap).

The last element is moved to the root position, and the heap is then "*bubbled down*" to restore the heap property.

3. **Peek**: `O(1)`
   Retrieve, but do not remove, the root element..

4. **Heapify (Convert Array into Heap)**: `O(n)`
   Convert an arbitrary array into a heap. This is commonly used as the first step in heap sort.

5. **Heap Sort**: `O(n log n)`

   A comparison-based sorting algorithm that uses a heap to sort elements in `O(n log n)` time.

   Heap sort involves first building a heap (`O(n)`) and then repeatedly removing the root (`O(log n)`) until the heap is empty. The sorting operation thus takes `O(n log n)` time in total.

Most Popular Heap Questions

Heap based questions are very common in coding interview questions. LEt's dive into some of the most popular coding interview questions based on Heaps

Problem 1: Kth Largest Element in an Array

Problem Statement

Given an integer array `nums` and an integer `k`, return the `kth` largest element in the array.

Solution

You could ask the following clarifying questions to the interviewer before jumping into the solution. You conversation may go as follows:

Clarifying Questions

Before I proceed, I'd like to ask a few clarifying questions:

1. **Array Size**:
   a. Candidate: Is there any constraint on the size of the array? For example, can the array be very large?
   b. Interviewer: The Array can be very large.
2. **Element Values**:
   a. Candidate: Can the elements of the array be negative, or are they guaranteed to be non-negative?

   b. Interviewer: The elements of the array can be negative.
3. **Duplicates**:
   a. Candidate: Can the array contain duplicate elements, and if so, do duplicates affect the value of the kth largest element?
   b. Interviewer: The array can contain duplicate elements. Find the kth largest element in the sorted order, *not the kth distinct element*.
4. **Value of k**:
   a. Candidate: Is k guaranteed to be a valid number, i.e., between 1 and the size of the array?
   b. Interviewer: Assume that `k` is guaranteed to be a valid number

[Candidate]
Great, thanks for the clarifications! Now that I understand the problem better, I'll first talk about the brute force approach and then the optimal approach.

Brute Force Approach

The simplest way to find the kth largest element is to sort the entire array in descending order and then return the element at the index `k-1`.

While this approach will work, it's not the most efficient given that the array can be very large. Sorting the array will take `O(n log n)`, where `n` is the number of elements in the array.

Sorting the entire array is unnecessary if we're only interested in the kth largest element.

Optimal Approach

Here is the optimal approach:

- We can optimize the solution by using a ***Min Heap***. The idea is to maintain a heap of size `k` while traversing the array. This heap will store the `top k largest` elements.
- After processing all the elements, the root of the heap will contain the kth largest element.

Outline of the steps for implementation:
1. Create a Min Heap of size `k`.
2. Iterate through the array:
   - Add the current element to the heap.
   - If the heap size exceeds `k`, remove the smallest element (i.e., the root of the Min Heap).
3. After processing all elements, the ***root of the Min Heap will be the kth largest element***.

Code Solution

Here's the Java code implementing the optimal solution:

```
import java.util.PriorityQueue;
```

```
public class KthLargestElement {

    public int findKthLargest(int[] nums, int k) {
        // Create a Min Heap with a capacity of k
        PriorityQueue<Integer> minHeap = new PriorityQueue<>(k);

        // Process each element in the array
        for (int num : nums) {
            // Add the element to the heap
            minHeap.offer(num);

            // If the heap size exceeds k, remove the smallest
element
            if (minHeap.size() > k) {
                minHeap.poll();
            }
        }

        // The root of the heap is the kth largest element
        return minHeap.peek();
    }

    public static void main(String[] args) {
        KthLargestElement solution = new KthLargestElement();
        int[] nums = {3, 2, 1, 5, -6, 4};
        int k = 2;
        System.out.println("The " + k + "th largest element is " +
solution.findKthLargest(nums, k)); // Output: 4
    }
}
```

Time and Space Complexity

- Time Complexity: Inserting an element into a Min Heap takes `O(log k)` time. Since we do this for all `n` elements, the total time complexity is `O(n log k)`.
- Space Complexity: The space complexity is `O(k)` for storing the heap.

This approach is more efficient, as `k` is small compared to the `size` of the array.

Problem 2: Top K Frequent Elements

Problem Statement

Given an integer array `nums` and an integer `k`, return the `k` most frequent elements. You may return the answer in any order.

Solution

Let's use the real life interview setting format to approach this problem.

Clarifying Questions

Candidate: Thank you for the question. Before I proceed, I'd like to ask a few clarifying questions:

1. **Array Size:**
   a. Candidate: Is there any constraint on the size of the array? Can the array be very large?
   b. Interviewer: The array can be very large, so consider both time and space efficiency in your solution. However, assume that it can fit in memory.
2. **Element Values:**
   a. Candidate: Can the elements of the array be negative, or are they guaranteed to be non-negative?
   b. Interviewer: The elements in the array can be negative, and there are no constraints on the range of values.
3. **k Value:**
   a. Candidate: Is it guaranteed that `k` is always valid, i.e., `k` will not be greater than the number of unique elements in the array?
   b. Interviewer: Yes, `k` is guaranteed to be a valid number, meaning it will not exceed the number of unique elements in the array.
4. **Frequency Tie:**
   a. Candidate: If two elements have the same frequency, can we return them in any order, or is there a specific order you prefer?
   b. Interviewer: If two elements have the same frequency, you can return them in any order. There's no requirement for a specific order in the case of ties.

Candidate: Great, thanks for the clarifications! Now that I understand the problem better, I'll first talk about the brute force approach and then the optimal approach.

Brute Force Approach

The brute force approach would be *counting the frequency of each element in the array* and *then sorting* these frequencies to find the k most frequent elements.

Outline of the brute force logic:
1. Traverse the array and use a hashmap to count the frequency of each element.
2. Sort the elements based on their frequency in descending order.
3. Extract the top k elements from this sorted list.

Efficiency:
- Time Complexity: Counting the frequency takes `O(n)` time. Sorting the frequencies will take `O(m log m)`, where `m` is the number of unique elements. Therefore, the total time complexity is `O(n + m log m)`.
- Space Complexity: The space complexity is `O(m)` for storing the frequencies in the hash map.

This approach will work, but *sorting the entire frequency map is unnecessary* if we only need the *top k frequent* elements.

Optimal Approach

To optimize, we can use a Min Heap, which is well-suited when we want to find the k most frequent elements.

Here is the outline of the approach:

1. Traverse the array to count the frequency of each element using a hash map.
2. Use a Min Heap to store the k most frequent elements:
   - Iterate over the frequency map.
   - Add each element to the heap. If the heap size exceeds k, remove the element with the smallest frequency.
3. The heap will then contain the k most frequent elements.
4. Extract the elements from the heap to form the result.

Code Solution

Here's the Java code implementing the optimal solution using a Min Heap:

```
public class KMostFrequentElements {

   public int[] topKFrequent(int[] nums, int k) {
        // Step 1: Build a frequency map
        Map<Integer, Integer> frequencyMap = new HashMap<>();
        for (int num : nums) {
            frequencyMap.put(num, frequencyMap.getOrDefault(num, 0) +
1);
        }

        // Step 2: Use a Min Heap to keep track of the k most
frequent elements
        PriorityQueue<Map.Entry<Integer, Integer>> minHeap =
                new PriorityQueue<>((a, b) -> a.getValue() -
b.getValue());

        for (Map.Entry<Integer, Integer> entry :
frequencyMap.entrySet()) {
            minHeap.offer(entry);
            if (minHeap.size() > k) {
                minHeap.poll(); // Remove the element with the
smallest frequency
            }
        }

        // Step 3: Extract the top k frequent elements from the heap
        int[] result = new int[k];
        int index = 0;
        while (!minHeap.isEmpty()) {
            result[index++] = minHeap.poll().getKey();
        }

        return result;
   }
```

```
    public static void main(String[] args) {
        KMostFrequentElements solution = new KMostFrequentElements();
        int[] nums = {1, 1, 1, 2, 2, 3, -4, 3, 1, 2, 4, -1};
        int k = 2;
        int[] result = solution.topKFrequent(nums, k);
        System.out.print("The top " + k + " most frequent elements
are: ");
        for (int num : result) {
            System.out.print(num + " ");
        }
        // Expected output: [1, 2] (Order may vary)
    }
}
```

Note: You should test the solution with multiple examples in the real life interview.

Time and Space Complexity

- Time Complexity: Building the frequency map takes `O(n)`. Maintaining the heap takes `O(m log k)`, where `m` is the number of unique elements, so the total time complexity is `O(n + m log k)`.
- Space Complexity: The space complexity is `O(m)` for storing the frequency map and `O(k)` for the heap.

Problem 3: Merge K Sorted Lists

Problem Statement

You are given an array of `k linked-lists` lists, each linked-list is *sorted* in ascending order.

Merge all the linked-lists into one sorted linked-list and return it.

Solution

Let's use the real life interview setting format to approach this problem.

Clarifying Questions

1. **Linked List Size:**
   a. Candidate: Is there any constraint on the size of each linked list or the total number of nodes across all linked lists? Can the combined size be very large?
   b. Interviewer: There's no specific constraint on the size of each linked list. The total number of nodes across all linked lists can be very large, so consider *efficiency* in your solution.
2. **Number of Linked Lists (k):**
   a. Candidate: Is there a constraint on the value of `k`, the number of linked lists? Can `k` be very large?
   b. Interviewer: There's no specific constraint on `k`; it can also be very large.

3. **Input Structure**:
    a. Candidate: How will the linked lists be provided? Should we assume they are provided as an array of `ListNode` objects?
    b. Interviewer: You can assume that the linked lists are provided as an *array* of `ListNode` objects, where each ListNode represents the head of a sorted linked list.
4. **Duplicate Values**:
    a. Candidate: Can the linked lists contain *duplicate* values, and should those be handled in any specific way?
    b. Interviewer: The linked lists can contain duplicate values. Your merged list should also maintain the sorted order, including any duplicates.
5. **Memory Constraints**:
    a. Candidate: Are there any memory constraints we should consider when designing the solution?
    b. Interviewer: There are no specific memory constraints, but an efficient use of memory is always preferred.

Candidate: Great! Let's dive into the problem now that I have a clear understanding of the requirements.

Brute Force Approach

The simplest approach is to merge all the linked lists into a single list, and then sort that list.

The outline for that approach is:

1. Traverse each of the `k` linked lists and add all the elements to a single list.
2. Once all the elements are in a single list, *sort the list.*
3. Finally, *convert* the sorted list back into a linked list.

Efficiency:

- The *time complexity* for this approach would be `O(n log n)`, where `n` is the total number of nodes across all `k` linked lists. This includes `O(n)` for extracting all elements and `O(n log n)` for sorting.
- The *space complexity* would be `O(n)` for storing the nodes in a separate list before converting it back to a linked list.

While this approach works, it's not the most efficient given the problem constraints. *Sorting the entire list is unnecessary* if we can *leverage the sorted nature* of the individual linked lists.

Optimal Approach

A more efficient approach would be to use a Min Heap (Priority Queue) to merge the `k` sorted linked lists.

The idea is to always pick the smallest element among the current heads of the linked lists, and then add that element to the merged list.

Here is the outline of this approach:

1. Initialize a Min Heap that will store the *head* of each linked list.
2. Extract the *minimum element* from the heap, which represents the smallest current node across the k linked lists.
3. Add this node to the *result* linked list.
4. If the extracted node has a *next node*, *insert that next node into the heap.*
5. *Repeat the process* until all nodes are processed.

Code Solution

Here's the Java code implementing the optimal solution using a Min Heap:

```
import java.util.PriorityQueue;

public class MergeKSortedLists {

    public static class ListNode {
        int val;
        ListNode next;

        ListNode(int x) {
            val = x;
        }
    }

    public ListNode mergeKLists(ListNode[] lists) {
        // Min Heap to store the nodes by their value
        PriorityQueue<ListNode> minHeap = new PriorityQueue<>((a, b)
-> a.val - b.val);

        // Add the head of each linked list to the heap
        for (ListNode node : lists) {
            if (node != null) {
                minHeap.offer(node);
            }
        }

        // Dummy node to form the merged linked list
        ListNode dummy = new ListNode(0);
        ListNode current = dummy;

        // Process the heap until it's empty
        while (!minHeap.isEmpty()) {
            // Extract the smallest node
            ListNode smallest = minHeap.poll();

            // Add this node to the merged list
            current.next = smallest;
            current = current.next;

            // If there's a next node, add it to the heap
            if (smallest.next != null) {
                minHeap.offer(smallest.next);
            }
```

```
        }

        // The merged linked list is pointed by dummy.next
        return dummy.next;
    }

    public static void main(String[] args) {
        // Example usage
        MergeKSortedLists solution = new MergeKSortedLists();

        // Create some test linked lists
        ListNode list1 = new ListNode(1);
        list1.next = new ListNode(4);
        list1.next.next = new ListNode(5);

        ListNode list2 = new ListNode(1);
        list2.next = new ListNode(3);
        list2.next.next = new ListNode(4);

        ListNode list3 = new ListNode(2);
        list3.next = new ListNode(6);

        ListNode[] lists = new ListNode[]{list1, list2, list3};

        ListNode result = solution.mergeKLists(lists);

        // Print the merged linked list
        System.out.print("Merged Linked List: ");
        while (result != null) {
            System.out.print(result.val + " ");
            result = result.next;
        }
        // Expected output: 1 1 2 3 4 4 5 6
    }
}
```

Time and Space Complexity

- **Time Complexity**: Inserting and removing elements from the Min Heap takes `O(log k)` time. Since each of the `n` nodes will be inserted and removed exactly once, the total time complexity is `O(n log k)`, where `n` is the total number of nodes and `k` is the number of linked lists.
- **Space Complexity**: The space complexity is `O(k)` for the Min Heap.

Problem 4: Find Median from Data Stream

Problem Statement

The median is the middle value in an ordered integer list. If the size of the list is even, there is no middle value, and the median is the mean of the two middle values.

- For example, for `arr = [2,3,4]`, the median is `3`.

- For example, for `arr = [2,3]`, the median is `(2 + 3) / 2 = 2.5`.

Implement the `MedianFinder` class:
- `MedianFinder()` initializes the MedianFinder object.
- `void addNum(int num)` adds the integer num from the data stream to the data structure.
- `double findMedian()` returns the median of all elements so far.

Solution

Let's use the real life interview setting format to approach this problem.

Clarifying Questions

1. **Data Stream Size**:
   - Candidate:Is there any constraint on the size of the data stream? Should we consider the possibility of very large data sets?
   - Interviewer: The data stream can be very large, so consider efficiency in both time and space when designing your solution.
2. **Order of Operations**:
   - Candidate: Can we assume that the addNum and findMedian methods will be called alternately, or do we need to consider cases where many numbers are added before finding the median?
   - Interviewer: You need to handle cases where multiple numbers are added consecutively before finding the median. Your solution should be efficient in such scenarios.
3. **Constraints on the Numbers**:
   - Candidate: Are there any constraints on the range of the numbers being added (e.g., can they be very large or very small)?
   - Interviewer: There are no specific constraints on the range of the numbers. The numbers can be very large or very small, including negative numbers.

[Candidate]
Key Observations:
- The problem requires us to *design a data structure* that efficiently supports two operations:
  - Adding a number to the data stream.
  - Finding the median of the numbers added so far.
- Median Definition:
  - For an odd number of elements, the median is the middle element.
  - For an even number of elements, the median is the average of the two middle elements.

Brute Force Approach

The brute force approach could be to
  - Maintain a dynamic list of elements.
  - Every time a new element is added, sort the list.
  - Find the median by accessing the middle element(s) of the sorted list.

Efficiency for the brute for approach is as follows:

- Time Complexity: Adding a number takes `O(n log n)` due to sorting, and finding the median takes `O(1)`.
- Space Complexity: The space complexity is `O(n)` to store the elements.

This approach is inefficient due to the need to sort the list after each insertion. We can improve this by leveraging data structures that maintain order more efficiently.

Optimal Approach

To efficiently find the median, we can use two heaps:

- Max Heap: To store the smaller half of the numbers.
- Min Heap: To store the larger half of the numbers.
- The Max Heap (left side) stores the largest element on top, and the Min Heap (right side) stores the smallest element on top. This allows us to balance the heaps and efficiently find the median:
- If the total number of elements is odd, the median is the top of the Max Heap.
- If even, the median is the average of the tops of both heaps.

Implementation outline:

1. **Adding a Number**:
    - If the Max Heap is empty or the number is less than or equal to the top of the Max Heap, add the number to the Max Heap.
    - Otherwise, add it to the Min Heap.
    - Balance the heaps so that the difference in size between the two heaps is no more than 1.
2. **Finding the Median**:
    - If the heaps are of equal size, the median is the average of the tops of both heaps.
    - If one heap has more elements, the median is the top of that heap.

Code Solution

Here's the Java code implementing the optimal solution using a Min Heap and a Max Heap:

```
import java.util.PriorityQueue;
import java.util.Collections;

class MedianFinder {

    // Max Heap for the lower half of the data
    private final PriorityQueue<Integer> maxHeap;

    // Min Heap for the upper half of the data
    private final PriorityQueue<Integer> minHeap;

    /**
     * Initialize your data structure here.
     */
    public MedianFinder() {
```

```
        // Max Heap to store the smaller half of the numbers
        maxHeap = new PriorityQueue<>(Collections.reverseOrder());

        // Min Heap to store the larger half of the numbers
        minHeap = new PriorityQueue<>();
    }

    /**
     * Adds a number into the data structure.
     */
    public void addNum(int num) {
        // Add to the max heap first (Max Heap contains the smaller
half)
        if (maxHeap.isEmpty() || num <= maxHeap.peek()) {
            maxHeap.offer(num);
        } else {
            minHeap.offer(num);
        }

        // Balance the heaps if needed
        if (maxHeap.size() > minHeap.size() + 1) {
            minHeap.offer(maxHeap.poll());
        } else if (minHeap.size() > maxHeap.size()) {
            maxHeap.offer(minHeap.poll());
        }
    }

    /**
     * Finds the median of the current data stream.
     */
    public double findMedian() {
        if (maxHeap.size() > minHeap.size()) {
            // Max Heap has more elements, so the median is the top
of the Max Heap
            return maxHeap.peek();
        } else {
            // Heaps are balanced, so the median is the average of
the tops of both heaps
            return (maxHeap.peek() + minHeap.peek()) / 2.0;
        }
    }

    public static void main(String[] args) {
        MedianFinder medianFinder = new MedianFinder();
        medianFinder.addNum(1);
        medianFinder.addNum(2);
        System.out.println("Median: " + medianFinder.findMedian());
// Output: 1.5
        medianFinder.addNum(3);
        System.out.println("Median: " + medianFinder.findMedian());
// Output: 2
    }
}
```

Time and Space Complexity

- Time Complexity:
    - `addNum(int num)`: Each insertion into the heaps takes `O(log n)` time, where `n` is the number of elements in the heap.
    - `findMedian()`: Finding the median takes `O(1)` time because it involves simply accessing the top elements of the heaps.
- Space Complexity:
    - The space complexity is `O(n)`, where `n` is the number of elements added so far, since we store all elements in the two heaps.

Problem 5: Meeting Rooms

Problem Statement

Given an array of meeting time intervals intervals where `intervals[i] = [start`$_i$`, end`$_i$`]`, return the minimum number of conference rooms required.

Solution

Let's break down the problem and solve it step by step, following our structured approach.

Clarifying Questions

1. **Overlapping Intervals**:
    - Candidate: Are the meeting intervals guaranteed to be well-formed, i.e., will the start time always be less than the end time for each interval?
    - Interviewer: Yes, each meeting interval is well-formed, with the start time less than the end time.
2. **Interval Format**:
    - Candidate: Can the intervals have the same start and end times? For example, can a meeting start and end at the same time, and how should that be handled?
    - Interviewer: Yes, a meeting can start and end at the same time. In such cases, it would still require a conference room for that moment in time.
3. **Interval Range**:
    - Candidate: Is there any constraint on the range of the start and end times? For example, can the times be very large?
    - Interviewer: There are no specific constraints on the range of the times, but you can assume they are within a reasonable range (e.g., within a 24-hour period).
4. Sorting Requirement:
    - Candidate: Should the intervals be considered in any particular order, or can I assume they are unsorted?
    - Interviewer: You can assume the intervals are unsorted and handle the sorting as necessary in your solution.

[Candidate]

Key Observations:

- The goal is to determine the minimum number of conference rooms required to host all meetings such that no two overlapping meetings are scheduled in the same room.
- We need to track overlapping intervals to determine how many rooms are required at any point in time.
- If multiple meetings are overlapping, we need a separate room for each meeting during that overlap.

Brute Force Approach

1. For each interval, check against every other interval to see if they overlap.
2. Count the maximum number of overlapping intervals at any point in time, which will give the number of rooms required.

Efficiency:

- Time Complexity: $O(n^2)$, where n is the number of intervals, because we compare each interval with every other interval.
- Space Complexity: $O(1)$, as we are not using any additional data structures except for a few variables.

This approach is inefficient because it checks every pair of intervals, leading to quadratic time complexity.

Optimal Approach

To optimize, we can leverage the start and end times of the meetings. By sorting these times, we can efficiently track the number of overlapping meetings using a Min Heap or a two-pointer technique.

Outline for the implementation:

1. Sort the intervals:
   - First, sort the intervals by their start time.
   - Alternatively, we can also sort the start and end times separately.
2. Use a Min Heap:
   - As we iterate over the sorted intervals, use a Min Heap to keep track of the end times of meetings currently using a room.
   - For each interval:
     - If the meeting with the earliest end time (top of the heap) ends before the current meeting starts, remove it from the heap.
     - Add the current meeting's end time to the heap.
   - The size of the heap at any point gives the number of rooms required.

Code Solution

Here's the Java code implementing the optimal solution using a Min Heap:

```
import java.util.Arrays;
import java.util.PriorityQueue;

public class MeetingRooms {
```

```
    public int minMeetingRooms(int[][] intervals) {
        // Edge case: if there are no meetings, no rooms are needed
        if (intervals == null || intervals.length == 0) {
            return 0;
        }

        // Step 1: Sort the intervals by start time
        Arrays.sort(intervals, (a, b) -> a[0] - b[0]);

        // Step 2: Initialize a Min Heap to track the end times of
meetings
        PriorityQueue<Integer> minHeap = new PriorityQueue<>();

        // Step 3: Iterate over the sorted intervals
        for (int[] interval : intervals) {
            // If the room due to free up the earliest is free,
remove it from the heap
            if (!minHeap.isEmpty() && minHeap.peek() <= interval[0])
{
                minHeap.poll();
            }

            // Add the current meeting's end time to the heap
            minHeap.offer(interval[1]);
        }

        // The size of the heap is the minimum number of rooms
required
        return minHeap.size();
    }

    public static void main(String[] args) {
        MeetingRooms solution = new MeetingRooms();

        int[][] intervals = {{0, 30}, {5, 10}, {15, 20}};
        System.out.println("Minimum number of conference rooms
required: " + solution.minMeetingRooms(intervals)); // Output: 2

        intervals = new int[][]{{7, 10}, {2, 4}};
        System.out.println("Minimum number of conference rooms
required: " + solution.minMeetingRooms(intervals)); // Output: 1
    }
}
```

Time and Space Complexity

- Time Complexity: `O(n log n)`, where `n` is the number of intervals. This complexity arises from sorting the intervals and the operations on the heap.
- Space Complexity: `O(n)`, as we store the end times of meetings in the heap.

Chapter 16: Sorting

Introduction

A solid understanding of sorting algorithms and their applications is essential for any candidate aiming to succeed in technical interviews.

This chapter will cover the key sorting algorithms, their time and space complexities, and their practical applications.

We will also discuss when to choose one sorting algorithm over another and walk through a few commonly asked sorting-based interview questions with detailed solutions in Java.

Importance of Sorting in Interviews

Understanding sorting allows you to think more clearly about data manipulation and is often the first step in optimizing a solution.

Key Reasons Sorting is Important:

- **Foundation for Other Algorithms**: Sorting is often the first step in solving more complex problems like searching, merging intervals, or detecting duplicates.
- **Efficiency:** Sorting allows for more efficient algorithms, especially when combined with searching (e.g., binary search) or other operations that benefit from *ordered data.*

Overview of Sorting Algorithms

There are many sorting algorithms, *each with its own strengths and weaknesses.*

Below are the most commonly used ones:

1. Bubble Sort

- Concept: Repeatedly steps through the list, compares adjacent elements, and swaps them if they are in the wrong order.
- Time Complexity: $O(n^2)$
- Space Complexity: $O(1)$
- When to Use: *Rarely used* in practice due to inefficiency, but it's useful for educational purposes to understand basic algorithmic concepts.

2. Selection Sort

- Concept: Divides the input into a sorted and an unsorted region, then *repeatedly selects the smallest element from the unsorted region* and moves it to the end of the sorted region.
- Time Complexity: $O(n^2)$

- Space Complexity: `O(1)`
- When to Use: Simple to implement, but *not efficient for large datasets.*

3. Insertion Sort

- Concept: Builds the sorted array one item at a time, *inserting each new item into its proper place in the sorted portion of the array.*
- Time Complexity: `O(n²)` average and worst-case, `O(n)` best-case when the array is nearly sorted.
- Space Complexity: `O(1)`
- When to Use: Efficient for small or nearly sorted arrays.

4. Merge Sort

- Concept: *Divides* the array into halves, sorts each half, and then *merges* the sorted halves.
- Time Complexity: `O(n log n)`
- Space Complexity: `O(n)`
- When to Use: *Stable sort, suitable for large datasets*, especially when memory isn't a constraint.

5. Quick Sort

- Concept: Picks a *pivot* element, *partitions the array into two halves around the pivot*, and recursively sorts the partitions.
- Time Complexity: `O(n log n)` average, `O(n²)` worst-case.
- Space Complexity: `O(log n)` due to recursion stack.
- When to Use: *One of the most efficient sorting algorithms* for large datasets, though *not stable.*

6. Heap Sort

- Concept: Utilizes a binary heap data structure to sort elements. It first builds a max heap and then repeatedly extracts the maximum element from the heap, rebuilding the heap each time.
- Time Complexity: `O(n log n)`
- Space Complexity: `O(1)`
- When to Use: Efficient for large datasets, but *not stable.*

7. Counting Sort

- Concept: *Counts the number of occurrences of each element* and uses this information to place elements into the correct position.
- Time Complexity: `O(n + k)`, where k is the range of the input.
- Space Complexity: `O(k)`
- When to Use: Efficient when the *range of input values is small*, not comparison-based.

8. Radix Sort

- Concept: Sorts numbers *digit by digit, using counting sort as a subroutine.*
- Time Complexity: `O(d * (n + k))`, where d is the number of digits and k is the range of digits.
- Space Complexity: `O(n + k)`
- When to Use: Useful for sorting large numbers or strings, especially when the range of digits is limited.

9. Bucket Sort

- Concept: *Distributes elements into a number of buckets*, sorts each bucket individually (using another sorting algorithm or recursively), and then concatenates the buckets.
- Time Complexity: `O(n + k)`
- Space Complexity: `O(n + k)`
- When to Use: Works well when the input is uniformly distributed over a range.

Choosing the Right Sorting Algorithm

When deciding which sorting algorithm to use, consider the following factors:

- **Data Size:** For small arrays, algorithms like Insertion Sort might be more efficient. For large datasets, algorithms like Merge Sort or Quick Sort are preferred.
- **Memory Constraints:** If memory is limited, algorithms like Heap Sort are advantageous as they have `O(1)` space complexity.
- **Stability:** If stability is required (i.e., maintaining *the relative order of records with equal keys*), Merge Sort or Insertion Sort is a good choice.
- **Input Characteristics:** For nearly sorted arrays, Insertion Sort is particularly efficient. If the input range is known and limited, Counting Sort, Radix Sort, or Bucket Sort may be the best option.

Summary of Key Concepts

- **Stable Sorting:** A sorting algorithm is stable if it maintains the relative order of equal elements. Merge Sort, Insertion Sort, Radix Sort, and Counting Sort are stable, while Quicksort and Heapsort are not.
- **In-Place Sorting:** An in-place algorithm sorts the elements without requiring extra space proportional to the size of the input. Quick Sort, Heap Sort, Insertion Sort, and Selection Sort are in-place, while Merge Sort is not.
- **Time Complexity:** Understanding the best, worst, and average case time complexities of sorting algorithms is crucial for making informed decisions during coding interviews.
- **Space Complexity:** Some algorithms require additional space for auxiliary arrays (e.g., Merge Sort), while others operate within the input array itself.

Popular Interview Questions on Sorting

Now, let's look at some of the most commonly asked coding interview questions based on Sorting algorithms.

Problem 1: Sort an Array

Problem Statement

Given an array of integers *nums*, sort the array in ascending order and return it.

Solution

Let's dive into the problem. We will solve it here using ***merge sort and quick sort*** algorithms, in a real interview setting *choose one implementation based on the constraints of the given problem.*

Clarifying Questions

Candidate: Is the input array guaranteed to have only integer values, and can it contain duplicates or negative numbers?
Interviewer: Yes, the input array will contain only integer values, and it can have both duplicates and negative numbers.

Candidate: Is there a specific size constraint on the array, or should my solution handle arrays of any size?
Interviewer: Your solution should be efficient and handle arrays of any size, but typically you can expect the array size to be within a reasonable range that a standard sorting algorithm can handle.

Example:
Candidate: Let me take an example to ensure we have a shared understanding of the expected input and output format.
For example, if the input array is `nums = [3, 6, -2, 5, -8, 4, 1]`, the expected output after sorting should be `[-8, -2, 1, 3, 4, 5, 6]`. Does that look correct?
Interviewer: Yes, that looks correct.

Brute Force Approach

A simple way to sort the array would be to use an algorithm like *bubble sort, selection sort, or insertion sort.* However, these algorithms have a time complexity of $O(n^2)$, we can do better than that using other algorithms which have time complexity of `O(n log n)`.

Optimal Approach

To solve this problem optimally, we can implement it using MergeSort or QuickSort algorithms:

1. **Merge Sort:** This is a *divide-and-conquer algorithm* that divides the array into two halves, recursively sorts each half, and then merges the two sorted halves.
2. **Quick Sort:** This is another *divide-and-conquer algorithm* that selects a pivot element, partitions the array around the pivot such that elements less than the pivot are on the left, and elements greater than the pivot are on the right. It then recursively sorts the left and right partitions.

Code Solution

```
public class SortArray {

    // Merge Sort Implementation
    public int[] mergeSort(int[] nums) {
        if (nums.length <= 1) {
            return nums;
        }
        mergeSort(nums, 0, nums.length - 1);
        return nums;
    }

    private void mergeSort(int[] nums, int left, int right) {
        if (left < right) {
            int mid = left + (right - left) / 2;
            mergeSort(nums, left, mid);
            mergeSort(nums, mid + 1, right);
            merge(nums, left, mid, right);
        }
    }

    private void merge(int[] nums, int left, int mid, int right) {
        int n1 = mid - left + 1;
        int n2 = right - mid;

        int[] leftArray = new int[n1];
        int[] rightArray = new int[n2];

        for (int i = 0; i < n1; ++i) {
            leftArray[i] = nums[left + i];
        }
        for (int j = 0; j < n2; ++j) {
            rightArray[j] = nums[mid + 1 + j];
        }

        int i = 0, j = 0;
        int k = left;
        while (i < n1 && j < n2) {
            if (leftArray[i] <= rightArray[j]) {
                nums[k] = leftArray[i];
                i++;
            } else {
                nums[k] = rightArray[j];
                j++;
            }
            k++;
        }

        while (i < n1) {
            nums[k] = leftArray[i];
            i++;
            k++;
        }
```

```
        while (j < n2) {
            nums[k] = rightArray[j];
            j++;
            k++;
        }
    }

    // Quick Sort Implementation
    public int[] quickSort(int[] nums) {
        quickSort(nums, 0, nums.length - 1);
        return nums;
    }

    private void quickSort(int[] nums, int low, int high) {
        if (low < high) {
            int pi = partition(nums, low, high);
            quickSort(nums, low, pi - 1);
            quickSort(nums, pi + 1, high);
        }
    }

    private int partition(int[] nums, int low, int high) {
        int pivot = nums[high];
        int i = (low - 1);
        for (int j = low; j < high; j++) {
            if (nums[j] <= pivot) {
                i++;
                int temp = nums[i];
                nums[i] = nums[j];
                nums[j] = temp;
            }
        }
        int temp = nums[i + 1];
        nums[i + 1] = nums[high];
        nums[high] = temp;
        return i + 1;
    }

    // Main method to test the sorting algorithms
    public static void main(String[] args) {
        SortArray sorter = new SortArray();

        int[] nums1 = {3, 6, -2, 5, -8, 4, 1};
        int[] nums2 = nums1.clone(); // Clone array for quick sort
test

        // Test Merge Sort
        int[] sortedMerge = sorter.mergeSort(nums1);
        System.out.println("Merge Sort Result: " +
java.util.Arrays.toString(sortedMerge));

        // Test Quick Sort
        int[] sortedQuick = sorter.quickSort(nums2);
```

```
        System.out.println("Quick Sort Result: " +
java.util.Arrays.toString(sortedQuick));
    }
}
```

Time and space complexity:

- **Merge Sort:**
  - Time Complexity: `O(n log n)` due to the division of the array and merging process.
  - Space Complexity: `O(n)` because of the auxiliary space required for the temporary arrays during merging.
- **Quick Sort:**
  - Time Complexity: Average `O(n log n)`. However, in the worst case (when the pivot is always the smallest or largest element), it can degrade to $O(n^2)$.
  - Space Complexity: `O(log n)` in the best case (when recursion depth is minimized), and `O(n)` in the worst case due to the recursion stack.

Problem 2: Merge Intervals

Problem Statement

Given an array of *intervals* where `intervals[i] = [start`$_i$`, end`$_i$`]`, merge all overlapping intervals, and return an array of the non-overlapping intervals that cover all the intervals in the input.

Solution

Let's work through this problem as if we are in a real life coding interview setting.

Clarifying Questions

Candidate: Before I start, I'd like to ask a few clarifying questions to make sure I fully understand the problem.

Candidate: Are the intervals provided in the input array sorted by their start times, or could they be in any order?
Interviewer: The intervals are not guaranteed to be sorted, so your solution should handle unsorted input.

Candidate: Can an interval have the same start and end time, effectively making it a point?
Interviewer: Yes, an interval can have the same start and end time. In that case, it's a point interval.

Candidate: What should be the output if there are no intervals or just one interval in the input array?

Interviewer: If there are no intervals, the output should be an empty array. If there is only one interval, the output should simply be that interval.

Candidate: Just to confirm, the intervals are defined using inclusive start and end times, correct?
Interviewer: Yes, the intervals use inclusive start and end times.

Example:
Candidate: Let's consider an example to make sure we're aligned on the expected behavior.
Suppose the input array of intervals is `[[1, 3], [2, 6], [8, 10], [15, 18]]`. Here, the intervals `[1, 3]` and `[2, 6]` overlap and can be merged into `[1, 6]`. The rest of the intervals do not overlap, so the expected output would be `[[1, 6], [8, 10], [15, 18]]`. Does that look correct?
Interviewer: Yes, that's correct.

Brute Force Approach

A brute force approach could involve checking every pair of intervals to see if they overlap and then merging them if they do. However, this approach would be inefficient, with a time complexity of $O(n^2)$ due to the pairwise comparison of intervals.

Optimal Approach

The optimal approach would involve *first sorting the intervals based on their start times.* Once sorted, we can iterate through the list and merge intervals as necessary. This way, we only need to go through the list once after sorting, achieving a time complexity of `O(n log n)` due to the sorting step, followed by a linear pass `O(n)` through the intervals.

Code Solution

I will implement this approach in Java now.

```
import java.util.ArrayList;
import java.util.Arrays;
import java.util.List;

public class MergeIntervals {

   public int[][] merge(int[][] intervals) {
        if (intervals.length <= 1) {
            return intervals;
        }

        // Sort intervals by start time
        Arrays.sort(intervals, (a, b) -> Integer.compare(a[0],
b[0]));

        List<int[]> mergedIntervals = new ArrayList<>();

        // Initialize with the first interval
```

```
        int[] currentInterval = intervals[0];
        mergedIntervals.add(currentInterval);

        for (int[] interval : intervals) {
            int currentStart = currentInterval[0];
            int currentEnd = currentInterval[1];
            int nextStart = interval[0];
            int nextEnd = interval[1];

            if (currentEnd >= nextStart) { // Overlapping intervals,
merge them
                currentInterval[1] = Math.max(currentEnd, nextEnd);
            } else { // No overlap, move to the next interval
                currentInterval = interval;
                mergedIntervals.add(currentInterval);
            }
        }

        return mergedIntervals.toArray(new
int[mergedIntervals.size()][]);
    }

    // Main method to test the merge intervals function
    public static void main(String[] args) {
        MergeIntervals mi = new MergeIntervals();

        // Test case 1
        int[][] intervals1 = {{1, 3}, {2, 6}, {8, 10}, {15, 18}};
        int[][] result1 = mi.merge(intervals1);
        System.out.println("Merged intervals: " +
Arrays.deepToString(result1));

        // Test case 2
        int[][] intervals2 = {{1, 4}, {4, 5}};
        int[][] result2 = mi.merge(intervals2);
        System.out.println("Merged intervals: " +
Arrays.deepToString(result2));

        // Test case 3
        int[][] intervals3 = {{1, 4}, {2, 3}};
        int[][] result3 = mi.merge(intervals3);
        System.out.println("Merged intervals: " +
Arrays.deepToString(result3));

        // Test case 4
        int[][] intervals4 = {{1, 4}, {5, 6}};
        int[][] result4 = mi.merge(intervals4);
        System.out.println("Merged intervals: " +
Arrays.deepToString(result4));
    }
}
```

Time and Space Complexity:

- The time complexity of this approach is `O(n log n)` due to the sorting step. The subsequent merging process is `O(n)`, resulting in an overall time complexity of `O(n log n)`.
- The space complexity is `O(n)` in the worst case due to the space required for the list of merged intervals and the sorting algorithm's additional space.

Problem 3: Meeting Rooms II

Problem Statement

Given an array of meeting time intervals `intervals` where `intervals[i] = [start`$_i$`, end`$_i$`]`, return *the minimum number of conference rooms required.*

Solution

Let's dive into this problem.

Clarifying Questions

Candidate: I'd like to ask a few clarifying questions to ensure I understand the problem correctly.

Candidate: Are the start and end times of the intervals inclusive or exclusive?
Interviewer: The start time is inclusive, and the end time is exclusive.

Candidate: Can the intervals overlap, and is it possible for some intervals to have the same start or end time?
Interviewer: Yes, intervals can overlap, and it's possible for intervals to have the same start or end times.

Candidate: What should be the output if there are no intervals or just one interval?
Interviewer: If there are no intervals, the output should be `0` because no rooms are required. If there is only one interval, the output should be `1`.

Example:
Candidate: Let's consider an example to make sure we're aligned on the expected behavior.

Suppose the input array of intervals is `[[0, 30], [5, 10], [15, 20]]`. Here, the intervals `[0, 30]` and `[5, 10]`overlap, and so do `[15, 20]` with `[0, 30]`. The minimum number of conference rooms required would be 2 because at most two meetings are overlapping at the same time.

Does that look correct?
Interviewer: Yes, that's correct.

Brute Force Approach

A brute force approach could involve checking each pair of intervals to determine if they overlap, but this would require *checking every interval against every other interval*, resulting in a time complexity of $O(n^2)$. This would be inefficient for large inputs, so let's move on to a more optimal approach.

Optimal Approach

The optimal approach involves *sorting the intervals by their start times and then using a min-heap (or priority queue) to keep track of the end times of meetings that are currently ongoing*. This way, we can efficiently determine the minimum number of rooms required.

The steps are as follows:

1. Sort the intervals by start time.
2. Use a *min-heap* to track the earliest ending meeting.
3. Iterate through the sorted intervals:
   - If the current meeting starts after or when the earliest meeting in the heap ends, we can reuse the room (remove the earliest meeting from the heap).
   - If not, we need a new room (add the current meeting's end time to the heap).
4. The size of the heap at the end will represent the minimum number of conference rooms required.

Code Solution

I'll now implement the solution using this approach.

```
import java.util.Arrays;
import java.util.PriorityQueue;

public class MeetingRooms {

    public int minMeetingRooms(int[][] intervals) {
        if (intervals.length == 0) {
            return 0;
        }

        // Sort intervals by start time
        Arrays.sort(intervals, (a, b) -> Integer.compare(a[0],
b[0]));

        // Min-heap to track the end times of meetings
        PriorityQueue<Integer> minHeap = new PriorityQueue<>();

        // Add the first meeting's end time to the heap
        minHeap.add(intervals[0][1]);

        for (int i = 1; i < intervals.length; i++) {
            // If the current meeting starts after the earliest
ending meeting ends, reuse the room
            if (intervals[i][0] >= minHeap.peek()) {
                minHeap.poll();
```

```
            }

            // Add the current meeting's end time to the heap
            minHeap.add(intervals[i][1]);
        }

        // The size of the heap is the minimum number of conference
rooms required
        return minHeap.size();
    }

    // Main method to test the minMeetingRooms function
    public static void main(String[] args) {
        MeetingRooms mr = new MeetingRooms();

        // Test case 1
        int[][] intervals1 = {{0, 30}, {5, 10}, {15, 20}};
        System.out.println("Minimum rooms required: " +
mr.minMeetingRooms(intervals1)); // Output: 2

        // Test case 2
        int[][] intervals2 = {{7, 10}, {2, 4}};
        System.out.println("Minimum rooms required: " +
mr.minMeetingRooms(intervals2)); // Output: 1

        // Test case 3
        int[][] intervals3 = {{1, 5}, {2, 6}, {4, 8}, {8, 9}};
        System.out.println("Minimum rooms required: " +
mr.minMeetingRooms(intervals3)); // Output: 3

        // Test case 4
        int[][] intervals4 = {{9, 10}, {4, 9}, {4, 17}};
        System.out.println("Minimum rooms required: " +
mr.minMeetingRooms(intervals4)); // Output: 2
    }
}
```

Time and Space Complexity

- The time complexity of this approach is `O(n log n)` due to the sorting step and the operations with the min-heap.
- The space complexity is `O(n)` in the worst case due to the space required by the min-heap to store the end times.

Problem 4: Kth Largest Element in an Array

Problem Statement

Given an integer array `nums` and an integer `k`, return the kth largest element in the array.

Note that it is the kth largest element in the sorted order, not the kth distinct element.

Solution

Clarifying Questions

Candidate: I'd like to ask a few clarifying questions to ensure I fully understand the problem.

Candidate: Can the array contain duplicate elements, and should those be considered when determining the kth largest element?
Interviewer: Yes, the array can contain duplicate elements, and they should be considered when determining the kth largest element.

Candidate: Is it safe to assume that the value of k will always be valid, meaning it will be between 1 and the length of the array?
Interviewer: Yes, you can assume that k will always be a valid index, so `1 ≤ k ≤ length` of the array.

Example:
Candidate: Let's consider an example to ensure we're aligned on the expected behavior.
Suppose the input array is `nums = [3, 2, 1, 5, 6, 4]` and `k = 2`.

The sorted array would be [1, 2, 3, 4, 5, 6], and the *2nd largest* element would be 5.
Does that look correct?
Interviewer: Yes, that's correct.

Approach

To solve this problem efficiently, I'll use the Quickselect algorithm, which is well-suited for finding the kth smallest or largest element in an unsorted array.

The ***Quickselect*** algorithm is a variation of standard quicksort algorithm which works by repeatedly partitioning the array and narrowing down the search space based on the position of the pivot.

Code Solution

```
import java.util.ArrayList;
import java.util.List;
import java.util.Random;

public class KthLargestElement {

    public int findKthLargest(int[] nums, int k) {
        List<Integer> list = new ArrayList<>();
        for (int num : nums) {
            list.add(num);
```

```
        }

        return quickSelect(list, k);
    }

    public int quickSelect(List<Integer> nums, int k) {
        int pivotIndex = new Random().nextInt(nums.size());
        int pivot = nums.get(pivotIndex);

        List<Integer> left = new ArrayList<>();
        List<Integer> mid = new ArrayList<>();
        List<Integer> right = new ArrayList<>();

        for (int num : nums) {
            if (num > pivot) {
                left.add(num);
            } else if (num < pivot) {
                right.add(num);
            } else {
                mid.add(num);
            }
        }

        if (k <= left.size()) {
            return quickSelect(left, k);
        }

        if (left.size() + mid.size() < k) {
            return quickSelect(right, k - left.size() - mid.size());
        }

        return pivot;
    }

    // Main method to test the findKthLargest function
    public static void main(String[] args) {
        KthLargestElement kle = new KthLargestElement();

        // Test case 1
        int[] nums1 = {3, 2, 1, 5, 6, 4};
        int k1 = 2;
        System.out.println("2nd largest element: " +
kle.findKthLargest(nums1, k1)); // Output: 5

        // Test case 2
        int[] nums2 = {3, 2, 3, 1, 2, 4, 5, 5, 6};
        int k2 = 4;
        System.out.println("4th largest element: " +
kle.findKthLargest(nums2, k2)); // Output: 4

        // Test case 3
        int[] nums3 = {2, 1};
        int k3 = 1;
        System.out.println("1st largest element: " +
```

```
kle.findKthLargest(nums3, k3)); // Output: 2

        // Test case 4
        int[] nums4 = {7, 6, 5, 4, 3, 2, 1};
        int k4 = 5;
        System.out.println("5th largest element: " +
kle.findKthLargest(nums4, k4)); // Output: 3
    }
}
```

Explanation:
The approach works as follows:

1. Pivot Selection: The *quickSelect* method selects a *random pivot* from the list of numbers.
2. Partitioning: The list is divided into three sublists:
   - *left* contains elements greater than the pivot.
   - *mid* contains elements equal to the pivot.
   - *right* contains elements less than the pivot.
3. Recursive Selection:
   - If the *size of the left* list is greater than or equal to `k`, then the kth largest element must be in the left list, and we recursively call *quickSelect* on it.
   - If the *size of left + mid* is less than `k`, then the kth largest element must be in the right list, and we recursively call *quickSelect* on it, adjusting `k` to account for the removed elements.
   - If `k` falls within the size of the mid list, the *pivot* itself is the kth largest element, and we return it.

Time and Space Complexity

- The average time complexity of the Quickselect algorithm is `O(n)`, which is very efficient for this problem. In the worst case (depending on the random pivot selection), it can degrade to $O(n^2)$, but this is rare.
- The space complexity of this implementation is `O(n)` due to the additional space required to store the sublists left, mid, and right.

Problem 5: 3 Sum

Problem Statement

Given an integer array nums, return all the triplets `[nums[i], nums[j], nums[k]]` such that `i != j, i != k, and j != k, and nums[i] + nums[j] + nums[k] == 0.`

Notice that the solution set must not contain duplicate triplets.

Solution

Let's dive into this problem as if we are in a real life interview setting.

Clarifying Questions

Candidate: I'd like to ask a few clarifying questions to ensure I fully understand the problem.

Candidate: Can the array contain duplicate elements, and should those duplicates be considered when finding the triplets?
Interviewer: Yes, the array can contain duplicate elements, but your solution should not include duplicate triplets in the result.

Candidate: What should be the output if the input array has fewer than three elements?
Interviewer: If the array has fewer than three elements, the output should be an empty list since it's impossible to form a triplet.

Example:
Candidate:
Let's consider an example to ensure we're aligned on the expected behavior. Suppose the input array is `nums = [-1, 0, 1, 2, -1, -4]`. The triplets that sum to zero are `[-1, -1, 2]` and `[-1, 0, 1]`.

Notice that we only include unique triplets, so the expected output is [[-1, -1, 2], [-1, 0, 1]]. Does that look correct?
Interviewer: Yes, that's correct.

Brute Force Approach

A brute force approach would involve checking all possible triplets, which would result in a time complexity of $O(n^3)$. However, this would be inefficient for large input arrays, so let's move on to a more optimal approach.

Optimal Approach

The optimal approach is to use sorting and the two-pointer technique.

Here's how it will work:

1. **Sorting**: First, we sort the array. Sorting helps in efficiently skipping duplicate elements and in applying the two-pointer technique.
2. **Two-pointer technique**: For each element `nums[i]`, we use two pointers, left and right, to find pairs that sum to `-nums[i]`.
3. **Avoid duplicates**: We skip duplicate elements during iteration to avoid adding duplicate triplets to the result.

Code Solution

I'll now implement the solution using the optimal approach.

```
import java.util.ArrayList;
import java.util.Arrays;
```

```
import java.util.List;

public class ThreeSum {

    public List<List<Integer>> threeSum(int[] nums) {
        List<List<Integer>> result = new ArrayList<>();
        Arrays.sort(nums); // Step 1: Sort the array

        for (int i = 0; i < nums.length - 2; i++) {
            if (i > 0 && nums[i] == nums[i - 1]) {
                continue; // Skip duplicate elements
            }

            int left = i + 1;
            int right = nums.length - 1;

            while (left < right) {
                int sum = nums[i] + nums[left] + nums[right];

                if (sum == 0) {
                    result.add(Arrays.asList(nums[i], nums[left],
nums[right]));
                    left++;
                    right--;

                    // Skip duplicates
                    while (left < right && nums[left] == nums[left -
1]) {
                        left++;
                    }
                    while (left < right && nums[right] == nums[right
+ 1]) {
                        right--;
                    }
                } else if (sum < 0) {
                    left++; // We need a larger sum, move the left
pointer
                } else {
                    right--; // We need a smaller sum, move the
right pointer
                }
            }
        }

        return result;
    }

    // Main method to test the threeSum function
    public static void main(String[] args) {
        ThreeSum ts = new ThreeSum();

        // Test case 1
        int[] nums1 = {-1, 0, 1, 2, -1, -4};
        System.out.println("Triplets: " + ts.threeSum(nums1)); //
```

```
Output: [[-1, -1, 2], [-1, 0, 1]]

        // Test case 2
        int[] nums2 = {0, 0, 0, 0};
        System.out.println("Triplets: " + ts.threeSum(nums2)); //
Output: [[0, 0, 0]]

        // Test case 3
        int[] nums3 = {};
        System.out.println("Triplets: " + ts.threeSum(nums3)); //
Output: []

        // Test case 4
        int[] nums4 = {-2, 0, 1, 1, 2};
        System.out.println("Triplets: " + ts.threeSum(nums4)); //
Output: [[-2, 0, 2], [-2, 1, 1]]
    }
}
```

Time and Space Complexity

- The time complexity of this approach is $O(n^2)$. Sorting the array takes `O(n log n)`, and then we iterate through the array using a two-pointer technique, which takes $O(n^2)$ in total.
- The space complexity is `O(1)` for the sorting and pointer operations, though the result list will require `O(k)` space, where `k` is the number of unique triplets found.

Chapter 17: Graphs

Introduction to Graphs

Graphs is a data structure consisting of ***nodes*** (also called *vertices*) and ***edges*** that connect pairs of nodes.

They are used to ***represent relationships between objects***.

For example, in a social network, nodes represent people, and edges represent friendships.

Types of Graphs

- **Directed vs. Undirected Graphs:**
  - **Directed Graph:** Edges have a direction, indicating a one-way relationship.
  - **Undirected Graph:** Edges do not have a direction, indicating a two-way relationship.
- **Weighted vs. Unweighted Graphs:**
  - **Weighted Graph:** Edges have weights, representing the cost or distance between nodes.
  - **Unweighted Graph:** All edges are equal, without any weight.
- **Cyclic vs. Acyclic Graphs:**
  - **Cyclic Graph:** Contains at least one cycle (a path that starts and ends at the same node).
  - **Acyclic Graph:** Contains no cycles.
- **Connected vs. Disconnected Graphs:**
  - **Connected Graph:** There is a path between any two nodes.
  - **Disconnected Graph:** Some nodes are isolated, with no path connecting them to others.

Graph Representation

- **Adjacency Matrix:** A *2D array* where `matrix[i][j]` is *true* (or the weight) if there is an edge between nodes `i` and `j`.
- **Adjacency List:** An *array of lists*, where each list at index `i` contains the neighbors of node `i`.
- **Edge List**: A *list of all edges*, where each edge is a pair (or triplet, if weighted) of nodes.

Common Graph Algorithms

Graph algorithms are essential for solving many types of problems. Below are some of the most important algorithms you should know for coding interviews.

1. Breadth-First Search (BFS)

BFS is used to explore the nodes of a graph *level by level*, starting from a given node. It's particularly useful for finding the shortest path in an unweighted graph.

- Use Cases: Shortest path in an unweighted graph, level-order traversal.
- Time Complexity: `O(V + E)`, where `V` is the number of vertices, and `E` is the number of edges.
- Space Complexity: `O(V)`.

2. Depth-First Search (DFS)

DFS explores *as far down a branch as possible before backtracking*. It can be implemented either iteratively with a stack or recursively.

- Use Cases: Path finding, topological sort, cycle detection.
- Time Complexity: `O(V + E)`.
- Space Complexity: `O(V)` for recursion stack.

3. Dijkstra's Algorithm

Dijkstra's algorithm *finds the shortest path from a source node to all other nodes in a weighted graph with non-negative weights.*

- Use Cases: Shortest path in a weighted graph.
- Time Complexity: `O((V + E) log V)` with a priority queue.
- Space Complexity: `O(V)`.

4. Topological Sort

Topological sort is used to *order the nodes of a Directed Acyclic Graph (DAG)* such that for every directed edge `u -> v`, node `u` comes before node `v` in the ordering.

- Use Cases: Task scheduling, resolving dependencies.
- Time Complexity: `O(V + E)`.
- Space Complexity: `O(V)`.

5. Union-Find (Disjoint Set)

Union-Find is used to *detect cycles in an undirected graph and to solve connectivity problems.*

- Use Cases: Cycle detection, connected components.
- Time Complexity: `O(α(V))`, where `α` is the Inverse Ackermann function.
- Space Complexity: `O(V)`.

Most Popular Graph Related Interview Questions

In this section, we will look at popular coding interview questions which can be solved by applying one of the five commonly used graph algorithms mentioned above.

Problem 1: Rotting Oranges

Problem Statement

You are given an `m x n` grid where each cell can have one of three values:

- `0` representing an *empty* cell,

- 1 representing a *fresh* orange, or
- 2 representing a *rotten* orange.

Every minute, any fresh orange that is 4-directionally adjacent to a rotten orange becomes rotten.

Return the minimum number of minutes that must elapse until no cell has a fresh orange. If this is impossible, return `-1`.

Solution

Let's dive into the problem as if we are in a real life interview setting.

Clarifying Questions

Thanks for the question! I'd like to ask a few clarifying questions before diving into the solution.

Candidate: Can the grid dimensions be very large, or are they constrained?
Interviewer: The grid can be up to 10 x 10, so it's relatively small.

Candidate: Is it guaranteed that there is at least one orange in the grid?
Interviewer: Yes, there is at least one orange in the grid.

Candidate: If there are no fresh oranges in the grid from the start, should I return `0` since no time is needed to rot all oranges?
Interviewer: Yes, that's correct. If there are no fresh oranges, you should return 0.

Candidate: Do the oranges only rot in the 4 main directions (up, down, left, right), or can they rot diagonally as well?
Interviewer: The oranges only rot in the 4 main directions (up, down, left, right).

Candidate: I think I have a good understanding of the problem now. I'll start with an example and then move on to discuss the approach.

Example

Let's consider an example grid:

```
[
 [2, 1, 1],
 [1, 1, 0],
 [0, 1, 1]
]
```

1. Initial State:
   - The rotten orange is at `(0,0)`.
2. After 1 minute:
   - The oranges at `(0,1)` and `(1,0)` will rot.
3. After 2 minutes:
   - The oranges at `(0,2)`, `(1,1)`, and `(2,1)` will rot.
4. After 3 minutes:
   - The orange at `(2,2)` will rot.

In this example, it takes 3 minutes for all the oranges to rot.

Brute Force Approach

Let's first think about a brute force approach. One idea might be to iteratively rot the adjacent oranges in each step and keep track of the time. We can repeat this process until no more oranges can be rotted.

However, this approach is inefficient because we would need to scan the grid multiple times for each minute, leading to a time complexity of `O((m * n) * (m * n))`, which could be slow for larger grids.

Optimal Approach

We can leverage *Breadth-First Search* (BFS) to efficiently solve this problem. BFS is ideal here because *it explores all the adjacent nodes* (oranges) level by level, which corresponds to each minute passing.

Here's the step-by-step plan:

1. **Initialize a queue**: We'll start by enqueuing all the rotten oranges. The idea is to spread the rotting effect simultaneously from all rotten oranges using BFS.
2. **Track time**: We'll use a counter to track the number of minutes elapsed.
3. **Perform BFS**: For each rotten orange, we'll rot its adjacent fresh oranges and enqueue them. After processing all rotten oranges at the current minute, we'll increase the time counter.
4. **Check for remaining fresh oranges**: After the BFS completes, if there are any fresh oranges left, it means it's impossible to rot all oranges, so we return `-1`.

Code Solution

Here's the Java code for the BFS approach:

```
import java.util.*;

public class RottenOranges {

    public int orangesRotting(int[][] grid) {
        int m = grid.length;
        int n = grid[0].length;
        Queue<int[]> queue = new LinkedList<>();
        int freshOranges = 0;

        // Step 1: Initialize the queue with all rotten oranges
        for (int i = 0; i < m; i++) {
            for (int j = 0; j < n; j++) {
                if (grid[i][j] == 2) {
                    queue.add(new int[]{i, j});
                } else if (grid[i][j] == 1) {
```

```
                    freshOranges++;
                }
            }
        }

        // If there are no fresh oranges, return 0
        if (freshOranges == 0) return 0;

        int minutesElapsed = 0;
        int[][] directions = {{1, 0}, {-1, 0}, {0, 1}, {0, -1}};

        // Step 2: BFS to rot adjacent oranges
        while (!queue.isEmpty()) {
            int size = queue.size();
            boolean hasRotting = false;

            for (int i = 0; i < size; i++) {
                int[] cell = queue.poll();
                int row = cell[0];
                int col = cell[1];

                for (int[] dir : directions) {
                    int newRow = row + dir[0];
                    int newCol = col + dir[1];

                    if (newRow >= 0 && newRow < m && newCol >= 0 &&
newCol < n && grid[newRow][newCol] == 1) {
                        grid[newRow][newCol] = 2;
                        queue.add(new int[]{newRow, newCol});
                        freshOranges--;
                        hasRotting = true;
                    }
                }
            }

            if (hasRotting) {
                minutesElapsed++;
            }
        }

        // Step 3: Check if all oranges have rotted
        return freshOranges == 0 ? minutesElapsed : -1;
    }

    public static void main(String[] args) {
        RottenOranges solution = new RottenOranges();

        int[][] grid1 = {
                {2, 1, 1},
                {1, 1, 0},
                {0, 1, 1}
        };
        System.out.println(solution.orangesRotting(grid1)); //
Expected output: 4
```

```
        int[][] grid2 = {
                {2, 1, 1},
                {0, 1, 1},
                {1, 0, 1}
        };
        System.out.println(solution.orangesRotting(grid2)); //
Expected output: -1

        int[][] grid3 = {
                {0, 2}
        };
        System.out.println(solution.orangesRotting(grid3)); //
Expected output: 0
    }
}
```

Time and Space Complexity

- The time complexity of this approach is `O(m * n)` because each cell is processed once during the BFS.
- The space complexity is also `O(m * n)` because, in the worst case, all oranges could be rotten, requiring us to store their positions in the queue.

Problem 2: Number of Islands

Problem Statement

Given an `m x n` 2D binary grid `grid` which represents a map of `'1'`s (land) and `'0'`s (water), return *the number of islands.*

An **island** is surrounded by water and is formed by connecting adjacent lands horizontally or vertically. You may assume all four edges of the grid are all surrounded by water.

Solution

Thank you for the question! I'd like to ask a few clarifying questions to ensure I fully understand the problem.

Clarifying Questions

Candidate: Can the grid have disconnected clusters of land, and are these clusters considered separate islands?
Interviewer: Yes, each disconnected cluster of land (group of '1's) is considered a separate island.

Candidate: Are diagonally adjacent lands considered part of the same island?
Interviewer: No, only horizontally and vertically adjacent lands are part of the same island.

Candidate: Is there a possibility of an empty grid, and if so, should the result be 0 since there would be no islands?
Interviewer: Yes, if the grid is empty, you should return 0.

Candidate: Will the grid always be rectangular, or could it have irregular dimensions?
Interviewer: The grid will always be rectangular.

Great, I think I have all the information I need. I'll start by discussing an example and then move on to the solution.

Example
Consider the following grid:
```
[  ['1', '1', '0', '0', '0'],
  ['1', '1', '0', '0', '0'],
  ['0', '0', '1', '0', '0'],
  ['0', '0', '0', '1', '1']
]
```

In this grid, we have three separate islands:
1. The first island is formed by the four 1s in the top-left corner.
2. The second island is formed by the single 1 in the center.
3. The third island is formed by the two 1s in the bottom-right corner.

The expected output for this grid is 3.

Approach

The optimal approach is to perform depth-first search to traverse the grid.

When we encounter a cell with a '1', we initiate a DFS to traverse all adjacent land cells connected to it, marking them as visited (or changing their value to '0') to ensure we don't count them again.

Each time we initiate a DFS, it indicates the discovery of a new island.

The main steps are:
1. Iterate over each cell in the grid.
2. When a land cell (1) is found, increase the island count and perform DFS to mark all connected land cells.
3. Continue this process until all cells are checked.

Code Solution

Here's the Java implementation using DFS:
```
public class NumberOfIslands {

    public int numIslands(char[][] grid) {
        if (grid == null || grid.length == 0) {
            return 0;
```

```
        }

        int numIslands = 0;
        int rows = grid.length;
        int cols = grid[0].length;

        for (int i = 0; i < rows; i++) {
            for (int j = 0; j < cols; j++) {
                if (grid[i][j] == '1') {
                    numIslands++;
                    dfs(grid, i, j);
                }
            }
        }

        return numIslands;
    }

    private void dfs(char[][] grid, int i, int j) {
        int rows = grid.length;
        int cols = grid[0].length;

        // Boundary check
        if (i < 0 || i >= rows || j < 0 || j >= cols || grid[i][j] ==
'0') {
            return;
        }

        // Mark this cell as visited by setting it to '0'
        grid[i][j] = '0';

        // Explore all four directions
        dfs(grid, i - 1, j); // Up
        dfs(grid, i + 1, j); // Down
        dfs(grid, i, j - 1); // Left
        dfs(grid, i, j + 1); // Right
    }

    public static void main(String[] args) {
        NumberOfIslands solution = new NumberOfIslands();

        char[][] grid1 = {
                {'1', '1', '0', '0', '0'},
                {'1', '1', '0', '0', '0'},
                {'0', '0', '1', '0', '0'},
                {'0', '0', '0', '1', '1'}
        };
        System.out.println(solution.numIslands(grid1)); // Expected
output: 3

        char[][] grid2 = {
                {'1', '1', '1'},
                {'0', '1', '0'},
                {'1', '1', '1'}
```

```
        };
        System.out.println(solution.numIslands(grid2)); // Expected
output: 1

        char[][] grid3 = {
                {'1', '0', '0', '1'},
                {'0', '0', '0', '0'},
                {'1', '0', '1', '1'}
        };
        System.out.println(solution.numIslands(grid3)); // Expected
output: 4

        char[][] grid4 = {
                {'0', '0', '0'},
                {'0', '0', '0'},
                {'0', '0', '0'}
        };
        System.out.println(solution.numIslands(grid4)); // Expected
output: 0
    }
}
```

Time and Space Complexity

- The time complexity of this approach is `O(m * n)` where `m` is the number of rows and `n` is the number of columns. This is because we visit each cell once.
- The space complexity is `O(m * n)` in the worst case due to the recursion stack if the grid is filled with land.

Problem 3: Network Delay Time

Problem Statement

You are given a network of `n` nodes, labeled from `1` to `n`. You are also given `times`, a list of travel times as directed edges `times[i] = (`u_i`, `v_i`, `w_i`)`, where u_i is the source node, v_i is the target node, and w_i is the time it takes for a signal to travel from source to target.

We will send a signal from a given node `k`. Return *the **minimum** time it takes for all the* `n` *nodes to receive the signal.* If it is impossible for all the `n` nodes to receive the signal, return `-1`.

Solution

Thank you for the problem statement. I'd like to ask a few clarifying questions before proceeding with the solution.

Clarifying Questions

Candidate: Are the nodes guaranteed to be connected, or could there be isolated nodes that make it impossible for some nodes to receive the signal?
Interviewer: The nodes might not be fully connected, so it's possible for some nodes to be unreachable from the starting node k.

Candidate:Are there any constraints on the values of n (the number of nodes) and the size of the times list?
Interviewer: You can assume that n is up to 100, and the times list could have up to 10,000 elements.

Candidate:Should the signal travel time be considered cumulative as it travels through multiple nodes?
Interviewer: Yes, the signal travel time accumulates as it travels from node to node.

Candidate:Are there any negative weights in the travel times, or are all weights positive?
Interviewer: All weights are positive, so there won't be any negative cycles.

Candidate: Great, I have a clear understanding of the problem. I'll start by discussing an example and then move on to the solution approach.

Example

Let's consider an example:

```
n = 4
times = [
  [2, 1, 1],
  [2, 3, 1],
  [3, 4, 1]
]
k = 2
```

In this example:

- The signal starts at node 2.
- It takes 1 unit of time to travel from node 2 to node 1.
- It takes 1 unit of time to travel from node 2 to node 3.
- It takes 1 unit of time to travel from node 3 to node 4.

The minimum time required for all nodes to receive the signal would be 2, since node 4 will be the last to receive it after 2 units of time.

Brute Force Approach

A brute force approach might involve trying to calculate the shortest path from the source node k to every other node using an exhaustive search. However, given the constraints, this approach would be inefficient. We need a more optimized method to handle the possible large size of the input.

Optimal Approach

The problem can be efficiently solved using *Dijkstra's Algorithm*.

Dijkstra's Algorithm is well-suited for finding the shortest path from a single source node to all other nodes in a graph with non-negative edge weights.

Here's the approach:

1. Use a *priority queue* to always expand the shortest path first.
2. Set the distance to the starting node `k` as `0` and all other nodes as `infinity`.
3. Pop the node with the *smallest distance* from the queue, update the distances to its neighboring nodes, and push them into the queue if the new distance is smaller.
4. Continue until all nodes are processed.
5. The *maximum distance in the distance array will be the time required* for all nodes to receive the signal. If any node remains unreachable (infinity), return `-1`.

Code Solution

Here's the Java code using Dijkstra's algorithm:

```
import java.util.*;

public class NetworkDelayTime {

   public int networkDelayTime(int[][] times, int n, int k) {
       Map<Integer, List<int[]>> graph = new HashMap<>();

       // Build the graph
       for (int[] time : times) {
           graph.computeIfAbsent(time[0], x -> new
ArrayList<>()).add(new int[]{time[1], time[2]});
       }

       // Min-heap to process nodes with the smallest known
distance first
       PriorityQueue<int[]> pq = new
PriorityQueue<>(Comparator.comparingInt(a -> a[1]));
       pq.add(new int[]{k, 0});

       // Distance array to store the shortest distance from node k
to each node
       int[] dist = new int[n + 1];
       Arrays.fill(dist, Integer.MAX_VALUE);
       dist[k] = 0;

       // Set to keep track of visited nodes
       boolean[] visited = new boolean[n + 1];

       while (!pq.isEmpty()) {
           int[] current = pq.poll();
           int node = current[0];
           int time = current[1];
```

```
            if (visited[node]) continue;
            visited[node] = true;

            if (!graph.containsKey(node)) continue;

            for (int[] neighbor : graph.get(node)) {
                int nextNode = neighbor[0];
                int travelTime = neighbor[1];

                if (!visited[nextNode] && dist[nextNode] > time +
travelTime) {
                    dist[nextNode] = time + travelTime;
                    pq.add(new int[]{nextNode, dist[nextNode]});
                }
            }
        }

        int maxTime = 0;
        for (int i = 1; i <= n; i++) {
            if (dist[i] == Integer.MAX_VALUE) return -1;
            maxTime = Math.max(maxTime, dist[i]);
        }

        return maxTime;
    }

    public static void main(String[] args) {
        NetworkDelayTime solution = new NetworkDelayTime();

        int[][] times1 = {
                {2, 1, 1},
                {2, 3, 1},
                {3, 4, 1}
        };
        System.out.println(solution.networkDelayTime(times1, 4, 2));
// Expected output: 2

        int[][] times2 = {
                {1, 2, 1}
        };
        System.out.println(solution.networkDelayTime(times2, 2, 1));
// Expected output: 1

        int[][] times3 = {
                {1, 2, 1},
                {2, 3, 2},
                {1, 3, 4}
        };
        System.out.println(solution.networkDelayTime(times3, 3, 1));
// Expected output: 3

        int[][] times4 = {
                {1, 2, 1},
                {2, 3, 2},
```

```
                {3, 1, 4}
        };
        System.out.println(solution.networkDelayTime(times4, 3, 2));
// Expected output: 3
    }
}
```

Time and Space Complexity

- The time complexity is `O((V + E) log V)`, where `V` is the number of nodes, and `E` is the number of edges. This comes from the fact that we process each edge once, and each operation with the priority queue takes `O(log V)` time.
- The space complexity is `O(V + E)` due to the space required to store the graph and the priority queue.

Problem 4: Course Schedule

Problem Statement

There are a total of `numCourses` courses you have to take, labeled from `0` to `numCourses - 1`. You are given an array called `prerequisites` where `prerequisites[i] = [`a_i`, `b_i`]` indicates that you must take course b_i first if you want to take course a_i.

Return the ordering of courses you should take to finish all courses. If there are many valid answers, return any of them. If it is impossible to finish all courses, return an empty array.

Solution

Thank you for the problem statement. I'd like to ask a few clarifying questions before I proceed.

Clarifying Questions

Candidate: Can there be multiple valid course orderings, and if so, should I return just one of them?
Interviewer: Yes, there can be multiple valid orderings. You can return any valid ordering.

Candidate:What should I return if there's a cycle in the prerequisites, making it impossible to complete all the courses?
Interviewer: If it's impossible to finish all the courses due to a cycle, you should return an empty array.

Candidate:Are the course numbers guaranteed to be within the range 0 to numCourses - 1?
Interviewer: Yes, all course numbers will be within this range.

Candidate:Thanks for the clarifications! I'll start with an example to illustrate the problem and then discuss my approach.

Let's consider an example:

```
numCourses = 4
prerequisites = [
  [1, 0],
  [2, 0],
  [3, 1],
  [3, 2]
]
```

In this example, dependencies are as follows:

- You must take course `0` before you can take courses `1` and `2`.
- You must also take courses `1` and `2` before you can take course `3`.

A valid course order would be `[0, 1, 2, 3]` or `[0, 2, 1, 3]`. The *key point* is that `0` must come before `1` and `2`, and both `1` and `2` must come before `3`.

Brute Force Approach

A brute force approach might involve generating all possible permutations of courses and checking if each permutation satisfies the prerequisite conditions. However, this approach would be inefficient given the large number of permutations for even a small number of courses.

Optimal Approach

The optimal approach involves using ***Topological Sorting*** of a Directed Acyclic Graph (DAG).

This problem can be modeled as a graph where each *course is a node*, and a directed edge from course b to course a (b -> a) indicates that course b must be taken before course a.

Here's the plan:

1. **Build the graph**: Represent the courses as nodes and the prerequisites as directed edges.
2. **Calculate in-degrees**: For each node (course), calculate its in-degree (the number of edges pointing to it).
3. **Perform BFS**: Start with all nodes that have an in-degree of 0 (i.e., courses with no prerequisites). Process these nodes and reduce the in-degrees of their neighbors accordingly. If a neighbor's in-degree drops to 0, add it to the queue.
4. **Check for a cycle**: If there are still nodes left with non-zero in-degree after processing all the courses, it means there's a cycle, and it's impossible to finish all the courses.

Code Solution

Here's the Java code using ***Kahn's Algorithm*** (BFS for *Topological Sorting*):

```
import java.util.*;

public class CourseSchedule {

    public int[] findOrder(int numCourses, int[][] prerequisites) {
        List<List<Integer>> graph = new ArrayList<>();
        int[] inDegree = new int[numCourses];
        Queue<Integer> queue = new LinkedList<>();
        int[] result = new int[numCourses];
        int index = 0;

        // Initialize graph
        for (int i = 0; i < numCourses; i++) {
            graph.add(new ArrayList<>());
        }

        // Build graph and calculate in-degrees
        for (int[] prereq : prerequisites) {
            int course = prereq[0];
            int prerequisite = prereq[1];
            graph.get(prerequisite).add(course);
            inDegree[course]++;
        }

        // Add courses with no prerequisites (in-degree 0) to the
queue
        for (int i = 0; i < numCourses; i++) {
            if (inDegree[i] == 0) {
                queue.add(i);
            }
        }

        // Process the courses in topological order
        while (!queue.isEmpty()) {
            int current = queue.poll();
            result[index++] = current;

            for (int neighbor : graph.get(current)) {
                inDegree[neighbor]--;
                if (inDegree[neighbor] == 0) {
                    queue.add(neighbor);
                }
            }
        }

        // If we managed to process all courses, return the result,
otherwise return an empty array
        if (index == numCourses) {
            return result;
        } else {
            return new int[0];
        }
    }
```

```
    public static void main(String[] args) {
        CourseSchedule solution = new CourseSchedule();

        int numCourses1 = 4;
        int[][] prerequisites1 = {
                {1, 0},
                {2, 0},
                {3, 1},
                {3, 2}
        };

System.out.println(Arrays.toString(solution.findOrder(numCourses1,
prerequisites1))); // Expected output: [0, 1, 2, 3] or [0, 2, 1, 3]

        int numCourses2 = 2;
        int[][] prerequisites2 = {
                {1, 0},
                {0, 1}
        };

System.out.println(Arrays.toString(solution.findOrder(numCourses2,
prerequisites2))); // Expected output: []

        int numCourses3 = 6;
        int[][] prerequisites3 = {
                {5, 2},
                {5, 0},
                {4, 0},
                {4, 1},
                {2, 3},
                {3, 1}
        };

System.out.println(Arrays.toString(solution.findOrder(numCourses3,
prerequisites3))); // Expected output: [0, 1, 3, 2, 4, 5]
    }
}
```

Time and Space Complexity

- The time complexity is `O(V + E)`, where `V` is the number of courses, and `E` is the number of prerequisite pairs. This is because each course and each edge is processed exactly once.
- The space complexity is `O(V + E)` due to the space required for the graph representation and the in-degree array.

Problem 5: Accounts Merge

Problem Statement

Given a list of accounts where each element `accounts[i]` is a list of strings, where the first element `accounts[i][0]` is a *name*, and the rest of the elements are *emails* representing emails of the account.

Now, we would like to *merge these accounts*. Two accounts definitely belong to the same person if there is some *common email* to both accounts.

Note that even if two accounts have the same name, they may belong to different people as people could have the same name.

A person can have any number of accounts initially, but all of their accounts definitely have the same name.

After merging the accounts, return the accounts in the following format: the first element of each account is the name, and the rest of the elements are emails in sorted order.

The accounts themselves can be returned in any order.

Solution

Thank you for the problem statement. I'd like to ask a few clarifying questions to ensure I fully understand the problem.

Clarifying Questions

Candidate: Should the emails in the final output be unique and sorted for each merged account?
Interviewer: Yes, the emails should be unique and sorted in lexicographical order.

Candidate: Are we guaranteed that the input will have at least one account, and that each account will have at least one email?
Interviewer: Yes, you can assume there's at least one account and each account has at least one email.

Candidate: Does the order of the accounts in the output matter, or can they be returned in any order?
Interviewer: The order of the accounts in the output doesn't matter.

Candidate: Thanks for the clarifications! I'll start with an example and then proceed to the solution.

Let's consider an example:

```
accounts = [
  ["John", "johnsmith@mail.com", "john00@mail.com"],
```

```
  ["John", "johnnybravo@mail.com"],
  ["John", "johnsmith@mail.com", "john_newyork@mail.com"],
  ["Mary", "mary@mail.com"]
]
```

In this example:

- The *first* and *third* accounts belong to the same person because they share the email *johnsmith@mail.com.*
- The second account belongs to the same person but doesn't share any emails with the other accounts.
- The fourth account belongs to a different person, "Mary".

The expected output after merging should be:

```
[
  ["John", "john00@mail.com", "john_newyork@mail.com",
"johnsmith@mail.com"],
  ["John", "johnnybravo@mail.com"],
  ["Mary", "mary@mail.com"]
]
```

Approach

This problem can be solved using a graph-based approach, specifically with ***Union-Find (Disjoint Set)*** to *group the emails that belong to the same person.*

Here's the plan:

1. Build a graph where each email is a node, and there's an edge between two nodes if they appear in the same account.
2. Union the emails using Union-Find to group them together.
3. Map the emails to the corresponding person and gather the emails for each connected component.
4. Sort the emails within each component and format the output.

Code Solution

Here's the Java code using the Union-Find approach:

```
import java.util.*;

public class AccountsMerge {

   public List<List<String>> accountsMerge(List<List<String>>
accounts) {
        Map<String, String> emailToName = new HashMap<>();
        Map<String, String> parent = new HashMap<>();
        Map<String, TreeSet<String>> unions = new HashMap<>();

        // Initialize Union-Find structure
        for (List<String> account : accounts) {
            String name = account.get(0);
            for (int i = 1; i < account.size(); i++) {
                String email = account.get(i);
```

```
                parent.put(email, email);
                emailToName.put(email, name);
            }
        }

        // Union emails within the same account
        for (List<String> account : accounts) {
            String firstEmail = account.get(1);
            for (int i = 2; i < account.size(); i++) {
                union(parent, firstEmail, account.get(i));
            }
        }

        // Group emails by their root parent
        for (List<String> account : accounts) {
            for (int i = 1; i < account.size(); i++) {
                String email = account.get(i);
                String rootEmail = find(parent, email);
                unions.computeIfAbsent(rootEmail, x -> new
TreeSet<>()).add(email);
            }
        }

        // Prepare the output
        List<List<String>> result = new ArrayList<>();
        for (String rootEmail : unions.keySet()) {
            List<String> emails = new
ArrayList<>(unions.get(rootEmail));
            emails.add(0, emailToName.get(rootEmail));
            result.add(emails);
        }

        return result;
    }

    private String find(Map<String, String> parent, String email) {
        if (!parent.get(email).equals(email)) {
            parent.put(email, find(parent, parent.get(email))); //
Path compression
        }
        return parent.get(email);
    }

    private void union(Map<String, String> parent, String email1,
String email2) {
        String root1 = find(parent, email1);
        String root2 = find(parent, email2);
        if (!root1.equals(root2)) {
            parent.put(root1, root2);
        }
    }

    public static void main(String[] args) {
        AccountsMerge solution = new AccountsMerge();
```

```
        List<List<String>> accounts1 = Arrays.asList(
                Arrays.asList("John", "johnsmith@mail.com",
"john00@mail.com"),
                Arrays.asList("John", "johnnybravo@mail.com"),
                Arrays.asList("John", "johnsmith@mail.com",
"john_newyork@mail.com"),
                Arrays.asList("Mary", "mary@mail.com")
        );
        System.out.println(solution.accountsMerge(accounts1));
        // Expected output:
        // [
        //   ["John", "john00@mail.com", "john_newyork@mail.com",
"johnsmith@mail.com"],
        //   ["John", "johnnybravo@mail.com"],
        //   ["Mary", "mary@mail.com"]
        // ]

        List<List<String>> accounts2 = Arrays.asList(
                Arrays.asList("Gabe", "Gabe0@m.co", "Gabe3@m.co",
"Gabe1@m.co"),
                Arrays.asList("Gabe", "Gabe3@m.co", "Gabe4@m.co",
"Gabe2@m.co"),
                Arrays.asList("Gabe", "Gabe4@m.co", "Gabe5@m.co")
        );
        System.out.println(solution.accountsMerge(accounts2));
        // Expected output:
        // [
        //   ["Gabe", "Gabe0@m.co", "Gabe1@m.co", "Gabe2@m.co",
"Gabe3@m.co", "Gabe4@m.co", "Gabe5@m.co"]
        // ]
    }
}
```

Time and Space Complexity

- The time complexity is `O(N * α(N))`, where `N` is the total number of emails, and `α(N)` is the inverse Ackermann function, which is very slow-growing, making it almost constant in practice.
- The space complexity is `O(N)`, where `N` is the total number of emails. This is because we are using extra space to store the parent pointers, the email-to-name mapping, and the unions.

Problem 6: Clone Graph

Problem Statement

Given a reference of a node in a connected undirected graph.

Return a *deep copy (clone)* of the graph.

Each node in the graph contains a `value (int)` and a `list (List[Node])` of its neighbors.

```
class Node {
    public int val;
    public List<Node> neighbors;
}
```

Solution

Thank you for the problem statement. I'd like to ask a few clarifying questions before proceeding.

Clarifying Questions

Candidate: Is the graph guaranteed to be connected, or could there be isolated nodes?
Interviewer: The graph is guaranteed to be connected.

Candidate: Can the graph contain cycles, meaning a node could eventually reference itself through its neighbors?
Interviewer: Yes, the graph can contain cycles, so the solution must handle such cases.

Candidate: Is the input graph mutable, or can I assume the input graph won't change during the operation?
Interviewer: You can assume the input graph won't change during the cloning operation.

Candidate: Should I worry about the node values being unique, or can there be multiple nodes with the same value?
Interviewer: There could be multiple nodes with the same value, so the value alone shouldn't be used to distinguish nodes.

Great, I think I have all the information I need. Let me dive into the approach and code solution now.

Approach

To clone a graph, we need to ensure that every node in the original graph is copied exactly once, and that the connections (edges) between nodes are preserved.

This problem can be approached using graph traversal algorithms such as Depth-First Search (DFS) or Breadth-First Search (BFS).

The key steps are:

1. Use a *hashmap* to keep track of cloned nodes. The keys will be the original nodes, and the values will be their corresponding cloned nodes.
2. Traverse the graph using DFS or BFS, and for each node:
    - If the node has already been cloned (exists in the hash map), return the cloned node.

   - Otherwise, create a clone of the node, and recursively clone all its neighbors.
3. Handle cycles by using the hash map to avoid reprocessing nodes that have already been cloned.

Code Solution

Here's the Java implementation using a recursive DFS approach:

```
import java.util.*;

class Node {
   public int val;
   public List<Node> neighbors;

   public Node() {
       val = 0;
       neighbors = new ArrayList<Node>();
   }

   public Node(int _val) {
       val = _val;
       neighbors = new ArrayList<Node>();
   }

   public Node(int _val, ArrayList<Node> _neighbors) {
       val = _val;
       neighbors = _neighbors;
   }
}

public class CloneGraph {

   private Map<Node, Node> visited = new HashMap<>();

   public Node cloneGraph(Node node) {
       if (node == null) {
           return null;
       }

       // If the node was already cloned, return the clone.
       if (visited.containsKey(node)) {
           return visited.get(node);
       }

       // Create a new node for the clone with the same value as
the original node.
       Node clone = new Node(node.val);
       visited.put(node, clone);

       // Recursively clone all the neighbors
       for (Node neighbor : node.neighbors) {
           clone.neighbors.add(cloneGraph(neighbor));
       }
```

```
        return clone;
    }

    public static void main(String[] args) {
        CloneGraph solution = new CloneGraph();

        // Example usage:
        // Creating a graph manually for testing
        Node node1 = new Node(1);
        Node node2 = new Node(2);
        Node node3 = new Node(3);
        Node node4 = new Node(4);

        node1.neighbors.add(node2);
        node1.neighbors.add(node4);

        node2.neighbors.add(node1);
        node2.neighbors.add(node3);

        node3.neighbors.add(node2);
        node3.neighbors.add(node4);

        node4.neighbors.add(node1);
        node4.neighbors.add(node3);

        // Cloning the graph
        Node clonedGraph = solution.cloneGraph(node1);

        // Print to verify (this is a simple check, real validation
would require deeper inspection)
        System.out.println("Original Node 1 Neighbors: " +
node1.neighbors.size());
        System.out.println("Cloned Node 1 Neighbors: " +
clonedGraph.neighbors.size());
    }
}
```

Time and Space Complexity

- The time complexity is `O(N + M)`, where `N` is the number of nodes and `M` is the number of edges. This is because we visit every node and every edge exactly once during the traversal.
- The space complexity is `O(N)`, where `N` is the number of nodes. This space is used by the recursion stack (in the DFS approach) and the hashmap to store the cloned nodes.

Problem 7: Graph Valid Tree

Problem Statement

You have a graph of `n` nodes labeled from `0` to `n - 1`. You are given an integer `n` and a list of edges where `edges[i] = [`a_i`, `b_i`]` indicates that there is an undirected edge between nodes a_i and b_i in the graph.

Return *true* if the edges of the given graph make up a valid tree, and otherwise return *false*.

Solution

I'd like to ask a few clarifying questions before proceeding.

Clarifying Questions

Candidate: What exactly defines a "valid tree" in this context?
Interviewer: A valid tree is an undirected graph that is connected and acyclic. This means there must be exactly `n - 1` edges for `n` nodes, and every node must be reachable from any other node.

Candidate: Can we assume that the input edge list has no duplicate edges?
Interviewer: Yes, you can assume that there are no duplicate edges in the input.

Great, I think I have all the information I need. Let me discuss the approach now.

Approach

I'll approach the problem using depth-first search or breadth-first search.

The key idea is to ensure that the graph is *connected and acyclic.* A valid tree must satisfy these two conditions:

1. **Connectivity**: Every node must be reachable from any other node.
2. **Acyclicity**: The graph must not contain any cycles.

Here's how we can solve the problem using DFS or BFS:

1. Start from any node.
2. Traverse the graph (using either DFS or BFS), marking nodes as visited.
3. If we encounter a node that has already been visited and is not the direct parent of the current node, then the graph contains a cycle.
4. After the traversal, if all nodes have been visited and no cycles were detected, then the graph is a valid tree.

Code using DFS Approach

```
import java.util.*;

public class GraphValidTreeDFS {

    public boolean validTree(int n, int[][] edges) {
```

```java
        if (edges.length != n - 1) {
            return false;
        }

        // Build the adjacency list
        List<List<Integer>> graph = new ArrayList<>();
        for (int i = 0; i < n; i++) {
            graph.add(new ArrayList<>());
        }
        for (int[] edge : edges) {
            graph.get(edge[0]).add(edge[1]);
            graph.get(edge[1]).add(edge[0]);
        }

        // Array to keep track of visited nodes
        boolean[] visited = new boolean[n];

        // Perform DFS to check for cycles and connectivity
        if (hasCycle(graph, 0, -1, visited)) {
            return false;
        }

        // Check if all nodes were visited (ensuring connectivity)
        for (boolean v : visited) {
            if (!v) {
                return false;
            }
        }

        return true;
    }

    private boolean hasCycle(List<List<Integer>> graph, int node, int
parent, boolean[] visited) {
        visited[node] = true;

        for (int neighbor : graph.get(node)) {
            if (!visited[neighbor]) {
                if (hasCycle(graph, neighbor, node, visited)) {
                    return true;
                }
            } else if (neighbor != parent) {
                // If visited and not parent, then it's a back edge,
indicating a cycle
                return true;
            }
        }

        return false;
    }

    public static void main(String[] args) {
        GraphValidTreeDFS solution = new GraphValidTreeDFS();
```

```
        int n1 = 5;
        int[][] edges1 = {
                {0, 1},
                {0, 2},
                {0, 3},
                {1, 4}
        };
        System.out.println(solution.validTree(n1, edges1)); //
Expected output: true

        int n2 = 5;
        int[][] edges2 = {
                {0, 1},
                {1, 2},
                {2, 3},
                {1, 3},
                {1, 4}
        };
        System.out.println(solution.validTree(n2, edges2)); //
Expected output: false (Cycle detected)

        int n3 = 4;
        int[][] edges3 = {
                {0, 1},
                {2, 3}
        };
        System.out.println(solution.validTree(n3, edges3)); //
Expected output: false (Not connected)
    }
}
```

Code using BFS Approach

```
import java.util.*;

public class GraphValidTreeBFS {

    public boolean validTree(int n, int[][] edges) {
        if (edges.length != n - 1) {
            return false;
        }

        // Build the adjacency list
        List<List<Integer>> graph = new ArrayList<>();
        for (int i = 0; i < n; i++) {
            graph.add(new ArrayList<>());
        }
        for (int[] edge : edges) {
            graph.get(edge[0]).add(edge[1]);
            graph.get(edge[1]).add(edge[0]);
        }

        // Array to keep track of visited nodes
```

```
        boolean[] visited = new boolean[n];

        // Use a queue for BFS
        Queue<Integer> queue = new LinkedList<>();
        queue.add(0);
        visited[0] = true;

        while (!queue.isEmpty()) {
            int node = queue.poll();

            for (int neighbor : graph.get(node)) {
                if (!visited[neighbor]) {
                    visited[neighbor] = true;
                    queue.add(neighbor);
                } else {
                    // If we see a visited neighbor, remove it from
the adjacency list to avoid revisiting
                    // If it's the parent, this removal prevents
recognizing it as a cycle
                    graph.get(neighbor).remove((Integer) node);
                }
            }
        }

        // Check if all nodes were visited (ensuring connectivity)
        for (boolean v : visited) {
            if (!v) {
                return false;
            }
        }

        return true;
    }

    public static void main(String[] args) {
        GraphValidTreeBFS solution = new GraphValidTreeBFS();

        int n1 = 5;
        int[][] edges1 = {
                {0, 1},
                {0, 2},
                {0, 3},
                {1, 4}
        };
        System.out.println(solution.validTree(n1, edges1)); //
Expected output: true

        int n2 = 5;
        int[][] edges2 = {
                {0, 1},
                {1, 2},
                {2, 3},
                {1, 3},
                {1, 4}
```

```
        };
        System.out.println(solution.validTree(n2, edges2)); //
Expected output: false (Cycle detected)

        int n3 = 4;
        int[][] edges3 = {
                {0, 1},
                {2, 3}
        };
        System.out.println(solution.validTree(n3, edges3)); //
Expected output: false (Not connected)
    }
}
```

Time and Space Complexity

Time Complexity:

- DFS/BFS Traversal: The time complexity is `O(V + E)`, where `V` is the number of vertices (nodes) and `E` is the number of edges.

Space Complexity:

- DFS: The space complexity is `O(V)` for the recursion stack and visited array.
- BFS: The space complexity is `O(V)` for the queue and visited array.

Problem 8: Cheapest Flights Within K Stops

Problem Statement

Given `n` cities connected by some number of flights. You are given an array flights where `flights[i] = [from`$_i$`, to`$_i$`, price`$_i$`]` indicates that there is a flight from city `from`$_i$ to city `to`$_i$ with cost `price`$_i$.

You are also given three integers `src`, `dst`, and `k`, return the cheapest price from `src` to `dst` with at most `k` stops. If there is no such route, return `-1`.

Solution

Thank you for the problem statement. I'd like to clarify a few points before proceeding.

Clarifying Questions

Candidate: Are the flights directed, meaning they only go one way from `from_i` to `to_i`?
Interviewer: Yes, the flights are directed.

Candidate: Is it possible for a flight to have zero cost, or will all costs be positive?
Interviewer: All costs are non-negative.

Candidate: Should we prioritize finding the path with the minimum cost, or the path with the minimum stops, when there is a tie in cost?
Interviewer: Your primary goal is to find the path with the *minimum cost*, considering up to k stops.

Great, with that understanding, I'll outline my approach and then proceed with the code.

Approach

This problem can be efficiently solved using a variation of ***Breadth-First Search (BFS) with a priority queue*** *(min-heap)*.

The idea is to explore the cheapest flight options first, while also keeping track of the number of stops made.

Here's the step-by-step approach:

1. **Graph Representation:**
   - We'll first convert the *list of flights into an adjacency list* to represent the graph. Each *city will be a node*, and *each flight will be a directed edge between two nodes* with a given cost.
2. **Priority Queue Initialization:**
   - We'll use a priority queue (min-heap) to explore the cheapest path first. Each element in the queue will be an array containing the current cost, the current city, and the number of stops made so far.
3. **Stops Tracking:**
   - We'll maintain an array called `stops` to keep track of the minimum number of stops needed to reach each city. This helps us avoid revisiting cities with more stops than necessary.
4. **BFS Traversal:**
   - We'll traverse the graph starting from the source city, expanding the cheapest paths first, and updating the stops array as we go. If we reach the destination city within the allowed stops, we'll return the cost.
5. **Handling Edge Cases:**
   - If we exhaust the queue without finding a valid path, we'll return -1 indicating that it's not possible to reach the destination within the given constraints.

Code Solution

Here's the Java code implementing this approach:

```
import java.util.*;

public class CheapestFlightsWithinKStops {

    public int findCheapestPrice(int n, int[][] flights, int src, int
dst, int k) {
        // Step 1: Initialize the graph
        Map<Integer, List<int[]>> adj = new HashMap<>();
        for (int[] flight : flights) {
```

```
            adj.computeIfAbsent(flight[0], value -> new
ArrayList<>()).add(new int[]{flight[1], flight[2]});
        }

        // Step 2: Initialize the stops array
        int[] stops = new int[n];
        Arrays.fill(stops, Integer.MAX_VALUE);

        // Step 3: Priority queue to explore the cheapest paths
first
        PriorityQueue<int[]> pq = new PriorityQueue<>((a, b) -> a[0]
- b[0]);
        // {current_cost, current_city, current_stops}
        pq.offer(new int[]{0, src, 0});

        // Step 4: Process the priority queue
        while (!pq.isEmpty()) {
            int[] temp = pq.poll();
            int current_cost = temp[0];
            int current_city = temp[1];
            int current_stops = temp[2];

            // Step 5: If the number of stops exceeds the limit or
is not optimal, skip this path
            if (current_stops > stops[current_city] || current_stops
> k + 1) {
                continue;
            }

            // Update the stops array for the current city
            stops[current_city] = current_stops;

            // If the current city is the destination, return the
current cost
            if (current_city == dst) {
                return current_cost;
            }

            // If the current city has no outgoing edges, continue
to the next node in the queue
            if (!adj.containsKey(current_city)) {
                continue;
            }

            // Explore all neighboring cities
            for (int[] neighbor : adj.get(current_city)) {
                int next_city = neighbor[0];
                int next_cost = neighbor[1];
                pq.offer(new int[]{current_cost + next_cost,
next_city, current_stops + 1});
            }
        }

        // Step 6: If no valid path is found within the constraints,
```

```
return -1
        return -1;
    }

    public static void main(String[] args) {
        CheapestFlightsWithinKStops solution = new
CheapestFlightsWithinKStops();

        int n1 = 3;
        int[][] flights1 = {
                {0, 1, 100},
                {1, 2, 100},
                {0, 2, 500}
        };
        int src1 = 0;
        int dst1 = 2;
        int k1 = 1;
        System.out.println(solution.findCheapestPrice(n1, flights1,
src1, dst1, k1)); // Expected output: 200

        int n2 = 3;
        int[][] flights2 = {
                {0, 1, 100},
                {1, 2, 100},
                {0, 2, 500}
        };
        int src2 = 0;
        int dst2 = 2;
        int k2 = 0;
        System.out.println(solution.findCheapestPrice(n2, flights2,
src2, dst2, k2)); // Expected output: 500

        int n3 = 4;
        int[][] flights3 = {
                {0, 1, 100},
                {0, 2, 300},
                {1, 2, 100},
                {2, 3, 100}
        };
        int src3 = 0;
        int dst3 = 3;
        int k3 = 1;
        System.out.println(solution.findCheapestPrice(n3, flights3,
src3, dst3, k3)); // Expected output: 400
    }
}
```

Time and Space Complexity

- Time Complexity: `O((n + E) * log n)`, where `n` is the number of cities and `E` is the number of flights. The `log n` factor comes from the *priority queue* operations.

- Space Complexity: `O(n + E)`, where `n` is the number of cities and `E` is the number of flights. This space is used to store the graph, the priority queue, and the stops array.

Problem 9: Is Graph Bipartite

Problem Statement

You are given an undirected graph with `n` nodes, numbered from `0` to `n - 1`.

The graph is represented by a 2D array `graph`, where `graph[u]` lists all nodes adjacent to node `u`.

The graph has no self-loops, no duplicate edges, and is undirected, meaning if `v` is in `graph[u]`, then `u` is in `graph[v]`.

The graph may also be disconnected.

> *A graph is bipartite if its nodes can be divided into two sets such that every edge connects nodes from different sets.*

Return `true` if the graph is bipartite, otherwise return `false`.

Solution

Thank you for the problem statement. I'd like to clarify a few things before diving into the solution.

Clarifying Questions

Candidate: Can the graph have multiple connected components, and should we consider each component separately when determining if the graph is bipartite?
Interviewer: Yes, the graph can have multiple components, and each component should be considered when determining if the graph is bipartite.

Candidate: Are there any constraints on the size of the graph, such as the number of nodes or edges?
Interviewer: The number of nodes n can be up to 100, and the graph array can contain up to 10,000 edges in total.

Candidate: Is the input graph guaranteed to be non-empty, or should we handle the case where n = 0?
Interviewer: You can assume that n is at least 1.

Great! I have a clear understanding now. I'll start by discussing the approach and then implement it in Java.

Approach

To determine if a graph is bipartite, we can use a ***graph coloring method.***

The idea is to try to color the graph using two colors such that no two adjacent nodes share the same color. If we can successfully color the graph in this manner, then the graph is bipartite; otherwise, it is not.

Here's the plan:

1. **Coloring the Graph:**
   - We will use two colors (say, 0 and 1).
   - Start by picking any unvisited node and color it with one color (say 0).
   - Then, attempt to color all its neighbors with the opposite color (1), and continue this process for the neighbors' neighbors, and so on.
   - If we ever find a situation where two adjacent nodes have the same color, then the graph is not bipartite.
2. **Handling Multiple Components:**
   - Since the graph may not be connected, we will need to repeat the above process for each component of the graph. We can iterate through each node and initiate the coloring process if the node has not been visited yet.
3. **DFS/BFS Choice:**
   - We can use either Depth-First Search (DFS) or Breadth-First Search (BFS) to implement this approach. I'll use BFS for this solution, but DFS would work just as well.

Code Solution

Here's the Java code implementing the BFS approach to check if the graph is bipartite:

```
import java.util.*;

public class IsGraphBipartite {

    public boolean isBipartite(int[][] graph) {
        int n = graph.length;
        int[] colors = new int[n];
        Arrays.fill(colors, -1); // -1 indicates that the node has
not been colored yet

        for (int i = 0; i < n; i++) {
            if (colors[i] == -1) { // If the node is uncolored, start
a BFS
                if (!bfsCheck(graph, i, colors)) {
                    return false;
                }
            }
        }
        return true;
    }

    private boolean bfsCheck(int[][] graph, int start, int[] colors)
```

```
{
        Queue<Integer> queue = new LinkedList<>();
        queue.offer(start);
        colors[start] = 0; // Start coloring with color 0

        while (!queue.isEmpty()) {
            int node = queue.poll();
            int currentColor = colors[node];
            int nextColor = 1 - currentColor; // Toggle between 0 and
1

            for (int neighbor : graph[node]) {
                if (colors[neighbor] == -1) { // If the neighbor has
not been colored
                    colors[neighbor] = nextColor;
                    queue.offer(neighbor);
                } else if (colors[neighbor] == currentColor) { // If
the neighbor has the same color
                    return false;
                }
            }
        }
        return true;
    }

    public static void main(String[] args) {
        IsGraphBipartite solution = new IsGraphBipartite();

        int[][] graph1 = {
                {1, 2},
                {0, 3},
                {0, 3},
                {1, 2}
        };
        System.out.println(solution.isBipartite(graph1)); // Expected
output: true

        int[][] graph2 = {
                {1, 3},
                {0, 2},
                {1, 3},
                {0, 2}
        };
        System.out.println(solution.isBipartite(graph2)); // Expected
output: true

        int[][] graph3 = {
                {1, 2, 3},
                {0, 2},
                {0, 1, 3},
                {0, 2}
        };
        System.out.println(solution.isBipartite(graph3)); // Expected
output: false
```

```
        int[][] graph4 = {
                {1},
                {0, 3},
                {3},
                {1, 2}
        };
        System.out.println(solution.isBipartite(graph4)); // Expected
output: true
    }
}
```

Time and Space Complexity

- Time Complexity: `O(V + E)`, where `V` is the number of vertices (nodes) and `E` is the number of edges. This is because we visit each node and edge exactly once.
- Space Complexity: `O(V)`, where `V` is the number of nodes. This space is used for the colors array and the BFS queue.

Problem 10: Reconstruct Flight Itinerary

Problem Statement

Given a list of airline tickets represented as pairs of departure and arrival airports, construct the itinerary starting from "JFK". The itinerary must use all tickets exactly once. If multiple valid itineraries exist, return the one that is lexicographically smallest.

Solution

Thank you for the question! I'd like to ask a few clarifying questions to ensure I fully understand the problem.

Clarifying Questions

Candidate: Are there any constraints on the number of tickets, or can the input size be large?
Interviewer: You can assume that the number of tickets is reasonably large, but it will fit into memory. The number of tickets can go up to around 10,000.

Candidate: Is it guaranteed that all tickets will form a valid itinerary, meaning we can always use all the tickets to create a complete path?
Interviewer: Yes, you can assume that all tickets form at least one valid itinerary.

Candidate: Should the output itinerary include all stops, including those that may be revisited, or just the unique ones?
Interviewer: The output should include all stops, even if some airports are visited more than once. The order must reflect the complete path using all tickets.

Candidate: If multiple itineraries have the same starting sequence but differ later on, how should we decide which one to return?
Interviewer: If multiple valid itineraries exist, you should return the one that is lexicographically smallest when read as a single string.
Candidate: Great, I think I have a good understanding of the problem. I'll start by discussing an example and then proceed with the implementation.

Example
Let's consider an example:
Input:
```
tickets = [["MUC", "LHR"], ["JFK", "MUC"], ["SFO", "SJC"], ["LHR",
"SFO"]]
```

Expected Output:
```
["JFK", "MUC", "LHR", "SFO", "SJC"]
```

The itinerary starts at "JFK" and follows the path that uses all the tickets exactly once.

Brute Force Approach

A brute force approach would involve *generating all possible permutations of the tickets*, then checking each one to see if it forms a valid itinerary starting from "JFK" and using all tickets exactly once.

Finally, we'd select the lexicographically smallest itinerary from the valid ones.

Efficiency:

- Time Complexity: This approach would be very inefficient, with a time complexity of `O((n!) * n)`, where `n` is the number of tickets. This is because we'd have to consider every possible permutation of the tickets and then validate each one.
- Space Complexity: The space complexity would also be high due to the storage required for all permutations.

This brute force approach is not practical for large inputs, so let's consider a more optimal solution.

Optimal Approach

The optimal approach leverages the graph traversal algorithm, specifically *Hierholzer's Algorithm*, which is used to ***find an Eulerian path in a graph***.

Here, each airport is a node, and each ticket is a directed edge from one node to another.

Here's how we can solve the problem:

1. **Graph Representation:**

  - We'll represent the tickets as a directed graph using an adjacency list. Each airport will be a node, and there will be directed edges between nodes corresponding to the tickets.
2. **Priority Queue for Lexicographical Order:**
   - For each node, we'll use a priority queue (min-heap) to store the destinations. This ensures that we always visit the smallest lexical airport first when there are multiple choices.
3. **DFS to Construct the Itinerary:**
   - We'll perform a Depth-First Search (DFS) starting from "JFK". As we traverse, we remove the tickets from the graph. When we reach an airport with no further destinations, we add that airport to the itinerary.
   - The itinerary is built in reverse, so after the DFS completes, we'll reverse the itinerary to get the correct order.

Code Solution

Here's how we can implement this in Java:

```
import java.util.*;

public class ReconstructItinerary {

   public List<String> findItinerary(List<List<String>> tickets) {
        // Step 1: Build the graph using a HashMap and PriorityQueue
for lexical order
        Map<String, PriorityQueue<String>> graph = new HashMap<>();
        for (List<String> ticket : tickets) {
            graph.computeIfAbsent(ticket.get(0), k -> new
PriorityQueue<>()).add(ticket.get(1));
        }

        // Step 2: Prepare a list to store the result itinerary
        LinkedList<String> itinerary = new LinkedList<>();

        // Step 3: Perform DFS from "JFK"
        dfs("JFK", graph, itinerary);

        // Step 4: The itinerary is built in reverse order, so no
need to reverse it manually
        return itinerary;
   }

   private void dfs(String airport, Map<String,
PriorityQueue<String>> graph, LinkedList<String> itinerary) {
        PriorityQueue<String> destinations = graph.get(airport);
        while (destinations != null && !destinations.isEmpty()) {
            String next = destinations.poll();
            dfs(next, graph, itinerary);
        }
        // Add the airport to the beginning of the itinerary
(reverse order)
        itinerary.addFirst(airport);
   }
```

```
    public static void main(String[] args) {
        ReconstructItinerary solution = new ReconstructItinerary();

        List<List<String>> tickets1 = Arrays.asList(
                Arrays.asList("MUC", "LHR"),
                Arrays.asList("JFK", "MUC"),
                Arrays.asList("SFO", "SJC"),
                Arrays.asList("LHR", "SFO")
        );
        System.out.println(solution.findItinerary(tickets1)); //
Expected output: [JFK, MUC, LHR, SFO, SJC]

        List<List<String>> tickets2 = Arrays.asList(
                Arrays.asList("JFK", "SFO"),
                Arrays.asList("JFK", "ATL"),
                Arrays.asList("SFO", "ATL"),
                Arrays.asList("ATL", "JFK"),
                Arrays.asList("ATL", "SFO")
        );
        System.out.println(solution.findItinerary(tickets2)); //
Expected output: [JFK, ATL, JFK, SFO, ATL, SFO]
    }
}
```

Time and Space Complexity

- The time complexity is `O(E * logE)`, where `E` is the number of flights. This is due to the priority queue operations in the graph traversal.
- The space complexity is `O(V + E)`, where `V` is the number of airports and `E` is the number of flights. This is due to the storage required for the adjacency list and the recursion stack.

Chapter 18: Tries

What is a Trie?

A Trie is a tree-like data structure that stores a *dynamic set of strings*, where each node represents a single character of a string.

The key property of a Trie is that ***all descendants of a node share a common prefix of the string associated with that node.***

This structure allows for efficient ***retrieval of strings***, making it ideal for tasks like autocomplete and spell checking.

Structure of a Trie

A trie is made up of *nodes* and *edges*. Each node represents a character of the alphabet, and the edges connect the nodes.

The root node is usually an empty string and does not contain any character. Every node in the trie can have as many children as there are letters in the alphabet, typically represented using an array or hash map.

Key Characteristics

- **Hierarchical Structure:** Tries are organized in a tree form where each level represents a character position in the string.
- **Efficient Retrieval:** Search operations can be performed in `O(M)` time, where `M` is the length of the string being searched.
- **Space Usage:** Tries can consume more space compared to other data structures like hash tables, especially when storing a large set of strings with little overlap.
- **Dynamic and Scalable:** They can easily handle dynamic datasets where strings can be added or removed efficiently.

Why Use Tries?

Understanding when and why to use Tries is crucial for tackling relevant interview problems effectively.

Advantages

- **Fast Search Operations:** Tries provide quick lookups for strings and prefixes, making them ideal for applications requiring real-time search suggestions.
- **Prefix-Based Queries:** They excel in scenarios where prefix matching is necessary, such as autocomplete features.

- **Sorted Data Retrieval:** Since nodes are often stored in a sorted manner, retrieving all keys in alphabetical order is straightforward.
- **Spell Checking:** Tries can efficiently check if a word exists in a dictionary and suggest corrections based on prefixes.

Disadvantages

- **High Memory Consumption:** They can use more memory compared to other data structures, especially when storing a large number of short strings.
- **Implementation Complexity:** Implementing a Trie correctly requires careful handling of edge cases and understanding of the underlying structure.

Popular Interview Questions on Trie

Let's look at a few most commonly asked coding interview questions on Tries.

Problem 1: Implement a Trie for Efficient String Operations

Problem Statement

Implement a *Trie* (prefix tree) that supports the following operations:

1. `Trie()`: Initializes the Trie.
2. `void insert(String word)`: Adds a word to the Trie.
3. `boolean search(String word)`: Returns true if the word exists in the Trie, otherwise returns false.
4. `boolean startsWith(String prefix)`: Returns true if any word in the Trie starts with the given prefix, otherwise returns false.

This data structure is useful for applications like *autocomplete and spell checking*.

Solution

Before I start coding, I'd like to ask a few clarifying questions to ensure I understand the requirements correctly.

Clarifying Questions

Candidate: Should the Trie be case-sensitive? For example, should "Apple" and "apple" be treated as different strings?
Interviewer: Yes, the Trie should be case-sensitive.

Candidate: Can we assume that the input strings will consist only of lowercase English letters, or should we handle other characters as well?
Interviewer: For simplicity, let's assume that the input strings will only consist of lowercase English letters ('a' to 'z').

Candidate: Should we consider cases where an empty string is inserted or searched for?
Interviewer: Let's assume that the input strings will always be non-empty.

Candidate: Are there any specific performance expectations for the operations, or is it sufficient to implement the basic operations efficiently?
Interviewer: The focus should be on implementing the basic operations efficiently. Performance considerations will naturally follow from a correct implementation.

Great! With that in mind, I'll start by explaining how we can implement the Trie and the operations you're asking for.

Example
Let's first sequence of operations as follows:

1. *Insert* Operations:
   - Insert `apple`
   - Insert `app`
2. *Search* Operations:
   - Search `apple` -> Should return `true`.
   - Search `app` -> Should return `true`.
   - Search `appl` -> Should return `false`.
3. *Prefix Search* Operations:
   - StartsWith `appl` -> Should return `true`.
   - StartsWith `apl` -> Should return `false`.

Approach

I'll implement the Trie class in **Java**, along with the *insert*, *search*, and *startsWith* methods.

Code

```
class Trie {
   private TrieNode root;

   // TrieNode definition
   private class TrieNode {
       TrieNode[] children;
       boolean isEndOfWord;

       TrieNode() {
           children = new TrieNode[26]; // For lowercase 'a' to 'z'
           isEndOfWord = false;
       }
   }

   // Initializes the trie object.
   public Trie() {
       root = new TrieNode();
   }

   // Inserts the string word into the trie.
   public void insert(String word) {
       TrieNode node = root;
       for (char c : word.toCharArray()) {
```

```
            int index = c - 'a'; // Map character to index
            if (node.children[index] == null) {
                node.children[index] = new TrieNode();
            }
            node = node.children[index];
        }
        node.isEndOfWord = true; // Mark the end of the word
    }

    // Returns true if the string word is in the trie.
    public boolean search(String word) {
        TrieNode node = root;
        for (char c : word.toCharArray()) {
            int index = c - 'a';
            if (node.children[index] == null) {
                return false;
            }
            node = node.children[index];
        }
        return node.isEndOfWord; // Only return true if it's the end
of a word
    }

    // Returns true if there is any word in the trie that starts
with the given prefix.
    public boolean startsWith(String prefix) {
        TrieNode node = root;
        for (char c : prefix.toCharArray()) {
            int index = c - 'a';
            if (node.children[index] == null) {
                return false;
            }
            node = node.children[index];
        }
        return true; // If we can traverse the entire prefix, return
true
    }

    // Main method to test the implementation
    public static void main(String[] args) {
        Trie trie = new Trie();

        trie.insert("apple");
        System.out.println(trie.search("apple"));   // true
        System.out.println(trie.search("app"));     // true
        System.out.println(trie.search("appl"));    // false
        System.out.println(trie.startsWith("app")); // true
        System.out.println(trie.startsWith("apl")); // false

        trie.insert("app");
        System.out.println(trie.search("app"));     // true
    }
}
```

Time and Space Complexity

- *Insert Operation*: The time complexity is `O(M)`, where `M` is the length of the word being inserted. The space complexity is also `O(M)` for storing the word in the Trie.
- *Search Operation*: The time complexity is `O(M)`, where `M` is the length of the word being searched. The space complexity is `O(1)` since we're just traversing the Trie.
- *StartsWith Operation*: The time complexity is `O(M)`, where `M` is the length of the prefix. The space complexity is `O(1)` for similar reasons.

Problem 2: Autocomplete System for Product Suggestions

Problem Statement

Given an *array of product names* and a *search word*, implement *a system that suggests up to three products from the array as you type each character of the search word.*

The suggested products must share a common prefix with the search word. If more than three products share the prefix, return the three lexicographically smallest products.

Return a list of lists containing the suggested products after each character of the search word is typed.

Solution

Before I start coding, I'd like to ask a few clarifying questions to make sure I understand the requirements fully.

Clarifying Questions

Candidate: Should the product names and searchWord be treated as case-sensitive? For example, should "Apple" and "apple" be considered different?
Interviewer: You can assume that all input will be in lowercase.

Candidate: Is the products array pre-sorted lexicographically, or do I need to handle sorting within the solution?
Interviewer: You should assume the products array is not pre-sorted, so you'll need to sort it as part of your solution.

Great, now let's walk through an example.

Example
Let's say you have the following:

```
Products: ["mobile", "mouse", "moneypot", "monitor", "mousepad"]
SearchWord: "mouse"
```

Step-by-Step Suggestions:

1. After typing `m`:
    - Possible matches: `"mobile", "moneypot", "monitor", "mouse", "mousepad"`
    - Suggested: `["mobile", "moneypot", "monitor"]`
2. After typing `mo`:
    - Possible matches: `"mobile", "moneypot", "monitor", "mouse", "mousepad"`
    - Suggested: `["mobile", "moneypot", "monitor"]`
3. After typing `mou`:
    - Possible matches: `"mouse", "mousepad"`
    - Suggested: `["mouse", "mousepad"]`
4. After typing `mous`:
    - Possible matches: `"mouse", "mousepad"`
    - Suggested: `["mouse", "mousepad"]`
5. After typing `mouse`:
    - Possible matches: `"mouse", "mousepad"`
    - Suggested: `["mouse", "mousepad"]`

Brute Force Approach

One possible approach is to iterate through the products array after each character of searchWord is typed and filter out the products that have the current prefix. After filtering, sort the resulting list lexicographically and pick the first three elements.

This approach, however, is not efficient.

- Time Complexity: `O(N * M * logM)`, where `N` is the number of characters in searchWord and `M` is the number of products. This includes the *sorting* operation after *filtering*.

Optimal Approach

A more efficient way to handle this is by ***using a Trie***.

We can insert all the product names into a Trie, and as we type each character of searchWord, we can traverse the Trie to find all possible matches.

This allows us to efficiently filter out products and retrieve the top three lexicographically smallest matches.

Code Solution

```
import java.util.*;

class Trie {
    private final TrieNode root;

    // TrieNode definition
    private static class TrieNode {
        Map<Character, TrieNode> children = new HashMap<>();
        PriorityQueue<String> words = new PriorityQueue<>();
```

```
        void addWord(String word) {
            if (words.size() < 3) {
                words.offer(word);
            } else if (word.compareTo(words.peek()) < 0) {
                words.poll();
                words.offer(word);
            }
        }
    }

    // Initializes the trie object.
    public Trie() {
        root = new TrieNode();
    }

    // Inserts the string word into the trie.
    public void insert(String word) {
        TrieNode node = root;
        for (char c : word.toCharArray()) {
            node.children.putIfAbsent(c, new TrieNode());
            node = node.children.get(c);
            node.addWord(word);
        }
    }

    // Returns a list of words with the given prefix
    public List<String> searchWithPrefix(String prefix) {
        TrieNode node = root;
        for (char c : prefix.toCharArray()) {
            if (!node.children.containsKey(c)) {
                return new ArrayList<>();
            }
            node = node.children.get(c);
        }
        List<String> result = new ArrayList<>(node.words);
        Collections.sort(result); // Sort to get lexicographically
smallest
        return result;
    }
}

class AutoCompleteSystem {
    public List<List<String>> suggestedProducts(String[] products,
String searchWord) {
        Trie trie = new Trie();
        Arrays.sort(products); // Sort the products
lexicographically

        // Insert all products into the Trie
        for (String product : products) {
            trie.insert(product);
        }
```

```
        List<List<String>> result = new ArrayList<>();
        String prefix = "";

        // For each character in searchWord, get suggestions
        for (char c : searchWord.toCharArray()) {
            prefix += c;
            result.add(trie.searchWithPrefix(prefix));
        }

        return result;
    }

    // Main method to test the implementation
    public static void main(String[] args) {
        AutoCompleteSystem solution = new AutoCompleteSystem();

        String[] products = {"mobile", "mouse", "moneypot",
"monitor", "mousepad"};
        String searchWord = "mouse";

        List<List<String>> suggestions =
solution.suggestedProducts(products, searchWord);

        for (List<String> suggestion : suggestions) {
            System.out.println(suggestion);
        }
    }
}
```

Time and Space Complexity

- ***Insert Operation***: `O(L * log M)`, where `L` is the total number of characters in all products and `M` is the number of products. Sorting the products array initially takes `O(M * log M)`, and inserting each word into the Trie takes `O(L)` time.
- ***Search Operation***: `O(N * log M)`, where `N` is the length of the searchWord. For each character typed, we traverse the Trie to get the top 3 suggestions, which is efficient due to the structure of the Trie.
- ***Space Complexity***: `O(L)`, where `L` is the total length of all the words in the products array. This is the space required to store the Tri

Problem 3: Word Dictionary with Wildcard Search

Problem Statement

Design a class called ***WordDictionary*** that can store words and check if a given word matches any of the stored words.

The word to be checked may contain the dot character `.`, which can match any letter.

Solution

Thank you for the problem statement! Before I dive in, I'd like to clarify a few things to ensure we're on the same page.

Clarifying Questions

Candidate: First, regarding the search method, you mentioned that the word may contain dots '.'. Just to confirm, should the dot be able to match exactly one character at any position in the word, similar to a wildcard?
Interviewer: Yes, that's correct. The dot '.' should match exactly one character in the word.
Candidate: Got it. Also, is there a limit on the number of words that can be added to the WordDictionary or any constraints on the length of the words?
Interviewer: There's no specific limit on the number of words, but you can assume that the total number of words and the length of each word will fit within typical memory constraints for a coding interview.

Candidate: Perfect, thanks for the clarification! Let's consider an example for better understanding.

Example:
Input:
```
WordDictionary wordDictionary = new WordDictionary();
wordDictionary.addWord("bad");
wordDictionary.addWord("dad");
wordDictionary.addWord("mad");
boolean result1 = wordDictionary.search("pad");
boolean result2 = wordDictionary.search("bad");
boolean result3 = wordDictionary.search(".ad");
boolean result4 = wordDictionary.search("b..");
```

Output:
```
result1 = false
result2 = true
result3 = true
result4 = true
```

Candidate: Now, let me walk through the approach.

Brute Force Approach

The brute force way to solve this problem would be to store all the words in a list and then, during the search operation, iterate through the list, checking each word to see if it matches the given search pattern.

If the word contains a dot '.', we would compare each character individually to see if it matches or if it can match any character.

However, The brute force approach could be quite inefficient, especially as the number of words increases. Each search would require iterating through all stored words, and for each word, potentially comparing every character.

Optimal Approach

The efficient approach would involve using a data structure that is *well-suited for prefix-based operations, such as a Trie.*

A Trie (prefix tree) allows us to efficiently add and search words, especially when dealing with wildcard characters like the dot '.'.

Code Solution

```
import java.util.HashMap;
import java.util.Map;

class WordDictionary {

   private final TrieNode root;

   // Initializes the object
   public WordDictionary() {
       root = new TrieNode();
   }

   // Adds word to the data structure
   public void addWord(String word) {
       TrieNode current = root;
       for (char ch : word.toCharArray()) {
           if (!current.children.containsKey(ch)) {
               current.children.put(ch, new TrieNode());
           }
           current = current.children.get(ch);
       }
       current.isWord = true;
   }

   // Returns true if there is any string in the data structure
that matches word or false otherwise
   public boolean search(String word) {
       return searchInNode(word, root);
   }

   private boolean searchInNode(String word, TrieNode node) {
       TrieNode current = node;
       for (int i = 0; i < word.length(); i++) {
           char ch = word.charAt(i);
           if (ch == '.') {
               for (TrieNode child : current.children.values()) {
                   if (searchInNode(word.substring(i + 1), child)) {
                       return true;
                   }
               }
               return false;
           } else {
               if (!current.children.containsKey(ch)) {
                   return false;
```

```
                }
                current = current.children.get(ch);
            }
        }
        return current.isWord;
    }

    // Trie Node class
    private static class TrieNode {
        Map<Character, TrieNode> children = new HashMap<>();
        boolean isWord = false;
    }

    // Main method for testing
    public static void main(String[] args) {
        WordDictionary wordDictionary = new WordDictionary();
        wordDictionary.addWord("bad");
        wordDictionary.addWord("dad");
        wordDictionary.addWord("mad");

        System.out.println(wordDictionary.search("pad")); // false
        System.out.println(wordDictionary.search("bad")); // true
        System.out.println(wordDictionary.search(".ad")); // true
        System.out.println(wordDictionary.search("b..")); // true
    }
}
```

Time and Space Complexity

- *Time Complexity*:
    - Add Word: The time complexity for adding a word is `O(M)`, where `M` is the length of the word.
    - Search Word: The time complexity for searching is `O(N * M)` in the worst case, where `N` is the number of nodes traversed (in the case of dots) and `M` is the length of the word. However, in practice, it will be much faster due to the Trie's efficiency.
- *Space Complexity*: The space complexity is `O(T)`, where `T` is the total number of nodes in the Trie.

Chapter 19: Dynamic Programming

In this chapter, we will explore the key ideas, strategies, and types of problems where dynamic programming is applied, along with practical tips for solving DP problems efficiently. We will also look at popular dynamic programming questions asked in coding interviews.

Understanding Dynamic Programming

Dynamic Programming is based on the principle of ***breaking down a complex problem into simpler subproblems and storing the results of these subproblems to avoid redundant computations.***

This approach is particularly useful for problems ***where the same subproblems are solved multiple times.***

There are two main approaches to implementing dynamic programming:

1. **Top-Down Approach (Memoization)**: This approach involves solving the problem *recursively* and storing the results of subproblems in a cache (often called memoization). Whenever the same subproblem is encountered again, the stored result is used instead of recalculating it.

2. **Bottom-Up Approach (Tabulation)**: This approach involves solving the problem *iteratively* by *building a table* (often a 2D array) from the smallest subproblems up to the original problem. This method avoids recursion and is usually more space-efficient.

Key Concepts in Dynamic Programming

To effectively solve dynamic programming problems, you need to understand the following key concepts:

- ***Optimal Substructure:*** A problem exhibits an optimal substructure if an optimal solution to the problem can be constructed efficiently from optimal solutions of its subproblems. For example, the shortest path problem in graphs has an optimal substructure.
- ***Overlapping Subproblems:*** A problem exhibits overlapping subproblems if the same subproblems are solved multiple times. This is where dynamic programming shines, as it avoids redundant computations by storing results.
- ***State Definition:*** The state in dynamic programming is *a representation of the subproblem at hand.* Defining the state correctly is crucial to formulating the dynamic programming solution.
- ***State Transition:*** The state transition involves moving from one state to another based on a recurrence relation. This transition is often expressed as a recursive formula.

- *Base Cases:* These are the simplest subproblems that can be solved directly without further recursion or iteration. Correctly identifying and handling base cases is essential for the correctness of the solution.

How to Solve Dynamic Programming Problems

When faced with a dynamic programming problem in a coding interview, you can follow a structured approach to arrive at the solution:

1. **Identify if DP is Applicable:**
   - Determine if the problem can be broken down into ***overlapping subproblems with optimal substructure.***
   - Look for keywords in the problem statement like "*maximum*," "*minimum*," "*count*," or "*ways*," which often indicate DP applicability.
2. **Define the State:**
   - Clearly ***define what each state*** represents in terms of the problem. The state should capture all the information necessary to solve the subproblem.
   - For example, in a knapsack problem, the state could be defined by the current item index and the remaining capacity of the knapsack.
3. **Formulate the State Transition:**
   - Write down the ***recurrence relation that describes how the current state depends on previous states.***
   - Ensure the recurrence covers all possible transitions between states.
4. **Identify Base Cases:**
   - Determine the ***simplest subproblems and their solutions***, which serve as the base cases for the recurrence relation.
   - For example, in the Fibonacci sequence, the base cases are `Fib(0) = 0 and Fib(1) = 1.`
5. **Implement the Solution:**
   - Choose between the ***top-down or bottom-up*** approach based on the problem's constraints.
   - Implement the solution in code, making sure to handle all edge cases and optimize for time and space complexity.
6. **Optimize Further (if necessary):**
   - Consider space optimization techniques like reducing a 2D DP table to a 1D array if the current state only depends on the previous state.
   - Analyze and refine your approach to reduce unnecessary computations.

Dynamic Programming Interview Questions

Now, let's solve the most commonly asked dynamic programming questions. Practicing these problems will provide you a strategy to solve any dynamic programming related coding interview questions.

Problem 1: Count Ways to Climb Stairs

Problem Statement

You need to climb a staircase with n steps to reach the top. Each time you climb, you can take either *1 step* or *2 steps*.

How many *unique ways* are there to reach the top of the staircase?

Solution

Before jumping into the solution, I'd like to clarify a few things to ensure we're on the same page.

Clarifying Questions

Candidate: Is it safe to assume that n is a positive integer, and the staircase has at least 1 step?
Interviewer: Yes, n will always be a positive integer.

Candidate: Are there any specific constraints on the value of n, like a maximum limit?
Interviewer: You can assume n to be reasonably large, but nothing extreme that would cause an overflow in calculations.

Candidate: Should I account for any special cases, like no steps at all?
Interviewer: If `n = 0`, you're already at the top, so there's 1 way to be at the top (doing nothing). But focus on `n >= 1`.

Candidate: Got it! To summarize, I need to find the number of distinct ways to reach the top of a staircase with n steps, where each move can be either 1 or 2 steps.

Example:
Now, Let's take an example:

```
Input: n = 3
Output: 3
```

Explanation:
For `n = 3`, there are three distinct ways to reach the top:

```
1. Step 1 -> Step 1 -> Step 1
2. Step 1 -> Step 2
3. Step 2 -> Step 1
```

Brute Force Recursive Approach

The first approach that comes to mind is using a *simple recursive solution.*

The idea is to explore all possible paths to reach the top by either taking 1 step or 2 steps at each point.

We can formulate the recursive approach as follows:

- **Base Case 1**: If `n == 0`, this means you are already at the top of the staircase. There is exactly 1 way to be at the top when you are already there (by doing nothing). So, `climbStairsRecursive(0)` should return 1.
- **Base Case 2**: If `n < 0`, this means you've taken more steps than needed, which is not a valid way to reach the top. Therefore, there are 0 ways to reach the top in this scenario. So, `climbStairsRecursive(n)` for `n < 0` should return 0.
- **Recursive Relation**: The number of ways to reach the nth step can be derived by considering:
    1. The number of ways to reach the $(n-1)^{th}$ step (and then take a 1-step move).
    2. The number of ways to reach the $(n-2)^{th}$ step (and then take a 2-step move).

Thus, the recursive formula is: `ways(n) = ways(n-1) + ways(n-2)`

Here is a Java code for this approach:

```
public class StaircaseClimbing {

    // Brute force recursive method to calculate the number of
distinct ways
    public int climbStairsRecursive(int n) {
        // Base cases
        if (n == 0) return 1; // Reached the top
        if (n < 0) return 0;  // Went beyond the top, not a valid
path

        // Recursive relation
        return climbStairsRecursive(n - 1) + climbStairsRecursive(n -
2);
    }

    public static void main(String[] args) {
        StaircaseClimbing staircase = new StaircaseClimbing();

        // Test case
        System.out.println(staircase.climbStairsRecursive(3)); //
Output: 3
    }
}
```

Time Complexity: The time complexity of this brute force solution is $O(2^n)$ because ***each step results in two recursive calls.***
Space Complexity: The space complexity is $O(n)$ due to the recursive call stack.

Top-Down DP Approach (Memoization)

The brute force approach ***recalculates the same subproblems multiple times***, leading to inefficiency.

To optimize this, we can use memoization to store the results of subproblems and reuse them.

Here's the code with memoization:

```
import java.util.HashMap;
import java.util.Map;

public class StaircaseClimbing {

    // Memoization map to store results of subproblems
    private Map<Integer, Integer> memo = new HashMap<>();

    // Top-down dynamic programming method with memoization
    public int climbStairsMemo(int n) {
        // Base cases
        if (n == 0) return 1;
        if (n < 0) return 0;

        // Check if the result is already computed
        if (memo.containsKey(n)) {
            return memo.get(n);
        }

        // Recursive relation with memoization
        int result = climbStairsMemo(n - 1) + climbStairsMemo(n - 2);
        memo.put(n, result); // Store the result in the map

        return result;
    }

    public static void main(String[] args) {
        StaircaseClimbing staircase = new StaircaseClimbing();

        // Test case
        System.out.println(staircase.climbStairsMemo(3)); // Output:
3
    }
}
```

Time Complexity: The time complexity is reduced to `O(n)` because we only compute each subproblem once.
Space Complexity: The space complexity is `O(n)` for the memoization storage and the recursive call stack.

Bottom-Up DP Approach (Tabulation)

We can further optimize the solution by using a bottom-up dynamic programming approach. This eliminates the overhead of recursion ***by iteratively building the solution from the base cases.***

The bottom-up approach to dynamic programming is essentially about building the solution from the simplest case upwards, step by step, until you reach the desired result. Instead of solving the problem recursively (from the top down), you start from the smallest subproblems (the base cases) and iteratively combine their solutions to solve the larger problem.

For this problem, Instead of recursively calculating the number of ways for each step and re-computing values, we can store the results as we go. This way, each value is computed exactly once.

We start from the base cases, `n = 1` and `n = 2`, and then iteratively compute the number of ways for each step up to `n`.

Here's the code for the bottom-up approach:

```
public class StaircaseClimbing {

    // Bottom-up dynamic programming method
    public int climbStairsDP(int n) {
        // Base cases
        if (n == 1) return 1;
        if (n == 2) return 2;

        // Variables to store the number of ways to reach the last
two steps
        int oneStepBefore = 2;
        int twoStepsBefore = 1;
        int allWays = 0;

        // Iterate from step 3 to n
        for (int i = 3; i <= n; i++) {
            allWays = oneStepBefore + twoStepsBefore;
            twoStepsBefore = oneStepBefore;
            oneStepBefore = allWays;
        }

        return allWays;
    }

    public static void main(String[] args) {
        StaircaseClimbing staircase = new StaircaseClimbing();

        // Test case
        System.out.println(staircase.climbStairsDP(3)); // Output: 3
    }
}
```

Time Complexity: The time complexity remains `O(n)` because we iterate through the steps from `3` to `n` once.
Space Complexity: The space complexity is reduced to `O(1)` because we only use a few variables to store intermediate results.

Problem 2: Jump Game: Reaching Last Position

Problem Statement

You are given an array of integers, `nums`, where each element represents the maximum distance you can jump forward from that position.

Starting at the first index, determine if you can reach the last index of the array.

Solution

Let's start by clarifying a few aspects of the problem.

Clarifying Questions

Candidate: Can the elements of the array be negative, or are they always non-negative integers?
Interviewer: The elements are always non-negative integers.

Candidate: If an element is `0`, that means I cannot move forward from that position, correct?
Interviewer: Yes, if you land on a `0`, you cannot move forward from that position unless you've already reached the last index.

Candidate: Is the length of the array always greater than or equal to 1?
Interviewer: Yes, the array has at least one element.

Candidate: Should I return *true* if I am already at the last index at the start?
Interviewer: Yes, if the array length is 1, you are already at the last index, so you should return *true*.

Candidate:
Great! So, the goal is to determine whether we can reach the last index of the array starting from the first index, given that each element in the array represents the maximum jump length from that position.

Example:
Let's take an example to clarify the problem:

- `Input: nums = [2, 3, 1, 1, 4]`
- `Output: true`

Explanation:

Starting at index 0, you can jump to index 1 or index 2. From index 1, you can jump to index 4, which is the last index. Hence, it is possible to reach the last index.

Brute Force Recursive Approach

Let's begin with the brute force recursive approach. The idea is to explore all possible paths from the first index to the last.

We will recursively try to jump from the current index to all possible next positions within the jump limit and check if any of those paths can lead to the last index. Recurrence relation can be defined as follows:

1. **Base Case:** If `index` is at or beyond the last index (`index >= nums.length - 1`), return `true` because you've reached or passed the last index.
2. **Recursive Case:**
   a. For each possible jump `i` from the current index (where `i` ranges from `1` to `nums[index]`):
      i. If any of these jumps can successfully reach the last index (i.e., if `canJump(index + i)` returns `true`), then return `true`.
   b. If *none* of the jumps lead to the last index, return `false`.

Here's the brute force recursive implementation:

```
public class JumpGame {

    // Brute force recursive method to check if we can reach the
last index
    public boolean canJumpRecursive(int[] nums, int index) {
        // Base case: if we've reached the last index, return true
        if (index >= nums.length - 1) return true;

        // Explore all positions we can jump to from the current
index
        int maxJump = nums[index];
        for (int i = 1; i <= maxJump; i++) {
            if (canJumpRecursive(nums, index + i)) {
                return true;
            }
        }

        // If none of the jumps lead to the last index, return false
        return false;
    }

    public static void main(String[] args) {
        JumpGame game = new JumpGame();

        // Test case
        int[] nums = {2, 3, 1, 1, 4};
        System.out.println(game.canJumpRecursive(nums, 0)); //
Output: true
    }
```

```
}
```

Time Complexity: The time complexity is $O(2^n)$ because, at each index, we may try to jump to every possible next position, resulting in an *exponential number of recursive calls.*
Space Complexity: The space complexity is `O(n)` due to the recursive call stack.

Top-Down DP Approach (Memoization)

The brute force approach is inefficient due to the ***overlapping subproblems.*** We can optimize it by using ***memoization*** to store the results of subproblems.

This way, we avoid recomputing whether we can reach the last index from a given position.

For this problem, the ***three key steps*** in converting brute force recursive solution to top down dynamic programming (memoization) solution are as follows:

1. **Add a Memoization Data Structure:**
   Example: `Map<Integer, Boolean> memo = new HashMap<>();`
2. **Check Memo Before Recursion:**
   Before calling the recursive function, check if the result for the current `index` is already in `memo`.
3. **Store the Result in Memo After Computation:**
   After computing the result for the current index, store it in a `memo` before returning.

Here's the top-down dynamic programming solution with memoization:

```
public class JumpGameMemo {

    // Memoization map to store results of subproblems
    private final Map<Integer, Boolean> memo = new HashMap<>();

    // Top-down dynamic programming method with memoization
    public boolean canJumpMemo(int[] nums, int index) {
        // Base case: if we've reached the last index, return true
        if (index >= nums.length - 1) return true;

        // Check if the result is already computed
        if (memo.containsKey(index)) {
            return memo.get(index);
        }

        // Explore all positions we can jump to from the current
index
        int maxJump = nums[index];
        for (int i = 1; i <= maxJump; i++) {
            if (canJumpMemo(nums, index + i)) {
                memo.put(index, true); // Store result as true
```

```
                return true;
            }
        }

        memo.put(index, false); // Store result as false if we can't
reach the last index
        return false;
    }

    public static void main(String[] args) {
        JumpGameMemo game = new JumpGameMemo();

        // Test case
        int[] nums = {2, 3, 1, 1, 4};
        System.out.println(game.canJumpMemo(nums, 0)); // Output:
true
    }
}
```

Time Complexity: The time complexity is reduced to `O(n)` because each subproblem is solved only once.
Space Complexity: The space complexity remains `O(n)` for the memoization storage and the recursive call stack.

Bottom-Up DP Approach (Tabulation)

We can further optimize the solution by using a bottom-up dynamic programming approach.

The bottom-up approach to the Jump Game problem is about working backward iteratively from the last index to determine if you can reach it from the start.

1. **Start from the End:**
   - Begin by assuming you need to reach the last index (`lastPos = nums.length - 1`).
2. **Work Backwards:**
   - Iterate backward through the array, checking for each position if you can reach `lastPos`.
   - If from any position `i`, the maximum jump (`nums[i]`) allows you to reach or surpass `lastPos`, then update `lastPos` to this position (`i`).
3. **Final Check:**
   - After processing all positions, if `lastPos` has moved to the start (index `0`), then it's possible to reach the last index from the start.

Here's the code for the bottom-up approach:

```
public class JumpGame {

    // Bottom-up dynamic programming method
    public boolean canJumpDP(int[] nums) {
        // Initialize the last position we need to reach
```

```
        int lastPos = nums.length - 1;

        // Iterate backwards from the second-to-last position to the
start
        for (int i = nums.length - 2; i >= 0; i--) {
            // If we can jump from the current position to or beyond
the lastPos, update lastPos
            if (i + nums[i] >= lastPos) {
                lastPos = i;
            }
        }

        // If lastPos has moved to the start, return true;
otherwise, false
        return lastPos == 0;
    }

    public static void main(String[] args) {
        JumpGame game = new JumpGame();

        // Test case
        int[] nums = {2, 3, 1, 1, 4};
        System.out.println(game.canJumpDP(nums)); // Output: true
    }
}
```

Time Complexity: The time complexity is `O(n)` because we iterate through the array once.
Space Complexity: The space complexity is `O(1)` since we only use a constant amount of extra space for the `lastPos` variable.

Problem 3: House Robber - Max Loot

Problem Statement

You are planning to rob houses along a street, where each house has a certain amount of money. However, you cannot rob two adjacent houses on the same night because their security systems are connected.

Given an array `nums` where each element represents the amount of money in a house, find the maximum amount of money you can rob without triggering the security systems.

Solution

Let's start by clarifying a few things about the problem.

Clarifying Questions

Candidate: Can the amount of money in each house be zero, or are all values guaranteed to be positive?
Interviewer: The amounts can be zero or any non-negative integer.

Candidate: Is there any constraint on the number of houses, or can there be any number of houses along the street?
Interviewer: The number of houses can vary, but for this problem, you can assume a reasonable number that won't cause memory issues.

Candidate: If there's only one house, should I simply return the amount of money in that house?
Interviewer: Yes, if there's only one house, you should return the amount of money in that house.

Got it! The goal is to maximize the amount of money we can rob without robbing two adjacent houses.

Example:

Let's consider an example to understand the expected input and output:

- `Input: nums = [2, 7, 9, 3, 1]`
- `Output: 12`

Explanation:
You can rob houses `1`, `3`, and `5` for a total of `2 + 9 + 1 = 12`, which is the maximum amount you can rob without triggering the alarms.

Brute Force Recursive Approach

The brute force approach involves considering all possible combinations of houses that can be robbed.

At each house, we decide ***whether to rob it or skip it***:

1. If we rob the current house, we skip the next one and move two steps forward.
2. If we skip the current house, we move one step forward.

We recursively compute the maximum money we can rob by exploring both options at each house.

Let `rob(index)` be a function that returns the maximum amount of money you can rob *starting from the house at position* `index`.

The **recurrence relation** can be defined as:
`rob(index)=max(nums[index]+rob(index + 2),rob(index + 1))`

Here's the brute force recursive implementation:

```
public class HouseRobberRecursive {
```

```
    public int rob(int[] nums) {
        return robRecursive(nums, 0);
    }

    // Brute force recursive method to calculate the maximum amount
of money
    private int robRecursive(int[] nums, int index) {
        // Base case: if we are out of bounds, return 0
        if (index >= nums.length) return 0;

        // Option 1: Rob the current house and skip the next one
        int robCurrent = nums[index] + robRecursive(nums, index + 2);

        // Option 2: Skip the current house and consider the next
one
        int skipCurrent = robRecursive(nums, index + 1);

        // Return the maximum of both options
        return Math.max(robCurrent, skipCurrent);
    }

    public static void main(String[] args) {
        HouseRobberRecursive robber = new HouseRobberRecursive();

        // Test case
        int[] nums = {2, 7, 9, 3, 1};
        System.out.println(robber.rob(nums)); // Output: 12
    }
}
```

Time Complexity: The time complexity is $O(2^n)$ because each house generates two possible recursive paths (robbing or skipping).
Space Complexity: The space complexity is $O(n)$ due to the recursive call stack.

Top-Down DP Approach (Memoization):

The brute force approach involves ***recalculating the maximum amount of money for the same subproblems multiple times***. We can optimize this by storing the results of subproblems using memoization.

Here's the top-down dynamic programming solution ***with memoization***:

```
public class HouseRobberMemo {
    // Memoization map to store results of sub-problems
    private final Map<Integer, Integer> memo = new HashMap<>();

    public int rob(int[] nums) {
        return robMemo(nums, 0);
    }

    // Top-down dynamic programming method with memoization
```

```
    private int robMemo(int[] nums, int index) {
        // Base case: if we are out of bounds, return 0
        if (index >= nums.length) return 0;

        // Check if the result is already computed
        if (memo.containsKey(index)) {
            return memo.get(index);
        }

        // Option 1: Rob the current house and skip the next one
        int robCurrent = nums[index] + robMemo(nums, index + 2);

        // Option 2: Skip the current house and consider the next
one
        int skipCurrent = robMemo(nums, index + 1);

        // Store the result in memo and return the maximum of both
options
        int result = Math.max(robCurrent, skipCurrent);
        memo.put(index, result);
        return result;
    }

    public static void main(String[] args) {
        HouseRobberMemo robber = new HouseRobberMemo();

        // Test case
        int[] nums = {2, 7, 9, 3, 1};
        System.out.println(robber.rob(nums)); // Output: 12
    }
}
```

Time Complexity: The time complexity is reduced to `O(n)` because each subproblem is solved only once.
Space Complexity: The space complexity is `O(n)` for the memoization storage and the recursive call stack.

Bottom-Up DP Approach (Tabulation):

To further optimize, we can use a bottom-up dynamic programming approach, ***where we iteratively calculate the maximum money*** we can rob up to each house, starting from the beginning.

The bottom-up approach builds the solution iteratively from the smallest subproblems (starting from the first house) to the overall problem (the last house). Instead of solving the problem recursively, you calculate the maximum money you can rob up to each house by making decisions ***based on previously computed results***.

Here's the bottom-up approach:

```
public class HouseRobber {
```

```
    // Bottom-up dynamic programming method
    public int robDP(int[] nums) {
        if (nums.length == 0) return 0;
        if (nums.length == 1) return nums[0];

        // Array to store the maximum money that can be robbed up to
each house
        int[] dp = new int[nums.length];

        // Initialize base cases
        dp[0] = nums[0];
        dp[1] = Math.max(nums[0], nums[1]);

        // Fill the dp array iteratively
        for (int i = 2; i < nums.length; i++) {
            dp[i] = Math.max(nums[i] + dp[i - 2], dp[i - 1]);
        }

        // The last element in dp array will have the answer
        return dp[nums.length - 1];
    }

    public static void main(String[] args) {
        HouseRobber robber = new HouseRobber();

        // Test case
        int[] nums = {2, 7, 9, 3, 1};
        System.out.println(robber.robDP(nums)); // Output: 12
    }
}
```

Time Complexity: The time complexity is `O(n)` because we iterate through the array once.
Space Complexity: The space complexity is `O(n)` because of the dp array.

Further Optimization

We can further optimize the space complexity by realizing that at any house, ***we only need to know the results for the last two houses.***

Therefore, we can reduce the space complexity to `O(1)`.

```
public class HouseRobberOptimized {

    // Optimized bottom-up dynamic programming method with O(1)
space
    public int robDPOptimized(int[] nums) {
        if (nums.length == 0) return 0;
        if (nums.length == 1) return nums[0];

        int prev2 = nums[0];
```

```
        int prev1 = Math.max(nums[0], nums[1]);

        for (int i = 2; i < nums.length; i++) {
            int current = Math.max(nums[i] + prev2, prev1);
            prev2 = prev1;
            prev1 = current;
        }

        return prev1;
    }

    public static void main(String[] args) {
        HouseRobberOptimized robber = new HouseRobberOptimized();

        // Test case
        int[] nums = {2, 7, 9, 3, 1};
        System.out.println(robber.robDPOptimized(nums)); // Output:
12
    }
}
```

Time Complexity: The time complexity remains `O(n)`.
Space Complexity: The space complexity is reduced to `O(1)` since we only use a few variables

---

Problem 4: Coin Change - Fewest Coins

Problem Statement

Given an array called `coins` representing different denominations of coins and an integer `amount` representing a total sum of money, find the minimum number of coins needed to make up that amount.

If it's not possible to make up the amount with the given coins, return `-1`.

Solution

Let's begin by clarifying the problem requirements.

Clarifying Questions

Candidate: Can the coins array contain duplicate denominations, or are all denominations unique?
Interviewer: The denominations are unique in the array.

Candidate: Is there any constraint on the maximum value of amount or the number of coins?
Candidate: Assume the amount can be a reasonably large integer, but it won't cause

overflow. The number of coin types in the coins array is also within reasonable limits.

Great! So, the goal is to determine the minimum number of coins needed to make up the given amount using the available denominations, or return `-1` if it's not possible.

Example:
Let's consider an example to understand the expected input and output format:

- `Input: coins = [1, 2, 5], amount = 11`
- `Output: 3`

Explanation:
The minimum number of coins needed to make `11` is `3` (using coins `5 + 5 + 1`).

Brute Force Recursive Approach

We could start by thinking of a recursive solution where, at each step, we subtract a coin denomination from the amount and recursively find the minimum number of coins needed for the remaining amount.

The idea is to ***reduce the problem size by choosing one coin at a time***. For each coin, you calculate the minimum coins needed for the remaining amount (`amount - coin`). The recursive function will return the minimum number of coins needed from all possible combinations.

To summarize,

1. **Base case:** When the `amount` is `0`, no coins are needed to make up that amount. Hence, return `0`.
2. **Recursive case:** For each coin in the `coins` array, recursively check if you can make up the `amount` by subtracting the value of the coin from the `amount`.
3. Keep ***track of minimum coin count*** during all these computations.

Here's the brute force recursive implementation:

```
public class CoinChangeRecursive {

   // Brute force recursive method to calculate the minimum number
of coins
   public int coinChangeRecursive(int[] coins, int amount) {
       // Base case: if amount is 0, no coins are needed
       if (amount == 0) return 0;

       // If amount is negative, return -1 to indicate it's not
possible
       if (amount < 0) return -1;

       int minCoins = Integer.MAX_VALUE;

       // Try every coin and find the minimum number of coins
needed
       for (int coin : coins) {
```

```
            int result = coinChangeRecursive(coins, amount - coin);
            if (result >= 0 && result < minCoins) {
                minCoins = result + 1;
            }
        }

        // If no valid result was found, return -1
        return minCoins == Integer.MAX_VALUE ? -1 : minCoins;
    }

    public static void main(String[] args) {
        CoinChangeRecursive cc = new CoinChangeRecursive();

        // Test cases
        int[] coins = {2};
        int amount = 3;
        System.out.println(cc.coinChangeRecursive(coins, amount)); //
Output: -1

        int[] coins2 = {1, 2, 5};
        int amount2 = 11;
        System.out.println(cc.coinChangeRecursive(coins2, amount2));
// Output: 3
    }
}
```

Time Complexity: The time complexity is $O(c^a)$, where c is the number of coins, and a is the amount, due to the exponential growth of recursive calls.
Space Complexity: The space complexity is $O(a)$ due to the recursive call stack.

Top-Down DP Approach (Memoization):

We can optimize the recursive approach by using *memoization* to store the results of subproblems, avoiding redundant calculations.

To further solidify our understanding of memoization dynamic programming approach. Here is detailed explanation (we will skip this for next problem onwards):

Identifying the Opportunity for Memoization:
To determine whether memoization can be used to optimize a problem, look for these ***key indicators***:

1. **Overlapping Subproblems:**
    - In the Coin Change problem, the same subproblems are solved multiple times during recursion. For example, when calculating the minimum coins needed for `amount = 11`, you might repeatedly calculate the minimum coins needed for `amount = 6` if different coins lead to that subproblem.
    - This *repetition is a clear sign that memoization can help*, as you can store the result of `amount = 6` the first time it's calculated and reuse it whenever needed.
2. **Optimal Substructure:**

    - The problem can be *broken down into smaller subproblems*, and the optimal solution to the overall problem depends on the optimal solutions to these subproblems.
    - In this case, the minimum number of coins needed to make up the `amount` depends on the minimum coins needed for the `amount - coin` for each coin in coins.
3. **Recursive Nature:**
    - The problem is naturally solved using recursion, where the solution involves making a *series of decisions that lead to smaller, similar problems*. Memoization is ideal for optimizing such recursive solutions.

How Memoization Works Here:

- **Store Results:** When you calculate the minimum coins needed for a specific amount, store that result in a memoization structure (like a map or an array).
- **Reuse Results:** Before you attempt to calculate the result for an amount, check if it's already been computed and stored. If it has, return the stored result instead of recalculating it.

Here's the top-down dynamic programming solution with memoization:

```
import java.util.HashMap;
import java.util.Map;

public class CoinChangeMemo {

    // Memoization map to store results of subproblems
    private Map<Integer, Integer> memo = new HashMap<>();

    // Top-down dynamic programming method with memoization
    public int coinChangeMemo(int[] coins, int amount) {
        // Base case: if amount is 0, no coins are needed
        if (amount == 0) return 0;

        // If amount is negative, return -1 to indicate it's not
possible
        if (amount < 0) return -1;

        // Check if the result is already computed
        if (memo.containsKey(amount)) {
            return memo.get(amount);
        }

        int minCoins = Integer.MAX_VALUE;

        // Try every coin and find the minimum number of coins
needed
        for (int coin : coins) {
            int result = coinChangeMemo(coins, amount - coin);
            if (result >= 0 && result < minCoins) {
                minCoins = result + 1;
```

```
            }
        }

        // Store the result in memo, if no solution found, store -1
        memo.put(amount, (minCoins == Integer.MAX_VALUE) ? -1 :
minCoins);

        return memo.get(amount);
    }

    public static void main(String[] args) {
        CoinChangeMemo cc = new CoinChangeMemo();

        // Test cases
        int[] coins1 = {2};
        int amount1 = 3;
        System.out.println(cc.coinChangeMemo(coins1, amount1)); //
Output: -1

        int[] coins2 = {1, 2, 5};
        int amount2 = 11;
        System.out.println(cc.coinChangeMemo(coins2, amount2)); //
Output: 3
    }
}
```

Time Complexity: The time complexity is `O(a * c)`, where a is the amount and c is the number of coins.
Space Complexity: The space complexity is `O(a)` for the memoization storage.

Bottom-Up DP Approach (Tabulation)

To further optimize the solution, let's convert it to a bottom-up approach, where we iteratively compute the minimum number of coins needed for each amount from `0` to `amount`.

The bottom-up approach builds the solution by iterating from the smallest subproblems (starting with `amount = 0`) and gradually solving larger subproblems until we reach the target amount. By solving the problem incrementally and storing the results, we can efficiently determine the minimum number of coins needed for the target amount.
Bottom up DP equation can be formulated as follow:
Let `dp(amount)` be the minimum number of coins needed to make up the given `amount`.

```
dp(amount)=min(dp(amount - coin))+1 for each coin in coins
```

Here's a code for the bottom-up approach:

```
import java.util.Arrays;
```

```
public class CoinChange {
       // Create a dp array to store the minimum coins needed for
each amount
        int[] dp = new int[amount + 1];
        Arrays.fill(dp, amount + 1); // Initialize with a large value
        dp[0] = 0; // Base case: 0 coins are needed to make amount 0

        // Fill the dp array
        for (int i = 1; i <= amount; i++) {
            for (int coin : coins) {
                if (i - coin >= 0) {
                    dp[i] = Math.min(dp[i], dp[i - coin] + 1);
                }
            }
        }

        // If dp[amount] is still the large value, return -1 as it's
not possible
        return dp[amount] > amount ? -1 : dp[amount];
    }

    public static void main(String[] args) {
        CoinChange cc = new CoinChange();

        // Test case
        int[] coins = {1, 2, 5};
        int amount = 11;
        System.out.println(cc.coinChangeDP(coins, amount)); //
Output: 3
    }
}
```

Time Complexity: The time complexity is `O(a * c)`, where a is the amount and `c` is the number of coins.
Space Complexity: The space complexity is `O(a)` because of the dp array.

Problem 5: Coin Change 2 - Count Combinations

Problem Statement

Given an array called `coins` representing different denominations and an integer `amount` representing a total sum of money, find the number of distinct combinations of coins that can make up that amount.

If it's not possible to make up the amount with any combination of the coins, return `0`.

Solution

Let's begin by clarifying the problem requirements.

Clarifying Questions

Candidate: Can the coins array contain duplicate denominations, or are all denominations unique?
Interviewer: The denominations are unique in the array.

Candidate: Is the order in which we use the coins important, or do only the combinations matter?
Interviewer: Only the combinations matter, not the order.

Candidate: If the amount is `0`, should I return `1` because there is exactly one way to make up 0 (using no coins)?
Interviewer: Yes, if the amount is `0`, you should return `1` because there is exactly one way to make up `0` by using no coins.

Candidate: Got it! So, the goal is to count the number of distinct ways to make up the given amount using the available coins, considering that each coin can be used an infinite number of times.

Example:
Let's consider an example to understand the input and output format:

- `Input: coins = [1, 2, 5], amount = 5`
- `Output: 4`

Explanation:
The four combinations are:

1. 5
2. 2 + 2 + 1
3. 2 + 1 + 1 + 1
4. 1 + 1 + 1 + 1 + 1

Brute Force Recursive Approach

The brute force approach involves trying all possible combinations of coins to see if they sum up to the given amount.

For each coin, we can either include it in the current combination or exclude it, and recursively explore both options.

Here's the brute force recursive implementation:

```
public class CoinChangeIIRecursive {

   // Brute force recursive method to count the number of
combinations
   public int countCombinations(int[] coins, int amount, int index)
{
       // Base case: if amount is 0, there's exactly one way to
make the amount (by using no coins)
       if (amount == 0) return 1;
```

```
        // If amount is negative or no more coins are left, there's
no valid combination
        if (amount < 0 || index == coins.length) return 0;

        // Option 1: Include the current coin and reduce the amount
        int include = countCombinations(coins, amount - coins[index],
index);

        // Option 2: Exclude the current coin and move to the next
coin
        int exclude = countCombinations(coins, amount, index + 1);

        // Return the sum of both options
        return include + exclude;
    }

    public static void main(String[] args) {
        CoinChangeIIRecursive cc = new CoinChangeIIRecursive();

        // Test case
        int[] coins = {1, 2, 5};
        int amount = 5;
        System.out.println(cc.countCombinations(coins, amount, 0));
// Output: 4
    }
}
```

Time Complexity: The time complexity is exponential `O(2^n)` where `n` is the number of coins because we explore all possible combinations.
Space Complexity: The space complexity is `O(n)` due to the recursive call stack.

Top-Down DP Approach (Memoization):

To avoid recalculating the number of combinations ***for the same amount and index***, we can use memoization to store the results of subproblems.

Here's the top-down dynamic programming solution with memoization:

```
import java.util.HashMap;
import java.util.Map;

public class CoinChangeIIMemo {

    // Memoization map to store results of subproblems
    private final Map<String, Integer> memo = new HashMap<>();

    // Top-down dynamic programming method with memoization
    public int countCombinationsMemo(int[] coins, int amount, int
index) {
        // Base case: if amount is 0, there's exactly one way to
make the amount
        if (amount == 0) return 1;
```

```
        // If amount is negative or no more coins are left, there's
no valid combination
        if (amount < 0 || index == coins.length) return 0;

        // Create a unique key for the memo map
        String key = amount + "-" + index;

        // Check if the result is already computed
        if (memo.containsKey(key)) {
            return memo.get(key);
        }

        // Option 1: Include the current coin
        int include = countCombinationsMemo(coins, amount -
coins[index], index);

        // Option 2: Exclude the current coin
        int exclude = countCombinationsMemo(coins, amount, index +
1);

        // Store the result in memo
        int result = include + exclude;
        memo.put(key, result);

        return result;
    }

    public static void main(String[] args) {
        CoinChangeIIMemo cc = new CoinChangeIIMemo();

        // Test case
        int[] coins = {1, 2, 5};
        int amount = 5;
        System.out.println(cc.countCombinationsMemo(coins, amount,
0)); // Output: 4
    }
}
```

Time Complexity: The time complexity is `O(n * a)` where `n` is the number of coins and `a` is the amount, as each subproblem is solved only once.
Space Complexity: The space complexity is `O(n * a)` due to the memoization storage and recursive call stack.

Bottom-Up DP Approach (Tabulation)

We can convert the solution to a bottom-up dynamic programming approach where we iteratively calculate the number of combinations for each amount using each coin.

In the bottom-up approach, we start by considering the smallest subproblems (amounts starting from `0`) and gradually build up to the target amount.

For each coin, we update the number of ways to make each possible amount by considering that coin.

Here's the code for bottom-up approach:

```
public class CoinChangeII {

    // Bottom-up dynamic programming method
    public int countCombinationsDP(int[] coins, int amount) {
        // Create a dp array to store the number of combinations for
each amount
        int[] dp = new int[amount + 1];
        dp[0] = 1; // There's one way to make amount 0 (using no
coins)

        // Fill the dp array
        for (int coin : coins) {
            for (int i = coin; i <= amount; i++) {
                dp[i] += dp[i - coin];
            }
        }

        return dp[amount];
    }

    public static void main(String[] args) {
        CoinChangeII cc = new CoinChangeII();

        // Test case
        int[] coins = {1, 2, 5};
        int amount = 5;
        System.out.println(cc.countCombinationsDP(coins, amount)); //
Output: 4
    }
}
```

Time Complexity: The time complexity is `O(n * a)` where `n` is the number of coins and a is the amount, as we iterate through each coin and each possible amount.
Space Complexity: The space complexity is `O(a)` due to the dp array.

Problem 6: Edit Distance - Min String Transformations

Problem Statement

Given two strings `word1` and `word2`, determine the minimum number of operations needed to convert `word1` into `word2`.

The allowed operations are:

1. Inserting a character.
2. Deleting a character.

3. Replacing a character.

Solution

Let's start by clarifying a few aspects of the problem.

Clarifying Questions

Candidate: Are the operations only applicable to individual characters, or can we apply them to substrings as well?
Interviewer: The operations apply to individual characters only.

Candidate: Is there any constraint on the length of `word1` and `word2`, or can they be of any length?
Interviewer: The strings can be of any length, but assume they are within reasonable limits that won't cause memory or performance issues.

Candidate: Are the strings case-sensitive, meaning that lowercase and uppercase characters are considered different?
Interviewer: Yes, the strings are case-sensitive.

Candidate: Great! So, the goal is to find the minimum number of operations (insert, delete, or replace) required to transform `word1` into `word2`.

Example:
Let's consider an example to clarify the input and output format:

- `Input: word1 = "horse", word2 = "ros"`
- `Output: 3`

Explanation:

- Replace `h` with `r`.
- Delete `o`.
- Delete `e`.

Brute Force Recursive Approach

The brute force approach involves considering all possible operations (insert, delete, replace) at each step and recursively calculating the minimum operations required.

Here's how we can approach this recursively:

1. Start iterating over two words one character at a time.
2. If characters match, then move on to the next characters.
3. If the current character does not match, consider all three operations as follows
   a. **Insert**: Insert a character from `word2` into `word1` and move to the next character in word2.
   b. **Delete**: Delete a character from `word1` and continue with the remaining characters.
   c. **Replace**: Replace a character in `word1` with the corresponding character in `word2` and move to the next character in both strings.

Here's the brute force recursive implementation:

```
public class EditDistanceRecursive {

   // Brute force recursive method to calculate the minimum edit
distance
   public int minDistanceRecursive(String word1, String word2, int
i, int j) {
       // Base case: If one of the strings is empty
       if (i == word1.length()) return word2.length() - j;
       if (j == word2.length()) return word1.length() - i;

       // If characters match, move to the next characters in both
strings
       if (word1.charAt(i) == word2.charAt(j)) {
           return minDistanceRecursive(word1, word2, i + 1, j + 1);
       }

       // Otherwise, consider all three operations
       int insertOp = minDistanceRecursive(word1, word2, i, j + 1);
       int deleteOp = minDistanceRecursive(word1, word2, i + 1, j);
       int replaceOp = minDistanceRecursive(word1, word2, i + 1, j +
1);

       // Return the minimum number of operations needed
       return 1 + Math.min(insertOp, Math.min(deleteOp, replaceOp));
   }

   public static void main(String[] args) {
       EditDistanceRecursive ed = new EditDistanceRecursive();

       // Test case
       String word1 = "horse";
       String word2 = "ros";
       System.out.println(ed.minDistanceRecursive(word1, word2, 0,
0)); // Output: 3
   }
}
```

Time Complexity: The time complexity is $O(3^m)$ where m is the length of the shorter string, due to the three recursive calls at each step.
Space Complexity: The space complexity is `O(m + n)` due to the recursive call stack.

Top-Down DP Approach (Memoization)

To avoid recalculating the same subproblems, we can use memoization to store the results of subproblems.

Here's the top-down dynamic programming solution with memoization:

```
import java.util.HashMap;
```

```
import java.util.Map;

public class EditDistanceMemo {

    // Memoization map to store results of subproblems
    private final Map<String, Integer> memo = new HashMap<>();

    // Top-down dynamic programming method with memoization
    public int minDistanceMemo(String word1, String word2, int i, int
j) {
        // Base case: If one of the strings is empty
        if (i == word1.length()) return word2.length() - j;
        if (j == word2.length()) return word1.length() - i;

        // Create a unique key for the memo map
        String key = i + "-" + j;

        // Check if the result is already computed
        if (memo.containsKey(key)) {
            return memo.get(key);
        }

        // If characters match, move to the next characters in both
strings
        if (word1.charAt(i) == word2.charAt(j)) {
            memo.put(key, minDistanceMemo(word1, word2, i + 1, j +
1));
            return memo.get(key);
        }

        // Otherwise, consider all three operations
        int insertOp = minDistanceMemo(word1, word2, i, j + 1);
        int deleteOp = minDistanceMemo(word1, word2, i + 1, j);
        int replaceOp = minDistanceMemo(word1, word2, i + 1, j + 1);

        // Store the result in memo and return the minimum number of
operations needed
        int result = 1 + Math.min(insertOp, Math.min(deleteOp,
replaceOp));
        memo.put(key, result);

        return result;
    }

    public static void main(String[] args) {
        EditDistanceMemo ed = new EditDistanceMemo();

        // Test case
        String word1 = "horse";
        String word2 = "ros";
        System.out.println(ed.minDistanceMemo(word1, word2, 0, 0));
// Output: 3
    }
}
```

Time Complexity: The time complexity is `O(m * n)` where `m` and `n` are the lengths of `word1` and `word2`, respectively, as each subproblem is solved only once.
Space Complexity: The space complexity is `O(m * n)` due to the memoization storage and recursive call stack.

Bottom-Up DP Approach (Tabulation)

Let's now convert the solution to a bottom-up dynamic programming approach, where we iteratively calculate the minimum number of operations needed for progressively larger substrings.

The dynamic programming equation can be formulated as follows:

For each pair of indices `i` and `j`:

- If the characters `word1[i-1]` and `word2[j-1]` are equal, then
  `dp[i][j] = dp[i-1][j-1]`
- If the characters `word1[i-1]` and `word2[j-1]` are different:
  `dp[i][j] = 1 + min(dp[i-1][j], dp[i][j-1], dp[i-1][j-1])`

Here's the code for bottom-up approach:

```
public class EditDistance {

   // Bottom-up dynamic programming method
   public int minDistanceDP(String word1, String word2) {
       int m = word1.length();
       int n = word2.length();

       // Create a dp array to store the minimum number of
operations needed
       int[][] dp = new int[m + 1][n + 1];

       // Initialize base cases
       for (int i = 0; i <= m; i++) {
           dp[i][0] = i; // If word2 is empty, delete all
characters of word1
       }
       for (int j = 0; j <= n; j++) {
           dp[0][j] = j; // If word1 is empty, insert all
characters of word2
       }

       // Fill the dp array iteratively
       for (int i = 1; i <= m; i++) {
           for (int j = 1; j <= n; j++) {
               if (word1.charAt(i - 1) == word2.charAt(j - 1)) {
                   dp[i][j] = dp[i - 1][j - 1]; // Characters match,
no new operation needed
               } else {
                   dp[i][j] = 1 + Math.min(dp[i - 1][j], // Delete
operation
```

```
                                    Math.min(dp[i][j - 1], // Insert
operation
                                              dp[i - 1][j - 1])); // Replace
operation
                }
            }
        }

        // The value at dp[m][n] contains the minimum edit distance
        return dp[m][n];
    }

    public static void main(String[] args) {
        EditDistance ed = new EditDistance();

        // Test case
        String word1 = "horse";
        String word2 = "ros";
        System.out.println(ed.minDistanceDP(word1, word2)); //
Output: 3
    }
}
```

Time Complexity: The time complexity is `O(m * n)` where `m` and `n` are the lengths of `word1` and `word2`, respectively.
Space Complexity: The space complexity is `O(m * n)` due to the dp table.

Problem 7: Unique Paths - Count Robot Paths

Problem Statement

You have a robot on an `m x n` grid that starts at the top-left corner (`grid[0][0]`) and needs to reach the bottom-right corner (`grid[m-1][n-1]`).

The robot can only move down or right at any point.

Given the dimensions `m` and `n`, find the number of unique paths the robot can take to reach its destination.

Solution

Let's begin by clarifying a few aspects of the problem.

Clarifying Questions

Candidate: Can the robot move diagonally, or is it limited to just down and right?
Interviewer: The robot is limited to moving only down or right.

Candidate: Are there any obstacles or is the grid completely open?
Interviewer: The grid is completely open with no obstacles.

Candidate:
Got it! The goal is to calculate the number of unique paths the robot can take from the top-left corner to the bottom-right corner of an `m x n` grid.

Example:
Let's consider an example for better understanding of the problem:

- `Input: m = 3, n = 2`
- `Output: 3`

Explanation:
The robot can take three different paths:

```
1. Right -> Right -> Down
2. Right -> Down -> Right
3. Down -> Right -> Right
```

Brute Force Recursive Approach

The brute force approach involves recursively exploring all possible paths from the top-left corner to the bottom-right corner. At each step, the robot can either move down or right.

The recursive formula is based on the idea that to reach any cell `(m, n)` in the grid, the robot must have come either from the cell directly above it `(m-1, n)` or from the cell directly to the left of it `(m, n-1)`.

Thus, the total number of unique paths to `(m, n)` is the sum of the paths to `(m-1, n)` and `(m, n-1)`:

Here's how we can approach this recursively:

```
public class UniquePathsRecursive {

   // Brute force recursive method to calculate the number of
unique paths
   public int countPathsRecursive(int m, int n) {
       // Base case: If the grid is a single row or a single column
       if (m == 1 || n == 1) return 1;

       // The total number of paths to (m, n) is the sum of the
paths from above and from the left
       return countPathsRecursive(m - 1, n) + countPathsRecursive(m,
n - 1);
   }

   public static void main(String[] args) {
       UniquePathsRecursive up = new UniquePathsRecursive();

       // Test case
       int m = 3;
       int n = 2;
       System.out.println(up.countPathsRecursive(m, n)); // Output:
3
```

```
    }
}
```

Time Complexity: The time complexity is exponential `O(2^(m+n))` because the function makes two recursive calls for each grid cell.
Space Complexity: The space complexity is `O(m + n)` due to the recursive call stack.

Top-Down DP Approach (Memoization)

We can optimize the recursive solution using *memoization* to store the results of subproblems, to avoid redundant calculations.

Here's the top-down dynamic programming solution with memoization:

```
import java.util.HashMap;
import java.util.Map;

public class UniquePathsMemo {

    // Memoization map to store results of subproblems
    private final Map<String, Integer> memo = new HashMap<>();

    // Top-down dynamic programming method with memoization
    public int countPathsMemo(int m, int n) {
        // Base case: If the grid is a single row or a single
column,
        // there is only one unique path to the destination.
        if (m == 1 || n == 1) return 1;

        // Create a unique key for the memo map based on the current
grid size
        String key = m + "," + n;

        // Check if the result is already computed and stored in
memo
        if (memo.containsKey(key)) {
            return memo.get(key);
        }

        // Calculate the number of unique paths to the current cell
by summing:
        // - The paths from the cell directly above (m-1, n)
        // - The paths from the cell directly to the left (m, n-1)
        int paths = countPathsMemo(m - 1, n) + countPathsMemo(m, n -
1);

        // Store the result in memo to avoid redundant calculations
        memo.put(key, paths);

        return paths;
    }
```

```
    public static void main(String[] args) {
        UniquePathsMemo up = new UniquePathsMemo();

        // Test case: Calculate the number of unique paths in a 3x2
grid
        int m = 3;
        int n = 2;
        System.out.println(up.countPathsMemo(m, n)); // Output: 3
    }
}
```

Time Complexity: The time complexity is `O(m * n)` because each subproblem is solved only once.
Space Complexity: The space complexity is `O(m * n)` due to the memoization storage and recursive call stack.

Bottom-Up DP Approach (Tabulation)

The bottom-up approach builds the solution by filling in a table where each cell represents the number of unique paths to reach that cell.

The value in each cell is the sum of the values from the cell above it and the cell to the left of it, as those are the only two directions the robot can come from.

Here's the code for bottom-up approach:

```
public class UniquePaths {

    // Bottom-up dynamic programming method
    public int countPathsDP(int m, int n) {
        // Create a 2D dp array to store the number of unique paths
        int[][] dp = new int[m][n];

        // Initialize the first row and first column with 1s since
there's only one way to reach those cells
        for (int i = 0; i < m; i++) {
            dp[i][0] = 1;
        }
        for (int j = 0; j < n; j++) {
            dp[0][j] = 1;
        }

        // Fill the dp array iteratively
        for (int i = 1; i < m; i++) {
            for (int j = 1; j < n; j++) {
                dp[i][j] = dp[i - 1][j] + dp[i][j - 1];
            }
        }

        // The value at dp[m-1][n-1] contains the number of unique
paths
        return dp[m - 1][n - 1];
```

```
    }

    public static void main(String[] args) {
        UniquePaths up = new UniquePaths();

        // Test case
        int m = 3;
        int n = 2;
        System.out.println(up.countPathsDP(m, n)); // Output: 3
    }
}
```

Time Complexity: The time complexity is `O(m * n)` because we iterate over each cell in the grid.
Space Complexity: The space complexity is `O(m * n)` due to the dp array.

Problem 8: Longest Common Subsequence

Problem Statement

Given two strings `text1` and `text2`, find the length of their longest common subsequence. If there is no common subsequence, return `0`.

A subsequence is a sequence that appears in the same relative order but not necessarily contiguously.

Solution

Let's begin by clarifying the problem requirements.

Clarifying Questions

Candidate: Can the subsequences be non-contiguous, as long as the order of characters is maintained?
Interviewer: Yes, the subsequences can be non-contiguous as long as the order is maintained.

Candidate: Are the strings case-sensitive?
Interviewer: Yes, the strings are case-sensitive.

Candidate:
Great! So, the goal is to find the *length of the longest common subsequence* between `text1` and `text2`.

Example:
Let's consider an example to clarify the input and output format:

- `Input: text1 = "abcde", text2 = "ace"`
- `Output: 3`

Explanation:
The longest common subsequence is `ace`, which has a length of 3.

Brute Force Recursive Approach

The brute force approach involves checking all possible subsequences of `text1` and `text2` and finding the longest one that is common to both.

This can be done recursively by comparing the characters of the current substrings and either *including* them in the subsequence or *excluding* them.

Here's how we can approach this recursively:

```
public class LongestCommonSubsequenceRecursive {

    // Brute force recursive method to find the length of the
longest common subsequence
    public int lcsRecursive(String text1, String text2, int i, int j)
{
        // Base case: if either string is exhausted
        if (i == text1.length() || j == text2.length()) return 0;

        // If characters match, include this character in the
subsequence
        if (text1.charAt(i) == text2.charAt(j)) {
            return 1 + lcsRecursive(text1, text2, i + 1, j + 1);
        }

        // Otherwise, consider excluding the character from either
string
        int excludeText1 = lcsRecursive(text1, text2, i + 1, j);
        int excludeText2 = lcsRecursive(text1, text2, i, j + 1);

        // Return the maximum length obtained
        return Math.max(excludeText1, excludeText2);
    }

    public static void main(String[] args) {
        LongestCommonSubsequenceRecursive lcs = new
LongestCommonSubsequenceRecursive();

        // Test case
        String text1 = "abcde";
        String text2 = "ace";
        System.out.println(lcs.lcsRecursive(text1, text2, 0, 0)); //
Output: 3
    }
}
```

Time Complexity: The time complexity is $O(2^n)$ where n is the length of the shorter string, due to the exponential growth of recursive calls.

Space Complexity: The space complexity is `O(m + n)` due to the recursive call stack, where `m` and `n` are the lengths of `text1` and `text2`, respectively.

Top-Down DP Approach (Memoization)

We can optimize the brute force approach using memoization to store the results of subproblems, avoiding redundant calculations.

Here's the top-down dynamic programming solution with memoization:

```
import java.util.HashMap;
import java.util.Map;

public class LongestCommonSubsequenceMemo {

    // Memoization map to store results of subproblems
    private final Map<String, Integer> memo = new HashMap<>();

    // Top-down dynamic programming method with memoization
    public int lcsMemo(String text1, String text2, int i, int j) {
        // Base case: if either string is exhausted
        if (i == text1.length() || j == text2.length()) return 0;

        // Create a unique key for the memo map
        String key = i + "-" + j;

        // Check if the result is already computed
        if (memo.containsKey(key)) {
            return memo.get(key);
        }

        int result;

        // If characters match, include this character in the
subsequence
        if (text1.charAt(i) == text2.charAt(j)) {
            result = 1 + lcsMemo(text1, text2, i + 1, j + 1);
        } else {
            // Otherwise, consider excluding the character from
either string
            int excludeText1 = lcsMemo(text1, text2, i + 1, j);
            int excludeText2 = lcsMemo(text1, text2, i, j + 1);
            result = Math.max(excludeText1, excludeText2);
        }

        // Store the result in memo
        memo.put(key, result);

        return result;
    }

    public static void main(String[] args) {
        LongestCommonSubsequenceMemo lcs = new
```

```
LongestCommonSubsequenceMemo();

        // Test case
        String text1 = "abcde";
        String text2 = "ace";
        System.out.println(lcs.lcsMemo(text1, text2, 0, 0)); //
Output: 3
    }
}
```

Time Complexity: The time complexity is reduced to `O(m * n)` because each subproblem is solved only once.
Space Complexity: The space complexity is `O(m * n)` due to the memoization storage and recursive call stack.

Bottom-Up DP Approach (Tabulation)

The bottom-up approach builds the solution by filling in a table where each cell represents the length of the longest common subsequence between the substrings of `text1` and `text2` up to that point.

Outline of the steps:

1. **Initialize the Table**:
    - Create a 2D array dp of size `(m+1) x (n+1)` where `m` and `n` are the lengths of `text1` and `text2`. Initialize `dp[0][*]` and `dp[*][0]` to `0` because an empty string has an LCS length of `0` with any string.
2. **Fill the Table:**
    - Iterate through each character of `text1` and `text2`.
    - If `text1[i-1]` matches `text2[j-1]`, set `dp[i][j] = dp[i-1][j-1] + 1`.
    - If they don't match, set `dp[i][j] = max(dp[i-1][j], dp[i][j-1])` to take the longer subsequence found so far.
3. **Final Result:**
    - The value in the bottom-right cell `dp[m][n]` contains the length of the longest common subsequence between `text1` and `text2`.

The equation `dp[i][j] = max(dp[i-1][j], dp[i][j-1])` effectively captures the ***decision-making process*** of whether to exclude the current character from either string to maximize the LCS length up to that point.

When `text1[i-1] != text2[j-1]`, the characters at position `i-1` in `text1` and `j-1` in `text2` are not the same, so you can't include both characters in the LCS. So you have one of the following options:

1. **Exclude the Current Character of `text1` (`dp[i-1][j]`):**
    - This represents the LCS length if you ignore the current character of `text1` and consider the LCS up to the previous character of `text1` and the entire `text2`.
2. **Exclude the Current Character of `text2` (`dp[i][j-1]`):**

- This represents the LCS length if you ignore the current character of `text2` and consider the LCS up to the previous character of `text2` and the entire `text1`.

The `max(dp[i-1][j], dp[i][j-1])` ensures that you take the best possible subsequence found by either excluding the character from `text1` or from `text2`.

Here's the code for bottom-up approach:

```
public class LongestCommonSubsequence {

   // Bottom-up dynamic programming method
   public int lcsDP(String text1, String text2) {
        int m = text1.length();
        int n = text2.length();

        // Create a 2D dp array to store the lengths of the longest
common subsequence
        int[][] dp = new int[m + 1][n + 1];

        // Fill the dp array iteratively
        for (int i = 1; i <= m; i++) {
             for (int j = 1; j <= n; j++) {
                  if (text1.charAt(i - 1) == text2.charAt(j - 1)) {
                       dp[i][j] = dp[i - 1][j - 1] + 1; // Characters
match, include in LCS
                  } else {
                       dp[i][j] = Math.max(dp[i - 1][j], dp[i][j - 1]);
// Take max from top or left
                  }
             }
        }

        // The value at dp[m][n] contains the length of the longest
common subsequence
        return dp[m][n];
   }

   public static void main(String[] args) {
        LongestCommonSubsequence lcs = new
LongestCommonSubsequence();

        // Test case
        String text1 = "abcde";
        String text2 = "ace";
        System.out.println(lcs.lcsDP(text1, text2)); // Output: 3
   }
}
```

Time Complexity: The time complexity is `O(m * n)` where `m` and `n` are the lengths of text1 and text2, respectively.
Space Complexity: The space complexity is `O(m * n)` due to the `dp` table.

Problem 9: Longest Increasing Subsequence

Problem Statement

Given an array of integers `nums`, find the length of the *longest increasing subsequence.*

A subsequence is a sequence derived from the array by deleting some or no elements without changing the order of the remaining elements.

Solution

Let's begin by clarifying the problem requirements.

Clarifying Questions

Candidate: Can the elements in the subsequence be non-contiguous, as long as they maintain their relative order in nums?
Interviewer: Yes, the elements can be non-contiguous but must maintain their relative order.

Candidate: If array `nums` has only one element, should I return `1` since the subsequence length would be 1?
Interviewer: Yes, if array nums has only one element, the length of the longest strictly increasing subsequence is `1`.

Candidate:
Great! So, the goal is to find the length of the *longest subsequence* in array nums where *each element is strictly greater than the one before it.*

Example:
Let's consider an example:

- `Input: nums = [10, 9, 2, 5, 3, 7, 101, 18]`
- `Output: 4`

Explanation:
The longest strictly increasing subsequence is `[2, 3, 7, 101]`, which has a length of 4.

Brute Force Recursive Approach

The brute force approach would be recursively exploring all possible subsequences and checking if they are strictly increasing. We keep track of the maximum length found.

Here's how we can approach this recursively:

```
public class LongestIncreasingSubsequenceRecursive {
```

```
    // Brute force recursive method to find the length of the
longest increasing subsequence
    public int lisRecursive(int[] nums, int prevIndex, int currIndex)
{
        // Base case: if we have reached the end of the array
        if (currIndex == nums.length) return 0;

        // Option 1: Exclude the current element and move to the
next
        int exclude = lisRecursive(nums, prevIndex, currIndex + 1);

        // Option 2: Include the current element if it forms an
increasing subsequence
        int include = 0;
        if (prevIndex == -1 || nums[currIndex] > nums[prevIndex]) {
            include = 1 + lisRecursive(nums, currIndex, currIndex +
1);
        }

        // Return the maximum length obtained
        return Math.max(include, exclude);
    }

    public static void main(String[] args) {
        LongestIncreasingSubsequenceRecursive lis = new
LongestIncreasingSubsequenceRecursive();

        // Test case
        int[] nums = {10, 9, 2, 5, 3, 7, 101, 18};
        System.out.println(lis.lisRecursive(nums, -1, 0)); // Output:
4
    }
}
```

Time Complexity: The time complexity is $O(2^n)$ where n is the length of array nums, due to the exponential number of subsequences.
Space Complexity: The space complexity is $O(n)$ due to the recursive call stack.

Top-Down DP Approach (Memoization)

We can optimize the recursive approach ***using memoization to store the results of subproblems***, to avoid redundant calculations.

Here's the top-down dynamic programming solution with memoization:

```
import java.util.HashMap;
import java.util.Map;

public class LongestIncreasingSubsequenceMemo {

    // Memoization map to store results of subproblems
    private final Map<Integer, Integer> memo = new HashMap<>();
```

```
    // Top-down dynamic programming method with memoization
    public int lisMemo(int[] nums, int prevIndex, int currIndex) {
        // Base case: if we have reached the end of the array
        if (currIndex == nums.length) return 0;

        // Create a unique key for the memo map
        int key = prevIndex * nums.length + currIndex;

        // Check if the result is already computed
        if (memo.containsKey(key)) {
            return memo.get(key);
        }

        // Option 1: Exclude the current element and move to the
next
        int exclude = lisMemo(nums, prevIndex, currIndex + 1);

        // Option 2: Include the current element if it forms an
increasing subsequence
        int include = 0;
        if (prevIndex == -1 || nums[currIndex] > nums[prevIndex]) {
            include = 1 + lisMemo(nums, currIndex, currIndex + 1);
        }

        // Store the result in memo and return the maximum length
obtained
        int result = Math.max(include, exclude);
        memo.put(key, result);

        return result;
    }

    public static void main(String[] args) {
        LongestIncreasingSubsequenceMemo lis = new
LongestIncreasingSubsequenceMemo();

        // Test case
        int[] nums = {10, 9, 2, 5, 3, 7, 101, 18};
        System.out.println(lis.lisMemo(nums, -1, 0)); // Output: 4
    }
}
```

Time Complexity: The time complexity is reduced to $O(n^2)$ because each subproblem is solved only once.

Space Complexity: The space complexity is $O(n^2)$ due to the memoization storage and recursive call stack.

- The number of subproblems is determined by the number of unique pairs `(prevIndex, currIndex)`.
- Since both `prevIndex` and `currIndex` can take n values, the total number of pairs is $n * n = n^2$.

Bottom-Up DP Approach (Tabulation)

Let's now convert the solution to a bottom-up dynamic programming approach where we iteratively calculate the length of the longest increasing subsequence for each element.

The bottom-up approach builds the solution by filling in a table (dp) where each entry `dp[i]` represents the length of the longest increasing subsequence that ends at index `i`.

The keys things to understand for bottom up approach:
Base Case:

- Each element can *start its own subsequence*, so initialize `dp[i]` to `1` for all `i`.

Filling the DP Table:

- For each element `nums[i]`, check all previous elements `nums[j]` where `j < i`. If `nums[i] > nums[j]`, update `dp[i]` to the maximum of `dp[i]` or `dp[j] + 1`.

Final Result: The length of the longest increasing subsequence is the maximum value in the dp array.

The equation can be formulated as follows:

Let `dp(i)` represent the length of the longest increasing subsequence ending at index `i`.

`dp(i) = max(1,1 + dp(j)) for all j < i and nums[j] < nums[i]`

Here's the code for bottom-up approach:

```
import java.util.Arrays;

public class LongestIncreasingSubsequence {

    // Bottom-up dynamic programming method
    public int lisDP(int[] nums) {
        int n = nums.length;
        if (n == 0) return 0;

        // Create a dp array to store the length of LIS ending at
each index
        int[] dp = new int[n];
        // Initialize each dp[i] to 1 (minimum subsequence length)
        Arrays.fill(dp, 1);

        // Fill the dp array iteratively
        for (int i = 1; i < n; i++) {
            for (int j = 0; j < i; j++) {
                if (nums[i] > nums[j]) {
                    dp[i] = Math.max(dp[i], dp[j] + 1);
                }
            }
        }
```

```
        // The result is the maximum value in the dp array
        int maxLength = 0;
        for (int length : dp) {
            maxLength = Math.max(maxLength, length);
        }

        return maxLength;
    }

    public static void main(String[] args) {
        LongestIncreasingSubsequence lis = new
LongestIncreasingSubsequence();

        // Test case
        int[] nums = {10, 9, 2, 5, 3, 7, 101, 18};
        System.out.println(lis.lisDP(nums)); // Output: 4
    }
}
```

Time Complexity: The time complexity is $O(n^2)$ because we check every pair of elements.
Space Complexity: The space complexity is $O(n)$ due to the dp array.

Problem 10: Partition Equal Subset Sum

Problem Statement

Given an array of integers `nums`, determine whether it is possible to partition the array into two subsets such that the sum of the elements in both subsets is equal.

Return `true` if it is possible, and `false` otherwise.

Solution

Let's begin by clarifying the problem requirements.

Clarifying Questions

Candidate: Are all the integers in the array positive, or can there be negative numbers as well?
Interviewer: The array contains only non-negative integers.

Candidate: If the total sum of the array is odd, should I immediately return false since it can't be divided equally?
Interviewer: Yes, if the total sum is odd, it can't be split into two equal parts, so you should return false.

Candidate: Is the array guaranteed to have at least one element?
Interviewer: Yes, the array will have at least one element.

Candidate:
Great! So, the goal is to determine *if we can split the array into two subsets with equal sums.*

Example:
Let's consider an example:

- `Input: nums = [1, 5, 11, 5]`
- `Output: true`

Explanation:
The array can be partitioned as `[1, 5, 5]` and `[11]`, both of which have the sum `11`.

Key Insight:
To solve this problem, the key insight is to recognize that if we can find a subset of array `nums` that sums to `sum(nums)/2`, then the rest of the array must sum to the same value.

Therefore, *the problem reduces to finding if there exists a subset with a sum equal to* `sum(nums) / 2`.

Brute Force Recursive Approach

The brute force approach involves exploring all possible subsets of array `nums` and checking if any subset sums to `sum(nums) / 2`.

Here's how we can implement this recursively:

```
public class PartitionEqualSubsetSumRecursive {

   // Brute force recursive method to check if a subset with a
given sum exists
   public boolean canPartitionRecursive(int[] nums, int index, int
targetSum) {
       // Base case: if targetSum is 0, we've found a subset that
sums to sum(nums) / 2
       if (targetSum == 0) return true;

       // If we've exhausted all elements or targetSum becomes
negative, return false
       if (index >= nums.length || targetSum < 0) return false;

       // Option 1: Include the current element in the subset
       boolean include = canPartitionRecursive(nums, index + 1,
targetSum - nums[index]);

       // Option 2: Exclude the current element from the subset
       boolean exclude = canPartitionRecursive(nums, index + 1,
targetSum);
```

```
        // Return true if either option leads to a valid subset
        return include || exclude;
    }

    public boolean canPartition(int[] nums) {
        int totalSum = 0;
        for (int num : nums) {
            totalSum += num;
        }

        // If total sum is odd, we can't partition it into two equal
subsets
        if (totalSum % 2 != 0) return false;

        // The target sum for each subset is half of the total sum
        return canPartitionRecursive(nums, 0, totalSum / 2);
    }

    public static void main(String[] args) {
        PartitionEqualSubsetSumRecursive solution = new
PartitionEqualSubsetSumRecursive();

        // Test case
        int[] nums = {1, 5, 11, 5};
        System.out.println(solution.canPartition(nums)); // Output:
true
    }
}
```

Time Complexity: The time complexity is $O(2^n)$ where n is the length of nums, due to the exponential number of subsets.
Space Complexity: The space complexity is O(n) due to the recursive call stack.

Top-Down DP Approach (Memoization)

We can optimize the recursive approach using memoization to store the results of subproblems, to avoid redundant calculations.

Here's the top-down dynamic programming solution with memoization:

```
import java.util.HashMap;
import java.util.Map;

public class PartitionEqualSubsetSumMemo {

    // Memoization map to store results of subproblems
    private final Map<String, Boolean> memo = new HashMap<>();

    // Top-down dynamic programming method with memoization
    public boolean canPartitionMemo(int[] nums, int index, int
targetSum) {
        // Base case: if targetSum is 0, we've found a subset that
```

```
sums to sum(nums) / 2
        if (targetSum == 0) return true;

        // If we've exhausted all elements or targetSum becomes
negative, return false
        if (index >= nums.length || targetSum < 0) return false;

        // Create a unique key for the memo map
        String key = index + "-" + targetSum;

        // Check if the result is already computed
        if (memo.containsKey(key)) {
            return memo.get(key);
        }

        // Option 1: Include the current element in the subset
        boolean include = canPartitionMemo(nums, index + 1, targetSum
- nums[index]);

        // Option 2: Exclude the current element from the subset
        boolean exclude = canPartitionMemo(nums, index + 1,
targetSum);

        // Store the result in memo and return true if either option
leads to a valid subset
        boolean result = include || exclude;
        memo.put(key, result);

        return result;
    }

    public boolean canPartition(int[] nums) {
        int totalSum = 0;
        for (int num : nums) {
            totalSum += num;
        }

        // If total sum is odd, we can't partition it into two equal
subsets
        if (totalSum % 2 != 0) return false;

        // The target sum for each subset is half of the total sum
        return canPartitionMemo(nums, 0, totalSum / 2);
    }

    public static void main(String[] args) {
        PartitionEqualSubsetSumMemo solution = new
PartitionEqualSubsetSumMemo();

        // Test case
        int[] nums = {1, 5, 11, 5};
        System.out.println(solution.canPartition(nums)); // Output:
true
    }
```

```
}
```

Time Complexity: The time complexity is reduced to `O(n * targetSum)` because each subproblem is solved only once.
Space Complexity: The space complexity is `O(n * targetSum)` due to the memoization storage and recursive call stack.

Bottom-Up DP Approach (Tabulation)

Now, let's convert the solution to a bottom-up dynamic programming approach where we iteratively build up to the solution.

We can use a 1D array to keep track of whether a subset with a given sum can be formed using the elements of `nums`.

The key idea is to start with a base case and then fill up the table iteratively.

Base Case:

- `dp[0] = true` because a sum of `0` can always be achieved with an empty subset.

Filling the DP Table:

- For each *number* in array *nums*, update the dp array from right to left, checking if the current number can help form a subset that sums to `targetSum`.

Final Result:
The value in `dp[targetSum]` indicates whether it's possible to form a subset with a sum equal to `targetSum`.

Here's the code for bottom-up approach:

```
public class PartitionEqualSubsetSum {

    // Bottom-up dynamic programming method
    public boolean canPartitionDP(int[] nums) {
        int totalSum = 0;
        for (int num : nums) {
            totalSum += num;
        }

        // If total sum is odd, we can't partition it into two equal
subsets
        if (totalSum % 2 != 0) return false;

        int targetSum = totalSum / 2;

        // Create a dp array to keep track of possible sums
        boolean[] dp = new boolean[targetSum + 1];
        dp[0] = true; // There's always a way to make a sum of 0
(use no elements)
```

```
        // Fill the dp array iteratively
        for (int num : nums) {
            for (int sum = targetSum; sum >= num; sum--) {
                dp[sum] = dp[sum] || dp[sum - num];
            }
        }

        // The value at dp[targetSum] tells us if we can partition
the array
        return dp[targetSum];
    }

    public static void main(String[] args) {
        PartitionEqualSubsetSum solution = new
PartitionEqualSubsetSum();

        // Test case
        int[] nums = {1, 5, 11, 5};
        System.out.println(solution.canPartitionDP(nums)); // Output:
true
    }
}
```

Time Complexity: The time complexity is `O(n * targetSum)` because we iterate over the array and update the possible sums.
Space Complexity: The space complexity is `O(targetSum)` due to the dp array.

Chapter 20: Object Oriented Design

Introduction

Understanding how to design robust, scalable, and maintainable systems using object-oriented principles is essential for demonstrating your ability to think like an architect.

This chapter will guide you through the core concepts of OOD, the types of questions you might encounter in interviews, and strategies to approach these problems effectively.

Core Object-Oriented Principles

To excel in object-oriented design questions, you must have a firm grasp of the following principles:

1. Encapsulation

Encapsulation is about *bundling data and methods that operate on that data within a single unit*, typically a class.

It helps in *hiding the internal state* of the object and *only exposing what is necessary*, thus promoting modularity and reducing complexity.

2. Abstraction

Abstraction involves *simplifying complex systems* by modeling classes appropriate to the problem domain. It allows you to focus on *essential characteristics while ignoring the irrelevant details*, which is crucial in large-scale system design.

3. Inheritance

Inheritance allows a class to *inherit properties and behaviors from another class*, promoting *code reuse* and establishing a natural hierarchy between classes.

4. Polymorphism

Polymorphism enables objects to be *treated as instances of their parent class, with the ability to override methods to define specific behaviors*. This principle is vital for designing flexible and extensible systems.

Common Object-Oriented Design Patterns

Familiarity with design patterns is critical for demonstrating your ability to *apply OOD principles* in real-world scenarios.

Here are a few key patterns that are frequently discussed in interviews:

- **Singleton Pattern:** Ensures a class has only one instance and provides a global point of access to that instance. This is often used in scenarios where a single instance of a class must coordinate actions across the system.
- **Factory Pattern:** The Factory Method pattern defines an interface for creating an object but lets subclasses alter the type of objects that will be created. This pattern is particularly useful when the exact type of object cannot be determined until runtime.
- **Observer Pattern:** The Observer pattern defines a one-to-many dependency between objects so that when one object changes state, all its dependents are notified and updated automatically. This pattern is widely used in event handling systems.
- **Strategy Pattern:** The Strategy pattern defines a family of algorithms, encapsulates each one, and makes them interchangeable. It lets the algorithm vary independently from the clients that use it.
- **Decorator Pattern:** The Decorator pattern allows behavior to be added to individual objects, either statically or dynamically, without affecting the behavior of other objects from the same class.

Types of Object-Oriented Design Questions

In coding interviews, object-oriented design questions typically fall into two categories (*most often you will encounter the first category of problems in coding interviews*):

- **Design a Class or System:** You may be asked to *design a class or a set of classes* to model a specific *problem domain*. For example, "*Design a parking lot system*" or "*Design a deck of cards*". In these questions, focus on *understanding the requirements*, *identifying the key objects*, and *defining the relationships* between them.
- **Design Patterns and Best Practices:** You might be asked to apply design patterns to solve a problem, like "*Implement a thread-safe singleton*" or "*Design an event management system using the observer pattern*". These questions test your ability to recognize patterns and apply them appropriately.

Approaching Object-Oriented Design Problems

Here's a structured approach to tackle object-oriented design questions in interviews:

1. **Clarify Requirements:** Start by asking clarifying questions to ensure you understand the problem. Identify the *core entities, their attributes, and their interactions*.
2. **Identify Key Objects and Relationships**: Break down the problem into objects and their relationships. Determine which classes need to be created, their responsibilities, and how they will interact with each other.
3. **Define Class Structure:** Create a basic class structure, including attributes and methods. Use UML diagrams or simple sketches to visualize the relationships between classes.

4. **Apply Design Patterns:** Identify *opportunities* to apply design patterns to solve recurring problems, enhance modularity, or simplify interactions between objects.
5. **Consider Edge Cases and Scalability:** Think about how your design will handle edge cases and how it might need to scale as requirements grow. Discuss potential trade-offs and optimizations.

Throughout the interview, explain your thought process clearly. Interviewers are often more interested in how you approach the problem than the final solution itself.

Popular Object Oriented Design Questions

Now, let's go over most commonly asked object oriented design questions and their complete solutions.

Problem 1: Design & Implement LRU Cache

Problem Statement

Design and implement a data structure that operates as a *Least Recently Used (LRU) cache.*

This cache should allow quick *retrieval and updates of key-value pairs* and efficiently manage the capacity by evicting the least recently accessed items when necessary.

Solution

Clarifying Questions

Candidate: Okay, to clarify, you want me to design an LRU cache that supports *two primary operations,* `get` and `put`, both of which should run in `O(1)` time complexity. The cache should have *a fixed capacity*, and if it exceeds this capacity, *the least recently used item should be evicted.* Does that sound correct?
Interviewer: Yes, that's correct.

Candidate: Great. For the LRU cache, would it be safe to assume that the *keys and values are both integers*?
Interviewer: Yes, you can assume that both keys and values are integers.

Candidate: Understood. Just to confirm, when you say "least recently used," do you mean that when I access or update an item, it becomes the most recently used, and any items that have not been accessed for the longest time should be removed first when the capacity is exceeded?
Interviewer: Exactly.

Candidate: Perfect. One last question: if the `put` operation is called with a key that already exists in the cache, should it update the value and also mark the key as the most recently used?
Interviewer: Yes, that's correct.
Candidate: Thanks for the clarification. Let me walk you through how I would approach this problem.

Example with Input and Expected Output:
Let's assume we initialize an LRU cache with a capacity of 2. Here's how the operations would play out:

```
LRUCache cache = new LRUCache(2);  // Cache capacity is 2
cache.put(1, 1);                   // Cache: [1] -> The cache contains
key 1 with value 1
cache.put(2, 2);                   // Cache: [2, 1] -> The cache now
contains key 1 and key 2
cache.get(1);                      // Returns 1, Cache: [1, 2] -> Key
1 is accessed, so it's moved to the front
cache.put(3, 3);                   // Evicts key 2, Cache: [3, 1] ->
Key 2 is the least recently used, so it's evicted
cache.get(2);                      // Returns -1 (not found), Cache:
[1, 3] -> Key 2 was evicted, so it's not found
cache.put(4, 4);                   // Evicts key 1, Cache: [3, 4] ->
Key 1 is the least recently used, so it's evicted
cache.get(1);                      // Returns -1 (not found), Cache:
[3, 4] -> Key 1 was evicted, so it's not found
cache.get(3);                      // Returns 3, Cache: [3, 4] -> Key
3 is accessed, so it's moved to the front
cache.get(4);                      // Returns 4, Cache: [4, 3] -> Key
4 is accessed, so it's moved to the front
```

Brute Force Approach

A brute force approach to solve this problem would involve *using a list to store the keys in the order of their usage.*

Every time we access or update a key, we would move it to the end of the list to mark it as recently used.

However, both the `get` and `put` operations would require scanning through the list to find the key, making them `O(n)` operations.

This approach wouldn't meet the `O(1)` time complexity requirement, so it's not suitable for our case.

Optimal Approach

To achieve `O(1)` time complexity for both `get` and `put` operations, we can use a combination of a **HashMap** and a **Doubly Linked List**.

The ***HashMap*** will store the keys and corresponding nodes in the linked list, allowing for `O(1)` access.

The **doubly linked list** will *maintain the order of access*, with the *most recently used item at the front* and the least recently used at the back. This allows us to efficiently *remove* and *add* nodes.

Whenever we access a key using `get`, we'll move the corresponding node to the front of the list. Similarly, when *inserting* or *updating* using put, we'll *move or add the node to the front.* If we *exceed the capacity*, we'll *remove the node at the back of the list.*

Code Solution

Here's how I would implement this in Java:

```
import java.util.HashMap;

class LRUCache {
    // Doubly Linked List Node
    static class Node {
        int key, value;
        Node prev, next;

        Node(int key, int value) {
            this.key = key;
            this.value = value;
        }
    }

    private final HashMap<Integer, Node> map;
    private final int capacity;
    private final Node head;
    private final Node tail;

    public LRUCache(int capacity) {
        this.capacity = capacity;
        this.map = new HashMap<>();
        this.head = new Node(0, 0);  // Dummy head
        this.tail = new Node(0, 0);  // Dummy tail
        head.next = tail;
        tail.prev = head;
    }

    public int get(int key) {
        if (map.containsKey(key)) {
            Node node = map.get(key);
            remove(node);
            insertToFront(node);
            return node.value;
        } else {
            return -1;
        }
    }
```

```
    public void put(int key, int value) {
        if (map.containsKey(key)) {
            Node node = map.get(key);
            node.value = value;
            remove(node);
            insertToFront(node);
        } else {
            if (map.size() == capacity) {
                // Remove from the tail
                Node lru = tail.prev;
                map.remove(lru.key);
                remove(lru);
            }
            Node newNode = new Node(key, value);
            map.put(key, newNode);
            insertToFront(newNode);
        }
    }

    private void remove(Node node) {
        node.prev.next = node.next;
        node.next.prev = node.prev;
    }

    private void insertToFront(Node node) {
        node.next = head.next;
        node.prev = head;
        head.next.prev = node;
        head.next = node;
    }

    // Main method with test cases
    public static void main(String[] args) {
        LRUCache cache = new LRUCache(2);
        cache.put(1, 1);
        cache.put(2, 2);
        System.out.println(cache.get(1));     // returns 1
        cache.put(3, 3);                      // evicts key 2
        System.out.println(cache.get(2));     // returns -1 (not
found)
        cache.put(4, 4);                      // evicts key 1
        System.out.println(cache.get(1));     // returns -1 (not
found)
        System.out.println(cache.get(3));     // returns 3
        System.out.println(cache.get(4));     // returns 4
    }
}
```

Time and Space Complexity

- **Time Complexity:** Both `get` and `put` operations run in `O(1)` time because they involve only HashMap lookups and updates, and doubly linked list insertions and deletions, all of which are `O(1)` operations.

- **Space Complexity:** The space complexity is `O(n)`, where `n` is the capacity of the LRU cache, since we store up to `n` keys and their corresponding nodes in the HashMap and doubly linked list.

Problem 2: Design & Implement Browser History Class

Problem Statement

Design and implement a class to *simulate a browser's history* functionality with a single tab.

The browser starts on a homepage and allows navigation to new URLs, going back and forward in the history, and managing the history when new pages are visited.

Solution

Clarifying Questions

Candidate: Just to clarify, you want me to design a class that ***manages the browser history*** with the following operations:

1. Start on a homepage.
2. Visit new URLs, which should clear any forward history.
3. Go back a specified number of steps in the history.
4. Move forward a specified number of steps in the history.

Does that capture the problem correctly?
Interviewer: Yes, that's exactly what I'm looking for.

Candidate: When you say "*visit a new URL*", does it mean that this action should clear all the forward history and start a new branch from the current page?
Interviewer: Yes, visiting a new URL should clear any forward history because you're essentially starting a new path in the browsing session.

Candidate: Understood. For the back operation, if the requested number of steps is more than the available history, should it just take the user as far back as possible and return the resulting URL?
Interviewer: Exactly. It should go back as far as possible and return the URL where it stops.

Candidate: And the same logic applies to the forward operation—if the requested steps exceed the available forward history, it should move as far forward as possible, right?
Interviewer: Yes, that's correct.

Candidate: Perfect. Let me first provide an example to illustrate how this should work.

Example with Input and Expected Output:

Let's walk through a scenario:

```
BrowserHistory browserHistory = new BrowserHistory("yahoo.com");   //
Start at "yahoo.com"
browserHistory.visit("google.com");      // Visit "google.com", now the
history is ["yahoo.com", "google.com"]
browserHistory.visit("facebook.com");    // Visit "facebook.com", now
the history is ["yahoo.com", "google.com", "facebook.com"]
browserHistory.visit("youtube.com");     // Visit "youtube.com", now
the history is ["yahoo.com", "google.com", "facebook.com",
"youtube.com"]
browserHistory.back(1);                  // Move back 1 step to
"facebook.com"
browserHistory.back(1);                  // Move back 1 step to
"google.com"
browserHistory.forward(1);               // Move forward 1 step to
"facebook.com"
browserHistory.visit("linkedin.com");    // Visit "linkedin.com",
clears forward history, now history is ["yahoo.com", "google.com",
"facebook.com", "linkedin.com"]
browserHistory.forward(2);               // Cannot move forward, so
stays at "linkedin.com"
browserHistory.back(2);                  // Move back 2 steps to
"google.com"
browserHistory.back(7);                  // Move back as far as
possible to "yahoo.com"
```

Brute Force Approach

A brute force approach would be *using a list to store the history* and an *index* to keep track of the current page.

The `visit` method would add a new URL to the list and truncate any forward history. The `back` and `forward` methods would simply adjust the *index*.

However, this approach would require `O(n)` time for `back` and `forward` operations in the worst case if we need to move across the entire history.

Optimal Approach

To achieve efficient operations, we can use ***two stacks***:

1. **Back Stack:** This will keep track of the pages visited before the current one, allowing us to *pop* from this stack when moving *back* in history.
2. **Forward Stack:** This will keep track of the pages that can be visited when moving forward in history. When we visit a new URL, we clear this stack since the forward history is invalidated.

This stack-based approach ensures that both the `back` and `forward` operations can be done in `O(steps)` time, and visiting a new URL is `O(1)` since we only push onto the stack.

Code Solution

Here's how I would implement this in Java:

```
import java.util.Stack;

class BrowserHistory {
   private final Stack<String> backStack;
   private final Stack<String> forwardStack;
   private String current;

   public BrowserHistory(String homepage) {
       backStack = new Stack<>();
       forwardStack = new Stack<>();
       current = homepage;
   }

   public void visit(String url) {
       backStack.push(current);     // Push current page to back
stack
       current = url;               // Set the new URL as current
       forwardStack.clear();        // Clear the forward history
   }

   public String back(int steps) {
       while (steps > 0 && !backStack.isEmpty()) {
           forwardStack.push(current);   // Move current page to
forward stack
           current = backStack.pop();    // Pop from back stack to
go back
           steps--;
       }
       return current;  // Return the current URL
   }

   public String forward(int steps) {
       while (steps > 0 && !forwardStack.isEmpty()) {
           backStack.push(current);   // Move current page to back
stack
           current = forwardStack.pop();  // Pop from forward stack
to go forward
           steps--;
       }
       return current;  // Return the current URL
   }

   // Main method with test cases
   public static void main(String[] args) {
       BrowserHistory browserHistory = new
BrowserHistory("yahoo.com");
       browserHistory.visit("google.com");
       browserHistory.visit("facebook.com");
       browserHistory.visit("youtube.com");
       System.out.println(browserHistory.back(1));    // returns
"facebook.com"
       System.out.println(browserHistory.back(1));    // returns
"google.com"
```

```
        System.out.println(browserHistory.forward(1)); // returns
"facebook.com"
        browserHistory.visit("linkedin.com");
        System.out.println(browserHistory.forward(2)); // returns
"linkedin.com"
        System.out.println(browserHistory.back(2));    // returns
"google.com"
        System.out.println(browserHistory.back(7));    // returns
"yahoo.com"
    }
}
```

Time and Space Complexity

- **Time Complexity:**
  - *visit*: `O(1)`, as we only push to the back stack and clear the forward stack.
  - *back*: `O(min(steps, n))`, where `n` is the size of the back stack.
  - *forward*: `O(min(steps, m))`, where `m` is the size of the forward stack.
- **Space Complexity:** `O(n + m)`, where `n` is the number of pages stored in the back stack, and `m` is the number of pages in the forward stack.

Problem 3: Implementing a Rate-Limited Logger System

Problem Statement

Design a logging system that *controls the printing of messages based on their timestamps.*

Each unique message can only be printed if *at least 10 seconds have passed* since the last time it was printed. If a message arrives too soon, it should not be printed.

Implement a method *`shouldPrintMessage`* which should return `true` if the message can be printed, otherwise it should return `false`.

Solution

Clarifying Questions

Candidate: Just to clarify, you want me to design a logger system that receives messages with their associated timestamps. The logger should ensure that each unique message is printed *at most once every 10 seconds*. If the same message arrives before 10 seconds have passed, it should not be printed. Is that correct?
Interviewer: Yes, that's correct.

Candidate: Are the timestamps provided in seconds, and can we assume that they will always increase or stay the same but never decrease?
Interviewer: Yes, the timestamps are given in seconds, and you can assume they are non-decreasing.

Example with Input and Expected Output:

Let's walk through an example:

```
Logger logger = new Logger();
logger.shouldPrintMessage(1, "foo");  // Returns true, "foo" is
printed
logger.shouldPrintMessage(2, "bar");  // Returns true, "bar" is
printed
logger.shouldPrintMessage(3, "foo");  // Returns false, "foo" is not
printed because it was printed at timestamp 1
logger.shouldPrintMessage(8, "bar");  // Returns false, "bar" is not
printed because it was printed at timestamp 2
logger.shouldPrintMessage(10, "foo"); // Returns false, "foo" is not
printed because it was printed at timestamp 1
logger.shouldPrintMessage(11, "foo"); // Returns true, "foo" is
printed because 10 seconds have passed since it was last printed
```

Brute Force Approach

A brute force approach can be implemented using a *list of all printed messages and their timestamps.*

Every time a new message arrives, we would scan through the list to check if the message was printed in the last 10 seconds.

However, this approach would be inefficient, with a time complexity of `O(n)` per message, where `n` is the number of stored messages.

Optimal Approach

A more efficient approach would be to *use a HashMap* to store each unique message and the last timestamp when it was printed. This allows us to check if a message should be printed in `O(1)` time.

Here's the plan:

- Use a `HashMap<String, Integer>` where the *key* is the message, and the *value* is the last timestamp when the message was printed.
- For each incoming message, check the HashMap to see if the message exists and whether the *difference between the current timestamp and the stored timestamp is 10 seconds or more.*
    - If it's been 10 seconds or more, update the timestamp in the HashMap and return *`true`*.
    - Otherwise, return *`false`*.

Code Solution

Here's how I would implement this in Java:

```
import java.util.HashMap;

class Logger {
```

```
    private final HashMap<String, Integer> messageTimestamps;

    public Logger() {
        this.messageTimestamps = new HashMap<>();
    }

    public boolean shouldPrintMessage(int timestamp, String message)
{
        if (!messageTimestamps.containsKey(message)) {
            // If the message is new, print it and record the
timestamp
            messageTimestamps.put(message, timestamp);
            return true;
        }

        int lastTimestamp = messageTimestamps.get(message);
        if (timestamp - lastTimestamp >= 10) {
            // If at least 10 seconds have passed since the last
print, update timestamp and print it
            messageTimestamps.put(message, timestamp);
            return true;
        } else {
            // Otherwise, do not print the message
            return false;
        }
    }

    // Main method with test cases
    public static void main(String[] args) {
        Logger logger = new Logger();
        System.out.println(logger.shouldPrintMessage(1, "foo"));  //
true
        System.out.println(logger.shouldPrintMessage(2, "bar"));  //
true
        System.out.println(logger.shouldPrintMessage(3, "foo"));  //
false
        System.out.println(logger.shouldPrintMessage(8, "bar"));  //
false
        System.out.println(logger.shouldPrintMessage(10, "foo")); //
false
        System.out.println(logger.shouldPrintMessage(11, "foo")); //
true
    }
}
```

Time and Space Complexity

- **Time Complexity:** The *shouldPrintMessage* function runs in O(1) time because we are using a HashMap for fast lookups and updates.
- **Space Complexity:** The space complexity is O(n), where n is the number of unique messages that have been logged because we store each unique message and its timestamp.

Problem 4: Design an In-Memory File System

Problem Statement

Design a data structure that simulates an *in-memory file system* with basic file and directory operations.

You should be able to *create* directories, *add content* to files, *list* directory contents, and *read* file contents.

Solution

Clarifying Questions

Candidate: Just to clarify, you want me to design a file system that supports the following operations:

1. `ls(String path)`: List the contents of a directory or return the file name if the path is a file.
2. `mkdir(String path)`: Create directories based on the given path, including any intermediate directories that don't exist.
3. `addContentToFile(String filePath, String content)`: Add content to a file, creating the file if it doesn't exist.
4. `readContentFromFile(String filePath)`: Read and return the content from a specified file.

Is that correct?
Interviewer: Yes, that's correct.

Candidate: For the `ls` command, when we list the contents of a directory, should the result be in lexicographic order?
Interviewer: Yes, the list should be in lexicographic order.

Candidate: Understood. For the `addContentToFile` command, if the file already exists, should the new content be *appended* to the existing content?
Interviewer: Yes, if the file exists, append the new content to the existing content.

Candidate: Should I assume that all paths are *absolute paths* starting from the root directory `/`?
Interviewer: Yes.

Example with Input and Expected Output:

Let's go through an example so that we agree on the expected input and output formats.

```
FileSystem fs = new FileSystem();

fs.mkdir("/a/b/c");                    // Creates directory structure
/a/b/c
```

```
fs.addContentToFile("/a/b/c/d", "hello");  // Creates file /a/b/c/d
with content "hello"

System.out.println(fs.ls("/"));       // Returns ["a"]
System.out.println(fs.ls("/a/b/c")); // Returns ["d"]
System.out.println(fs.readContentFromFile("/a/b/c/d")); // Returns
"hello"

fs.addContentToFile("/a/b/c/d", " world"); // Appends " world" to
/a/b/c/d

System.out.println(fs.readContentFromFile("/a/b/c/d")); // Returns
"hello world"
```

Brute Force Approach

A brute force approach would involve storing the entire file system in a flat list or hash map, where each entry represents either a file or a directory. However, this approach would be inefficient for *hierarchical operations* like `ls` and `mkdir`, as it would require traversing the entire structure to find or modify paths.

Optimal Approach

A more efficient approach would involve using a *tree-like structure*, where:

- Each directory is represented as a *node* with a mapping to its child directories and files.
- Files are represented as *leaf nodes* with associated content.

Here's how I would design it:

- The ***root*** of the file system is a node representing `/`.
- Each directory node contains a `HashMap<String, Node>`, where the key is the name of the directory or file, and the value is the corresponding node.
- Each file node contains a *StringBuilder* to store the file content.

Code Solution

Here's how I would implement this in Java:

```
import java.util.*;

class FileSystem {
   private static class Node {
       boolean isFile = false;
       StringBuilder content = new StringBuilder();
       TreeMap<String, Node> children = new TreeMap<>();
   }

   private final Node root;

   public FileSystem() {
       root = new Node();  // Root directory
   }
```

```
    public List<String> ls(String path) {
        Node node = traversePath(path);
        if (node.isFile) {
            return new
ArrayList<>(Collections.singletonList(path.substring(path.lastIndexO
f('/') + 1)));
        } else {
            return new ArrayList<>(node.children.keySet());
        }
    }

    public void mkdir(String path) {
        traverseAndCreatePath(path);
    }

    public void addContentToFile(String filePath, String content) {
        Node node = traverseAndCreatePath(filePath);
        if (!node.isFile) {
            node.isFile = true;
        }
        node.content.append(content);
    }

    public String readContentFromFile(String filePath) {
        Node node = traversePath(filePath);
        return node.content.toString();
    }

    // Helper method to traverse the path and return the node
    private Node traversePath(String path) {
        Node curr = root;
        if (path.equals("/")) return curr;
        String[] parts = path.split("/");
        for (String part : parts) {
            if (part.isEmpty()) continue;
            curr = curr.children.get(part);
        }
        return curr;
    }

    // Helper method to traverse the path and create nodes if they
don't exist
    private Node traverseAndCreatePath(String path) {
        Node curr = root;
        String[] parts = path.split("/");
        for (String part : parts) {
            if (part.isEmpty()) continue;
            curr.children.putIfAbsent(part, new Node());
            curr = curr.children.get(part);
        }
        return curr;
    }

    // Main method with test cases
```

```
    public static void main(String[] args) {
        FileSystem fs = new FileSystem();
        fs.mkdir("/a/b/c");
        fs.addContentToFile("/a/b/c/d", "hello");
        System.out.println(fs.ls("/"));            // ["a"]
        System.out.println(fs.ls("/a/b/c"));       // ["d"]
        System.out.println(fs.readContentFromFile("/a/b/c/d")); //
"hello"
        fs.addContentToFile("/a/b/c/d", " world");
        System.out.println(fs.readContentFromFile("/a/b/c/d")); //
"hello world"
    }
}
```

Time and Space Complexity

- **Time Complexity:**
    - `ls(path)`: `O(m + n log n)`, where `m` is the length of the path and `n` is the number of entries in the directory.
    - `mkdir(path)`: `O(m)`, where `m` is the length of the path.
    - `addContentToFile(filePath, content)`: `O(m + c)`, where `m` is the length of the path and `c` is the length of the content to be added.
    - `readContentFromFile(filePath)`: `O(m + c)`, where `m` is the length of the path and `c` is the length of the content.
- **Space Complexity:** `O(m + c)`, where `m` is the total number of directories and files, and `c` is the total length of content in all files.

Problem 5: Implement a Randomized Set

Problem Statement

Design a data structure that supports *inserting*, *removing*, and *retrieving* a random element, all in average `O(1)` time complexity.

Solution

Clarifying Questions

Candidate: To clarify, you want me to design a class that supports the following operations:

1. `insert(int val)`: Adds an integer to the set if it's not already present.
2. `remove(int val)`: Removes an integer from the set if it's present.
3. `getRandom()`: Returns a random integer from the set, where each element has an equal probability of being selected.

And all these operations need to be done in average `O(1)` time complexity. Does that capture the problem correctly?
Interviewer: Yes, that's correct.

Candidate: For the *getRandom()* function, should the random selection be uniform, meaning each element in the set has an equal probability of being chosen?
Interviewer: Yes, that's correct. Each element should have an equal chance of being returned.

Candidate: Understood. Can we assume that the values inserted into the set are unique integers?
Interviewer: Yes, you can assume that the values are unique integers.

Candidate: Thanks for the clarification. Let me walk you through how I would approach this problem.

Example with Input and Expected Output:

```
RandomizedSet randomSet = new RandomizedSet();
randomSet.insert(1);  // Returns true, set = {1}
randomSet.remove(2);  // Returns false, set = {1}
randomSet.insert(2);  // Returns true, set = {1, 2}
randomSet.getRandom();  // Returns 1 or 2 randomly
randomSet.remove(1);  // Returns true, set = {2}
randomSet.insert(2);  // Returns false, set = {2}
randomSet.getRandom();  // Returns 2
```

Brute Force Approach

A brute force approach would involve storing the elements in a list and using the list's operations for *insert*, *remove*, and *getRandom*. However, this wouldn't achieve O(1) time complexity for the *remove* method because removing an element from the middle of the list is an O(n) operation.

Optimal Approach

To achieve O(1) time complexity for all operations, we can use a combination of a *HashMap* and a *List*.

- **HashMap<Integer, Integer>**: The key is the value to be inserted, and the value is the index of that value in the list. This allows us to find the index of any element in O(1) time.
- **ArrayList<Integer>**: The list stores the actual elements. It allows O(1) time for adding elements at the end and for accessing elements by index.

Here's how the operations works:

- **Insert**: We check if the value is already in the HashMap. If not, we add it to the end of the list and record its index in the HashMap.
- **Remove**: We find the index of the element to remove using the HashMap. To remove it efficiently, we swap it with the last element in the list and then remove the last element. We update the HashMap accordingly.
- **GetRandom**: We simply pick a random index from the list and return the element at that index. This ensures O(1) time complexity for random access.

Code Solution

Here's how I would implement this in Java:

```
import java.util.*;

class RandomizedSet {
   private final List<Integer> list;
   private final HashMap<Integer, Integer> map;
   private final Random rand;

   public RandomizedSet() {
       list = new ArrayList<>();
       map = new HashMap<>();
       rand = new Random();
   }

   public boolean insert(int val) {
       if (map.containsKey(val)) {
           return false; // Value already in set
       }
       map.put(val, list.size());
       list.add(val);
       return true;
   }

   public boolean remove(int val) {
       if (!map.containsKey(val)) {
           return false; // Value not found in set
       }
       int index = map.get(val);
       int lastElement = list.get(list.size() - 1);
       list.set(index, lastElement);  // Move last element to the
index of the element to be removed
       map.put(lastElement, index);   // Update the index of the
last element in the map
       list.remove(list.size() - 1);  // Remove the last element
from the list
       map.remove(val);               // Remove the element from the
map
       return true;
   }

   public int getRandom() {
       return list.get(rand.nextInt(list.size()));
   }

   // Main method with test cases
   public static void main(String[] args) {
       RandomizedSet randomSet = new RandomizedSet();
       System.out.println(randomSet.insert(1));  // true
       System.out.println(randomSet.remove(2));  // false
       System.out.println(randomSet.insert(2));  // true
       System.out.println(randomSet.getRandom());  // 1 or 2
       System.out.println(randomSet.remove(1));  // true
       System.out.println(randomSet.insert(2));  // false
       System.out.println(randomSet.getRandom());  // 2
```

```
    }
}
```

Time and Space Complexity

- **Time Complexity:**
    - *insert(val)*: `O(1)` because we add the element to the end of the list and update the map.
    - *remove(val)*: `O(1)` because we swap the element with the last one and remove it from the list, then update the map.
    - *getRandom()*: `O(1)` because we use the *rand.nextInt* method to get a random index and return the element at that index.
- **Space Complexity:** `O(n)`, where `n` is the number of elements in the set because we store all elements in both the list and the map.

Problem 6: Designing a Hit Counter for Tracking Recent Activity

Problem Statement

Design a hit counter that tracks the number of hits received in the past 5 minutes (300 seconds).

The system should record hits with a timestamp and be able to return the count of hits within the last 5 minutes efficiently.

Solution

Clarifying Questions

Candidate: To clarify, you want me to design a hit counter system that can record hits with a timestamp and return the number of hits received in the past 5 minutes from a given timestamp. The timestamp is given in seconds, and the timestamps are monotonically increasing. Does that capture the problem correctly?
Interviewer: Yes, that's correct.

Candidate: For the `hit` method, should it handle multiple hits at the same timestamp, and do I need to account for them separately?
Interviewer: Yes, multiple hits at the same timestamp should be handled, and they should be recorded appropriately.

Candidate: Understood. For the `getHits` method, should it only consider hits within the last 300 seconds from the given timestamp and ignore anything before that?
Interviewer: Yes, only the hits within the last 300 seconds should be counted.

Candidate: Got it. Let me take an example and then approach the solution.

Example with Input and Expected Output:

```
HitCounter counter = new HitCounter();
counter.hit(1);           // Hit at timestamp 1
counter.hit(2);           // Hit at timestamp 2
counter.hit(3);           // Hit at timestamp 3
System.out.println(counter.getHits(4));   // Returns 3, all hits are
within the last 5 minutes
counter.hit(300);         // Hit at timestamp 300
System.out.println(counter.getHits(300)); // Returns 4, all hits are
within the last 5 minutes
System.out.println(counter.getHits(301)); // Returns 3, the hit at
timestamp 1 is now outside the 5-minute window
```

Brute Force Approach

A brute force approach might involve storing every hit's timestamp in a list. Every time getHits is called, we would iterate through the list and count the number of hits that fall within the last 300 seconds.

However, this approach would be inefficient for large numbers of hits as it could require scanning the entire list, leading to `O(n)` time complexity for the getHits method.

Optimal Approach

To achieve efficient operations, we can *use a queue where each element is a pair* (*tuple*) containing the *timestamp and the count of hits at that timestamp.*

Here's how it works:

- **Use Queue:** Each element in the queue is a tuple of `(timestamp, hitCount)`. This allows us to efficiently keep track of the hits and their corresponding timestamps.
- `hit(int timestamp)` method: When a hit is recorded, if the queue is empty or the last element's timestamp is different from the current timestamp, we add a new element to the queue. Otherwise, we simply increment the hit count of the last element.
- `getHits(int timestamp)` method: We remove elements from the front of the queue if they are older than 300 seconds relative to the current timestamp. Then, we *sum up the counts of the remaining elements in the queue* to get the total number of hits in the last 5 minutes.

Code Solution

Here's how I would implement this in Java:

```
import java.util.LinkedList;
import java.util.Queue;

class HitCounter {
    private final Queue<int[]> hitsQueue;
    private static final int TIME_WINDOW = 300;

    public HitCounter() {
```

```
        this.hitsQueue = new LinkedList<>();
    }

    public void hit(int timestamp) {
        if (!hitsQueue.isEmpty() && hitsQueue.peek()[0] == timestamp)
{
            hitsQueue.peek()[1]++;
        } else {
            hitsQueue.offer(new int[]{timestamp, 1});
        }
    }

    public int getHits(int timestamp) {
        while (!hitsQueue.isEmpty() && timestamp -
hitsQueue.peek()[0] >= TIME_WINDOW) {
            hitsQueue.poll();  // Remove hits that are older than 5
minutes
        }

        int totalHits = 0;
        for (int[] hit : hitsQueue) {
            totalHits += hit[1];
        }

        return totalHits;
    }

    // Main method with test cases
    public static void main(String[] args) {
        HitCounter counter = new HitCounter();
        counter.hit(1);
        counter.hit(2);
        counter.hit(3);
        System.out.println(counter.getHits(4));    // 3
        counter.hit(300);
        System.out.println(counter.getHits(300)); // 4
        System.out.println(counter.getHits(301)); // 3
    }
}
```

Time and Space Complexity

- **Time Complexity:**
    - `hit(int timestamp)`: `O(1)` because adding a new hit or updating the last hit is done in constant time.
    - `getHits(int timestamp)`: `O(1)` on average because old hits are efficiently removed from the front of the queue, and the remaining hits are counted in `O(n)` time, where `n` is the number of elements in the queue. Since the maximum number of elements in the queue is bounded by the time window (300 seconds), this operation is efficient.

- **Space Complexity**: O(n), where n is the number of hits within the last 300 seconds. The space used by the queue is proportional to the number of unique timestamps within this window.

Problem 7: Implement a Tic-Tac-Toe

Problem Statement

Design a ***Tic-Tac-Toe game*** on an n x n board where two players take turns placing their marks.

The game should determine if a player wins by placing n of their marks consecutively in a row, column, or diagonal.

Implement methods to initialize the board and make moves, returning the status of the game after each move.

Solution

Clarifying Questions

Candidate: To clarify, you want me to design a Tic-Tac-Toe game that supports:
1. *Initializing* a board of size n x n.
2. Allowing *two players* to alternate placing their marks on the board.
3. *Determining if a player wins* by placing n of their marks in a row, column, or diagonal.

After each move, the game should return 0 if there is no winner, 1 if *player 1* wins, or 2 if *player 2* wins. Is that correct?
Interviewer: Yes, that's correct.
Candidate: For the *move* method, if a player wins after their move, should the game immediately terminate, or should I just return the winner without making any further moves?
Interviewer: The game should return the winner, and no further moves should be allowed after a win.

Candidate: Understood. Should I assume that all moves are valid, meaning they will always be within bounds and placed on an empty spot?
Interviewer: Yes, you can assume that all moves are valid.

Candidate: Got it. Let me take an example and then discuss the approach .

Example with Input and Expected Output:

```
TicTacToe toe = new TicTacToe(3);
System.out.println(toe.move(0, 0, 1)); // Player 1 moves at (0, 0) ->
Returns 0 (No winner)
System.out.println(toe.move(0, 2, 2)); // Player 2 moves at (0, 2) ->
Returns 0 (No winner)
```

```
System.out.println(toe.move(2, 2, 1)); // Player 1 moves at (2, 2) ->
Returns 0 (No winner)
System.out.println(toe.move(1, 1, 2)); // Player 2 moves at (1, 1) ->
Returns 0 (No winner)
System.out.println(toe.move(2, 0, 1)); // Player 1 moves at (2, 0) ->
Returns 0 (No winner)
System.out.println(toe.move(1, 0, 2)); // Player 2 moves at (1, 0) ->
Returns 0 (No winner)
System.out.println(toe.move(2, 1, 1)); // Player 1 moves at (2, 1) ->
Returns 1 (Player 1 wins)
```

Brute Force Approach

A brute force approach would involve updating the board after each move and checking all rows, columns, and diagonals for a winning condition.

However, this approach would require scanning the entire board after each move, leading to $O(n^2)$ time complexity per move, which is inefficient for large boards.

Optimal Approach

To achieve an efficient solution, we can *avoid scanning the entire board by using counters:*

- **Row Counters:** An array called *rows* of size `n` where `rows[i]` keeps track of the number of marks by a player in `row i`.
- **Column Counters:** An array called *cols* of size `n` where `cols[j]` keeps track of the number of marks by a player in `column j`.
- **Diagonal Counters:** Two variables *diagonal* and *antiDiagonal* to track the marks in the main diagonal (top-left to bottom-right) and the anti-diagonal (top-right to bottom-left).

Here's how it would work:

- When a player makes a move, *increment* the corresponding row, column, and diagonal counters.
- If any counter reaches `n`, the player wins.

Code Solution

Here's how I would implement this in Java:

```
class TicTacToe {
   private final int[] rows;
   private final int[] cols;
   private int diagonal;
   private int antiDiagonal;
   private final int n;

   public TicTacToe(int n) {
       this.n = n;
       this.rows = new int[n];
       this.cols = new int[n];
```

```
        this.diagonal = 0;
        this.antiDiagonal = 0;
    }

    public int move(int row, int col, int player) {
        int toAdd = (player == 1) ? 1 : -1;

        // Update row and column counts
        rows[row] += toAdd;
        cols[col] += toAdd;

        // Update diagonal counts if applicable
        if (row == col) {
            diagonal += toAdd;
        }
        if (row + col == n - 1) {
            antiDiagonal += toAdd;
        }

        // Check if this move caused a win
        if (Math.abs(rows[row]) == n || Math.abs(cols[col]) == n ||
                Math.abs(diagonal) == n || Math.abs(antiDiagonal) ==
n) {
            return player;
        }

        return 0; // No winner yet
    }

    // Main method with test cases
    public static void main(String[] args) {
        TicTacToe toe = new TicTacToe(3);
        System.out.println(toe.move(0, 0, 1)); // 0
        System.out.println(toe.move(0, 2, 2)); // 0
        System.out.println(toe.move(2, 2, 1)); // 0
        System.out.println(toe.move(1, 1, 2)); // 0
        System.out.println(toe.move(2, 0, 1)); // 0
        System.out.println(toe.move(1, 0, 2)); // 0
        System.out.println(toe.move(2, 1, 1)); // 1 (Player 1 wins)
    }
}
```

Time and Space Complexity

- **Time Complexity:** O(1) for each move, as we are only updating and checking counters.
- **Space Complexity:** O(n) for the rows and columns arrays, as well as the diagonal counters.

Problem 8: Design TinyURL Service - Encode and Decode

Problem Statement

Design a URL shortening service that converts a long URL into a short URL and can convert the short URL back into the original long URL.

The encoding and decoding mechanisms are up to you, but you must ensure that the conversion is consistent so that a short URL always decodes to the correct long URL.

Solution

Clarifying Questions

Candidate: Is there any specific length that the short URL needs to be, or can it be of any length as long as it's shorter than the original URL?
Interviewer: There's no specific length requirement, but it should be reasonably short compared to the original URL.

Candidate: Got it. Let me take an example to clarify the input and output.

Example with Input and Expected Output:

```
TinyURL tinyUrl = new TinyURL();
String shortUrl =
tinyUrl.encode("https://mysite.com/search/encode-decode-tinyurl");
System.out.println(shortUrl);  // e.g., "http://tinyurl.com/4e9iAk"
System.out.println(tinyUrl.decode(shortUrl));  //
"https://mysite.com/search/encode-decode-tinyurl"
```

Brute Force Approach

A brute force approach would be to simply *hashing* the long URL to create a unique identifier for the short URL.

However, this approach could lead to hash collisions, where different URLs produce the same hash, which could be problematic.

Optimal Approach

A more robust approach involves using a *HashMap* to store mappings between long URLs and short URLs, ensuring that each URL has a unique identifier. Use base-62 based encoding strategy.

Here's the plan:

- **HashMap to Store the Mapping:** We'll use two HashMaps:
  - One to map long URLs to short URLs (*longToShortMap*).
  - Another to map short URLs back to long URLs (*shortToLongMap*).
- **Encoding Strategy:**
  - When encoding, we generate a unique identifier for the short URL, which can be a *base-62 encoded string of a sequence number* or a random string. We then store this mapping in both HashMaps.

- **Decoding Strategy:**
    - When decoding, we simply look up the short URL in the *shortToLongMap* to retrieve the original long URL.

This approach ensures that each long URL is uniquely encoded to a short URL, and we can efficiently decode it back.

Code Solution

Here's how I would implement this in Java:

```
import java.util.HashMap;
import java.util.Random;

class TinyURL {
   private final HashMap<String, String> longToShortMap;
   private final HashMap<String, String> shortToLongMap;
   private final String baseHost;
   private final String chars;
   private final Random rand;

   public TinyURL() {
       this.longToShortMap = new HashMap<>();
       this.shortToLongMap = new HashMap<>();
       this.baseHost = "http://tinyurl.com/";
       this.chars =
"0123456789abcdefghijklmnopqrstuvwxyzABCDEFGHIJKLMNOPQRSTUVWXYZ";
       this.rand = new Random();
   }

   public String encode(String longUrl) {
       if (longToShortMap.containsKey(longUrl)) {
           return longToShortMap.get(longUrl);
       }

       String shortUrl;
       do {
           StringBuilder sb = new StringBuilder();
           for (int i = 0; i < 6; i++) {

sb.append(chars.charAt(rand.nextInt(chars.length())));
           }
           shortUrl = baseHost + sb.toString();
       } while (shortToLongMap.containsKey(shortUrl));

       longToShortMap.put(longUrl, shortUrl);
       shortToLongMap.put(shortUrl, longUrl);

       return shortUrl;
   }

   public String decode(String shortUrl) {
       return shortToLongMap.get(shortUrl);
```

```
    }

    // Main method with test cases
    public static void main(String[] args) {
        TinyURL solution = new TinyURL();
        String longUrl =
"https://mysite.com/search/encode-decode-tinyurl";
        String shortUrl = solution.encode(longUrl);
        System.out.println("Encoded URL: " + shortUrl);
        System.out.println("Decoded URL: " +
solution.decode(shortUrl));
    }
}
```

Time and Space Complexity

- **Time Complexity**:
  - `encode(String longUrl)`: `O(1)` on average, since we are simply generating a random string and inserting it into a HashMap.
  - `decode(String shortUrl)`: `O(1)`, since we are just performing a HashMap lookup.
- Space Complexity: `O(n)`, where `n` is the number of unique URLs stored, since we are storing mappings in two HashMaps.

Problem 9: Serialization and Deserialization of a Binary Tree

Problem Statement

Design an algorithm to serialize a binary tree into a string and then deserialize that string back into the original binary tree structure.

The serialization and deserialization methods should accurately preserve the structure and values of the tree.

Solution

Clarifying Questions

Candidate: To clarify, you want me to design an algorithm that can convert a binary tree into a string representation (serialization) and then convert that string back into the original binary tree structure (deserialization). Is that correct?
Interviewer: Yes, that's correct.

Candidate: Can I assume that the binary tree can contain both positive and negative integer values and that it might be sparse (i.e., some nodes might be null)?
Interviewer: Yes, you can assume the tree may contain any integer values, and it can be sparse with null nodes.

Candidate: Understood. Should I use a specific traversal method for serialization, such as pre-order, in-order, or post-order, or is that up to me?
Interviewer: That's entirely up to you. Just ensure that the deserialization can reconstruct the tree correctly.

Candidate: Got it. Let me walk you through how I would approach this problem.

Approach

I'll use *pre-order traversal* for serialization, as it allows us to easily reconstruct the tree during deserialization by following the order in which nodes are visited.

Here is how two methods would work:

- **Serialization**: We will traverse the tree in pre-order and represent each node as a string. If a node is null, we'll represent it with a special marker (e.g., "null"). We'll use commas to separate node values.
- **Deserialization**: During deserialization, we will split the string by commas to get the node values and reconstruct the tree by recursively assigning left and right children based on the order in which they were serialized.

Example:
Let's serialize and deserialize the following binary tree:

```
    1
   / \
  2   3
     / \
    4   5
```

Serialization Output: `1,2,null,null,3,4,null,null,5,null,null`
Deserialization Output: The *original tree structure* should be reconstructed.

Code Solution

Here's how I would implement this in Java:

```
import java.util.*;

class TreeNode {
    int val;
    TreeNode left;
    TreeNode right;

    TreeNode(int x) {
        val = x;
    }
}

public class BinaryTreeSerializeDeSerialize {

    // Serializes a tree to a single string.
    public String serialize(TreeNode root) {
```

```
        StringBuilder sb = new StringBuilder();
        serializeHelper(root, sb);
        return sb.toString();
    }

    private void serializeHelper(TreeNode root, StringBuilder sb) {
        if (root == null) {
            sb.append("null,");
        } else {
            sb.append(root.val).append(",");
            serializeHelper(root.left, sb);
            serializeHelper(root.right, sb);
        }
    }

    // Deserializes your encoded data to tree.
    public TreeNode deserialize(String data) {
        String[] nodes = data.split(",");
        Queue<String> queue = new LinkedList<>(Arrays.asList(nodes));
        return deserializeHelper(queue);
    }

    private TreeNode deserializeHelper(Queue<String> queue) {
        String val = queue.poll();
        if (val.equals("null")) {
            return null;
        }
        TreeNode root = new TreeNode(Integer.parseInt(val));
        root.left = deserializeHelper(queue);
        root.right = deserializeHelper(queue);
        return root;
    }

    // Main method with test cases
    public static void main(String[] args) {
        BinaryTreeSerializeDeSerialize codec = new
BinaryTreeSerializeDeSerialize();
        TreeNode root = new TreeNode(1);
        root.left = new TreeNode(2);
        root.right = new TreeNode(3);
        root.right.left = new TreeNode(4);
        root.right.right = new TreeNode(5);

        String serialized = codec.serialize(root);
        System.out.println("Serialized tree: " + serialized);

        TreeNode deserializedRoot = codec.deserialize(serialized);
        System.out.println("Deserialized tree (root value): " +
deserializedRoot.val);
    }
}
```

Time and Space Complexity

- **Time Complexity:**
  - `serialize(TreeNode root)`: `O(n)`, where `n` is the number of nodes in the tree. We visit each node once during pre-order traversal.
  - `deserialize(String data)`: `O(n)`, where `n` is the number of nodes in the tree. We process each node from the serialized string to reconstruct the tree.
- **Space Complexity:**
  - `O(n)` for both serialization and deserialization, as we store the serialized string and the reconstructed tree.

Problem 10: Parking System

Problem Statement

Design a parking system to manage a parking lot with three types of parking spaces: big, medium, and small.

Each type has a fixed number of available slots. The system should allow cars to park in spaces that match their size, and it should indicate whether parking is successful based on available space.

Solution

Clarifying Questions

Candidate: To clarify, you want me to design a parking system that:

1. Initializes with a specific number of parking slots for big, medium, and small cars.
2. Allows cars to park if there is an available slot for their size, returning true if successful and false if not.

Is that correct?
Interviewer: Yes, that's correct.

Candidate: For simplicity, should I assume that the parking slots for each car type are independent of one another, meaning a big car cannot park in a medium or small slot, and vice versa?
Interviewer: Yes, each car can only park in a slot that matches its type.

Candidate: Understood. Should I also assume that the system will handle cars arriving one by one, and once a car is parked, it won't be moved or removed?
Interviewer: Yes, you can assume that once a car is parked, it stays in that slot, and the system handles one car at a time.

Candidate: Got it. Let me walk you through how I would approach this problem.

Approach

I would use a simple approach with three counters to track the available slots for each car type.

- I'll maintain three integer variables (big, medium, small) to represent the number of available slots for each car type.
- During initialization, I'll set these counters based on the input values.
- `Parking (addCar(int carType))`: For each car that wants to park, I'll check the corresponding counter:
  - If there is at least one slot available, I'll decrement the counter and return true.
  - If no slots are available, I'll return false.

Example with Input and Expected Output:

```
ParkingSystem parkingSystem = new ParkingSystem(1, 1, 0);  //
Initialize with 1 big, 1 medium, and 0 small slots
System.out.println(parkingSystem.addCar(1)); // Returns true (1 big
slot available)
System.out.println(parkingSystem.addCar(2)); // Returns true (1 medium
slot available)
System.out.println(parkingSystem.addCar(3)); // Returns false (0 small
slots available)
System.out.println(parkingSystem.addCar(1)); // Returns false (0 big
slots available)
```

Code Solution

Here's how I would implement this in Java:

```
class ParkingSystem {
   private int big;
   private int medium;
   private int small;

   public ParkingSystem(int big, int medium, int small) {
       this.big = big;
       this.medium = medium;
       this.small = small;
   }

   public boolean addCar(int carType) {
       if (carType == 1) {
           if (big > 0) {
               big--;
               return true;
           } else {
               return false;
           }
       } else if (carType == 2) {
           if (medium > 0) {
               medium--;
               return true;
```

```
            } else {
                return false;
            }
        } else if (carType == 3) {
            if (small > 0) {
                small--;
                return true;
            } else {
                return false;
            }
        }
        return false; // Just in case carType is invalid (though
guaranteed to be 1, 2, or 3)
    }

    // Main method with test cases
    public static void main(String[] args) {
        ParkingSystem parkingSystem = new ParkingSystem(1, 1, 0);
        System.out.println(parkingSystem.addCar(1)); // true
        System.out.println(parkingSystem.addCar(2)); // true
        System.out.println(parkingSystem.addCar(3)); // false
        System.out.println(parkingSystem.addCar(1)); // false
    }
}
```

Time and Space Complexity

- Time Complexity: O(1) for the *addCar* method, as we're simply checking and updating a counter.
- Space Complexity: O(1) since we're using only three integer variables to track the available slots.

Big O Notation - Quick Reference

Complexity Class	Description	Example
Constant Time: `O(1)`	Execution time remains the same regardless of input size.	Accessing an element in an array by index.
Logarithmic Time: `O(log n)`	Execution time increases logarithmically as input size increases.	Binary search in a sorted array.
Linear Time: `O(n)`	Execution time increases linearly with input size.	Iterating through all elements in an array.
Linearithmic Time: `O(n log n)`	Execution time increases by a factor of *n log n*.	Efficient sorting algorithms like Merge Sort and Quick Sort.
Quadratic Time: $O(n^2)$	Execution time increases *quadratically* as input size increases.	Nested loops over the input (e.g., Bubble Sort).
Cubic Time: $O(n^3)$	Execution time increases cubically as input size increases.	Three nested loops.
Exponential Time: $O(2^n)$	Execution time *doubles* with each additional element.	Recursive solutions to the Fibonacci sequence.
Factorial Time: `O(n!)`	Execution time increases *factorially* with input size.	Generating all permutations of a set.

Common Data Structures & Time Complexities

Data Structure	Access	Search	Insertion	Deletion
Array	`O(1)`	`O(n)`	`O(n)`	`O(n)`
Linked List	`O(n)`	`O(n)`	`O(1)`	`O(1)`
Hash Table	`O(1)`	`O(1)`	`O(1)`	`O(1)`
Binary Search Tree (Balanced)	`O(log n)`	`O(log n)`	`O(log n)`	`O(log n)`
Heap	`O(n)`	`O(n)`	`O(log n)`	`O(log n)`

Common Algorithms & Time Complexities

Category	Algorithm	Complexity
Searching Algorithms	Linear Search	O(n)
	Binary Search	O(log n)
Sorting Algorithms	Bubble Sort	$O(n^2)$
	Insertion Sort	$O(n^2)$
	Selection Sort	$O(n^2)$
	Merge Sort	O(n log n)
	Quick Sort	O(n log n) on average, $O(n^2)$ worst-case
	Heap Sort	O(n log n)
Graph Algorithms	Depth-First Search	O(V + E)
	Breadth-First Search	O(V + E)
	Dijkstra's Algorithm	O((V + E) log V) with a min-heap
Dynamic Programming	Fibonacci Sequence	O(n)
	Longest Common Subsequence	O(n * m)
	Knapsack Problem	O(n * W), where W is the capacity

About the Author

With over 20 years of experience in the software industry, I have conducted and participated in hundreds of technical interviews. My deep understanding of coding interview format & its expectations, combined with a passion for teaching, has led to the creation of this comprehensive guide.

As a mentor and educator, I specialize in helping software engineers strengthen their problem-solving skills and master the core concepts needed to succeed in technical interviews.

This book is a reflection of my expertise and commitment to empower others in their career journeys.